CORRECTIONAL MANAGEMENT

Change
and Control
in Correctional
Organizations

David Duffee

Associate Professor
Graduate School of Criminal Justice
New York State University at Albany

PRENTICE-HALL, INC. Englewood Cliffs, New Jersey 07632

Library of Congress Cataloging in Publication Data

DUFFEE, DAVID,
    Correctional management.

    (Prentice-Hall series in criminal justice)
    Bibliography: p.
    Includes index.
    1. Corrections—United States—Administration.
I. Title.
HV9469.D83   658'.91'36460973   79-14241
ISBN 0-13-178400-5

PRENTICE-HALL SERIES IN CRIMINAL JUSTICE,
James D. Stinchcomb, series editor

*To the spirit of teaching in friendship and
friendship in learning displayed by my teachers,
Vincent O'Leary and R. Richard Ritti*

*Editorial/production supervision and interior design by Natalie Krivanek
Cover design by Alon Jaediker
Manufacturing buyer: John Hall*

© 1980 by Prentice-Hall, Inc., Englewood Cliffs, N.J. 07632

Printed in the United States of America

10 9 8 7 6 5 4 3 2 1

Prentice-Hall International, Inc., *London*
Prentice-Hall of Australia Pty. Limited, *Sydney*
Prentice-Hall of Canada, Ltd., *Toronto*
Prentice-Hall of India Private Limited, *New Delhi*
Prentice-Hall of Japan, Inc., *Tokyo*
Prentice-Hall of Southeast Asia Pte. Ltd., *Singapore*
Whitehall Books Limited, *Wellington, New Zealand*

CONTENTS

PART TWO—MANAGING THE INTERNAL ORGANIZATION 71

PART THREE—MANAGING INNOVATION
IN CORRECTIONS   181

PART FIVE—THE ENVIRONMENT OF CORRECTIONS AND THE MANAGEMENT OF THE SYSTEM 335

PART ONE

AN INTRODUCTION TO THE MANAGEMENT OF CORRECTIONS

INTRODUCTION

This volume is concerned with change and control in correctional systems and with the management of correctional organization. There is an attempt throughout to be generic rather than specific about managerial concerns, practices, and problems. In other words, the emphasis is on managerial activity that is relevant within a variety of correctional agencies and settings. At the same time, all the materials presented here are the outgrowth of research and action in actual correctional settings. Hence, specific correctional organizations are from time to time examined in detail. The point is that the guiding assumptions, theory, and hypotheses presented here have been examined for their utility in the world of practice.

The nature and scope of the practice under investigation deserve some comment. Correctional programs, supervision techniques, and classification and counseling principles are not, in and of themselves, topics of this book. Although such topics deserve and have received lengthy treatments of their own, they concern the direct labeling of, supervision of, control of, and service provision to offenders. Although these activities might be called the *management of offenders*, those who engage in these activities, such as counselors, teachers, and guards, are working *in* an organization, not *on* it. In contrast, the activities concerning us here are those that focus *on* the organization of correctional activity instead of on a person, a group, or an activity within the organization. This work does not concentrate on "front-line" correctional staff (i.e., the officials who work directly with offenders), and there is no commitment to dealing solely with parole chiefs, superintendents, commissioners, and other high-level correctional executives.

In fact, the concept of management does not deal with one or several sets of *people* at all. As we argue in Chapter 1, correctional management is a patterned set of activities that provides stability, control, and direction to an organization or set of organizations charged with the punishment of sentenced criminal offenders. It is conceivable that the activities of correctional management might be conducted by parolees or inmates as well as by parole supervisors and wardens. While examples of "con-run" prisons may be less frequent today than 40 years ago, the fact that inmates *have* run prisons (even through informal and corrupt channels) demonstrates that management is where you find it. All active, ongoing (surviving) systems are managed with some degree of effectiveness, although the actual management is not always done by a system's designated managers.

A key assumption to this work is that the persons responsible for correctional administration are effective to the extent that they are heavily involved in the change and control of the organization. Put another way, correctional administrators implement public policy effectively when the nature and demands of that policy are compatible with the structure and process of the organization that is to carry out the policy. When public goals are not effectively carried out, administrators can attempt to change the structure of the organization so that it more nearly accomplishes the goals that have been set for it, or they can change public policy so that it legitimizes the operational goals that the organization has been accomplishing in spite of public policy.

There are several good examples in the correctional field of the failure of administrators to guide their organizational structures in the directions specified by public policy. An early example would be the attempt by nineteenth-century reformers to administer penitence through the creation of the cellblock, fortress prison. Isolation, hard work, silence, and the Bible were supposed to instill in the incarcerated offender guilt for the offense committed and insight into the proper mode of behavior. The goals of administration were not achieved, however, because the management of the fortress prison "corrupted" administrative requirements. Silence could only be enforced through brutal, corporal punishments, isolation led to mental instability instead of religious awakening, overcrowding led to the end of isolation and to insufficient work to keep all inmates industriously employed, etc. More importantly, the administration of the reform goals required absolute dominance of the penitents. But management of the prison required a modicum of cooperation from the captives. Cooperation is difficult to obtain through complete subjugation, and the actual operative prison became a series of compromises between the security force and the inmates. These compromises provided the inmates with sufficient room to maneuver, communicate, and choose whatever opportunity arose for the formation of an *inmate culture*, the values of which contradicted the administrative goals of the prison. In brief, administrative intent and organizational structure were not congruent. Organizations of human beings naturally tend toward elaborating means of cooperation, but the policy of administrators did not allow for such cooperation.

The structure of the fortress prison was so incompatible with the goals of inmate reform that the need to change the structure or change the goals of the prison was evident by the end of the Civil War. In some institutions, such as Sing Sing, the choice was made to maintain the structure and abdicate the original administrative reform policy. The Sing Sing warden openly opted for an extremely punitive, harsh regime whose new goals were the production of suffering for its own sake. This goal the management of the fortress prison could accommodate.

Other executives and other prison reformers, however, were not satisfied with that approach. While they did not steadfastly adhere to the religious ideas of penitence, they espoused new statements of reform (centered around vocational and educational advancement) and attempted to create a new prison structure to implement that administrative policy. The reformatory was born, an attempted change in correctional structure that did not fare much better than the first.

Today, there is another perceived discrepancy between correctional organization and administrative policy. The claim now is that rehabilitation is not possible under the coercive conditions that the criminal process presents. Many influential spokesmen for and critics of the system claim that treatment goals should be abandoned as unreasonable expectations of the current correctional organization. In the place of such goals, these people say, we should institute more realistic objectives, which a coercive set of agencies (with some modification) might reasonably be expected to implement. One of the spokesmen, David Fogel, suggests that although a correctional organization probably cannot change people, it at least can be fair in the administration of criminal penalties. This correctional reform history and the reasons for the current state of confusion are reviewed in Chapter 2.

In Chapter 3 we will discuss in detail the various aspects of correctional management and we will attempt to ask and partially answer the following questions: (1) *To what extent can changes in correctional organization be accomplished?* (2) *To what extent can these feasible changes achieve the objectives of administrative policy?*

CORRECTIONS AS MANAGEMENT

The above two questions might be restated as the following one question: *Which administrative policies for correctional systems present manageable options for the organizations that must implement those policies?* This question does not assume that any publicly chosen policy should accommodate the present problems, dysfunctions, and conceptions that exist in currently operating systems. That assumption would amount to throwing in the towel and accepting the current lamination of human errors, oversights, and wishful thoughts as the *only* possible world. On the other hand, this question does not make the opposite assumption that certain sets of moral entrepreneurs or power elites can legislate and implement *any* goals for corrections that they wish to choose and expect those conditions to be achieved. Instead, the question is based on the following assumptions: (1) that certain degrees of freedom exist within ongoing systems that allow certain amounts of change in desired directions (improvement) and (2) that organizations of human beings (whether prisons, synagogues, or football teams) will tend to evolve in certain directions *regardless* of what chief executives or other policy makers might want. It, therefore, becomes extremely important to identify exactly how much freedom for change does exist and to identify which policy choices are most likely to be able to accommodate *and* take advantage of the fundamental tendencies of organization that are likely to happen.

This is both a theoretical approach and a pragmatic or practical one. It suggests that the prudent administrative policy is based on empirically validated statements about organizational behavior and that this organized behavior is variable enough that value (or policy) choices are both possible *and* necessary.

There are many "fundamental tendencies of organization" that will be discussed throughout this book. A key one discussed in Chapter 3 is that organized groups of people tend to elaborate (or invent) modes of cooperation (assuming they did not have those channels in the first place). This tendency toward cooperation will occur even in organizations in which one group was coerced into participation in the first place. The full definition of *cooperative* will take some time. Let it suffice now to mean the ability of two or more groups (or units) to negotiate a state of interaction in which each unit can achieve (or maintain) objectives satisfactory to itself while permitting each other group to do likewise. Rarely, of course, would cooperation mean that each group achieved *everything* it wanted or the *highest level* of what it wanted. Achieving the *best* possible set of goals for one group might easily mean that another group could achieve *nothing* that it was satisfied with. Hence, co-operation is frequently a state of compromise, a state of give and take. This is especially true in corrections where the offenders' highest objective of being free from supervision contradicts the correctional staff's highest objectives of gaining complete conformity to rules and regulations. But cooperation between staff groups and offenders is frequently observed. It occurs both legally (i.e., obtaining a parole date in return for participation in group counseling) and illegally (i.e., guard ignores minor infractions of contraband rules in return for a quiet or peaceful cellblock).

One fundamental question, then, is how much cooperation can be achieved legally? A second, perhaps more difficult question, would be under what policies can all involved groups simultaneously achieve *most* of their objectives or the highest feasible level of their objectives? These questions are fundamental managerial questions *wherever* they arise. For example, industrial executives may wish to know how best to integrate or coordinate the goals of a marketing division with the goals of a manufacturing division. Or they may want to know how to provide a customer with the most satisfactory product achievable at a price that still provides the company with a reasonable profit. Or they may want to know how to negotiate a union contract that is satisfactory to both workers and management.

Such questions, however, when they are asked within correctional organizations are slightly different from when they are asked in retail firms or manufacturing plants. Since corrections itself is the task of *managing people* (rather than managing people to sell X or produce Y), such management questions become: How can we manage (coordinate, produce cooperation, etc.) this organization in order to achieve the best possible management (situation of cooperation among people)? In other words, the product of correctional organization is management, or the creation of satisfactory interactions among different groups of people. This peculiar characteristic of public organizations for social control is the last topic of this part of the book. Following these introductory explorations, Part Two examines the management of the internal aspects of correctional organization.

1

The
Importance of
Management
to Corrections

Justifications of a book-length investigation of a subject matter are rather foolhardy in the same book that goes on to discuss the subject; the very attempt at justification tends to raise doubts about the importance of the topic. Authors of algebraic texts and books of pornographic jokes do not preface their efforts with attempts to justify their activity; they assume the reader is interested and has his own explanations of importance. Writers on management, however, if not their readers, are frequently not so sure of their subject matter, or of their reader's motivations and interest. Douglas McGregor began his famous *Human Side of Enterprise* with the observation that managers frequently assume their work to be a practical matter, for which there is no better teacher than experience.[1] The implication is either that management cannot be learned in books or that books cannot describe experience. If the first assumption were true,

[1] Douglas McGregor, *The Human Side of Enterprise* (New York: McGraw-Hill, 1960).

managers might have to wonder why other complex human undertakings, such as law and medicine, have a vast professional literature. If the second assumption were true, they might have to wonder why they themselves so frequently commit experience to paper, in the form of operations manuals, production records, tables of organization, and budgets.

Perhaps better explanations of the reluctance to rely on the written word as a means of learning about management have to do with the nature of management activity and its origins in the evolution of organizations. Management of a complex enterprise, whether it produces widgets or psychological services, is rarely the original organizational competency possessed by the incumbent of managerial status. The president of the American Widget Company likely was hired 20 years ago as a widget maker (and he may still pride himself as a producer of widgets, rather than as a manager of production). The president of a psychological consulting firm likely has a Ph.D. in psychology, rather than in management. In other words, management activity is often a very worldly set of activities taken on by men and women who were trained in other things. Their promotion to management activity is frequently a reward for effective technical activity of a specific sort, rather than a prediction that they will know how to manage well. It is usually assumed by them, and by the managers who promoted them, that management of an organization requires knowledge and experience in the frontline, in the "real work" of the organization, and that managing that real work is something that anyone with enough of that experience (and the right opportunity) might be able to do. Moreover, not only is management often a secondary or later skill developed by an individual, management as a distinct organizational role, separate from the "real work" of the organization, is also a relatively late specialty in the evolution of organizations.[2]

If these characteristics of management and managers are becoming gradually less manifest in business and industry, they are still fairly descriptive of correctional management. There were no texts on correctional management until 1975,[3] and there was little awareness of correctional agencies as organizations that needed management until at least 1960.[4] As late as 1969 it was true that most correctional managers had no formal training in management but had been

[2]Daniel Katz and Robert Kahn, *The Social Psychology of Organizations* (New York: Wiley, 1966), pp. 80–82.
[3]Alan R. Coffey, *Correctional Administration* (Englewood Cliffs, N.J.: Prentice-Hall, 1975).
[4]Richard Cloward et al., *Theoretical Studies in the Social Organization of the Prison* (New York: Social Science Research Council, March, 1960).

promoted from within the system, from positions as guards, counselors, parole officers, etc., where their training, if any, had related to the supervision of offenders, not to the coordination of large, complex organizations.[5]

Contributing to the slowness with which correctional management has been recognized as a professional specialty in its own right is the remarkable slowness with which management has been recognized as influencing the behavior of offenders, and hence the quality of correctional organization performance. Criticism of correctional effectiveness is by no means a new pastime. The social reform movements that resulted in the institution of the penitentiary, of parole, and of separate systems for juvenile offenders were all based on either observations or beliefs about the inability of correctional agencies to correct deviant behavior or to protect the community from harm. But most of these criticisms, and many later ones as well, generally were justified by alleged new information about the nature of the offender and the morphology of crime. That managerial practice could make correctional programs more effective, or that certain managerial practice could keep different programs from being effective, was frequently a side issue, if covered at all. As late as 1973 the National Council on Crime and Delinquency could devote an entire publication to the notion that the system of correctional organization, rather than the offender, was open to change.[6]

> It is likely that correctional managers are unable—or unwilling—to see that organizational policies and administrative requirements may actually contribute to client failure instead of client success.

Why this has been true is hard to determine. Obviously, if correctional managers have not perceived management itself as a unique activity that requires its own skills and theories, it will be hard to recognize the effect of that activity on other behaviors in the organization. It requires theory, or the assumed relationship between variables, to make manifest the impact of management on something else. But there are probably far deeper reasons than this for the reluctance of correctional managers to examine the impact of their own activity and the structure of their organizations on the behavior of offenders and staff. The greater of these perhaps has to do with the status of the offender and the beliefs about the role of the offender that are imbedded in our culture. The offender has variously

[5] Elmer K. Nelson and Catherine Lovell, *Developing Correctional Administrators*, Final Research Report to the Joint Commission on Correctional Manpower and Training (Washington, D.C.: Government Printing Office, 1969), pp. 23–33.
[6] *Crime and Delinquency* (July, 1973).
[7] Alvin Cohen, "The Failure of Correctional Management," *Crime and Delinquency* (July, 1973), 236.

been seen as ill, bad, or deprived, but in any event less competent to direct his own behavior than other people and less able to meet our culture's criteria of success. Moreover, convicted offenders are coerced into organizational roles—managers know they do not want to be doing what the organization demands of them. Under these circumstances, it is easy to blame the offender for the organizational failure because it is expected that the offender will fail. In much the same way, public school students who routinely do the worst in academic work, and who are unable to abide by normal classroom discipline, traditionally have been shunted off to the lowest tracks in the school system where their innate inability to perform (and to conform) is blamed for their continued poor performance. Only recently have our educational institutions recognized the contribution of teacher practice, educational material, and school-day organization to the failure of students.[8]

This expectation of failure on the part of the individual performs some functions for the organization. Change in organization is costly, disorderly, and conflict-producing. Change in normal organizational routines very frequently challenges not only internal, organizational beliefs about the way things should be done, and about normal relationships of power, prestige, and status, but this change may also prove threatening to much broader social values and traditions about how society works, and for whom it works best. Hence, recognition that correctional management may be a cause of continued offender deviance can set up large chain reactions that will disturb not only the way staff relate to offenders and to each other, but also the way in which the correctional enterprise may relate to the social system, the kind of support it may demand from the political and economic system, and the perception by society of the very things thought best and most valuable in the social order. For example, the notion that correctional organization (both physical and social) can impede an offender's ability to remain free of crime at the very least may suggest that the correctional system requires greater economic support than it has traditionally enjoyed and at the most it can suggest that political structures for responding to crime in fact function to maintain deviance if not increase it. Thus, the suggestion that correctional management has a responsibility for crime reduction in some way is not only threatening to management itself, it can also threaten the very social fabric that supports corrections and correctional management as they are.

[8]See, for example, Peter W. Greenwood, Dale Mann and Milbrey Wallin McLaughlin, *Federal Programs Supporting Educational Change, Vol. III: The Process of Change* (Santa Monica: Rand Corporation, April, 1975).

It may sound from the above discussion that the study of correctional management is routinely a radical exercise and that commitment to it is itself a manifestation of individual, social, or political deviance. Such is not the case. There is a wide variety of managerial practices and managerial innovations that is rather mundane, if not neutral, in its social and political implications. There are many ways in which managers and their expert staff can concentrate on increasing efficiency of operations without disturbing any of the basic tenets of correctional philosophy or of the social and political order. Personnel requirements can be updated, salary structure upgraded, training programs instituted, and prisons renovated without too much damage to traditional beliefs about offenders or correctional treatment. But in a world as complex and interdependent as ours, there are relatively few managerial practices whose maintenance or initiation does not have political and ethical consequences of some sort. If the implementation of some new management precepts and practices might appear radical, others may appear reactionary (and obviously some decisions may appear both ways to different groups). Managerial strategies that would reduce the frequency and ardour of inmate unrest or that would defuse the increasing union militancy of correctional staffs might appear to some people as subtle but powerful political machinations to keep an inequitable social structure at status quo. Even recent moves toward deinstitutionalization are seen as communist plots by some and as capitalist conspiracies by others.[9] Because criminal punishment as a social enterprise emerges from the core of our political structure and social values, the management of punishment has large potential to make significant changes in the future of our society.

Correctional managers have frequently behaved like ostriches by hiding their eyes to the potentials and dangers of this political and social maelstrom. But the sands of their protection are wearing thin. As we shall see in the next chapter, most correctional innovations in the last 150 years have origins outside the operating correctional complex. Correctional managers have often refused to take leadership in the controversial system that they run, with the result that new managers are appointed by the side that wins any particular controversy. But the changes in public value that often result in changed correctional administration are now so frequent that it is clear to many managers that their safety, if any exists, resides in their ability to enter the fray instead of hiding from it. This entrance to a

---

[9]Peter B. Meyer and David Duffee, "Alternatives to Incarceration: Humane Corrections or Low Cost Social Control?" Paper presented at the National Conference on Criminal Justice Evaluation, Washington, D.C., March 10, 1977.

position of conscious and planned leadership will require new forms of management and the utilization of new social technologies that have not in the past been seen as appropriate parts of the correctional management repertoire. These new strategies and techniques are no less the teachings of experience than the methods previously used. They are frequently experiences from which correctional managers have not learned in the past, and they will require methods of learning and means of analyzing experience that correctional managers have infrequently used.

MANAGEMENT AND OTHER ORGANIZATIONAL ACTIVITIES

Organizations are composed of individuals and groups, created in order to achieve certain goals and objectives, operated by means of differentiating functions that are intended to be rationally coordinated and directed, in existence through time on a continuous basis.[10]

Management of organizations is not synonymous with organizations themselves, and organizations are not merely the sum of their parts. Management includes the act of influencing, if not completely setting organizational goals and objectives, the decisions about how the organization should be differentiated or specialized in order to achieve subtasks leading to overall goals, and the activity of co-ordinating the specialized units, divisions, or components of the organization so that the different tasks fit together. Management also entails the processing, and sometimes the resolution, of the inevitable conflicts that will arise during the course of exchange across the specialized units as well as garnering support for the organization from groups, organizations, and broader processes and structures in the environment so that the organization can continue to do its work or do it more effectively. The activities of setting goals, articulating internal structure, resolving conflicts, and guiding exchange with the environment, taken together, are much of the reason that organizations can maintain their identity over time.

The complexity of management increases as organizations evolve and take on a wider variety of functions and employ larger numbers of people in more diverse specializations in order to get work done. The sole owner of a corner grocery store may be the only worker as well as the manager. The work of management as distinct from the work of clerking, stocking, butchering, etc., may not be very clear. Colonial jails and many rural jails today may require the efforts of only one or two people, and perhaps not their full-time effort at

[10]Edward E. Lawler III and John Grant Rhode, *Information and Control in Organizations* (Santa Monica: Goodyear, 1976), p. 32.

that. The sheriff in some less densely populated counties may have major law enforcement duties, act as an officer of the court, and run a jail and a grocery store at the same time.

Organizations begin, generally, as primitive production structures by which a single individual, or a small group, solves specific environmental problems as the need arises. For example, in some stateless, subsistence level tribes the entire work of "criminal justice," from apprehension to judgment to correction, may be a sporadic undertaking of village elders (or the whole tribe) engaged in only at the time when a theft or an altercation occurs. Under our definition, this activity would not even be categorized as an organization because it lacks continuity over time.[11]

Organizations develop from this simple state as the problems handled by the production structure become more frequent and/or as a greater amount of stability and predictability and expertise is required to get the production work done satisfactorily. At this point a maintenance system develops that elaborates rules for membership in the organization and rules for performance and devises and distributes rewards for membership and performance. As the organization "tightens down" on the manner by which work is done, and on the behavior allowed by organizational members, the organization also evolves an informal system that provides outlets for human goals that are not met by task demands.[12]

It is at this point in the development of the organization that management becomes a distinct activity, although it may still not require the full working effort of a designated manager. For example, the single parish constable in nineteenth-century English villages was not a manager of police activity. However, the growing inability to get the village populace to perform policing duties voluntarily and spontaneously created the demand for organization, the hiring of specialists, and the administration of the specialists' activities by designated managers. From these demands was generated the legislation that formed the London Police Department in 1829.[13]

As organizations continue to grow, and as the tasks assigned to them become more complex, managerial activity also becomes more demanding and increasingly different from the primary, or production, tasks of the organization. Maintenance structures and permanent organizational employees generate in organizations a life of their own that is separate from the community in which they spring and

---

[11]William Chambliss and Robert Siedman, *Law, Order and Power* (Reading, Mass.: Addison-Wesley, 1971), pp. 28–35.

[12]Katz and Kahn, *The Social Psychology of Organizations*, pp. 80–81.

[13]Charles Reith, *The Blind Eye of History: A Study of the Origins of the Present Police Era* (Montclair, N.J.: Patterson Smith, 1974).

that is autonomous to some extent from the immediate environmental demands for change. Hence, management in large and complex organizations also includes the activities by which the organization is related to the community: There is a need to manage not only the internal, but also the external environment.

It is somewhere within this stage of development that organizational management becomes itself a set of specialties, usually performed by more than one set of individuals. Some managers specialize in specific units of organization, for example, in being the captain of a guard shift or the supervisor of a probation district within a larger citywide probation department. Some managers specialize in recruitment, training, evaluation of personnel, and in the mediation of personal goals of members with the rules and regulations of the organization. Correctional departments now include separate departments for training personnel officers responsible for devising new positions, revising old ones, and determining that personnel are performing the job they were hired to do and are not punished for nonperformance of tasks out of their position. Other managers are responsible for coordinating the work of separate units. For example, a Deputy Superintendent for Treatment might make sure that classification of new inmates is synchronized with the programs available to inmates in the general population or that caseworkers in the prison prepare papers on time for the parole board or a disciplinary action committee. Other managers, usually at the highest level of authority, rarely see the internal operations of their organization and spend great amounts of time communicating with outside groups, ascertaining that parole and institutional policies do not conflict or that judges understand the reasons for inmate furloughs or that the state department of real estate is providing sufficient service to the department of correction for obtaining halfway house property, etc.

Management, then, is a complex, relatively abstract set of activities that becomes progressively important to each organization as it becomes more complex and progressively important to organized society as we become increasingly dependent on organizations for the performance of basic social functions. Management of a correctional organization *is not* the guarding, counseling, counting, cajoling, punishing, or helping of offenders. It *is* deciding which activities should be carried out and it is coordinating the efforts by which they are carried out.

Equally important to understanding how correctional management differs from other correctional activities is the ability to locate and identify managerial activity where it occurs. It is essential to the understanding of why correctional organizations work as they do *not* to confuse the arbitrary designations of specific offices with the actual functions of management. One must distinguish between *management* and *managers*. Those persons nominally known as the executives of an organization are usually located in the higher positions of organizational authority and prestige. In corrections, wardens, commissioners, parole supervisors, captains, and directors of research are identified in tables of organization as the managers of the organization. But it is not always true that the work that keeps an organization coordinated, integrated, and coherent through time is the work of these individuals or these individuals alone. If a designated manager spends too much of his time with the daily production activity of his organization, someone else will assume, formally or informally, the activity of management.[14]

In correctional organizations a shift captain may spend too much time actually supervising offenders himself, or a halfway house director may spend too much time counseling his residents. When these situations occur, it is likely that the actual managerial work will be done by another manager, by a particularly responsible front-line staff, or by a group of offenders. The complaints, decreasing but still frequent, that "the cons really run this place" are not necessarily complaints made by a power hungry custodial force. They may, instead, be a common-sense version of the observation that integration of different prison activities, or the adjudication of conflict between groups, is in reality carried on by nonmanagerial staff because the supposed managers are either unwilling or unable to provide the guidance that would keep the organization productive or stable.

It would seem likely that the more a designated manager knows about management, and the more he consciously practices the implementation of managerial theory, the less likely will management be an activity carried on informally by other groups in the organization. The more planned and sophisticated the strategies used by managers to guide their organization, the more likely is it that the managers, rather than somebody else, will be responsible for what happens in the organization, and the more will they be able to change the organization so that it more accurately approaches the objectives and policies formulated by the managers.[15]

It would be both mistaken and foolhardy to assume that any

[14] Chester I. Barnard, *The Functions of the Execution* (Cambridge, Mass.: Harvard University Press, 1968), p. 6.

[15] Douglas McGregor, *The Professional Manager*, ed. by Caroline McGregor and Warren G. Bennis (New York: McGraw Hill, 1967) pp. 58–68.

manager or set of managers can be completely responsible for the activity of organization. Indeed, one of the reasons that correctional organizations have survived so long, and with reasonably little disruption, despite faulty executive leadership, is that complex organizations for the most part manage themselves; [16] this is neither a silly observation nor a suggestion that quality executive leadership is not necessary. It is a characteristic of complex systems that much of both their work power and staying power are attributable to the very nature of complexity. The interacting, sometimes conflicting, often unwieldy parts of a diverse and complicated system possess both a great deal of redundancy and a great deal of self-initiative. When one part fails, another part may pick up its functions, and when one way of getting something done breaks down, another method can often be quickly invented that will do the job.

The self-managing aspect of organizations is both advantageous and troublesome. On the one hand, it means that severe dysfunctions by one group or unit can often be compensated for by exceptional behavior by another unit. On the other hand, it means that managers frequently find changing the organization from its present state almost impossible—the organization keeps on doing things in its "own way" regardless of what the managers would like.

This characteristic of complex systems also implies special roles for correctional managers that they have often failed to recognize. Managers in complex systems tend to be most effective when they take advantage of the self-direction of organizations rather than fight against it.[17] Managers should learn how to guide the natural forces of progression and change in the organization in certain directions rather than insist that things be done in one certain way as predetermined by the executive at the top. For example, correctional executives have long guarded against interaction and comradeship between correctional officers and inmates. Yet, without the very ability of guards and inmates to compromise and negotiate a mutually satisfactory state of affairs, the prison would scarcely escape riot. Instead of forbidding this natural and inevitable interaction between staff and offenders, correctional managers could find ways to harness that interaction to mutually beneficial ends. But until lately correctional managers have ignored the greatest potential of this kind of interaction.

Another role of correctional management is made possible by utilizing the self-guidance of the organization. If much of the internal daily operation of the organization can be left to the properly

16Ibid., p. 37.
17Stafford Beer, *Decision and Control* (New York: Wiley, 1966), pp. 345–369.

structured interaction of staff and offenders, managers can also spend a great deal more time in policy making and in ethical considerations than they presently do. To the extent that managers actively tackle the philosophical and political ambiguities that surround correctional work, they are less likely to leave the answering of these questions to outside groups that are less familiar with the daily problems and real potentials of correctional organization.

CORRECTION AS A FORM OF MANAGEMENT

So far we have concentrated on generic issues about management, or things that would make management principles developed elsewhere applicable to correctional settings and problems. There are, of course, differences which may be equally important to effective correctional management. For example, all organizations tend to differ from each other to the extent that their production processes—and the environmental problems they were destined to handle—are different. The tasks of production lend their own structure to organization. For example, the standardized and routine behaviors effective for the organization of work in automobile assembly plants would be terribly ineffective in the production of an Indianapolis 500 race car, and they would be equally damaging to the work of a research and development unit staffed by chemists and engineers.

Similarly, the structure of public organizations is likely to be different from that of private organizations, and the organization for the processing, guarding, or care of people is going to differ markedly from the organization of manufacturing firms. Katz and Kahn remark that the principle differences between the people-processing organization and the object-processing organization are the indeterminacy and the self-determinacy of the "things" being processed.[18] People, no matter how coerced and downtrodden, can ultimately say no to the demands placed upon them. Therefore, argue Katz and Kahn, people-processing organizations require a different organization of decision making: the front-line worker must use a great deal of discretion if he is to handle successfully the needs of the client, the demands of the consumer, or the expectations of the worshipper.[19] Therefore, we would expect that correctional organizations, in general, will have different decision and control structures than organizations that do not work on or with people.

Correctional organizations may have things in common with hospitals, the Boy Scouts, and churches that they do not share with

[18]Katz and Kahn, *The Social Psychology of Organizations*, p. 117.
[19]Ibid.

I.B.M. and General Motors. We must also recognize, however, that correctional agencies do work differently from the way that churches, scout troops, and mental institutions work. A key difference, according to Etzioni, is how power is distributed. In correctional organizations, almost all power rests with staff, the compliance of the offender is coerced, and as a result the offender is basically alienated from the organization.[20] Although McGregor would caution us that the appearance of unilateral power and the coercion of the lowest organizational echelon may be taken too seriously, he reluctantly admits that severe coercion may qualitatively change the principles of organization that might adhere:

> I find the evidence substantial for the assertion that unilateral power is *in fact* a fiction, except possibly under the most extreme conditions of physical coercion.[21]

If the coercive nature of prisons and other correctional undertakings once let correctional managers excuse themselves from adherence to general management principles, such is no longer the case. The fundamental shift in the distribution of power that is at the heart of many changes in American organization is at last sweeping correctional organization along in its tide. Perhaps the most striking of these changes in correction so far have been initiated by the courts. Courts in Louisiana, Arkansas, and Pennsylvania have declared entire prison organizations unconstitutionally cruel and unusual.[22] A court in Rhode Island substantially rewrote correctional classification criteria and utilized inmate input in the redrafting.[23] Similarly, courts have recently changed the procedures for parole and probation revocation,[24] and they have insisted that prison disciplinary hearings concerning statutory good time be substantially more orderly, open, and amenable to the inmates' influence than prison administrators were willing to accept on their own.[25] It is likely that correctional administration will have to learn to predict and presage such court action in the future; if they don't, they will fail.[26] A great part of that action by managers will center on changes in predominant

---

[20]Amitai Etzioni, *A Comparative Analysis of Complex Organizations* (New York: Free Press, 1961), pp. 3–21.

[21]McGregor, *The Professional Manager*, p. 94.

[22]*Holt* v. *Sarver*, 390 F. Supp. 362 (E. D. Ark., 1970); *Jackson* v. *Hendrick*, 40 Law Week 2710 (Ct. Comm. Pls. Pa., 1972); *Hamilton* v. *Schiro*, Civil No. 69–2443 (E. D. La., June 25, 1970).

[23]*Morris* v. *Travisano*, 310 F. Supp. 857 (D.R.I., 1970).

[24]*Morrissey* v. *Brewer*, 408 U.S. 471 (1972); *Gagnon* v. *Scarpell*, 411 U.S. 778 (1973).

[25]*Wolff* v. *McDonnell*, 418 U.S. 539 (1974).

[26]David Duffee, Thomas Maher, and Stephen Lagoy, "Administrative Due Process in Community Preparole Programs," *Criminal Law Bulletin* (Sept./Oct., 1977), 396–400.

managerial strategies from ones that depend on coercion and punishment to ones that depend on negotiation, compromise, and sharing of power with both lower-level staff and offenders.[27]

It should not be assumed, though, that the reduction in unilateral power, and the sharing of power with offenders, is a new phenomenon or one for which correctional organization itself is not responsible. Gresham Sykes' classic study of a traditional maximum security prison, operating in the 1950's, demonstrated conclusively that power was shared with the lowest levels of staff and with inmates, regardless of strong attempts by administrators to retain it for themselves.[28] In essence, Sykes' observations about the management of the Trenton Prison are enough to ease McGregor's worry that unilateral power may not apply in coercive settings. Sykes' study demonstrated that the American prison (and then a fortiori all other forms of American correctional organization) cannot be coercive enough that general principles of management should not apply. Sykes' basic thesis is that American culture does not permit the brutal and oppressive techniques that might conceivably make total power a reality. Consequently, correctional staff *must* negotiate and compromise with offenders in order to gain from them some element of cooperation with organizational goals.[29] One might add to this argument that as long as correctional administrators tend to hide from this fundamental fact of cooperation and the need for it, most forms of cooperation which exist in corrections will be guided by the informal rather than the formal structure of the organization, and most of its positive potential will be lost.

As management is willingly or unwillingly brought to the recognition of shared power, mutual decision making, and the group responsibility for task accomplishment, another characteristic of corrections opens to study:

> Prisons differ significantly, if not uniquely, from other organizations because their personnel hierarchies are organized down to the lowest level for the administration of the daily activities of men. The guard, who is the lowest-level worker in a prison, is also a manager.[30]

This observation about prison is also true of any other correctional organization. Parole officers, probation officers, house managers in

[27]National Advisory Commission on Criminal Justice Standards and Goals, *Corrections* (Washington, D.C.: Government Printing Office, 1974), pp. 439–453.

[28]Gresham Sykes, *The Society of Captives* (Princeton, N.J.: Princeton University Press, 1971).

[29]Ibid., pp. 40–62.

[30]Donald Cressey, "Contradictory Directives in Complex Organizations: The Case of the Prison," in Lawrence Hazelrigg (ed.), *Prison Within Society* (Garden City, N.Y.: Doubleday, 1969), p. 494.

halfway house facilities, all at the bottom of the official hierarchy, are all managers of other individuals. The managerial aspect of front-line correctional work is probably most evident in the closed environment of the prison in which all the activities of the offender are subject to regulation by staff. Nevertheless, all correctional staff have significant responsibility for the management of the lives of other people.

Stated in a different way, we can say that corrections itself is a form of management. This aspect of correctional organization is closely related to the more generic quality of all people-processing organizations. But there is more to Cressey's statement than just a reiteration of Katz and Kahn's dictum that front-line workers in people-processing organizations must use more discretion than must their counterparts in object-processing systems. The notion of correctional work as management itself is a specification of that more general characteristic, and the correctional version has its own unique implications. If it is true that front-line corrections' staff function as managers, not only must they use more discretion than other bottom-level staff, they also need to perceive the offender in somewhat different fashion from what would be true of personnel dealing with clients or consumers. A client who goes to a service organization in order to get aid in handling a problem, or a patient who goes to a hospital for treatment of a disease, or a consumer who seeks a product from a sales firm can legitimately be perceived by the organizational staff as outside the organization. But an offender, in reality, is none of these—he is a member of the organization.

Perceiving offenders as *members* of the organization is not really a new frame of reference. There is a strong argument that offenders have always been treated as members of the correctional agency, at least for certain aspects of organizational activity. The whole selection process of offenders for punishment, through prosecution and sentencing, tends to focus on which individuals, for reasons other than guilt, are amenable to correctional processing. One of the major issues in the guilty plea process, for example, is how much time an offender will spend in the system.[31] But correctional organizations, most notably prisons, have treated offenders as members in other ways as well. Most of the maintenance work in prisons, as well as farm work and manufacturing of certain state-used products, is done by offenders. In some southern correctional systems, notoriously Arkansas, certain prisoners have traditionally been used to guard and

---

[31]For a full development of this argument, see David Duffee and Robert Fitch, *An Introduction to Corrections: A Policy and Systems Approach* (Santa Monica: Goodyear, 1976), pp. 28–70.

punish other prisoners. And, in other treatment and/or reintegration oriented systems, some offenders have been used as adjuncts to staff, participating in group therapy leadership, parolee supervision, data processing, and so on.

But the full implications of offenders as organizational members have not been elaborated or systematically studied. At its base, this aspect of corrections should mean that offenders should be seen as individuals with whom correctional work is completed instead of individuals upon whom correctional work is done. It is in this twisting of the normally perceived relationship between staff and offender that some of the most glaring deficiencies of usual correctional organization and management can be seen. The correctional organization does not "produce" offenders (rehabilitated, punished, or deteriorated). Instead, correctional organizations produce patterns of behavior, or interaction systems involving several groups of people, including offenders, correctional staff, police, employers, families, and even victims. As such, correctional systems should not be concerned primarily with who offenders are, what they feel, or what they do, but rather with how any number of groups, organizations, and behavior support systems intersect for the production of behavioral consequences that are advantageous or disadvantageous for all concerned.

Unless correctional organization can function in this manner, it is unlikely that it will ever contribute to the social order the kinds of outcomes that will be satisfactory to any but a small fraction of the population that is dependent on it and makes demands of it. But there are as of now many characteristics of correctional structure and process, notably influenced by correctional management, that militate against this kind of organizational production. The greatest of these is the persistent penchant to treat human beings as objects, and hence to perpetuate the very same behavior that makes individuals victims rather than human beings.[32] This and other aspects of corrections are changing slowly, but change can always be retarded or facilitated by the quality of correctional management.

CHANGES IN CORRECTIONAL ADMINISTRATION

Meyer identifies four key obstacles to change in the correctional system: (1) conflicting value systems, (2) goal ambiguity, (3)

---

[32]Richard Korn, "Of Crime, Criminal Justice and Corrections," *University of San Francisco Law Review*, (Oct., 1971), 27–75.

inadequate information, and (4) decisions based on faulty criteria.[33] By and large, all four obstacles are characteristics of usual correctional management practice, and thus their lifting requires the support of management.[34]

In 1976 Harry More suggested that the problem facing corrections in the next decade will require the flattening of the organizational hierarchy, the democratizing of the correctional decision-making process, the decentralization of correctional services to the local, community level, and the use of state and federal expertise in a supportive and consultative, rather than a directive, capacity.[35] These suggestions reiterate the findings of a national survey of correctional management made in 1969.[36] While many correctional practitioners seem to favor such changes, the slowness of change tends to point to some built-in roadblocks that inhibit action.

One key problem, according to Malcolm Feeley, is not the presence of too much bureaucracy and formal organization in criminal justice, but on the contrary, the lack of it:

> What one finds in the system of criminal justice is a highly formalized and defined set of rules, norms, and goals, but also an organization which possesses no corresponding set of incentives and sanctions which act to systematically enforce them. Any far-reaching discussion of reform and proposals for change in the administration within the American system of criminal justice would have to deal with this problem of the nature and distribution of compliance-inducing mechanisms.[37]

Stated another way, criminal justice agencies, correctional ones among them, tend to lack the basic ability of effective organizations to get their people to do what is required. The ability to sanction and motivate successfully is a characteristic of mature management.

---

[33]John C. Meyer, "Change and Obstacles to Change in Prison Management," in George G. Killinger, Paul F. Cromwell, Jr., and Bonnie J. Cromwell, *Issues in Corrections and Administration* (St. Paul: West, 1976), pp. 144–146.

[34]Ibid.

[35]Harry W. More, Jr., *Criminal Justice Management* (St. Paul: West, 1977), pp. 227–232.

[36]Nelson and Lovell, *Developing Correctional Administrators*, pp. 85–95.

[37]Malcolm M. Feeley, "Two Models of the Criminal Justice System: An Organizational Perspective," *Law and Society Review* (Spring, 1973). 423.

2

Correctional
History
and the
Development of
Correctional
Management

From a long-term, historical perspective, the American correctional enterprise has plodded listlessly along a road that has no milestones. There has been little interest in selecting, let alone arriving at a final, satisfactory destination. The long list of correctional leaders who have sequentially assumed control of the cart have never been able to muster sufficient resources or sufficient understanding, or a satisfactory mix of both, to enlist the sympathy of the public or the confidence of experts for significant periods of time. Every once in a while a new driver uses a new whip or a new carrot and the old cart is jounced forward or sideways for some explainable, if not rational, reason. But few of these motions have been ultimately counted as progress, since research on the destination and the means of getting there has usually been lacking.

Beginning with the President's Commission on Law Enforcement and the Administration of Justice, and the related allocations coming from the Omnibus Crime Bill, we seemingly entered a new era: new modes of transportation and new road maps were in sight. Moreover, the general public has become so short of resources and patience and so pressed by even greater problems than the ones of crime and its control that we can confidently predict an increasing lack of tolerance for our past approaches. Correctional management, as part of the criminal justice system, will be held accountable for resources used and energy expended. Significant output must be demonstrated soon.

New breakthroughs and drastic changes are somewhat subdued perhaps by the fact that this new era is founded on hard evidence about the failure of past innovations. Or, to put it more precisely, the innovations we are now discussing involve the rejection (almost on an ideological level) of the validity of one-method solutions to complex problems.

One important part of the difference is that current discoveries and breakthroughs are to a great extent based on the scientific method. The insistence on independent and scientific evaluation of new programs and projects makes claims of unqualified success very difficult if not impossible to issue. And yet one can see some danger in this situation: that we might begin to claim as success our ability to measure and control the operations and output of correctional processes and miss the point that this new ability in and of itself is only a routine by which we establish and keep track of our line of work. Successful research may be a gain in valid information. But successful corrections will remain the production of change in offenders and the community so that the incidence of crime is reduced and/or that community dissatisfaction with troublesome behavior is redefined. We must not forget that the goals of the correctional reformers over the past 175 years were generally desirable, even if their methods were ineffective.

THE GOAL OF CHANGE
AND THE CONCLUSION OF FAILURE

While correctional systems need any number of managerial innovations, such as the equity of certain personnel plans, the efficiency of different computer systems, or the stability of different halfway houses, it would appear right now that a crucial management focus is on the achievement of change in specific directions. Several recent reviews of the correctional literature suggest that not much is changing. Both Bennett and Cohn, for example, have recently cited a string of studies to demonstrate that the correctional system is incapable of changing people.[1] Cohn uses these evaluations as a basis for

[1] Lawrence A. Bennett, "Should We Change the Offender or the System?" *Crime and Delinquency* (July, 1973), 332–343, and Al Cohn, "The Failure of Correctional Management," *Crime and Delinquency* (July, 1973), 323–331.

suggesting that we ought to change management rather than change offenders,[2] while Bennett points out that changes in the system have often yielded desired outcomes when changes directed at offenders failed to achieve those outcomes.[3]

In general, there would appear to be two major strategies arising from reactions to different interpretations of various evaluations of correctional effectiveness. Empey, to some extent, and Richard Korn much more markedly, may be taken to represent a group that suggests that we have knowledge about successful change techniques that can be applied on the individual and group level.[4] Korn, for example, suggests that we should make available to the average correctional offender the same kinds of change relationships that rich, non-offenders purchase to aid in the solution of personal problems.[5] It is true that a great deal of psychotherapy or group counseling could be purchased for the cost of incarcerating an offender in an institution for a year. But what is more important here than the specific speaker or the specific suggestion is the general claim that effective change strategies exist for application to individuals or small groups and that corrections is ineffective because the bureaucratic and totalitarian nature of the "delivery" system, such as the maximum security prison, neutralizes whatever change potential that group therapy, counseling, etc., may have. Thus, there is one group of experts that states that the change techniques on the individual and group level should be maintained and the organizations that interfere with their use should be abandoned. In the place of probation, prison, and parole, we should invent a new set of structures that are compatible with, or deliver effectively, the change-production activities on the personal and group level.

There is another side, most notably represented by two important papers by Cressey[6] and Bennett,[7] that suggests none of our present change techniques is effective and that new techniques should be invented that conform to the needs of or that are effective within the constraints of the present or somewhat modified organizational

---

[2] Cohn, "The Failure of Correctional Management."

[3] Bennett, "Should We Change the Offender or the System?"

[4] Lamar Empey, "Offender Participation in the Correctional Process: General Theoretical Issues," in *Offenders as a Correctional Manpower Resource* (Washington: Government Printing Office, 1967), pp. 5–21; Richard Korn, "Issues and Strategies of Implementation in the Use of Offenders in Resocializing Other Offenders," in *Offenders as a Correctional Manpower Resource*, pp. 60–81.

[5] Korn, "Issues and Strategies of Implementation," and Korn, "Of Crime, Justice and Corrections," *University of San Francisco Law Review* (Oct., 1971), 27–75.

[6] Donald Cressey, "The Nature and Effectiveness of Correctional Techniques," *Law and Contemporary Problems* (Autumn, 1958), 754–771.

[7] Bennett, "Should We Change the Offender or the System?"

systems that we are more or less stuck with. Cressey goes so far as to suggest that changing offenders will not be effective until we can develop techniques that can be used by a minimally educated official within a large, bureaucratic organization during an eight-hour shift.[8] Even more recently other critics of the system have updated the Cressey–Bennett arguments with a slightly different twist. Morris,[9] Fogel,[10] van den Haag,[11] and others have suggested that the correctional system, or a coercive system, cannot be used effectively to induce behavioral change at all. They suggest that the goals of "correction" or "treatment" should be abandoned and the existing correctional structures modified for the implementation of just and humane punishment. Suggestions such as these contrast markedly with the suggestions by Korn. One side says, save the effective change techniques and do away with ineffective organizations. The other side says, do away with ineffective techniques and maintain the organization.

There is, of course, some distortion at this level of generality, because "taking away the techniques" will change if not destroy the organization as we now know it; on the other side, the effective techniques have not been demonstrated effective with the populations that are housed in the now, allegedly, ineffective organizations. However, this summary does not do too much damage to either argument, and one can see some validity in both. There is, on the one hand, a concern for improving interactions between individuals, and there is, on the other hand, a concern for maintaining the social structure in which the individuals find themselves. Of most concern, however, is not the validity of either argument, but the implicit *rejection* of the scientific method in either suggestion. In order to make this clear, it may help to return for a moment to correctional history.

REVOLUTIONARY CORRECTIONS
AND EVOLUTIONARY SCIENCE

Although it is true that the correctional horse and cart have been plodding along over the last 175 years, the outside historian's vantage point may not be the best place from which to examine the reasons for this unimpressive pace. The history of corrections is marked by

---

[8] Cressey, "The Nature and Effectiveness of Correctional Techniques."

[9] Norval Morris, *The Future of Imprisonment* (Chicago: University of Chicago Press, 1974).

[10] David Fogel, *We Are the Living Proof* (Cincinnati: Anderson, 1975).

[11] Ernest van den Haag, *Punishing Criminals* (New York: Basic Books, 1975).

ideological and technical upheavals in which one approach was over-thrown and another approach wholeheartedly adopted. Although the pace of corrections has been slow, the internal *method* of loco-motion has been "revolutionary." Old goals and old means have been given up without any systematic evaluation of achievements or failures. New goals and new methods have been adopted without a great deal of planning and without any systematic plan for evaluating process and outcome. Moreover, the new has been grafted to the old without any careful consideration of how the operational realities of this grafting process would change either the retained or the new mechanisms. And, as is true of any highly controversial social activity, such as changing people, new plans and techniques contradictory in principle and operation have been instituted simultaneously to satisfy different publics and different power groups in an established policy-making hierarchy.

The penitentiary system, for example, began because people were dissatisfied with the goals and methods of punishment used in the eighteenth century. By the time that the cellblock was constructed in the courtyard of the Walnut Street jail in 1790, new goals included saving criminals from the iniquities of vice-laden cities, isolating them from contaminating social contacts, instilling the virtues of hard labor, and providing the solitude necessary for penitence. Although these goals were a revolutionary upheaval in the notions of why a man should be punished and how it might be done, techniques of the old jail were utilized, such as isolation and labor, and harnessed to new goals. Although the psychology of personality was new in those days, it would not appear that the same care and concern for individ-uals as human beings were given to the correctional reform planning as was evident in, say, the planning that occurred in the Constitu-tional Convention only a few years before. The reformers, so en-amored with their just and good purpose, were unsympathetic to the "perverse" nature of the human will and to the unintended but predictable exigencies of human organization. The concern with anticipated and desired outcome overrode the realistic appraisal of human and organizational behavior.[12]

Approximately 70 years after the penitentiary movement, the social work revolution arrived with similar force and similar conse-quences for the developing correctional system. The principles of humanitarian reform laid down with now ironic certainty at the first American Prison Congress in 1870 implicitly and explicitly rejected the real outcomes apparent after 40 years of prison

[12] See David Rothman, *The Discovery of the Asylum* (Boston: Little, Brown, 1971), pp. 79–108.

administration.[13] In place of the operating penitentiary, which had clearly become a human cage operating on administrative principles that could have been borrowed from a municipal zoo,[14] the new reformers, armed with the new social work principles and methods, again assaulted the public and the entrenched penal regime with new goals and purposes of operation and with new means of individualizing the correctional process.

These people had a tremendous impact, which is manifest in the initiation of parole at the Elmira reformatory,[15] the formal recognition of probation in the Boston courts,[16] and culminating in the new Chicago system for juveniles in 1899.[17]

And yet at least two major caution signs should have been immediately evident. First, this reform at the turn of the twentieth century proceeded as if the Quaker innovators of the 1790's had never spoken. People might have wondered whether and in what ways the harsh prison realities of Auburn, Sing Sing, etc., of the 1860's were related to the beneficent goals of the prison reformers. But no one stopped to wonder. Second, while the new principles and practices *again* had a revolutionary sound and form, the actual organizational changes that occurred were slow, developmental shifts in the ongoing operations of existing agencies. The social work reforms were instituted with little regard for the way in which the social and historical matrix of corrections would reshape these reforms when they had become part of the operating correctional organization. For example, the principles and rationale for parole were in their fundamentals contradictory to the principles and rationale of the penitentiary. The isolating institution was based on a theological confidence in the goodness of the individual human soul and the unregenerative and irreversible criminogenic influence of the new American cities.[18] Parole, like probation, was based on a fundamental confidence in the potential goodness of human companionship and mutual influence that could only be found *within* the community. And yet the community-oriented strategy was

---

[13] Negley Teeters, "State of Prisons in the United States: 1870–1970," in George C. Killinger and Paul F. Cromwell, Jr., *Penology* (St. Paul: West, 1973), pp. 59–62.

[14] See "The Report to the Warden of Sing Sing," in Rothman, *The Discovery of the Asylum*, pp. 101–102.

[15] See David Duffee and Robert Fitch, *An Introduction to Corrections: A Policy and Systems Approach* (Santa Monica: Goodyear, 1975), p. 122.

[16] David Dressler, *The Practice and Theory of Probation and Parole* (New York: Columbia University Press, 1959), p. 18.

[17] Sanford Fox, *The Law of Juvenile Courts in a Nutshell* (St. Paul: West, 1971), 258–259.

[18] See Rothman, *Discovery of the Asylum.*

grafted, in the form of parole, directly onto the individual-oriented strategy provided by the penitentiary. Similarly, the movement to save the children was plopped, like a transparency, upon the existing correctional mechanisms used on adult offenders.[19]

Approximately 50 years later a different revolution occurred, less sweeping and ideological than the first two, but revolutionary just the same. Following the work of Lewin and others with small group dynamics during World War II,[20] group therapy swept through both adult and juvenile systems in the 1950's as a panacea for the increasingly evident blight in insitutional and field service organizations. With the Highfields[21] and Provo[22] institutional and parole experiments in Minnesota[23] and elsewhere, the strategies of changing individuals changed from a strictly casework approach to an approach based on the belief that peer influence and support could be harnessed to alter an individual's values, to upset the homeostatic equilibrium of the inmate culture, and to generate positive changes in social climate and personal correctional outcomes.[24] Within a short time major papers were issued concerning the qualitative differences in this approach and the more traditional approaches. Correctional officers could be seen in many institutions listening politely to the foment and frustration of inmates assigned to their "discussion groups" or "rap sessions." The principles spread quickly to related areas as people noticed that groups could effect changes not only in offenders but in staff as well. Treatment teams consisting of custodians, counselors, and maintenance workers were given the responsibilities previously reserved for a prestigious centralized classification committee.[25] Researchers began to speak of perceiving offenders and nonprofessional correctional workers as

[19] John Griffiths, "Ideology in Criminal Procedure or a Third Model of the Criminal Process," *Yale Law Review* (Jan., 1970), 359–417.

[20] See Kurt Lewin, "Studies in Group Decision," in Darwin Cartwright and Alvin Zander (eds.), *Group Dynamics* (Evanston, Ill.: Row Peterson, 1953), pp. 287–301.

[21] H. Ashley Wenks, "The Highfields Project and Its Success," in Norman Johnston, Leonard Savitz, and Marvin Wolfgang, eds., *The Sociology of Punishment and Correction* (New York: Wiley, 1970), pp. 525–536; Lloyd McCorkle, Albert Elias, and F. Lovell Bixby, *The Highfields Story* (New York: Holt, 1958).

[22] Lamar Empey, *Alternatives to Incarceration*, Office of Juvenile Delinquency and Youth Development Studies in Delinquency (Washington, D.C.: Government Printing Office, 1967), pp. 37–40.

[23] Nathan Gary Mandel and William H. Parsonage, "An Experiment in Adult Group Supervision," *Crime and Delinquency*, (Oct., 1965), 313–325.

[24] David Street, Robert Vinter, and Charles Perrow, *Organization for Treatment* (New York: Free Press, 1966).

[25] Charles Hagan and Charles Campbell, "Team Classification in Federal Institutions," *Federal Probation* (March, 1968), 30–35.

peers in the group dynamic process. In the 1960's the concept became tied to a new interest in manpower development and New Careers was born.[26]

While there was less insistence that this group therapy-group dynamics revolution performed the miracles or achieved the universal scope of the previous reforms, the implications that "everyone can benefit from group work" was a fairly familiar sound in institutions and other operating agencies, if not in the scholarly literature.

While some group work theorists identified early the difficulties that this technique of change might encounter within the bureaucratic framework of established operating agencies, the lengths that the administration or the vaguely perceived "system in general" could go to co-opt the group involvement or to refuse flatly its introduction were somewhat surprising.[27] The research data that strong group processes were generally antithetic to the usual bureaucratic organizational structure, while frequently observed in business and industry at that point,[28] were slow in reaching the proponents of group work in corrections.

In review, correctional programs "progressed" from 1800 to 1960 in a rather unusual fashion. Every 50 to 75 years there emerged new groups that were interested in correction and that were dissatisfied with the goals, methods, and outcomes of their predecessors. Each new group of reformers rallied around new correctional goals, espoused "new," or at least warmed over ideologies, and successfully took the reins of power from previous correctional policy makers and managers. Each group then instituted its "reforms"—frequently finding that the implemented reform bore little resemblance to the espoused goals. The correctional enterprise would jog on again at its usual slow rate until a new set of outsiders decided that it had found a new and better way to run the show.

Although change in correctional policy and program has rarely been effective in this century and a half of correctional history, the change has not evolved slowly. On the contrary, change in correction has been the result of revolts against antiquated beliefs and values, followed by overthrows in the leadership and sponsorship of persons with older beliefs and values. In other words, change has been

---

[26] Department of Health, Education and Welfare, *Experiment in Culture Expansion,* report on the proceedings of a conference "On Using the Products of a Social Problem in Coping with the Problem," held at the California Rehabilitation Institution, Norco, Calif., July 11, 12, 13, 1963.

[27] See Korn, "Issues and Strategies of Implementation," and Elliot Studt, Sheldon Messinger, and Thomas Wilson, *C-Unit: The Search for Community in Prison* (New York: Russell Sage, 1968).

[28] Chris Argyris, *Personality and Organization* (New York: Harper & Row, 1957) and *Integrating the Individual and the Organization* (New York: Wiley, 1964).

revolutionary. And, as with many political revolutions, we should not be too surprised that the correctional regime implemented by the new group is neither very much better nor very much different from the regime toppled by the new ideas.

There is very little in all of this that smacks of science, or the scientific method, or even of plain hard rational thinking. In contrast, changes based on scientific thinking and findings would proceed slowly and in a different sense of slowness. The changes would be gradual and frequent, and they would be based on examining outcomes in relation to the independent variables that had produced the outcomes. Small adjustments in process and program structure would be made as alterations in the measured outcomes indicated that one process or structure was more advantageous than another. In addition, there would be much less willingness within a scientifically guided enterprise to throw all the organizational eggs into one basket. No single process or program would become the single major investment of the enterprise; therefore, failures in one activity would not mean that a revolution was necessary.

CURRENT TRENDS IN CORRECTIONS

This leads us directly to the current "revolutions" in correctional thinking and practices. Although these revolutions have followed much more quickly on the heels of the group movements than the social work reform did on the heels of the penitentiary movement, the rapidity of these new changes can easily be attributed to the quickening force of social change in general rather than to scientific evaluations of correctional effectiveness, of which there have not been many.

One emergent trend is perhaps academically anchored in the 1960 publication of *Theoretical Studies in the Social Organization of the Prison*,[29] but it also had nonacademic antecedents more internal to the system. One of these that must be recognized is the work of the Joint Commission on Correctional Manpower and Training, especially the research report prepared by Nelson and Lovell.[30] There was also the stepped-up activity by the National Council on Crime and Delinquency (N.C.C.D.) and other agencies in the training and organizational development area. With the preparation and opening of several permanent state correctional academies in this past decade,

---

[29] Richard Cloward et al., *Theoretical Studies in the Social Organization of the Prison* (New York: Social Science Research Council, 1960).
[30] Elmer K. Nelson and Catherine Lovell, *Developing Correctional Administrators*, final research report of the Joint Commission on Correctional Manpower and Training (Washington, D.C.: Government Printing Office, 1969).

the revolution of "training and organizational development" is certainly a reality.

The training and organizational development movement in corrections draws most of its strength from the apparent success of similar efforts in business and industry. Organizational development (O.D.) much like the earlier group therapy movement, can trace its origins to the work of Kurt Lewin and his followers. One aim of organizational development, according to one of its best-known adherents,

is that of creating conditions which enable the individual to achieve his own goals *best* by directing his efforts toward organizational goals.[31]

Organizational development is "the name that is being attached to *total-system*, planned-change efforts"[32] for reaching that objective. Unlike some of the earlier changes in corrections, organizational development does not portend a sweeping change in power and policy and its method is at least in its leading examples guided routinely by scientific inquiry and diagnostic and evaluation research.[33] However, organizational development seems to lend itself, much like earlier changes, to strong ideological commitment and to the routine application of tried and true change techniques in situations in which their application is inappropriate, or the resources necessary for their implementation insufficient. Perhaps more troublesome, however, in the case of organizational development as applied to corrections, is the *implied* caveat of organizational developers that the planned change method can solve the organizational deficiencies and improve goal attainment without much regard for the constraints imposed upon the organization by its political and economic environment. As such, organizational development tends to be a conservative force, ameliorating present organizational behaviors to the political–economic status quo. There is little scientific investigation of how the organization is linked to the environment and of whether or not the goals imposed on the organization by the environment are possible. Very seldom is the social desirability of the goals of the organization questioned, even if the goals are effectively achieved.[34]

Another current movement in corrections is the more publicized

---

[31] Douglas McGregor, *The Professional Manager*, Caroline McGregor and Warren Bennis eds. (New York: McGraw-Hill, 1967), p. 78.

[32] Richard Beckhard, *Organizational Development: Strategies and Models* (Reading, Mass.: Addison-Wesley, 1969), p. 7.

[33] See, for example, Chris Argyris, *Intervention Theory and Method* (Reading, Mass.: Addison-Wesley, 1970).

[34] Walter R. Nord, "The Failure of Current Applied Behavioral Science—A Marxian Perspective," *Journal of Applied Behavioral Science*, (Winter 1974), 557–578.

one of community correction, or deinstitutionalization. This trend is clearly related to the arguments of Korn (discussed earlier), Menninger,[35] and others who suggest that changing people is indeed the proper domain of correction and that the proper organizations or delivery systems need to be created by which to deliver these change services effectively. The argument goes that large institutions, as well as traditionally organized probation and parole services, do not do an adequate job of integrating the individual offender into the community order where he or she will have to live. Furthermore, institutional corrections damages the very social interaction skills on which the offender will have to depend in order to live legally in the community. Hence, small residential programs and new types of correctional field services must be provided to the offender that will better enable him or her to compete in free society; equally important, correctional officials need training and organizational support by which to begin affecting the community social structure to obtain for offenders greater access to opportunities in which they can use their new skills.[36]

Community-based correction and reintegration became popular terms in the late 1960's, after the President's Commission on Law Enforcement and the Administration of Justice did much to highlight both the antiquated physical facilities and social philosophy behind our major correctional institutions.[37] Community correction was based partially on practical observation that large, fortress prisons were unmanageable, partially on the insurgence of outside reformers clamoring for humane treatment for offenders, and partially on emergent theories of deviance that related individual illegality to community structure rather than to individual pathologies.[38]

As is true with the organizational development movement, community correction has much to recommend it, and yet its elaboration through 1977 displays some of the same earmarks of failure that have undone earlier reforms. First, community corrections has, until very recently, demonstrated very little knowledge of community. Many community corrections discussions proceed (1) as if the entrance of the offender under supervision into the community is

---

[35] Karl Menninger, *The Crime of Punishment* (New York: Viking, 1969).
[36] See, for example, Dennis C. Sullivan, *Team Models in Probation* (Hackensack, N.J.: National Council on Crime and Delinquency, 1971); Elliot Studt, *Reintegrating the Offender with the Community*, Criminal Justice Monograph (Washington, D.C.: Government Printing Office, 1973), pp. 42–53, Vernon Fox, *Community-Based Corrections* (Englewood Cliffs, N.J.: Prentice-Hall, 1977).
[37] President's Commission on Law Enforcement and the Administration of Justice, *Task Force Report: Corrections* (Washington, D.C.: Government Printing Office, 1967).
[38] For example, Richard Cloward and Lloyd Ohlin, *Delinquency and Opportunity* (New York: Free Press, 1960).

always a "good" and (2) as if most communities are basically the same. The enormous differences in the reception of community correctional programs in different communities has highlighted the faultiness of both assumptions.[39] Second, community correctional programs have rarely demonstrated greater effectiveness in reducing further crime by offenders than the institutional programs they replace.[40] Third, community corrections seems firmly entrenched in the "treatment is possible camp," despite clamors from other groups that coerced treatment is impossible or that community corrections is merely a more subtle form of coercive control designed to decrease costs to the government without providing the offender with a better net social situation.[41]

Another movement, following with remarkable rapidity on the heels of the community corrections trend, has been an almost opposite movement; yet some spokesmen seem able to speak of both community corrections and this newer movement at the same time. It is more difficult to label this last trend; it has several foci and somewhat different versions. For want of a better term, let us call it the "just punishment" movement. Like community corrections, this new penal philosophy was generated by the wave of dissatisfaction with modern institutional correction, especially with the medical model of correction, which assumed that offenders could be treated for deviance much as people can be treated for physical diseases. But, unlike the community corrections movement, the just punishment philosophy rejects the efficacy of coerced behavioral change altogether—or at least it claims that it does so. In place of the objective of correcting behavior, the just punishment objective is frequently stated as the reduction of penal activities to their bare essentials, to their only real sphere of competence, that is, punishing a person for the crime he or she has committed.[42] The just punishment movement criticizes a variety of current correctional practices and structures. Among the most commonly mentioned are indeterminant sentencing, the related parole decision (and consequently parole supervision as well), and the use of promised early release by prison administrators to obtain the "participation" of inmates in prison treatment programs. This trend has led so far to the restructuring of the sentencing

[39] See, for example, Robert B. Coates and Alden D. Miller, "Neutralization of Community Resistance to Group Homes," in Yitzhak Bakal (ed.), *Closing Correctional Institutions* (Lexington, Mass.: Lexington Books, 1974), 67–84.
[40] Harry E. Allen and Clifford E. Simonsen, *Corrections in America: An Introduction* (Beverly Hills: Glencoe Press, 1975).
[41] See Andrew Scull, *Decarceration* (Englewood Cliffs, N.J.: Prentice-Hall, 1977).
[42] See van den Haag, *Punishing Criminals*; Morris, *The Future of Imprisonment*; and Andrew von Hirsch, "Prediction of Criminal Conduct and Preventive Confinement of Convicted Persons," *Buffalo Law Review* (Winter 1972), 717–758.

codes in Maine, Indiana, and California, to the open repudiation of treatment programs by the Director of the Federal Bureau of Prisons, and to a flurry of sentencing debates and drafts of new legislation in the federal system and elsewhere.

It may seem surprising that some of the foremost adherents to the just punishment movement are, or have been, strong proponents of community correction and critics of the fortress prison as well. For example, David Fogel does not relent in his searing attacks on the prison, even as he marshals evidence against the possibility of treatment.[43] The ability to favor the two things at the same time is apparently based on two strategies: (1) the possibility of replacing prisons with halfway houses or similar small, community located programs without relating the use of these to indeterminate sentences and (2) divesting the correctional agencies of any responsibility for human services and relegating these reintegration programs to the same social agencies that would handle them for noncorrectional clients. Nevertheless, there would seem to be some incompatibility between the two trends unless the agency of correction could find new methods of reducing the stigma of correction to the point that outside agencies would willingly handle convicted clients and unless the just punishment model could find some equitable means of distributing community rather than institutional punishment to offenders that is not based on predictions of their behavior in the community.

Again, it should be pointed out that there is presently little if any evidence to support just punishment as an effective means of correction any more than there is to support community correction. These new trends are based on evidence that the fortress prison and coerced treatment do not work frequently or well.[44] But they are not based on the finding that the suggested alternatives are more effective at the same goals or at some other quantifiable goal. To the extent that just punishment is based on the assumption that deterrence, or deterrence and retribution in combination, will be achieved through these activities, some empirical evidence favoring these means would seem called for. On another level, the evidence logically sought might be more internal to the system instead of related to external outcomes. For example, many people argue that new sentencing codes based on the crime rather than on the character of the offender will reduce sentencing disparity or will make prisons "more manageable" and less frequently centers of corruption and violence. Data on this

---

[43] Fogel, *We Are the Living Proof.*

[44] Douglas Lipton, Robert Martinson, and Judith Wilks, *The Effectiveness of Correctional Treatment* (New York: Praeger, 1975).

should be gathered. There are also strong ethical arguments favoring this trend, as there have been for any other correctional change. In this case, people argue that a reduction in official discretion and the elimination of the gaming between correctional staff and offenders that is based on the release decision (or other treatment related rewards) will provide a more humane and a fairer system of punishment. It is unclear at this time which argument swings the greater weight—the value argument or the data-based outcome argument. If it is the former, there is, of course, little in the way of empirical evidence that can settle the issue. Decisions on what is fairer or more humane may be related to observations of what is actually taking place in the system, but they will always depend on valuations of the observed data that are based on beliefs and ideological frames of reference. It might cause us to wonder, however, whether or not the elimination of discretion (such as parole) will increase even the manageability of correctional facilities when that very discretion was first introduced in order to remove some of the inhumane practices of control that grew up in their absence.[45]

CORRECTIONAL CHANGE
AND CORRECTIONAL TREATMENT

Both the goals of correction and the value of any one of its outcomes are likely to be ambiguous and controversial as long as corrections, or punishment, exists. This is not surprising, since the very act of punishment implies some level of controversy and conflict between the party committing the perceived offense and the party doing the punishing. Criminal punishment is one way of handling social conflict. Hence, there is nothing in the above movements, and nothing really in the rest of this book, that the reader should anticipate to be conflict *resolving.* Some correctional actions may reduce conflict in the short term, but increase it in the long run. Others may do the opposite. Even more likely is the outcome that correctional action will reduce some types of conflict or conflicts in certain places while simultaneously increasing other types of conflict or making the same disagreements reappear in other places.

Nevertheless, there is one distinction in terminology that may help us to reduce some of the confusion in current competing philosophies and some of the contradictory expectations about the discussion of correctional management, namely, correctional *treatment* and correctional *change* (or even change in corrections) should not be

[45] See Rothman, *The Discovery of the Asylum* and Lester Douglas Johnson, *The Devil's Front Porch* (Lawrence, Kansas: The University of Kansas Press, 1970).

understood to be the same thing. Presently, there is widespread doubt about the efficacy of treatment in correctional settings, and many outside reformers and correctional practitioners flatly state that treatment of the individual should not be taken as a correctional objective. Nevertheless, there are few persons committed to correctional administration (or to attacks on the current patterns of administration) who would deny the appropriateness of describing corrections, or punishment, as an activity of *change*. Although some may argue that the term "change" is too vague and general to be of much use, it is frequently helpful to seek a higher-level abstraction or a more systemic level of discourse as a place to begin when the dilemmas of social policy seem insurmountable.[46] Any penal response to an act is done with some expectation of change in the offender, in the punisher, or in the social relationship between the two. We might say that a penal response is taken to an action in order to maintain the stability in the status network that connects the actors. If a father punishes a son for coloring on the living room wall, some might say that the father expects the son to change his behavior in the future, and others might say that the father expects to maintain his superior status vis-à-vis his son, at least with respect to coloring living room walls. We might not all agree that the punishment (in whatever form) is a treatment for the son, but we would probably all agree that the lack of response from the father would change both familial relations as well as the color of the room while the commission of punishment may change the son's mode of expression as well as his perception of his relationship to his father and hence his future actions. Admittedly, criminal punishment is much more complex than that, but again it is done to maintain a legal order or to change the interaction pattern of the actors.

It should also be obvious that one does not create change; change in interaction patterns among people is omnipresent. Correction is an activity by which we expect to channel change in certain directions and concomitantly to keep it from going in other directions (this is how we can talk of it as being *both* for certain types of change and for maintenance of other patterns at the same time). Correction is one form of the management of social interaction and as such is concerned with the change and control in the means and end values of people who live together. Correctional management is concerned with change and control in the organizations charged with this type of social management.

---

[46] Leslie Wilkins, *Social Deviance* (Englewood Cliffs, N.J.: Prentice-Hall, 1965), pp. 132–135.

CORRECTIONAL MANAGEMENT AND CHANGES IN CORRECTIONAL PHILOSOPHY

In the next chapter we shall discuss in detail some of the changes in the strategies for managing large, complex organizations. Obviously, there are many differences between management of an industrial firm or an insurance company or a bank or a church and the management of a correctional system. One of the major differences, of course, is the use of legitimate coercion. Prison wardens and parole officers have the authority to shove some people around without providing mutually satisfactory compensation for the shoving. Clearly, large, far-flung corporate conglomerates are reaching a stage of autonomy from either external regulation or internal pressure in which they can very frequently do very much what they want (i.e., closing a factory despite strong objections from a town dependent on the factory for employment[47]). Nevertheless, corporations cannot legally force lower employees to maintain membership, but correctional organizations frequently maintain the membership longest of the offenders whose participation is least contributory to the stable operation of the organization.

Despite such marked differences, many persons have lately made the claim that a sound management practice and theories currently used in business and industry can and should be transferred and applied to the management of correctional organizations. For example, Nelson and Lovell have measured correctional managerial behavior on criteria widely used in profit-making firms and other government organizations.[48] O'Leary et al. suggest that organizational development principles that have been developed in commercial organizations can be effective for improving the relationships between correctional executives and front-line staff and between correctional staff and offenders.[49] Of the few recent texts on correctional management, most consist of nothing more than descriptions of management practice in planning, supervision, and evaluation that is in use elsewhere and suggestions for its application to correctional agencies.[50]

[47] Peter B. Meyer, "Communities as Victims of Corporate Crimes," paper prepared for the Second International Symposium on Victimology, Boston, September 8, 1976.
[48] Nelson and Lovell, *Developing Correctional Administrators.*
[49] Vincent O'Leary, David Duffee, and Ernst Wenk, "Developing Relevant Data for a Prison Organizational Development Program," *Journal of Criminal Justice,* 5, 2, (Summer, 1977) pp. 85–104.
[50] See, for example, Alan R. Coffey, *Correctional Administration* (Englewood Cliffs, N.J.: Prentice-Hall, 1975); Harry W. More, Jr., (ed.), *Criminal Justice Management* (St. Paul: West, 1977); George G. Killinger, Paul F. Cromwell, Jr., and Bonnie J. Cromwell (eds.), *Issues in Corrections and Administration* (St. Paul: West, 1976).

One of the primary assumptions of most management theory is that the organizational manager must play a key role in (1) the integration of the various suborganizations or specialized units in the organizational system, (2) the adjudication of conflicts between various hierarchical levels in the organization, and (3) the articulation of the organization and its external environment.[51]

> Organizations which do not depend upon immediate environmental transactions can make more use of ritualism to build walls between themselves and their environments.[52]

Correctional managers have traditionally taken advantage of the separation of their immediate organizational goals from the need of the organization to be successful in the environment. And they have indeed utilized a plethora of ritual guises to reduce the amount of interaction with outside forces.[53] When these guises were effective and when the resultant separation from the environment was maintained, correctional management may indeed have been very different from the management of other types of organization. Whether or not this was true, the isolation had certain short-run advantages. Correctional managers could usually change or maintain organizational patterns of behavior based not on the relationship of that behavior to its yield for society but on the managers' own beliefs and values about what they thought was right or "good" correction or on their own idiosyncratic assumptions and hunches about how best to supervise their employees and maintain their executive status. In the short run, operating on assumptions, however untested for validity, and on belief, however unique to the believer, is in many ways cheaper and more comforting to the incumbent manager than would be the alternatives of using the scientific inquiry method as a means of accepting and rejecting practices of change and control. However, the short-run advantages of the "corrections-as-an-island" form of management has had its attendant long-range problems. The most obvious of these is that the very assumption of isolation or empiredom is in reality faulty. Its use has time and again made both the correctional manager and his organization vulnerable to effective outside attack; without systematic and continuous means by which to keep track of change in external value and belief, all correctional structures sooner or later (and increasingly sooner) have become unable to meet successfully the changing external

---

[51] Daniel Katz and Robert Kahn, *The Social Psychology of Organizations* (New York: Wiley, 1966), p. 94.
[52] Ibid., p. 105.
[53] Street, Vinter, and Perrow, *Organization for Treatment*, pp. 10–11.

criteria of correctional success. Correctional managers have discovered too late that the public correctional enterprise will ultimately be subject to judgments about its societal outcomes or to criteria of correctional effectiveness.

In the past these judgments have been sporadic and infrequent enough that the new managers, seated in power after any particular correctional revolution, always fell victim to the same faulty assumptions held by their predecessors. As a result, new changes in correctional program and structure have usually been generated by outside groups: new political powers, groups possessing new techniques of social change, or groups possessing new interpretations of what it means to be fair, humane, or protective of the social order.

If other types of organizations were as vulnerable to changes in external social value and belief as these, they would probably falter altogether. Correctional organizations have remained—despite revolutionary changes—because none of the emergent, overthrowing groups has been so radical as to suggest that corrections itself should be abolished. In contrast to the typical correctional organization's mode of dealing with a changing environment, most successful businesses (and various branches of government as well) have remained viable because their executives have displayed leadership in either changing the environmental expectations and demands on the organization (through advertising and public relations) or by changing the organization to fit better the changing demands of the environment (through the development of new products and services or vast overhauls in the manner by which the organization does its work).[54]

A method of management that might reduce somewhat the revolutionary jarrings of past reform movements and increase the adaptability of corrections uses the scientific method. This approach, as opposed to others, is an evolutionary rather than revolutionary one. It involves actually *doing* research on the system and directing changes based on these research findings instead of borrowing research findings from other fields and applying them fully and foolhardily to the correctional system. One term for this approach might be the "strategy of incremental approximation," or as Empey has aptly called it, the "strategy of search."[55]

---

[54] Katz and Kahn, *The Social Psychology of Organizations*, p. 92. For similar problems of dealing with external change in other organizations, see McGregor, *The Professional Manager*, pp. 138-139.

[55] Lamar Empey, "Implications: A Game with No Winners," in Anthony J. Mannochio and Jimmy Dunn, *The Time Game* (New York: Dell, 1972), pp. 241-253.

TRENDS IN SYSTEMATIZING CORRECTIONS

Many activities have lately come together as agents for the initiation and maintenance of the scientific, evolutionary method of change in corrections. Certainly, a major one has been the President's Crime Commission. The most marked general contrast between the reports of this commission and the work of the Wickersham Commission in 1931 is the use of the systems perspective in describing and analyzing crime and the activities of justice agencies. In many ways, the concept of the "criminal justice system" was born with this commission. If such a commission did not exist, the justice agencies' perceptions of themselves and of other agencies and the academic community's approach to criminal justice as an area of study would have been drastically different. Second, the Crime Commission provided the strongest (but not the first) forum from which to justify and support the role of research in criminal justice.[56]

Much more recent, but perhaps just as influential in the long run, is the work of the National Advisory Commission on Criminal Justice Standards and Goals.[57] Although discussion about research findings or areas in which research is needed was less germane to the Standards and Goals reports than the Crime Commission reports, research and its importance are underscored in two important ways. First, the Advisory Commission emphasizes the fact that all recommendations are based on research about what has happened in specific places rather than on beliefs about what should be good for everybody. Second, the Commission makes specific recommendations concerning research as an integral part of every justice activity and organization and as a means of modifying and adding to the list of recommendations over time.

A third influencing agent is Project Search. This agency has been active in the last several years in calling together administrators and researchers who are interested in the problems and practices of criminal justice research and in forming a system or a number of related systems for information collection, storage, retrieval, and analysis that should be instrumental in pulling together for the first time a set of diverse and conflicting organizations and operations by providing them with a common language.[58]

[56] President's Commission on Law Enforcement and the Administration of Justice, *Task Force Report: Corrections.*
[57] National Advisory Commission on Criminal Justice Standards and Goals, *Corrections* (Washington, D.C.: Government Printing Office, 1974).
[58] See, for example, Ernest Cresswell (ed.), Proceedings of the Second International Symposium on Criminal Justice Information and Statistics Systems (Sacramento: SEARCH Group Inc., 1974).

To the extent that this activity is fruitful, we have taken a giant step away from the precipice of another ideological overthrow. One major thrust in this direction, and the fourth agent of evolution, is a Project Search endeavor known as Offender-Based Transactions Statistics (O.B.T.S.). There is firm agreement at this point that the concepts underlying the Offender-Based Transaction Statistics and the system that can operationalize them are a major development in studying the criminal justice system as a system.[59] Consequently, the use of O.B.T.S. can be a major phase in the evolution of criminal justice agencies from an historical to a purposive system that selects its goals, plans to carry them out, implements strategies, evaluates consequences, reformulates its goals, replans, and so on. At that point, human beings will have created an organizational animal that learns, and learns how to learn, so that changes in the future should be gradual and continual rather than fitful and disruptive.

Correctional management still has a long way to go before it even approaches the sophistication and rigor with which other organizations routinely manage change and control of internal organizational operations and interactions with the external environment. National commissions and national research and development corporations are still several steps removed from the daily management of prisons, probation and parole offices, halfway houses, and the like. In order for correctional managers to become more responsible for the changes that will take place in their organizations and more responsive to changes in social demands on the correctional system, they will have to bring to the daily guidance of staff behavior and staff–offender interaction a much wider use of explicit organization theory and planned managerial practice based on and altered in response to feedback from systematically gathered information about organizational goals and objectives, staff supervision practices, the quality of the overall environment of the organization, and most importantly the consequences of organizational behavior on the ultimate outcomes which relate the organization to its public constituency.

The inclusion of such organizational variables in a continual data collection process and the use of the findings in the formulation of organizational policy can provide managers with the basis for slower and more gradual changes in program and structure as well as for more effective organizational behavior. A more pro-active, research-based management of organization should enable a correctional system to plan more effectively to implement plans consistent with

[59] See, for example, Carl E. Pope, "Sentence Dispositions Accorded Assault and Burglary Offenders: An Exploratory Study in Twelve California Counties," paper prepared for the annual meetings of the Society for the Study of Social Problems, New York, 1976.

overall goals and to initiate changes based on data and the prediction of long-term trends rather than on the well-intentioned guesses about what is good for offenders or desired by society.

But in order for such a system of management to work, there is the long tradition of revolutionary cures for correctional ills to overcome. Just as the past reformers were too concerned with the rightness of their recommendations to consider the implications of the organizational process systematically, there is some evidence now that persons in positions of administrative and financial power in the criminal justice system are too eager to foster innovation such as new correctional programs or new sentencing systems without incorporating the research findings and research and development procedures developed in the last 20 years, without which innovation is an aimless and dangerous concept.

3

Organizational Structure and Basic Management Functions

There may be any number of ways to analyze the behavior and structure of complex organizations. The selection of a basic frame of reference is somewhat dependent on the purposes of the analyst and somewhat dependent on the techniques for observation, categorization, and measurement that are available. It is not surprising then that the basic notions about organizations have changed considerably during the twentieth century as both cultural changes have influenced the frames of reference, notions of humans, society, and human purpose and as the growing technology of social science has permitted more complex conceptualizations and more sophisticated measurement.

Complex organizations themselves may be older than recorded history, and in many ways the basic tenets of organization and management have not changed appreciably in 2000 years. Julius Caesar may have been as savvy an administrator as exists today, and the remarkable durations of both the Roman Empire and the Roman

Catholic Church indicate that effective organization has not been dependent on the existence of social science to explain what is happening. Yet the value placed on the human being has changed drastically (perhaps more so in the last 100 years than in all the years before), and the explosions of production, information, transportation, and other technologies have irreversibly altered the size and complexity of organization, the numbers of organizations important to our daily living, the demands organizations make on us, and the demands we make on them.[1]

These changes have come to mean that the science of organization is now the science of human living, and the role of organizational management as much as any other modern activity will affect the ability of society to survive. And yet the practice of management, predating any systematic and scientific study of its nature and duties, has been alarmingly impervious to any fundamental change in its basic outlooks, goals, and modes of operation. Management, even of the most sophisticated and professionally based organizational activities, has often remained the province of apprenticeship learning.

This situation is not merely the fault of management itself. Until very recently many significant innovations in management practice and major contributions to organizational and management theory have been the legacy of our greatest managers rather than behavior recommended on the basis of organizational research and design.[2] Surprisingly, one of the reasons that it took so long for the science of management to break away from the practice of management and to begin to provide leadership for management practice was the long-standing subservience of organizational study to the goals and to the frame of reference held by management. Early studies of organization and early management science usually accepted the goals of management at face value and accepted as their task the advisory function of telling management how it might do better what it was doing anyway. It was not until management theory broke out of this trap and began to question the whole why and wherefore of management that real advances were made.[3]

---

[1] Geoffrey Vickers, *Making Institutions Work* (New York: Halsted, 1973).

[2] For example, Alfred P. Sloan's revolutionary reorganization of General Motors into a decentralized, federated system may be taken as an example of practical innovation; see Daniel Katz and Robert Kahn, *The Social Psychology of Organizations* (New York: Wiley, 1966), p. 89; Chester I. Barnard's major theoretical work on management may be taken as an example of a practicing executive's contribution to conceptual and theoretical development (the likes of which has rarely been equaled since), *The Functions of the Executive* (Cambridge, Mass.: Harvard University Press, 1938, Thirtieth Anniversary Edition, 1968).

[3] This observation and the following discussion on the development of management theory draw heavily on Chris Argyris, *Personality and Organization* (New York: Harper & Row, 1957), pp. 54–75 and 123–162.

THE DEVELOPMENT OF MANAGEMENT SCIENCE

Many experts agree that the study of management (as distinct from the more basic study of organization) began in earnest with the efforts of Frederick Winslow Taylor. Taylor began his famous treatise (1911) with a dictum that is remarkably close in form, if not in meaning, to management guidelines written decades later:

> The principle object of management should be to secure the maximum prosperity for the employer, coupled with the maximum prosperity for each employee.[4]

Taylor's hopes (or promise) for his principles of management were not lacking in optimism, if somewhat short on prescience:

> What constitutes a fair day's work will be a question for scientific investigation, instead of a subject to be bargained for and haggled over. Soldiering will cease because the object for soldiering will no longer exist. The great increase in wages which accompanies this type of management will largely eliminate the wage question as a source of dispute. But, more than all other causes, the close, intimate cooperation, the constant personal contact between the two sides, will tend to diminish friction and discontent.[5]

By *management*, Taylor meant primarily, if not solely, the organization of the work of production; by the *science of management* he meant primarily the ability of managers and their expert staff, with the cooperation of the workers, to analyze all the activities that went into task accomplishment and to devise the most efficient set of activities that would accomplish each task. It was his assumption that this engineering of the work, work space, and workers would drastically reduce the time and expense of production, increase profits, increase wages, increase markets, and round again. These ideas had indeed very significant impacts on the efficiency of industrial organization as they functioned at the time. But they were based, in large measure, on the very assumptions about the internal and external economy of organization that had given rise to the problems that Taylor sought to correct. For one, his ideas on the physical and social engineering of work were tied directly to basic assumptions about capitalism, to the notion that the market was essentially unlimited (and free) and that the best interests of the workers and the best interests of the employers were, if not identical, at least happily congruent. It has not taken a worldwide adoption of a Marxian perspective to overthrow these basic assumptions. It has become increasingly clear that not only can increased production

---

[4] Frederick Winslow Taylor, *The Principles of Scientific Management* (New York: Norton, 1967).
[5] Ibid., p. 143.

bring on uncontrolled inflation but also that increased efficiency in work, brought on by both the engineering of work and the displacement of workers with technology, can increase profit and prosperity to the employer while doing relative damage to the prosperity of the worker.

But more important for our concern with corrections is that Taylor's principles of management are inapplicable, or even damaging, to the organization of the work of governing human beings and that his principles focused the manager on internal matters of efficiency in blatant ignorance of faulty political and economic assumptions about the linkage of the organization to the external environment.

A growing body of public administration theory in the next three decades elaborated on Taylor's engineering principles and extended the study of management to include a broader array of organizational activities. Gulick and Urwick, for example, attempted to describe the entire organization as a large machine that had been rationally constructed for the accomplishment of tasks.[6] To the extent that Gulick and Urwick generalized from the activity of physical labor to the expanding number of service and governmental organizations, their ideas were presumably wider in application than Taylor's and were concerned with the organization of management into different specialities rather than simply with the management of production itself.

Public administration theory concentrated on the elements of formal organization. Little attention was given to explaining the informal culture that exists within an organization; there was little apparent interest in explaining why organizational members should want to carry out the roles and functions assigned to them by the "rationally" constructed organizational design. Basic concepts within this school were *task specialization* (fractionating work into specialties requiring the smallest amount of effort and intrapersonal coordination), *chain of command* (vertical structuring of the organization into a network of control that can integrate the various specialties), *unity of direction* (location of direction for each organizational unit in the hands of one and only one leader), and *span of control* (the limitation of leadership responsibility to a small number of subordinates over whom the leader can maintain direct and efficient control).[7] The basic assumption behind using these concepts

[6] Luther Gulick and L. Urwick, *Papers on the Science of Administration* (New York: Institute of Public Administration, 1927); and L. F. Urwick, *Scientific Principles and Organization* (New York: American Management Association, Institute of Management Series, No. 19, 1938).

[7] Argyris, *Personality and Organization*, pp. 59–66.

was that if the organization were divided into highly distinct manifestly interrelated parts, the confusion and waste in the management of organization would be reduced, just as task specialization alone would reduce inefficiency in the production line.

The advances here over Taylor are several. First, this body of theory is not so limited to industrial work as Taylor's had been. Clearly, the science of management was gaining some independence in its thinking from specific types of organization or management problems which might give rise to the study. Second, the public administration theory was clearly interested not simply in rules of behavior that would grow out of the nature of the production effort but in rules that would govern the relationships of organizational members to each other, at least in their official capacities. It is interesting that this expansion of management study emerged as organizations (industrial or otherwise) progressively run by officials or salaried managerial employees instead of by owners or employers. No longer was the best interest of the organization seen as resting directly on the prosperity of the owners (who by this time were often a diverse set of stockholders or a government representing diverse interests). Instead, the best interest of the organization now seems more closely tied to the efficiency and effectiveness of the organization for its own sake, although most management theorists closely identified the organization with the desires of the management that ran it.

A major breakthrough in the management of organizations emerged from the famous Hawthorne studies that were conducted in the Hawthorne plant of the Western Electric Company. This work began under much the same assumptions and goals that had directed Taylor and much of the public administration approach. A team of research scientists entered Hawthorne at management's request in order to determine how working conditions affected production and under what conditions efficiency of production would be greatest. Much of the work was routine sociophysical engineering that had become the hallmark of scientific management, but there were some findings that startled the researchers so greatly that a major new school of management opened in the aftermath of explaining the "findings." In brief, the core of the research accident was the finding that some workers in the Hawthorne plant did better under poorer physical conditions than they did under the normal conditions that the researchers had planned to improve. In one series of tests, women working in a delicate wiring operation produced more units and with better quality results under candlelight conditions than with normal lighting. Moreover, morale, the researchers noted, improved markedly from the start of the experiments, despite the presence of researcher meddling and unusual working conditions.[8]

These findings seemed unusual at the time, because they seemed a direct contradiction to the rational and engineering theories of organizational behavior. Their explanation, however, was equally rational, but as it turned out, equally incomplete. The unexpected behavior of the women in the relay assembly unit had to do with the facts that the women were:

(1) made "subjects" of an "important" experiment, (2) encouraged to participate in decisions affecting their work, (3) given veto power over their superiors. . . .[9]

In other words, the workers were placed in the position of structuring their own work situation, had much of the direct and close supervision lifted from them, and were made to feel important both to themselves and to the organization. As a consequence, both the "morale" of the work group and production rose.

The hypothesis generated by these observations, which rapidly grew into a managerial cliché, is that high morale leads to high production. The greatest value of this and other similar studies that followed was the turning of managerial attention to the goals of the organizational participant and exploring ways in which these goals could be met when they were not identical with those of the organization. Management science was finally directed at the informal structure of the organization instead of at its formal elements. Moreover, management science began to separate itself from the incorrect assumptions that the people of organization could be treated simply as other kinds of machines, as adjuncts to machines, or even simply as individuals. It was becoming clear that individuals are related and influenced in their behavior by group and organizational membership and that management would not be successful in predicting worker behavior by treating workers as so many isolated atoms to be arranged at management's discretion:

It is a commonplace of systems theory that the behavior of the whole (at any level) cannot be predicted solely by knowledge of its subparts. Conventional organization theory, however, does attempt to predict the behavior of the organization on the basis of assumptions about individuals.[10]

[8] Conrad M. Arensberg, "Behavior and Organization: Industrial Studies," in John H. Rhoser and Musafer Sherif, *Social Psychology at the Crossroads* (New York: Harper, 1951).

[9] Argyris, *Personality and Organization*, p. 69.

[10] Douglas McGregor, *The Professional Manager* (New York: McGraw-Hill, 1967), p. 40.

Hence, management turned its attention to "how to direct the enthusiasm and motivation of informal groupings toward the accomplishment of the collective task."[11]

The steps taken to tackle this problem have been varied, but for the convenience of summary, we can group them into three main categories: (1) the human relations approach, (2) the human resources approach, and (3) the organizational development approach.

The human relations approach to management has, rightly or wrongly, been associated with the early work of Elton Mayo, F. J. Roethlisberger, and W. J. Dickson.[12] Their work, which demonstrated the interaction of morale and production factors in organization, sent them and others to seek ways to raise the morale of workers and to establish and maintain the workers' commitment to the organization. Management's reaction to this work was somewhat short of full acceptance; managers often called it the "soft sell" approach. But over time it became a mainstay of management practice and resulted in a burgeoning of personnel and employee relations departments that became saddled with the job of keeping workers happy.

Although this approach to management became popular, it was never successfully demonstrated that the accidental findings of the Hawthorne research applied everywhere, or even applied in a majority of cases. As has often happened in industrial and correctional mangement alike, startling and apparently useful discoveries have frequently been turned into ideologies that have changed the practice of management without solid empirical bases to justify the sweeping adoption of a practice or principle. Moreover, the human relations approach was not, in the long run, a very significant departure from the public administration approach that preceded it. Human relations experts were still operating under the assumption that what management wants out of an organization is valid and achievable and that social science could find ways to make workers conform to organizational expectations. Taylor, Gulick, and others of the earlier schools merely called for the "loyalty" of the workers and urged management to build morale so that workers would sacrifice themselves to the demands placed on them. The human relations people were more sophisticated than that, but they merely added some "human

---

[11] Daniel Katz and Robert Kahn, *The Social Psychology of Organizations* (New York: Wiley, 1966), p. 81.

[12] Elton Mayo, *The Human Problems of an Industrial Civilization* (Boston: Division of Research, Harvard Business School, 1946) and F. J. Roethlisberger, *Management and the Worker* (Cambridge: Harvard University Press, 1949).

elements" to the variables that management had to manipulate in order to get the work done.

Perhaps the greatest deficiency of the human relations approach was that the management activities undertaken as a means of raising morale were very seldom associated with the structure of work itself; instead, they were add-ons to the organization, for example, coffee breaks, better benefits, organizationally sponsored outings, and even staff psychologists. These additions were not designed to change the fundamental relationship of the worker to his work or to his superiors. Rather, they were often designed as "loss leaders"—affordable sacrifices by management to workers in order to get the workers to do things management's way on the production floor. In other words, the human relations school suggested some compromise between the relentless push to achieve organizational goals through mechanically set rules and regulations and the desire of the organizational member to achieve his goals as a human being. But it did not suggest that the formal organization itself needed to change.

The management patterns established under human relations theory were not faddish enough to disappear overnight. But another major shift in management occurred in the 1950's when organizational researchers, again working in the tradition of the times, encountered organizational phenomena significantly great in its departures from their expectations to signal that something was wrong with theory. Rensis Likert summarizes the findings that proved troublesome:

> As was expected, the data show that among the work groups which tend to accept company goals, high peer-group loyalty is associated with higher productivity. On the other hand, among the work groups which tend to reject company goals, high peer-group loyalty is associated with lower productivity.[13]

Thus, it became arguable that morale, or in the above case group cohesion, could be associated with behavior contradictory to the organizational purpose and that some groups might fashion their morale on innovative means of avoiding organizational rules and standards.[14] From these and similar findings, the human resources school received its impetus.

The human resources approach was significantly different from earlier management approaches on several scores. For one, science

[13] Rensis Likert, *New Patterns of Management* (New York: McGraw-Hill, 1961), pp. 31–32.

[14] See especially William F. Whyte (ed.), *Money and Motivation* (New York: Harper & Row, 1955).

became a more integral part of the design of management strategy. Also, the science used became more varied, was based on a broader range of theory, and was wedded less to the goals of management. Most crucial, perhaps, was a change in the underlying assumptions about the structure and dynamics of organizations. As the term "human resources" might imply, the management strategies developing at this time were founded on an ecological model of organization. Likert, McGregor, and other leaders of this school were concerned with locating all the resources available to organizations and were especially concerned with cultivating the resources they saw on the *Human Side of Enterprise*.[15] They argued that the human resources in an organization, such as leadership, initiative, commitment, and innovation, were variable quantities that could be conserved and developed or that could be wasted and depleted, just as were the physical and financial resources that managers needed to rely on.

Unlike their predecessors, the proponents of human resources were not so willing to knuckle under to the espoused goals of management and to the traditional beliefs about workers that held sway at that time. They rejected the idea that workers could be treated as machines (even very complex ones), and they argued that management had operated under faulty notions of human motivations and human needs. Influenced strongly by the psychology of Abraham Maslow,[16] human resources theorists argued that human beings were not innately stupid, lazy, and slavish but instead were self-activating, intelligent, and self-directing. Moreover, the higher needs of individuals were not met through external rewards of money, security, comfortable working conditions, and the like. Instead, as workers gained the more basic biological and social needs, their goals tended toward those of self-expression, autonomy, and self-actualization.[17]

Management's long-standing complaints that workers were unwilling to work unless prodded and were unable to do more than the simplest tasks without constant supervision were considered by these researchers to be the results of a vicious circle. Management gave workers no power in making decisions about work, constantly refused worker-initiated efforts to alter their jobs and make them interesting, paid workers off for inherently dissatisfying roles, and then found workers disgruntled, willing to sabotage management strategy, and demanding higher and higher financial rewards. Human relations theorists hypothesized that the goals of individuals must be

[15] Douglas McGregor, *The Human Side of Enterprise*. See also Likert, *New Patterns of Management* (New York, McGraw-Hill, 1961) and Robert Blake and Jane Mouton, *The Managerial Grid* (Houston: Gulf, 1964).
[16] Abraham Maslow, *Eupsychian Management* (Homewood, Ill.: Irwin, 1965).
[17] See McGregor, *The Human Side of Enterprise*.

somehow imbedded in the very nature of work; by striving for the satisfaction of their own highest needs workers would accomplish the goals of the organization as well.

While strategies growing out of these assumptions have been varied, apparently two key strategies involve changes in the type of management directives thought to be most effective and involve related changes in the distribution of power in the organization.[18] Although different theorists have expressed it in different ways, a major strategy in human resources management has been utilizing the informal structure of the organization as one of the basic means of getting work done. These theorists have suggested that organizational participants will need less supervision, will have greater commitment to organizational goals, and will, in the long run, be more efficient and effective if they have a hand in making decisions about how work should be done and if they are allowed to work in groups or teams rather than individually.

It is here, perhaps, that management theory departs most markedly from the usual management practices in correctional agencies. While management in many organizations has gone the route of being less directive and more supportive, management in corrections still tends toward handling workers as individuals and continues to direct in a very prescriptive fashion the behavior of workers instead of allowing staff to formulate their own work plans based on their knowledge of their fellow workers and the problems of the job.

The human resources school has faded slowly and sometimes indistinguishably into another more current approach to management, the organizational development (O.D.) approach. This approach is not very different from the human resources approach. Indeed, some management experts are closely associated with both approaches. Organizational development, however, is usually associated with a somewhat broader and more systematic base than is the human resources approach. The human resources school tends to focus primarily on the management–worker relationship or to deal with the issue of supervision and the structure of the work force. Organizational development grew out of that tradition to include other activities as well, such as the relationship of the organization to its markets or the patterns of communication in the organization. At its worst, O.D. is little more than a fad, in which all the problems of an organization are "made to fit" a "bag of tricks" that certain organization trainers carry with them. For example, in some circles, O.D. has meant *only* the practice of sending out certain executives to management training seminars, T-groups, or sensitivity sessions.

---

[18] McGregor, *The Professional Manager*, pp. 94–95.

While these relatively standard techniques of O.D. may be its best known characteristics, O.D. itself is a much broader and sounder set of theory and management strategy aimed at solving organizational problems or at making organizations more effective.

Chin and Lippit, Watson, and Westley classify organizational development as the "normative-reeducative" approach to change.[19] By this, they mean that O.D. is a type of planned change that assumes human beings will do their best at work and that ineffective organizational behavior is a result of organizational constraints and policies that set up unnatural tendencies toward mistrust, competition, and selfishness among people who would normally trust, cooperate, and help others achieve their goals. They believe that planned change requires reducing the forces that tend to make people distrust and compete and increasing the forces that would make people do the opposite. O.D. assumes that simple rational demonstrations of why one approach or behavior is "better" than another and overtly coercive attempts to make people behave in one way regardless of how they feel both have dysfunctional elements that will reduce the overall effectiveness of the planned change effort. If planned change is to be effective in organizations, it must engage those who are responsible for carrying out the change in the deliberations about why change is important and in planning the alternatives to be taken. Argyris sums up the basics of the O.D. effort as: (1) providing valid information, (2) creating conditions for free and informed choice, and (3) developing commitment to the options.[20]

If operations research can be understood to be the research into the processes and structure of organization, organizational development is little more or less than the democratizing of operations research. It is a process of change based on research into the consequences of present behavior and includes the systematic use of research in the change process to reexamine the organization as new behavior is undertaken. While organizational development frequently includes the use of outside "change agentry" as a basis for beginning a change process, one goal of organizational development is instilling the capacity for change into the organization so that outside resources are not continually needed as a means of improving effectiveness. In contrast to the other management strategies that preceded it, O.D. is a management perspective that treats science, or research, as an integral part of the management process instead of treating it as

[19] R. Chin, "Models and Ideas About Changing," paper prepared for the Symposium on Acceptance of New Ideas, University of Nebraska, Nov., 1963, and R. Lippitt et al., *The Dynamics of Planned Change* (New York: Harcourt Brace Jovanovich, 1958).
[20] Chris Argyris, *Intervention Theory and Method* (Reading, Mass.: Addison-Wesley, 1971).

something that could occasionally help management out. Moreover, O.D. perceives that management, not the managers, needs improving. Relying very much on the distinction that we made in Chapter 1, O.D. seeks to make the whole organization effective instead of making one group in the organization (the managers) effective in controlling other groups in the organization. This management approach, much more so than the other management approaches we have looked at, requires an "open-system" model of the organization. It is to this model that we turn our attention in the next section, but before we do it is important to caution against seeing O.D. as a final answer to organizational problems. It is not. Indeed, it is probable that within a generation O.D. will seem as outmoded as the human relations approach or the public administration approach. If the O.D. precepts are carried out, the following should happen: Science will discover a new means of behaving that will be more effective than the old means (at least for new purposes). But it is the change in *purpose* that is most important. As we have traced the development of management science, it has become clear to us that the role of science in management has changed, as has the role of management. If we still see the basic goal of organization as prosperity for the employers, then things may not have changed a great deal since 1911. But the outlook of management and management science has increasingly broadened and has become increasingly systematic. What was once a fairly pecuniary interest in the structure of production has become a more complex and multifaceted concern that is progressively oriented toward the organization as a whole and toward organizational functions and interactions with a complex environment. We have now reached the point where the manager's overriding concern with the internal structure and dynamics of the organization is itself a conservative and debilitating concern and where the concern with interorganizational and broad institutional networks of value and behavior are more important. To understand why this has happened, it is important to study the organization as an open, interactive system and to study the particular nature of public organizations, including correctional ones, in the political economy of the twentieth century.

ORGANIZATIONS AS OPEN SYSTEMS

Although organizations have become increasingly important to life in the twentieth century, complaints about their rigidity, insensitivity, and inefficiency have also increased. Even though Americans seem to have a natural distaste for nepotism, traditionalism, and autocracy and have been vehement defenders of rule by law rather than by men, Americans constantly attack organizations that operate under their own internal rules or laws and are impervious to the desires of the workers. Front-line workers who are controlled by the rules and standards set by management are not the only ones upset by the difficulties involved in having organizations meet their needs. Equally important to correctional organization is the dissatisfaction of the people served by the organization. In the case of corrections, we find equally vociferous complaints that the organization is too easy, lax, and offender-oriented and that the organization is brutal, inhumane, and order-oriented.

> The increased problems with clients growing out of rigidity of organizational behavior is a specific illustration of the failure to recognize the true character of organizations as open systems in constant interaction with a dynamic environment.[21]

In the 1950's and when the human relations school of management was in vogue, it is true that the interactive nature of the organization and its environment was often downplayed, if studied at all. The organization was taken as the focal point, or more specifically, the problems confronted by managers as conceptualized by managers during the daily task of supervision was the usual focal point. Organizational designs, for example, tables of organization, were usually drawn without much consideration for the organization as an entity in its own right and for having a life and a culture of its own that could and would behave in certain ways, regardless of the purposes that managers wanted to achieve. The organization was thought of as a machine that like any other industrial machine would engage in the activities it was built for and would be operated by the people who had constructed it. Most management experts did not see the faulty elements of their analogy, for they could *not* construct the organization as they could a machine. Organizational participants are not constructed through managerial fancy; they come to organizations to achieve their own goals, not the goals of the organization. Moreover, persons in the environment who come to an organization with demands for products or service or advice cannot plug into an organization as they would a vending machine and have the desired product drop out a slot. On the contrary, they confront human beings who have to interpret both the capacity of the organization to deliver as well as the desires of the public for service.

Because the model or theory of organization held by both managers and others was not altogether accurate, strains in organizational

[21] Katz and Kahn, *The Social Psychology of Organizations,* p. 75.

operation were bound to occur. Employees did not behave as direct-ed, people were not satisfied with the service rendered, and feedback to management suggested that alterations were necessary. Production had to be stepped up, waste decreased, quality control tightened, and so on. Utilizing the same machine model of organization in making alterations as they had in generating the original difficulties, managers usually sought to correct organizational problems, particularly in large organizations, by tightening control, giving middle management less discretion, imposing closer supervision on rank and file, and raising standards of production by introducing new control devices.

Generally, the mechanical or external control systems used in organizations have tended to produce more of the same behavior that they were intended to control or do away with. The more precise the rules, the more errors are made, and the more that management relies on external indicators of production (by counting activities completed), the more often workers concentrate on follow-ing the rules by which they are evaluated rather than on completing the work that the rules supposedly describe. For example, Skolnick observed this rate-producing behavior among Oakland police. Detec-tives who were evaluated in terms of clearance rates routinely cleared arrests by attributing the offenses to apprehended offenders, regard-less of whether or not the offender would be punished for these additional claimed offenses and despite the fact that the public was no safer for the practice.[22] He also observed the practice of burglary detectives to classify "cold" burglaries (that is burglaries for which evidence was incomplete) as "suspicious circumstances" instead of as crimes, thereby keeping down the reported crime rate.[23]

McGregor argues that by using mechanical control systems most organizations produce in their employees the primary motivation of escaping punishment rather than achieving goals, because the negative sanctions attached to not meeting rates are certain but the positive external sanctions for exceeding the rates are only possible.[24] In the police case, for instance, the certainty of a reprimand for refusing to meet a traffic ticket quota may be certain, but the chances for a raise or promotion or better assignment are only possible.

Lawler and Rhode suggest that control systems in organizations can produce four types of dysfunctional behavior:[25] (1) Employees can become bureaucratic or ritualistic and behave to satisfy rules rather than achieve goals. (2) Employees, especially middle managers,

[22] Jerome Skolnick, *Justice Without Trial* (New York: Wiley, 1966), pp. 174–176.
[23] Ibid., pp. 169–173.
[24] McGregor, *The Professional Manager*, pp. 125–127.
[25] Edward E. Lawler III and John Grant Rhode, *Information and Control in Organiza-tions* (Santa Monica: Goodyear, 1976), p. 109.

can become strategic, behaving in ways that will make their own units look good, even if their behavior detracts from the overall goals of the organization. For example, managers of production may drive machines too hard in order to meet a monthly production quota; the result is that repair and maintenance bills will be charged to another department or to another month and will skyrocket. Similarly, Skolnick observed burglary officers who overlooked their informant's narcotic offenses and narcotic officers who did not enforce burglary laws against their informants.[26] (3) Employees can produce invalid data so that the standards are met on paper but do not reflect the behavior of the organization. (4) Organizational members can simply resist the efforts of control, particularly in organizations in which union contracts, civil service specifications, or other agreements about work to be done may not include mention of working with newly imposed control standards.

Research had generally found that

> The more important an organization considers an activity the more likely measures of it are to be distorted. . . . (I)mportant activities are more likely to produce rigid bureaucratic behavior and strategic behavior.[27]

This situation would be particularly true when the measures relied on are subjective, calling for judgments on the part of the persons responsible for the activity, or leave discretion to the organizational participant who is being evaluated. Hence, in correctional work one can expect to find a great deal of distortion on measures that provide the greatest room for public criticism or are most important for offenders. Reclassification decisions, especially those involving grading up to better working conditions or to greater amounts of freedom, are likely to be so affected.[28]

There are no easy answers to these problems of organizations. The power and efficiency of organizations that we see as advantages are also disadvantages. Nevertheless, there are means by which managers can reduce some of this dysfunctional behavior and achieve more completely the goals of the organization. One basic step is to shift from the use of a machine model of organization to the use of an open-system model.

It should be made clear that the open-system model is only that—a model. It is a specific means of organizing complex phenomena and generalizing from myriad and small bits of data to a set of ordered relationships that are more understandable. But it should be clear by

---

[26] Skolnick, *Justice Without Trial*, p. 129.
[27] Lawler and Rhode, p. 108.
[28] See, for example, the chapters in this text on classification and information systems.

now that all managers operate under some basic assumptions, theories, and models of organization, whether they call them rules of thumb, hunches, personal style, or something else. The use of an open-system model does not change the processes by which managers understand the organization, but it does seem more effective than other models for classifying the elements of organization and predicting basic organizational behavior.

Systems theory is not new. Mathematical and other logical systems and systems theories are very old, but the use of systems theory as a means of analyzing organization is far more recent, perhaps finding American roots in the work of Barnard and Selznick[29] but not flowering until its application to defense problems during World War II.[30]

A system, as defined by Ackoff and Emory, is

> A set of interrelated elements, each of which is related directly or indirectly to every other element, and no subset of which is unrelated to any other subset.[31]

There are a wide variety of systems, from very abstract sets of mathematical relations to very concrete systems of roadways. There are systems whose elements are stationary and defined by their physical relationship, for example, a Japanese rock garden, and there are systems that are very active and changing and defined by their function, for example, a system of football players. There are systems that are, for all intents and purposes, unchanging and unaffected by an environment, for example, a geometric figure, and there are other systems whose existence depends on their ability to take in energy, transform it, and exchange outputs with an environment.

Organizations of people would be classified as open systems. Within this system more specific categories would be classified according to the nature of environmental exchanges that take place, the complexity of the structure that transform the input, and the sophistication of the controls by which internal structure is altered and environmental exchange is governed. Some human systems are relatively stable in structure and are relatively limited in terms of the type of outputs they can deliver. Football teams can vary in terms of the defensive and offensive tactics they may use and in the quality with which they execute any of these strategies. But football teams do not change in size, unless the rules of the game change, and they

---

[29] Philip Solznick, *T.V.A. and the Grassroots* (New York, Harper & Row, 1948); Barnard, *The Functions of the Executive.*

[30] See generally Stafford Beer, *Decision and Control* (New York: Wiley, 1966).

[31] Russell L. Ackoff and Fred E. Emory, *On Purposeful Systems* (Chicago: Aldine Atherton, 1972), p. 18.

cannot go on to the production of widgets or symphonic music if the public demand for football entertainment slackens. Other human systems are far more complex and can change not only the structure by which they achieve goals but also the goals (or rules of the game). While all open systems can change somewhat, the speed and adaptability of change by open systems give rise to another form of classification that has to do with the processes of change employed and the means served by such change. Some open systems tend always toward a specific class of output but have no way to change the degree to which that output meets a more generalized set of environmental needs. These systems might be termed goal-oriented. Correctional systems are oriented toward certain societal goals, such as protection or rehabilitation, but the correctional systems are often unable to ascertain how any set of system activities contributes or detracts from these goals, and they do not seem able to consider systematically whether or not a different set of activities of system structures would better meet the social demand for protection or rehabilitation any better than the activities and structures currently used. Other systems might be termed "learning systems" or goal-directed systems, for they not only specify more concretely the goals to be undertaken, but they also seem able to compare the outputs produced to a general model of output desired and then to change internal behaviors in order to alter outputs. One might say that some of today's subsystems in corrections are learning systems, but the system in its entirety is not so sophisticated. For example, the system of guards and inmates in a prison does seem to learn rather rapidly how to adjust its output so that both guards and inmates are relatively satisfied and so that the prison management does not increase the negative sanctions on the unit as a whole. In contrast, the larger system of prisoners, guards, and managers does not seem able to evaluate the function of the quiet cellblock, or ascertain whether this quietness contributes to the broader goals of protection or rehabilitation.

A complete and exacting discussion of organizations as open systems would entail far greater time and detail than this work will allow. Our main purpose, that of exploring how management in corrections is currently carried out and how it can be improved, requires a familiarity with the basic concepts of systems theory and the application of these concepts to human organization. Research on managerial behavior and examples of new managerial behavior based on the treatment of organizations as open systems can be presented here, but a convincing demonstration of why such theory is applicable and fuller ramification of its possibilities are deserving of coverage in their own right. A variety of works are available with which a manager can begin his or her research.[32]

Our major concerns here are with the vertical and horizontal structures of organizations and how they elaborate to fulfill (and/or to change) system goals. The basic subsystems on the horizontal dimension of organization are built to get work done; the vertical structure imposes control and coordination upon the specialized work units. We also need to spend some time with the organizational environment of public organizations, because it is the organizational environment that constrains and shapes the goals of public organizations and the manner in which the work structure will react to demands for control and change.

A number of organizational theorists postulate that the two key dimensions of organizational structure are the horizontal dimension and the vertical dimension.[33]

> Vertical differentiation involves differences along such dimensions as the amount of authority or power individuals have to influence organizational actions, the degree of responsibility they have for these actions, and the number of individuals they supervise or manage.[34]

Although an official's position in an organizational hierarchy will greatly influence the type and quality of rewards associated with the job, the vertical structure of organization does more than delineate gradations of reward. Its most powerful consequence, perhaps, is its division of organizational members into two or more classes. In its simplest form, this is the polarity between the managers who exercise authority and the workers who obey it.[35] Lawler and Rhode are somewhat more discriminating; they divide the organization into three classes: those who make the decisions, those who maintain the system, and those who are measured and controlled by the system.[36] Parsons' classes are fairly similar: the workers on the technical level who are responsible for the actions of procurement, production and disposal, the officials on the managerial or administrative level who

[32] On human organizations as systems, see Ackoff and Emery, *On Purposeful Systems*. For an excellent introduction to open system characteristics and their application to complex organizations, see Katz and Kahn, *The Social Psychology of Organizations*. For a more difficult work that not only focuses on operations research in organizations but also develops the potential of general systems theory for human affairs in general, see Stafford Beer, *Decision and Control*. For an introduction to the application of systems theory to correctional organization, the reader might refer to David Duffee, *Correctional Policy and Prison Organization* (Beverly Hills: Sage-Halsted, 1975).

[33] Katz and Kahn, *The Social Psychology of Organizations*, p. 83; Lawler and Rhode, *Information and Control*, p. 35.

[34] Lawler and Rhode, *Information and Control*, p. 8.

[35] Katz and Kahn, *The Social Psychology of Organizations*, p. 84.

[36] Lawler and Rhode, *Information and Control*, p. 8.

are responsible for controlling technical-level conflicts and coordinating technical-level activities, and the officers on the institutional level who are responsible for integrating the organization into its environment.[37]

The vertical dimension in correctional agencies has been treated in a number of ways. The classic distinction, of course, is between the class of controllers (staff) and the class of controlled (offenders). Etzioni finds the impermeability of this class line the defining characteristic of the coercive organization and claims that it alone is responsible for the alienation of the offender from correctional goals.[38] Correctional observers have identified this class or vertical structure as a primary generator of the "inmate subculture" in both prisons[39] and mental institutions.[40] Other observers have been more reserved in their attributing staff–offender conflict to the dynamics of the vertical structure alone. Irwin and Cressey, for example, argue that the vertical structure of the prison reiterates the power structure in the community.[41] Cressey, Jacobs and Retsky, and Duffee have been cautious about the dichotomous nature of the prison vertical structure and have stressed the middle position of the front-line staff, as distinct from the executive staff, as a third class.[42]

The horizontal dimension of the organization is a consequence of the elaboration of the overall tasks into subparts and specialties and of overall goals into more specific objectives. The work specializations of an organization naturally differ depending on the overall goals. Manufacturing firms may break down into production, design and engineering, procurement, sales, and budgeting or accounting divisions. Consulting firms may have specialized units for each type of advice to be rendered, or for each type of research technology to be used, and other units for personnel, and contracts management. Correctional specializations have been slow to develop. The earliest penitentiaries were largely organized for the military operation of guarding, specializing not so much by function as by time of operation into shifts. But even the earliest prisons had divisions, or specialists, in

[37]Talcott Parsons, *Structure and Process in Modern Societies* (New York: Free Press, 1960), p. 69.
[38]Amitai Etzioni, *A Comparative Analysis of Complex Organizations* (New York: The Free Press, 1961).
[39]Gresham Sykes, *Society of Captives* (Princeton, N.J.: Princeton University Press, 1971); Donald Clemmer, *The Prison Community* (Indianapolis: Bobbs-Merrill, 1958).
[40]Erving Goffman, *Asylums* (Garden City, N.Y.: Doubleday, 1961).
[41]John Irwin and Donald R. Cressey, "Thieves, Convicts and the Inmate Culture," *Social Problems* (Fall, 1962), 142–155.
[42]James B. Jacobs and Harold G. Retsky, "Prison Guard," *Urban Life* (April, 1975), 5–29; David Duffee, "The Correctional Officer Subculture and Organizational Change," *Journal of Research in Crime and Delinquency*, (July, 1974), 155–172; Donald R. Cressey, "Limitations on Organization of Treatment in the Modern Prison," in Richard Cloward et al., *Theoretical Studies in Social Organization of the Prison* (New York: Social Science Research Council, Pamphlet 15, March, 1960), pp. 78–110.

charge of accounting and had groups responsible for maintenance and industry.

As the goals for correctional organizations changed, the older divisions or specialties did not disappear; instead, new ones were added to address new problems or to deliver new services. Education became important, as did field supervision (in the form of parole), and counseling and casework. Contemporary correctional organizations that are centralized in large departments or bureaus not only have major divisions for institutional and field work but also special organizations for classification and diagnosis and for prerelease and reintegration, such as halfway houses and work release centers.

Because of the ambiguity of correctional goals, not all correctional organization theorists agree on the best way to categorize correctional organization divisions. Cressey, for example, argues that prison organization is basically divided on the horizontal dimension into three separate units for keeping, using, and caring for inmates.[43] Other researchers have argued that the functional division between keeping (guarding) of offenders and caring for (treating) offenders is not clear-cut, and that at least in some institutions both the custodial force and the treatment force are equally responsible for the behavior changes, if any, that take place in offenders.[44] Duffee has generalized from this observation to suggest that all front-line personnel, whether uniformed or white-collar, should be considered part of a "production subsystem" responsible for the production of change.[45]

Probation and parole units, whether part of a larger correctional department or separate and autonomous organizations, are generally less complex in their specialization than are large prisons. Generally, the front-line agent is responsible for all the work directly involving the offender. Hence, while prison literature often focuses on the conflict between treatment and custody divisions of the organization,[46] much probation and parole literature concentrates on the inherent conflicts in the field officer role.[47]

Most organizational theorists suggest that there are several basic subsystems, or sets of specialized activities, that characterize the horizontal dimension of most complex organizations. Selznick[48]

[43] Donald R. Cressey, "Limitations on Organization of Treatment in the Modern Prison," and "Contradictory Directives in Complex Organizations: The Case of the Prison," *Administrative Science Quarterly* (June, 1959), 1-19.
[44] David Street, Robert Vinter, and Charles Perrow, *Organization for Treatment* (New York: Free Press, 1966).
[45] Duffee, *Correctional Policy and Prison Organization.*
[46] Oscar Grusky, "Role Conflict in Organizations: A Study of Prison Camp Officials," in Lawrence Hazelrigg (ed.), *Prison Within Society* (Garden City, N.Y.: Doubleday, 1969), pp. 455-476.
[47] Elliot Studt, *Surveillance and Service in Parole* (Los Angeles: Institute of Government and Public Affairs, U.C.L.A., 1972); Daniel Glaser, *The Effectiveness of a Prison and Parole System* (Indianapolis: Bobbs-Merrill, 1969), pp. 291-299.
[48] Selznick, *T.V.A. and the Grassroots*, p. 248.

and Argyris[49] are satisfied with three: (1) the subsystem for production, (2) the subsystem for maintenance, and the (3) subsystem for organizational exchange with the environment. Katz and Kahn make a strong case for being more elaborate: in addition to production and maintenance, they specify boundary activity, such as procurement of resources and disposal of output, and adaptive activity for research, development, and organizational change. They also identify the management subsystem as a distinct unit, although they stress that this last unit cuts across all the others as a means of integration.[50]

> Organizations cannot be understood wholly in terms of the interaction of past, present, and future environmental requirements and personal needs of members. The very structures created to meet these demands exert a force in their own right.[51]

Understanding the behavior of the organization, then, requires (1) an analysis of goals, as constrained and/or demanded by the environment and as set by organizational decision makers, (2) an understanding of the task specializations into which the organization is differentiated, and (3) an understanding of the vertical structure of authority and reward. It is the intersection of work function and hierarchical position that largely determines how organizational groups will behave.[52] And it is the position of corrections in the hierarchy of American values and the domain corrections controls in the realm of American social problems that determine the relationship of correctional systems to other systems in American society. If the positioning of values is politics, and if the division of labor forms an economy, then it is to the political economy of public organizations that we should now turn our attention.

THE POLITICAL ECONOMY OF PUBLIC ORGANIZATIONS[53]

While the systems concepts applicable to the analysis of correctional organizations may be very similar to the key concepts in the

---

[49] Chris Argyris, *Integrating the Individual and the Organization* (New York: Wiley, 1964).
[50] Katz and Kahn, *The Social Psychology of Organizations*, pp. 75–109.
[51] Ibid., p. 84.
[52] Ibid.
[53] This section relies heavily on Gary L. Wamsley and Mayer N. Zald, "The Political Economy of Public Organizations," *Public Administration Review* (Jan./Feb., 1973), 62–73, and on notes prepared by R. Richard Ritti, Professor of Organizational Behavior, Pennsylvania State University, for a weekly discussion group on organizations and public policy. The author would also like to thank the other members of that group, Joe A. Miller and Peter B. Meyer, for their help in the development of these ideas.

analysis of other complex organizations, there are differences in degree, if not in kind, of variables most influential in public, tax-supported, government organizations, as compared to the variables most important in understanding the behavior of private organizations, particularly profit-making organizations. The greatest of these differences, perhaps, is the lack in public organizations of clear and measurable objectives, such as increase in markets or maximization of profits. Goals in public organizations are often associated, if not identical, with core cultural symbols, such as justice, welfare, health, and education. While the American public and the managers of these organizations can often point to the absence of these "things," it is frequently difficult to point to what they are, or even to the activities that might contribute to them.

In contrast to many private, profit-making firms, the internal structure of public organizations is less in the control of the organization itself and is more immediately tied to the beliefs about productivity that exist in the environment. While the type, amount, and channels of exchange with outsiders used in profit-making firms are often dependent on the nature of the products made and sold, and hence by the structure of the labor specialization in its production subsystem, the type of products or the services rendered, and the way that work is structured, in public organizations are often determined by the type, amount, and channels of exchange that these organizations have with their legitimating environment.

A very good example of this relationship between the internal structure of the public enterprise and the public environment is provided by the history of modern police forces. These organizations, established in Great Britain and the United States in the first half of the nineteenth century, were closely associated with the desire of the nineteenth-century industrialists to be separated from, or protected from, direct contact with their labor forces and from the complaints from the working class about inequitable distribution of resources. The modern police organization intervened between the propertied and monied class and the "dangerous classes" (as they were called) and effectively diverted political dissent from owners and employers to the police force itself.[54] It is not surprising that in the class struggle of the nineteenth century the modern police agency was structured internally to defend property and prevent public disorder rather than to enforce laws that might favor the working class and the unemployed.

[54] Allan Silver, "The Demand for Order in Civil Society: A Review of Some Themes in the History of Urban Crime, Police, and Riot," in David Bordua (ed.) *The Police* (New York: Wiley, 1967), pp. 1–25; Cyril D. Robinson, "The Mayor and the Police—The Political Role of the Police in Society," in George L. Mosse (ed.), *Police Forces in History* (London: Sage, 1975), pp. 277–315.

Public organizations are established to perform activities necessary to the operation of communities and larger social systems. Most of the activities traditionally have been among those that private organizations could not or would not provide, either because the services or products were not profitable or were seen by powerful public groups as those that all individuals should have access to or benefit from without having to trade something of greater value. That is, public organizations are frequently engaged in performing services that are perceived to be due to citizens because of their *membership* in the community or the state instead of services to be provided in exchange for other services or products or for financial recompense.[55]

The absence of the legitmacy to profit from the provision of services of this category has effectively limited the types of auspice under which the services could be provided. Stated another way, public organizations have been established to provide services whose value is difficult to determine within normal economic distribution patterns and are determined instead in accordance with political power.

One may say that the value of public organizations is of greater centrality to the dominant culture than private, profit-making firms because the life or survival of the public organization is not tested by its ability to provide a certain quality or quantity of output under criteria of consumer demand. This means that while the value, or essentiality, of the service is not questioned, the economics of its provision (or the specialization of labor) is not generally determinable in terms of the effects of that economy on the products turned out. The agency is primarily evaluated in terms of its *mission* rather than in terms of the consequences of its performance. The major function of the public organization is its manifestation of some characteristic of a cultural pattern. Its function is its ability to provide the symbol(s) of a culture.

This does not mean that organizations of public services need not do anything or that significant conflicts do not arise concerning the provision of such services. Indeed, one function of the public organization is to provide a means by which public, political debate is resolved, or at least tempered, in the sense that the issues of debate are taken out of the realm of immediate, public scrutiny and placed under the authority of organizational executives. It is much as if the conflicting groups in the political system said, "We cannot agree on how to do this, or even on what it is, but we can agree that it has to be done, and therefore we establish this organization to do it."

[55] Vickers, *Making Institutions Work*, pp. 11–17.

Many public organizations deal with activities such as welfare, punishment, education, and so forth, in which the conflicting interest groups can agree on the importance of maintaining the symbol (i.e., education is good, wrongdoers are punished) but cannot agree on the specifics of its implementation (i.e., should the "three R's" or "emotional maturity and social skills" be the emphasis in secondary education?).

Empowering a public organization to take on the responsibility for such services deflects and/or diffuses the cultural conflict in at least two ways: (1) The organization as a physical entity, existing in a semiautonomous state vis-à-vis its legitimating environment, enables conflicting groups in society to concentrate their direct interaction in spheres in which there is more agreement (i.e., economic exchange) and isolates conflict to narrowly constricted spheres (as in budget hearings for the public organizations); (2) the delegation of responsibility for symbolic services to organizations reduces the visibility of the conflict or disagreement itself, so that basic divisions in society, or the mobilizing points for irresolvable conflict, are less visible. Although the public organization is not free from internal conflict concerning the distribution of its resources, it can generally rely on public confidence or deference to "professional expertise" as a way of avoiding public debate about the means chosen to accomplish ends or about whether or not conflicting goals assigned to the organization can be accomplished within the same organization.[56]

Public organizations, such as correctional departments, welfare departments, and mental health centers, have the additional problem of dealing with clients who are not the legitimizers of the organization itself. Most of the personnel hired, and their role technologies, are focused on the people with whom the system has direct contact; yet the reasons for organizational existence relate to the legitimating forces rather than to the people served. In this situation, there is likely to be a disparity between the goals of the executives who interface with outside groups who seek from the organization their utility in maintaining symbols and the goals of the front-line staff who interface with the individuals who are supervised, processed, or treated.

For example, executives in a department of correction may consider a program valuable if it reduces recidivism and thus protects the public. Front-line staff may value a program if it provides greater

---

[56] See George Dession, "Psychiatry and the Conditioning of Criminal Justice," *Yale Law Journal* (Jan., 1938), 319–340.

services or meets more needs of their clients.[57] Welfare executives may evaluate programs in terms of whether or not they meet federal regulations, but front-line staff may be more concerned with whether a new program makes it easier or more difficult to deal with welfare receipients. This disparity between the public "client" faced by executives and the service client faced by staff is likely to mean that the criteria of effectiveness that are required at one level are seen as irrelevant or counterproductive at another level.

Public organizations, like other organized economies, require both some slack resources and discretion in selecting the means with which to deal with environmental uncertainties and internal conflicts. Profit-making firms usually obtain slack and flexibility (or diversity) to the extent that previously engaged resources are successful in returning investable income. Public organizations do not obtain slack and diversity in this way. Rather, they are more dependent on the maintenance of diversity in the symbols that legitimate their missions. In other words, if these organizations are to grow, they require the existence of more than one significant authorizing group, or at least one authorizing group that seeks multiple symbolic missions from its public organizations.[58] Hence, these organizations are in significant trouble to the extent that (1) their mission is identified too closely with the values of any one public interest group, (2) several interest groups coalesce around the value of one symbolic mission, or (3) the dominant interest group opts for one interpretation of a symbol, or mission, at the expense of others.

Public organizations would then appear to operate under greatest strain when (1) there are powerful rationalizing influences in government that seek to order and prioritize among goals, (2) there is a demand for systemic research that attempts to link one program with another or to link programmatic assumptions with specific consequences, and (3) there are significant levels of disbelief in the environment that one set of public organizations can achieve the goals of competing and/or conflicting groups in society.

These strain-producing factors, and their consequences, are no more readily observable today than in correctional systems. Two of the greatest rationalizing influences, the economic recession in the early 1970's and the tightened governmental budget, have influenced not only a reordering of public goals but they have also brought into question government's role in providing many services or programs

---

. [57]David Duffee, Peter B. Meyer, and Barbara D. Warner, *Offender Needs, Parole Outcome and Program Structure in the Bureau of Correction Community Services Program* (Harrisburg, Pa.: Governor's Justice Commission, Sept., 1977), pp. 10–25.
[58]Marshall W. Meyer, "Organizational Domains," *American Sociological Review* (Oct., 1975), 599–615.

for which there is little demonstrated benefit. Just as important as the lack of financial resources are the increasing drain on natural resources and the shift in public concern from law and order to survival.

As a result of the changes in goal priorities, there has been a shift in the type of research engaged in. Instead of focusing on research and related action programs whose objectives are solving human problems, or reducing crime, or increasing learning, and so forth, research now focuses on evaluation of program effects. Correctional agencies have been pressured to demonstrate how action x, y, or z leads to specified objectives. This demand calls for research and program competencies well beyond the capacities of most correctional agencies. Lastly, the inability to demonstrate the attainment of program objectives has thrown into question the value of the correctional organization as it exists today, especially its competence in meeting the competing demands on it made by different and often conflicting goals. Because it has been doubted that the correctional organization provides either change in offender behavior or safety to communities, there have been strong demands that correctional organizations narrow their missions and concentrate on security, fairness, and administrative efficiency instead of on more vaguely optimistic individually oriented goals.

The changes in the correctional political economy will place new demands on correctional managers. Managers will have to learn how to translate broad, conflict ridden legislative mandates into objectives that are both achievable and satisfactory to broad segments of the body politic. Managers will have to make more sophisticated forays into the world of public decision and policy making and make more concentrated efforts at controlling the behavior of their organizations. If the attempts at internal control are not to fall into the same traps that stymied mechanistic management in industry, correctional managers will have to import research expertise into their organizations and to harness that expertise to the task of bringing both the informal and formal structures of organization closer together. Correctional organizations will have to shift from pursuing missions to achieving objectives.

PART TWO

MANAGING
THE
INTERNAL
ORGANIZATION

INTRODUCTION

A major portion of managerial time and effort is directed toward altering behavior within the organization or maintaining desired patterns of behavior within the boundaries of the system. The managerial task of ordering, evaluating, and changing the internal structure and dynamics of organization has been analyzed in a variety of ways. Probably more important than the different means of explaining this management job are several points that all management studies tend to agree on: managers, whether they understand it or not, are managing a system that is constantly interacting with its environment and in which each organizational subdivision, or system component, affects each other subdivision. Moreover, while many managers may describe their job in terms of "keeping the thing together," if they are pressed to explain how they do this, they will describe a series of unending changes and alterations as the basis of "keeping things together." In other words, management of an organization, even under noncrisis, rather stable conditions, is a task involving constant change.

This part of the book is concerned with describing the activities of management that are involved in managing, or controlling and changing, the internal aspects of the organization under normal, noncrisis conditions. The attempt has been made to present concepts in a sequence that makes the concepts easy to understand and that highlights the relationships between the different facets of this aspect of management. It should be stressed, however, that in actual, ongoing operations, a manager cannot attend to one part of his job first, and then the next, and so on. Because different parts of the organization affect each other, the different facets of the managerial job are also systematically interrelated and affect each other mutually.

Nevertheless, the first three chapters in this part relate the activities by which a manager decides what an organization should do, how the manager relates to his or her subordinates the accomplishment of these goals, and the impacts on organizational structure of both this goal-setting and daily guidance activity. Chapter 4 is concerned with organizational goals and the formulation of organizational policy in correction. First, several notions of organizational goal are reviewed and then Herbert Simon's concept of organizational goal as a complex goal-set is introduced. Based on this model of goal, four correctional policies are elaborated. These four policies relate to the manner in which the manager stresses concern for the individual offender and concern for the community as he or she decides on the structure of the organization.

Chapter 5 examines the means by which managers feed back to their organization information about goal achievement in an attempt to get the organization to accomplish more closely the policies established for the organization. The relationship between correctional policy and managerial feedback style is examined, with some suggestions why some managerial supervision styles may lead the organization away from the goals espoused by management.

Chapter 6 examines the impact of correctional policy and managerial feedback on the internal climate, or interaction patterns, established between staff and offenders in correctional settings. It is demonstrated that healthy or unhealthy organizational climates are frequently the product of the goal-setting and feedback activities that set the constraints on the internal organizational system.

Finally, Chapter 7 examines a distinct and generally problematic aspect of correctional organizations: the structure of the classification system through which decisions about offenders are made and by which offenders are allocated to different organizational programs or subdivisions. Classification decisions will greatly affect the extent to which various organizational programs and divisions will be able to supervise offenders effectively. Hence, it is very important that the organizational patterns used in the classification process mesh with the structures used for supervision and control. But classification decisions are heavily dependent on information; and, as we shall see, the accuracy and types of information generated are again related to correctional policy, to basic philosophies of correction, and to the organizational climates generated by the managerial tasks of goal setting and feedback.

4

Formulating Correctional Goals: The Interaction of Environment, Belief, and Organizational Structure[1]

(David Duffee and Vincent O'Leary)

Discussions about correctional goals are probably as tortuous, confused, and conflict-producing as any other discussions of goals in American public organizations. Part of the controversy is directly related to the centrality of values implied in the activity of criminal punishment. The strong notions of justice, due process, fairness, and citizenship expressed in the Declaration of Independence and in the Constitution, have made the process and relationships in control and sanctioning paramount organizational issues. The essentiality of criminal punishment in this American schema of order and freedom is manifested in the complexity with which the decision to

[1] This chapter draws heavily on Vincent O'Leary and David Duffee, "Correctional Policy: A Classification of Goals Designed for Change," *Crime and Delinquency* (Oct., 1977), 373–386; Herbert Simon, "On the Concept of Organizational Goal," *Administrative Science Quarterly* (June, 1964), 1–22; and on discussions in the seminar on organization and social policy at Pennsylvania State University, particularly R. Richard Ritti, "Comments on the Concept of Organizational Goal," notes prepared for that seminar, Jan. 14, 1977.

punish is shared by the three branches of government. It is typical that all three branches contribute to the implementation of a penalty against a criminal: the legislative in proscribing conduct and levying penalties, the judicial in a specific length and type of penalty, and the executive both in the administration of the penal agencies and in altering judicial decisions through parole, commutation, and pardon.

Although a great deal of effort has gone into establishing a process for deciding on and carrying out a punishment, considerably less energy has been expended in determining exactly what a specific class of penalties should accomplish or in designing the organized means by which this end is incrementally met. Even if agreement is reached within a particular jurisdiction concerning broad aims of rehabilitation, incapacitation, or deterrence, dissension is rampant over how these desired consequences are to be measured (or over what behaviors are to be taken as indicators of them) and over the selection of paths that might best reach these indicators.

Because of the conflict, ambiguity, and rapid change that attend philosophic and legal discussions about the substantive goals of correction, the process by which any set of these goals becomes a controlling factor in the management of correctional organization and the steps managers need to take to implement goals are widely ignored. People have frequently believed, or acted as if they believed, that settling (however temporarily) on some statement of intent or rationale for punishment would automatically settle the issues concerning implementation. This assumption is often not expressed openly, but it remains both a strong influence and a great deficiency in the deliberation of correctional goals, whether it is manifested by social reformers, legislators, or the actual managers of the correctional agencies.

The very nature of organizations as semiautonomous, self-activating, complex systems, replete with their own informal culture, rules, regulations, and productions structures, means that organizational goals are very different from the philosophical or legal deliberations about goals. It is simply not true that organizations do, or even could, embody or implement the "goals" expressed about it or for it by the acts of external groups who legitimize the organization and delegate to it the authority to carry out a certain societal function.

ORGANIZATIONAL GOALS

Organizational goals are not the desires expressed about the organization by any particular interest group, nor the intents and rationales embodied in authorizing legislation, nor public statements concerning goals by executive leaders, nor even the functions that the organization might serve for society or for a larger complex system. Organizational goals are organizational policies, or "abstractions or generalizations about organizational behavior at a level which involves the structure of the organization."[2] By structure, organizational theorists mean the patterned behavior of organizational participants and units that taken together explain the changes in inputs taken into the organization. Organizational goals "do not coincide with the goals of owners, or of top management, but have been modified by managers and employees at all echelons."[3] (Or, in keeping with our observations about offenders as members, are modified as well by the persons being punished.)

Herbert Simon defines organizational goals as

> Value premises that can serve as inputs to decisions. By *motives*, we mean the causes, whatever they are, that lead individuals to select some goals rather than others as premises for their decisions.[4]

Simon emphasizes that organizational goals are not single objectives or targets that an organization can reach, and they are not individual desires (or motives) of the persons running the organization. Instead, he argues that organizational goals are multiple sets of constraints on the organization, each part of which must be satisfied if the organization is to solve problems or take a specific course of action. Hence, it would be inaccurate to say that an organizational goal is to maximize profit. Rather, the goal set might be to gain the greatest profit possible, given the current market and producing the type of product the organization has the capacity to produce, by using means that satisfactorily meet the demands of labor. There are, in other words, a multiple set of constraints on organizational action. There may be many better ways of maximizing profit, given a different product, a different union contract, or a different set of organizational technologies. Similarly, there may be better ways of making a specific product, and there may be better or more satisfying conditions for labor than those provided by the company, but an organization has to solve a number of problems simultaneously, and the organizational goal should be taken as the overall solution, not the subobjectives that go into the solution.

Simon points out that if one gathered all the value premises, or bases for decisions, into one set of statements about organizational activity, most persons in the organization could probably agree upon

[2] Daniel Katz and Robert Kahn, *The Social Psychology of Organizations* (New York: Wiley, 1966), p. 259.
[3] Simon, "On the Concept of Organizational Goal," p.2.
[4] Ibid., p.4.

their merit. It is likely, for example, that the various levels of the correctional organization could agree that "security is necessary, rehabilitation is desirable, order and fairness in procedure are important, safety and protection of both staff and offenders are good," and so on.

With complex organizations, however, the different value premises take on different weights to different people and organizational units. Organizations do not solve their multiple constraint problems simultaneously; instead they break down the different parts of the complex goal into functional units and specialties. As it becomes the duty of one part of the organization to deal directly with one set of constraints, the importance of that constraint, or the actions taken to meet it, become more important than other constraints of the organization.

If all parts of the organization could be satisfied, there might be little organizational conflict.

> Actual decisions, however, involve trade-offs between values. At the very least, resources must be allocated by some means to a set of programs or functions which share these resources . . . Differences arise over which particular components of the goal set are to be optimized; that is, to be treated as generators of decisions as opposed to those which will be treated as tests.[5]

The distinction that Simon makes between goals as "decision generators" and goals as "decision tests" is crucial. Both tests and generators are important, but they influence decisions in different ways:

> The goals may be used directly to synthesize proposed solutions (alternative generation). Second, the goals may be used to test the satisfactoriness of a proposed solution (alternative testing).[6]

Because decisions makers in different parts of the organization divide goals differently between generators and tests, bitter conflict can arise over what the organization should be doing. "Within separate functions there is, in part, a trained incapacity of decision makers to see the legitimacy of generators other than the ones commonly used by their own function."[7]

In corrections this conflict is evident frequently, especially in prisons. Custodial managers often generate alternative shift schedules, perimeter security designs, and security grades to various prison jobs on the value premise that security is important. The managers may use as tests for that decision that the final security plan should not

---

[5] Ritti, "Comments on the Concept of Organizational Goal."
[6] Simon, "On the Concept of Organizational Goal," p. 7.
[7] Ritti, "Comments on the Concept of Organizational Goal." p. 2.

disgruntle the inmates too much, and thus cause additional security problems, or that disciplinary procedures must meet certain constitutional standards and departmental directives, or that counseling and educational programs need sufficient flexibility if they are to work. But the interests in a "test" are much narrower than the interests in a "generator." The primary concern is getting the custodial division's work done as best as possible; the secondary or test concern is that the security plan does not interfere too greatly with the programs in other divisions. The treatment division of a prison may have very contradictory value premises, generating alternatives on the bases of treatment objectives and modifying them only to the extent that they would fail the "test" of being too unsafe.

Not only do the tests and generators differ across organizational functions, but they may also vary at different levels in the organizational hierarchy. What may be for a lower-level manager a generator of action may be for his or her superior only a test, or vice versa. For example, the author analyzed a halfway house division of a major correctional department in which these hierarchical conflicts between tests and generators were very evident. The halfway house managers and their staff were primarily committed to staff and offender roles that would maximize the number of community services available to the residents and minimize the number of offender problems that prolonged the period of reintegration. The division chief, on the other hand, attempted to maximize the uniformity of procedures in the division and the obedience of staff and residents to rules and regulations conceived and drafted at the central office. While the front-line staff tested decisions on the basis of whether they met or conformed to the rules, the division manager tested decisions on whether or not they allowed staff the minimum amount of discretion that enabled the program to run. Each side in this conflict perceived the other as having displaced goals, although when an outside observer asked each party what the long-range effects of the program should be, the answers were relatively similar.[8]

It is also important to understand that the particular solution that organizations elaborate in order to meet complex constraints may not be satisfactory in terms of organizational survival. If an organization is to survive over the long haul, the value premises that it chooses to maximize should be relatively similar to the ones in the environment as the "functions of the organization."

[8] David Duffee, Peter B. Meyer, and Barbara D. Warner, *Offender Needs, Parole Outcome and Program Structure in the Bureau of Correction Community Services Division* (Harrisburg, Pa.: Governor's Justice Commission, 1977).

What the sociologist calls the functional requisites for survival can usually give us good clues for predicting organizational goals; however, if the functional requisites resemble the goals, the similarity is empirical, not definitional. What the goals are must be inferred from observation of the organization's decision-making processes, whether these processes be directed toward survival or suicide.[9]

The models of organizational constraints, or sets of value premises, described in the following pages are an attempt to elaborate some major ways in which correctional organizations have attempted to meet multiple constraints in the past. The models all involve value trade-offs of different sorts, and the trade-offs have formed, through correctional history, a fairly solid pattern of correctional options, each with separate tests and generators.

A MODEL OF CORRECTIONAL POLICIES

Among persons concerned with social reform few arguments are debated with as much vigor as those concerning the value premises of the agents of change, a favorite point of attack being the methods used to analyze and control social problems. The argument is made that methods are inexorably linked to values and that not nearly enough attention has been paid to the consequences that given change/control techniques are likely to achieve.[10] Whatever the merits of this criticism elsewhere, it is particularly apt when directed toward programs designed for change of convicted offenders. Attempts to make explicit the assumptions undergirding correctional efforts have been rare. Consequently, judgments of the desirability of any goal have lacked solid foundation, and devices for measuring the effectiveness of methods used to achieve one purpose or another have been difficult to construct.

A stress on goals shifts the focus away from an exclusive concern with the offender and his or her characteristics and toward a view that places the offender within a correctional system continuously accommodating itself to a larger social order; it calls special attention to the manner in which a correctional system organizes to achieve its goals, establishes relationships with offenders, and defines its priorities through the allocation of power and resources. The major assumption underlying this line of inquiry is that one can understand a correctional system and the behavior of the persons within it only

[9] Simon, "On the Concept of Organizational Goal," p. 20.
[10] For an example of this kind of criticism, see Elliott Currie and Jerome Skolnick, "A Critical Note on Conceptions of Collective Behavior," *Annals of the American Academy of Political and Social Science* (Sept., 1970), 34–35. A rejoinder follows on pp. 46–55.

by understanding the processes by which correctional value premises are elaborated in organizational structure.[11]

This chapter deals with the examination of correctional goals using methods that facilitate systemic change in correctional agencies. The essential strategy has been a "survey feedback technique" in which measures of goals and discrepancies in their attainment are presented to key groups of officials in the correctional systems.[12] The reasons for concentrating on correctional *goals* as the content of the feedback can be summarized as follows:

1. It is important to effective change efforts to be able to categorize programs in such a way that one can specify those whose aims are conguent or incongruent with other programs or with higher-level goals.
2. The identification and development of administrative and organizational structures and processes that support various organizational goals depend on a measure of those goals.
3. Judgments about staff actions and the appropriateness of the perceptions and behaviors of offenders are directly related to the aims of the system.

This chapter presents a classification of correctional goals that was subsequently scaled and used as a feedback instrument in correctional organization change activities. Two criteria were specified in its development: (1) the classification scheme had to cover the entire correctional spectrum; (2) it had to include an explicit statement about the assumptions underlying the methods used to change offenders.

The need to deal with the entire correctional system emerged from two considerations. First, correctional planning and managerial concerns are increasingly focused on the entire range of functions—from presentence investigation to discharge from parole. Classifications of goals limited to institutional programs have had the obvious disadvantage of not dealing with important correctional functions—

[11] This kind of analysis has had a long tradition in criminological research. See, for example, Donald Clemmer, *The Prison Community* (New York: Holt, Rinehart and Winston, 1958); Donald R. Cressey (ed.), *The Prison: Studies in Institutional Organization and Change* (New York: Holt, Rinehart and Winston, 1961); David Street, Robert D. Vinter, and Charles Perrow, *Organization for Treatment* (New York: Free Press, 1966); and E. K. Nelson and Catherine Lovell, *Developing Correctional Administrators* (Washington, D.C.: Joint Commission on Correctional Manpower and Training, Nov., 1969).

[12] The process has been widely used in organizational change efforts especially since Mann's pioneering work. See Floyd Mann, "Studying and Creating Change," in W. Bennis, K. Benne, and R. Chin, *The Planning of Change* (New York: Holt, Rinehart and Winston, 1961), pp. 605-15.

parole decision making, probation supervision, and prerelease activities. Already two-thirds of the nation's correctional population is handled outside of traditional institutions, and every sign points to a widening use of community-based programs. To deal with today's programs and the likely ones of the future, a classification system must be able to account for this entire band of activity.

Second, a system view of correction emphasizes the interdependence of the whole process. What is done in institutions has an effect on parole systems; and, similarly, probation activities have an effect on prisons. And the effects are reflected in more than the simple flow of offenders across the system. In numerous jurisdictions, probation, institutional, and parole systems operate in splendid isolation, each with sharply different philosophies. Serious and costly dysfunctions in program are the result. It is more common than not to find the same offender treated successively: (1) to individual supportive counseling while he or she is on probation, on the assumption that crime is a reflection of an emotional disability; (2) to group counseling while the offender is in prison, in the belief that effective attitude change can occur only in offender peer groups; and (3) to close observation while the offender is on parole, since it is argued that most crime originates through association with other offenders. These differences in goals have been described and studied within prisons and within probation and parole systems;[13] few attempts have been made to investigate them systematically across the span of correctional programs.

If he or she wants to be effective, the correctional manager of any particular agency, or set of functions, will need a broader conception of goals than the manager dealing only with the internal objectives of the agency. The manager will need to work with an explicit policy that links his or her units to others and that links the system to other social institutions.

The additional requirement that the classification system account for offenders' motivations is based largely on practical grounds of effective change efforts. It is very possible to describe sets of goals for correctional programs without linking them to motivational concepts. The Street–Vinter–Perrow system of institutional classification, in terms of a custody-treatment orientation, is a case in point.[14]

---

[13] See Street, Vinter, and Perrow, *Organization for Treatment*; Lloyd Ohlin, Herman Piven, and Donnell Pappenfort, "Major Dilemmas of the Social Worker in Probation and Parole," *NPPA Journal* (July, 1956), 211–25; Daniel Glaser, *The Effectiveness of a Prison and Parole System*, abbr. ed. (Indianapolis: Bobbs-Merrill, 1969), 293–99.

[14] Street, Vinter, and Perrow, *Organization for Treatment*. See also Donald Cressey, "Limitations on Organization of Treatment in the Modern Prison," in Richard Cloward et al., *Theoretical Studies in Social Organization of the Prison* (New York: Social Science Research Council, March, 1960), pp. 78–110.

Whatever else their merits, classification schemes that do not specifically account for motivation appear less effective in generating responses that lead to action when used as instruments to feed back data to persons in an organization.[15] Therefore, the classification scheme developed here accounts specifically for beliefs about offender motivations. For this reason, it begins with consideration of a theory of influence processes and the ways they are linked to various correctional strategies.

INFLUENCE PROCESSES IN CORRECTIONS

Herbert Kelman has described and experimentally demonstrated three processes by which persons are influenced by others to adopt new behaviors.[16] He labels his first category of planned change *compliance* and describes it as an influence process that depends on the change agent's ability to mediate external rewards and punishments. The target of change complies with new behavioral demands, Kelman argues, not out of the changee's inner conviction that the new behavior is intrinsically desirable to him or her, but out of the change agent's capacity to impose sanctions. The course of desired behavior is relatively specific, delimited in rules, orders, or the constraints of the environment and the changee is required to adopt it. This influence depends on the influence agent's capacity to maintain surveillance and his or her power to exert continuous demands for external change. The new behavior tends to be maintained by the changee only as long as the demands for the new behavior are enforced.

Another class of planned change, labeled *identification* by Kelman, arises when an individual adopts a behavior because it maintains a satisfying relationship with another person or group. The behavior is grounded in the relationship; as long as the relationship is salient, the changes can be influenced by it. The new behavior is maintained not because it is valuable in itself, but because of its meaning to the

---

[15] We have not yet made any systematic study of the reasons for this apparent characteristic. It may well be attributable to the personal style of the writers in their change efforts, or to the norms and expectations of correctional personnel, or to a more personalized reaction to data that have explicit motivational constructs. Argyris' comments on the advantages arising from the "emphasis on the cognitive and the deemphasis on emotionality" are another explanation for these apparent results. Chris Argyris, *Integrating the Individual and the Organization* (New York: Wiley, 1964), pp. 290–93.

[16] Herbert Kelman, "Compliance, Identification and Internalization: Three Processes of Attitude Change," *Journal of Conflict Resolution* (April, 1958), 51–60. For another attempt to employ Kelman's notions in a correctional setting, see Jay Hall, Martha Williams, and Louis Tomaino, "The Challenge of Correctional Change: The Interface of Conformity and Commitment," *Journal of Criminal Law, Criminology and Police Science* (Dec., 1966), 493–503.

change agent and the value of the relationship with the change agent to the changee. When the importance of that relationship diminishes, so will the likelihood of the new behavior.

The third type of change, *internalization,* describes those influences accepted by an individual because he or she finds them useful in solving a problem or because they are congruent with the individual's value system. The content of the influence attempt has intrinsic value. Motivation rests in opportunities for alternative behaviors not previously perceived as existent or possible. The power of the influence agent depends on the agent's credibility and expertness. Influence under these conditions tends to be incorporated into the changee's value system, and its retention is independent of continuing external demands or a continuing relationship between the change agent and the changee.

Kelman's classification system is general. It applies to more influence situations than are found in corrections. (And it would apply as well to attempts to influence correctional officials through training, education, organizational development, or other management efforts at change in the organization.) What makes correctional changee's value system, and its retention is independent of continuing the type of control imposed on offenders and the quality of the consequences for failing to change. Kelman's influence system can be made more directly relevant to corrections if these elements are added and some of the resultant dilemmas are posed.

CORRECTIONAL COMPLIANCE

Advocates of correctional compliance argue that their task is to induce law-abiding behavior by requiring the observance of community standards and that the most effective means of getting that observance is a system of rewards and punishments. Offender attitudes in and of themselves are irrelevant; it is assumed that if an offender evinces a certain behavior long enough, he or she will develop the appropriate attitudes to sustain it. The central problems under this influence style are (1) the maintenance of surveillance over the offender and (2) the development of legally and socially acceptable reward and punishment techniques that will encompass a substantial portion of the offender's behavior.

Under this influence strategy, control is typically authoritarian. The agents and the organization as a whole impinge actively and directly on the offender. Concomitantly, the organization makes severe behavioral demands on staff; agents and their superiors have demanding schedules to meet and a great deal of surveillance work to engage in. Sanctioning activity by staff is frequent and pervades the atmosphere of the organization and the relationship of staff and offenders. Various rules are set to govern a wide range of behavior, and these rules are to be followed rigidly. When an offender does not conform, the offender is punished; when the offender conforms, the offender is rewarded. Punishment takes the form of deprivation of privileges and the exercise of more stringent control; punishment is imposed not only for a failure to change—such as the commission of a new crime—but also for breaking regulations during the change process. Freedom is reduced to a degree suggested by the seriousness of the break in conformity.

CORRECTIONAL IDENTIFICATION

This type of correctional strategy is manifested by programs that minimize the directness and explicitness of demands to observe community or organizational standards. The emphasis is on helping the offender to understand himself or herself more fully and to develop more mature social relations, on the assumption that such social and psychological influences will result in favorable changes in the offender's behavior. Often, there is great concern with the offender's early life experiences, the effects of which must be identified and analyzed if the offender's core attitudes are to be altered.

The primary instrument of change in identification strategies is the relationship of staff to the offender. In an extreme form, staff may attempt to avoid any reference to standards external to the relationship, relying on the power of trust, support, and acceptance to give direction to the offender's behavior. Although these common psychotherapeutic techniques have been widely emulated in correctional counseling, the climate necessary for identification is very limited in correctional settings. Most typically, desired community values are transmitted through carefully nurtured relationships with staff or offender groups. The chief problems with this strategy in correctional settings are: (1) the extent of choice actually permitted the offender (who has been coerced into the relationship) and (2) the dependency on the relationship as a basis for maintaining desired behavior (when the staff responsible for the offender frequently change during the correctional process).

Under the identification strategy, punishment is also frequent, but it is masked by differences in presentation and by delays between the undesirable behavior and the sanction. Punishment is not an inevitable consequence of a break in regulations; it is mediated by an assessment of the changee's attitude. Typically, a change agent may talk over a behavioral mistake with the changee, who, if his or her explanation is satisfactory, will probably receive another chance. Punishment is likely to be imposed when the offender shows he or she does not care that he or she has deviated from the program or broken from the norms supporting the relationship to staff. Above all, punishment is presented as part of the treatment or change program. During a counseling session the agent may explain why restriction is necessary, that is, for the good of the offender. Often a punishment may be temporary and lack the finality it has in the compliance strategy.

CORRECTIONAL INTERNALIZATION

Correctional agencies that stress internalization attempt to cope simultaneously with community standards and offender attitudes. The offender makes choices among various options that are based on his or her prior experiences; and new experiences are provided the offender by which he or she gains a chance to test the viability of his or her new choices within the community. The motivation for change arises from the offender's perception of new and viable behaviors available to him or her. Activities directed toward the community include not only creating for the offender greater access to social institutions and resources but also developing within the community a greater tolerance for the life-styles represented by various groups of offenders. The chief dilemmas inherent in this strategy are: (1) the degree of tolerance that can be reasonably expected in the community, (2) the ability of correctional staff actually to make resources more readily available, and (3) the readiness of an offender to engage in various degrees of alternative testing without again breaking community standards and thereby reducing community tolerance during the change process.

Under this approach, control is more democratic than is true of compliance or identification. Control rests on the belief that offenders will conform most completely to those programs to which they are committed, and that commitment increases when those governed by the program or plan have had a stake in its formulation. Decision making is shared by various staff and offenders. On one hand, control is neither exercised autocratically nor subversively, under the guise of treatment. On the other hand, control is not abdicated; both staff and offenders are controlled by the inherent demands of the activity in which they are engaged.

Although used less frequently than in other strategies, punishment is used in internalization programs. Rules are few but explicit, and they are specifically linked to clear and important security measures and the observance of legal behavior. Typically, staff and offenders have clear opportunities to influence the shape of the rules and methods of enforcement. Punishment of the offender is part of the reality-testing exercise. The approach is not simply a matter of following rules and accepting a specific set of societal values; instead, staff and offenders decide what kinds of behavior would avoid other legal or social negative consequences. The whole organization operates to clarify situations and alternative actions so that punishment is no longer an external imposition for breaking rules or displeasing staff. Instead, punishment is perceived as the negative consequence of ineffective behavior, and more attention is devoted to how to make behavior more effective (or goal achieving) in the future.

DECISION GENERATORS IN CORRECTIONS

Now that processes aimed at influencing individuals have been linked to more generalized correctional concerns, it becomes possible to develop a system of classifying correctional organizations, a system that might permit us to make explicit some of the assumptions under which various correctional systems seem to be operating. It should also help us predict the staff and offender behaviors likely to be found in such organizations and their probable consequences.

The primary question here concerns the decision generators used by correctional managers in making their decisions. The change strategies that we have traced above are all found in the correctional system, but their presence is determined by correctional organizational constraints. What set of constraints do correctional managers seek to maximize? Under which set of constraints is internalization, identification, or compliance seen as appropriate role patterns for staff and offenders?

Although the philosophical debates about correctional or penal goals may be irresolvable through empirical inquiry, we can determine with some accuracy which constraints correctional managers are most attentive to. A recently completed study of juvenile detention practices in the United States concludes that the extent to which youths are detained pending adjudication reflects either a concern for community protection or a concern for the protection of the youngster.[17] Similarly, Scheurell identifies two competing constraints that vie for the probation manager's attention. One is to maximize the benefits accruing to the client through supervision and casework; the other is to maximize the protection of the agency through enforcing rules and regulations.[18] Ohlin et al. came to a

---

[17] Don Gottfredson, *Measuring Attitudes Toward Juvenile Detention* (New York: National Council on Crime and Delinquency, 1968).
[18] Robert P. Scheurell, "Valuation and Decision Making in Correctional Social Work," *Issues in Criminology* (Fall, 1969), 101–108.

similar conclusion concerning both probation and parole:

> The correctional agency is under community pressure. Anticipating possible criticism, administration organizes the agency and its policies in self-protection which contradicts the client centered approach. This divergence of interest between the administrator (supervisor) and correctional social worker presents problems in the areas of supervision of the correctional social worker, the rules of supervision and informal policies about agency–community conflicts. These problem areas do not present difficulties only in supervisory conferences, but in day-to-day functioning of the correctional social worker.[19]

Cressey has made similar observations about all correctional "professional" work:

> The professional ideology of social work, i.e., client's welfare is more important, conflicts with agency demands and community expectations for a correctional setting.[20]

The New York Governor's Special Committee on Criminal Offenders displayed very similar concerns in their 1969 suggestions about sentencing policy; the Committee suggested that a judge should sentence to determinate terms when he or she felt that the community was sufficiently upset about a crime that harsh punishment was warranted in order to "prevent anomie" and that a judge should sentence to indeterminate terms and allow the correctional authority considerable discretion when he or she felt that the principle objective was to change the offender's behavior.[21]

Although Gresham Sykes' study of the Trenton, New Jersey, prison was conducted much earlier, he observed rather similar influences or constraints operating on that organization but in a slightly different way. He argues that the generator in the Trenton prison was to obtain complete control of the inmate and that the test was that the control methods used must not violate basic American beliefs about humaneness and fairness. As a consequence, said Sykes, the techniques of control that should have been generated under totalitarian assumptions or goals were not used because they violated the test about humaneness. Therefore, the staff had a continual struggle to gain compliance from the inmates.[22] Looking at more recent prisons for adults[23] and institutions for juveniles,[24]

---

[19] Lloyd Ohlin, Herman Piven, and Donald Pappenfort, "Major Dilemmas of the Social Worker in Probation and Parole," p. 217.

[20] Donald R. Cressey, "Professional Correctional Work and Professional Work in Corrections," *National Probation and Parole Association Journal* (January 1959), 4.

[21] New York Governor's Special Committee on Criminal Offenders, *Preliminary Report* (New York: State of New York, Nov., 1969), 55–60.

[22] Gresham Sykes, *Society of Captives* (Princeton, N.J.: Princeton University Press, 1971).

[23] Donald R. Cressey, "Contradictory Directions in Complex Organizations: The Case of the Prison," *Administrative Science Quarterly* (March, 1959), 1–19.

[24] Street, Vinter, and Perrow, *Organization for Treatment.*

others have remarked that the custody constraint observed by Sykes remains, but that other primary constraint now is treatment instead of basic humaneness. After the exhaustive study on the evaluation of correctional treatment programs by Martinson and others, it is possible that the predominant interest will shift back to custody and fairness.[25]

The balance of these concerns for the offender and protection has often been posed as a central dilemma for correctional organization. Managers often have to choose between one set of decision generators and the other set. The relative emphasis that a manager places on each set is the basis for the following classification of correctional goals. The classification system is formed by placing (1) emphasis on the community and (2) emphasis on the offender against each other.[26] By assuming that managers could display high and low concern for either dimension, one can derive four basic organizational policy sets in corrections (see Figure 4.1).[27] When we develop this kind of typology, we are considering organizations, not individuals; we are characterizing whole systems regardless of the differences among individual workers. And, obviously, we are oversimplifying if we fail to recognize the myriad combinations of styles that can and actually do exist.

THE REFORM MODEL

This model, in the lower-right corner of Table 4.1, is characterized by maximum emphasis on community standards and minimum emphasis on the individual offender. The basic influence style is correctional compliance. The organization's mission is to make sure that the offender does not cause the community any more inconvenience, expense, or injury. The offender's conduct is expected to be more generally conforming; the offender should become not only a more law-abiding person but a better husband or wife, employee, citizen, and so forth.

The reform model is based on behavior change or, perhaps more

[25] Robert Martinson, "What Works? Questions and Answers About Prison Reform," *The Public Interest* (Spring, 1974), 22–54.

[26] A preliminary description of some of the elements of the models is found in Vincent O'Leary, "Correctional Assumptions and Their Program Implications," *Proceedings of the National Conference on Pre-release* (Huntsville, Texas: Institute of Contemporary Corrections and the Behavioral Sciences, Nov., 1967).

[27] These four models of policy are reflections of current expressions of influence strategy. Their appearance may change without significant effect on the consequence of institutional relations or program impact. See Daniel Glaser, "The Prospect for Corrections," paper prepared for the Arden House Conference on Manpower Needs in Corrections, mimeo., 1964; Clarence Schrag, "Contemporary Corrections: An Analytical Model," paper prepared for the President's Commission on Law Enforcement and Administration of Justice, mimeo., 1966.

accurately, on behavior molding.[28] Minimizing the stigma attached to a conviction is not a concern; rather, the threat of stigmatization may be used to control the offender. Correctional staff aim to instill proper habits in offenders. Typically, offenders are expected to follow a rigid and conforming routine and to acquire a vocational skill. Recreation and counseling are secondary and are used to relieve the drudgery of work routine. Much correctional officer and parole officer activity tends to be of the police type (regulatory and investigatory).

The staff try to be "firm but fair." Except for specialists, such as teachers, staff are not required to be highly educated and need not be specially skilled in social science disciplines, but they must be good administrators; they must be able to plan their work and the inmates' schedules. It is highly desirable that they be dedicated to the ideals and values of the larger society.

In this system, offenders have few rights. They have privileges granted by the state, in a unilateral and standardized fashion, in accordance with the degree of their conforming behavior. In the same manner, these privileges may be taken away. The decision process by which some offenders take up one job and others another, or by which some are paroled and others are not, has "low visibility." The staff has complete discretion and is not to be questioned or argued with. The reform policy opposes granting rights to inmates and resists interferences by the adversary legal system, which dissipates the authority necessary for proper control and encourages inmates to fight legal battles instead of learn new habits.

In the reform model, parole board members usually represent the community's dominant values and attitudes and are chosen for their familiarity with the kind of offender behavior that is conducive to permanent and steady employment. Above all, they attempt to make certain that only those inmates who would be productive in society will be released before their sentence expiration date.

Prerelease, work release, and other such programs are used infrequently in this kind of organization. Prison classes may be conducted in proper behavior for community living, but, generally, programs that lessen the extent of custody before release are discouraged because they weaken the control necessary for changing habits. These programs, and parole itself, may be perceived by

---

[28] In many respects some recent applications on behavioral modification techniques represent a modern version of this philosophy. Some elements of the models that Street, Vinter, and Perrow call obedience/conformity and reeducation/development are similar to the reform model (see *Organization for Treatment*, p. 21). They are also similar to Glaser's punitive-type parole officer (*The Effectiveness of a Prison and Parole System*, p. 294).

officials in this system as a clemency-granting device for offenders who have already demonstrated their ability to conform.

THE REHABILITATION MODEL

This model, in the upper-left corner of Table 4.1, is characterized by a high emphasis on the individual offender and low emphasis on the community. Correctional identification is the basic influence style. With supportive control and punishment presented as therapy,

Table 4.1 Models of Correctional Policies

		Emphasis on the Community	
		Low	High
Emphasis on the Offender	High	Rehabilitation (Identification Focus)	Reintegration (Internalization Focus)
	Low	Restraint (Organizational Focus)	Reform (Compliance Focus)

the atmosphere sought in this policy approaches that of a hospital. The label "sick" is substituted for the stigma "criminal." The language—particularly the vocabulary of diagnosis and prognosis—and the entire concept of criminality as a personal disability tend to be borrowed from medicine.[29] Classification committees stress offenders' attitudes and only secondarily their habits or skills. An atmosphere of understanding and support is sought as a means of offenders' developing insight into their attitudes and fostering relationships with staff. Programs of inmate self-expression or creativity are often stressed.

Unless the need for trained professionals drives the organization to locate near the sources of such staff, the rehabilitation prison is a remote, independent unit where, free from the contamination of societal pressures, skilled practitioners work with inmates in individualized programs. Ideally, the parole officers are skilled counselors who interview parolees periodically to discuss and solve the parolees' personal problems.

The therapist is the idealized staff figure. More than in any other model, a bifurcation between treatment and custodial staff occurs in the rehabilitation policy. This split is generated by the belief that

[29] Street, Vinter, and Perrow, *Organization for Treatment*, p. 21, includes a nearly identical "treatment model," Glaser describes a welfare-type parole officer that is also very close to this model (*Effectiveness of a Prison and Parole System*).

therapy is the sphere of trained professionals. Custodial personnel are charged merely with maintaining a peaceful atmosphere and supervising inmates between the active phases of treatment programs. The parole officer follows the ideology of psychotherapy and attempts to foster self-understanding and self-acceptance on the part of the parolee.

The rehabilitation model, like the reform model, is opposed to legal interventions, but it does so for different reasons. It takes the view that staff are beneficently motivated and should not be hampered in their rehabilitative work by lawyers' "jargon and sophistry." The harmonious atmosphere necessary for therapeutic change is not compatible with the procedural rights given normal and healthy citizens. It is absurd, argues the therapist in this model, to contest in adversary fashion what is best for offenders. The legal argument for disclosure of records and decision rationales is especially dangerous, since the therapist's knowledge should be privileged and his or her work unhampered by the pace and openness of legal communication.

The parole board's staffing and operations differ considerably from that of the reform model's board. Ideally, its members are professionals of the behavioral and medical disciplines who can accurately review an inmate's record and make decisions based on the inmate's progress in the treatment prescribed for him or her. Rules tend to be deemphasized. Parole is prescribed for inmates who are healthy enough to return to society; similarly, a revocation order, though not an immediate consequence of rule infraction, is often based on the parolee's "need for further treatment."

Work release and prerelease take a different tack under this model. Classes may be conducted in which inmates are encouraged to explore their feelings about returning home or returning to the job routine. A healthy and helpful relationship between parole officer and parolee is emphasized.

THE RESTRAINT MODEL

This model, in the lower left-hand corner of Table 4.1, is characterized by minimal concern for both the community and the offender. In this model it is believed that people change only if they want to. Therefore, no member of the staff is actively responsible for trying to change anyone. This model merely accepts the people the court sends and tries to make supervision of offenders as routine and trouble-free as possible for both offenders and staff. Punishment is not prescribed to change the offender but only to control the offender or calm him or her down. The appearance of efficiency is important in helping the organization to survive and perhaps to prosper.

This model may include large and remote prisons, but it might also emerge in a community-oriented department. In either case, the restraint model is probably the result of the failure of another model or the product of a two-model clash that ends in stalemate. Its philosophy is that the only possible achievements are "keeping the lid on" and "maintaining a good front." Both staff and inmates are "serving their own time."[30]

Restraint staff observe and control offenders. Any punishment that must be given or any change in routine that must occur may be presented with the explanation that "someone above ordered it," "the Department wants it," or "that's the rule." Higher education for staff is not required, except in technical skills necessary for maintenance (and perhaps for prison officials). Individual staff staff members are expected to do their own jobs and no one depends on or demands too much from others, except as such demands may be related to organizational output or appearance. The parole officer, like the prison worker, is an observer of behavior; he or she recommends revocation when required by policy, especially if needed "to keep the heat off the agency."[31]

Due process and other legal considerations are discouraged, because adversary procedure does not promote a smooth, orderly routine. Furthermore, the larger the number of challenged decisions or lawyer-included hearings, the more the paperwork and the greater demand for explanations.

The parole board that uses the restraint policy is singly responsive to public opinion. No inmate whom the public disfavors will be paroled and no parolee who makes his or her presence felt in the community will escape revocation. The board is highly concerned with maintaining the system and most of all with protecting its members against criticism. Prerelease programs may be used to keep the inmates quiet, but work release is often considered too disruptive to be valuable. In this model, effectiveness of administration is equated with smoothness of operation.

In comparison to the popularity of the reform and rehabiliation

[30] Some manifestations of this model may also be explained in terms of bureaucratic pathologies, such as "ritualism" in which the means replace the ends or goals. See Robert Merton, "Social Structure and Anomie" in Robert Merton, (ed.), *Social Theory and Social Structure* (New York: Free Press, 1968), pp. 182–214.

[31] Glaser's passive-type parole officer demonstrates many of the same characteristics (*Effectiveness of a Prison and Parole System*, p. 294).

models, the popularity of the restraint model has been weak in recent years. Nevertheless, restraint policy has perhaps always been the most frequently implemented policy, although systematic surveys of correctional policy in the United States are lacking. In recent years, however, the restraint policy has taken on some new dimensions, for dissatisfaction with rehabilitation has grown both in the field and in the external reform and academic circles. Fogel, Morris, van den Haag, and others have recently argued that not only is treatment a low-probability objective, but that effective techniques of change cannot be implemented properly in the coercive correctional environment.[32] Consequently, the basic tenet of restraint, that no offender can be made to change, is suddenly looking much more persuasive to both practitioners and outsiders. If correctional managers can find a way to implement the restraint policy in such a way that it would include appropriate concern for due process, it may well gain ascendancy as a correctional policy.

THE REINTEGRATION MODEL

This model, in the upper-right corner of Table 4.1, stresses both the community and the offender. Correctional internalization is the predominant influence style. Unlike the reform model, the reintegration model does not superimpose rules and regulations unilaterally on offenders. Instead, offenders work with a range of alternatives. Unlike the emphasis in the rehabilitation model, the central concern is not the offender's feelings in relationship to staff; feelings are examined rationally for their effect on situations and for situational effects on them. Short-term use may be made of compliance processes to enable offenders to deal better with reality, but the major stress is on altering community resource structures and on an internalization process in which mistakes in the implementation of an offender's goals are corrected by a demonstration of their ineffectiveness in reaching those goals.[33]

This model attempts to reduce the stigma attached to criminality that acts as a blockade to reintegration in the community. Emphasis on the community does not only mean a stress on maintaining its values, but it also means a stress on promoting changes within its

[32] Norval Morris, *The Future of Imprisonment* (Chicago: University of Chicago Press, 1974); Ernst van den Haag, *Punishing Criminals* (New York: Basic Books, 1975); David Fogel, *We Are the Living Proof* (Cincinnati: Anderson, 1975).
[33] Under any of the models, similar differential responses toward individual offenders can be observed. For example, reform model behaviors can range from intimate paternalism to detached austerity. The rehabilitation model can include many typologies which require different behavior on the part of treaters but which always finally center on a defect within the offender.

institutional structure to provide opportunities for offenders and to reduce systematic discrimination because of economic or cultural patterns.

In this model, confinement has specific objectives and is used as infrequently as possible. The preferred program is community supervision. Ideally, the institutions are close to the community of return. Parole officers are located in the neighborhoods where parolees live and work; they try to intervene in the community as well as in the life of the parolee. All agents are involved with community institutions—businesses, churches, schools, and so forth. The parole officer is the parolee's advocate as well as counselor and mediator.

There is no "ideal" staff member in this model. All staff members are valued for the change-producing skills that they can bring to the team effort.[34] Custodial staff are expected to participate as actively in the task of change as are professional staff. Moreover, the distinctions between "professional" and "custodial" are blurred, and volunteers and community workers are also sought.

In contrast to the reaction it receives in other models, in the reintegration model due process is not viewed as incompatible with the task of correctional change. Offenders and staff develop programs jointly; openness and confrontation are encouraged.

The parole board members in this model have no ideal background. They act as reviewers of programs that involve many other persons and as an appellate body that studies the decisions of institution and community-based staff. Revocation is used as a last resort. Policies are clearly spelled out and regulations are clear and few in number. Parole rules are worked out among the parole officer, the institution, the board, and the parolee. Prerelease and work release programs are near the core of the reintegration model. Breaks with the community are minimized; lines of communication are kept open.

NEW POLICY COMBINATIONS AND CONFLICTS

Spurred on particularly by the work of Elmer K. Nelson and Vincent O'Leary as Assistant Directors of the President's Commission on Law Enforcement and the Administration of Justice,[35] the reintegration policy has also been popular in the 1970's. Like the

---

[34] For a good description of team work efforts in probation supervision and probation organization, see Dennis C. Sullivan, *Team Work in Probation* (New York: National Council on Crime and Delinquency, 1969).

[35] See President's Commission on Law Enforcement and the Administration of Justice, *Task Force Report: Corrections* (Washington, D.C.: Government Printing Office, 1967).

resurgence of the restraint policy that has appeared recently, the popularity of reintegration is based partly on disatisfaction with institutional models of correction. But, whereas the restraint model would respond to that dissatisfaction by reducing or eliminating the change emphases found in rehabilitation and reform, reintegration has responded by arguing for the reduction or elimination of incarceration. Hence, reintegration and restraint together represent the two most current organizational manifestations of the debate discussed in Chapter 2 between Bennett, Cohn, and Cressey on the one hand and Korn and Empey on the other.

It is possible that we shall shortly see in corrections a melding of both reintegration and restraint in some way, with strategies of bureaucratic control stressed in the remaining institutions and the strategies of integration stressed in community programs. This melding, while a realistic possibility, would seem to contain many built-in points of conflict and inefficiency. It may not work much better than the combination of prison and parole did when formally instituted at Elmira in the 1870's. One problem is that offenders subject to restraint practices in prison would be unprepared for the change emphasis of the community programs. Equally problematic would be the difficulties in communication between the rule and regulation conscious institutional administrators and the active proponents of community change found in reintegration programs.[36]

Another option for combining the concerns of both restraint and reintegration is suggested by David Fogel. He argues that the correctional mission should be primarily one of restraint, with an emphasis on the just implementation of penalties. According to Fogel, offender needs for education, counseling, employment and job training, etc., would be met by the same agencies that provide these services to other citizens.[37] Hence, reintegration functions would be provided to offenders by agencies formally outside the correctional system.

Problems with this combination are also evident. It is unclear why offenders who are coerced by correctional employees into various types of activities and patterns of living would perceive the outside social agency workers as any less coercive than the officials of the state to whom they were directly subject. Some experts argue that the offenders' antagonism toward both correctional staff and outside social workers would be reduced if correctional staff no longer utilized the demand that inmates better themselves by participating in programs as a means of control.

[36] For a detailed analysis of these problems, see David Duffee, Frederick Hussey, and John Kramer, *Criminal Justice: Organization, Structure and Analysis* (Englewood Cliffs, N.J.: Prentice-Hall, 1978).
[37] David Fogel, *We Are the Living Proof.*

It is probably true that the coercive nature of social services would be drastically affected by their separation from the correctional system proper. For example, parole and parole workers would no longer exist because inmate behavior in prison would no longer be a criterion for deciding on release date. Thus, the types of social services presently provided by parole officers, along with a mix of other responsibilities, would be transferred to other agencies and agents, some of whom might not even know that a particular client was an offender.

This separation of correctional and social service work, however, generally fails to explain why the outside agencies would be willing to deal with correctional clients, whom such agencies often perceive as bad risks,[38] or why correctional administrators would be willing or able to achieve the kind of relationship with service agencies that would facilitate effective social service delivery by these agencies. It is typical that organizations cooperate most effectively with other agencies that they perceive to have congruent or similar goals and skills.[39] That social agency staff would see restraint correctional agencies as similar or congruent organizations is doubtful, especially if correctional workers believed that change in human beings cannot be facilitated by a professional staff or a bureaucratic agency of the state. In other words, in the new combinations of correctional supervision and social service delivery that are now surfacing, the same conflicts among decision generators that now riddle correctional organizations might create similar conflict across organizations.

GENERATORS AND TESTS IN CORRECTIONAL DECISION MAKING

Simon's analysis of organizational goal stresses that goal conflict is built into the way organizations attempt to solve the problems created by complex constraints. One may consider the organizational task one of solving a series of simultaneous equations in order to find the unique value for each value premise that enters into the various functions of the equations. But the organization seeks to find those particular values for these different functions by parceling them out to different divisions and organizational units. Hence, the values that seem appropriate to one division as it attempts to solve

---

[38] Wallace Mandell, "Making Correction a Community Agency," *Crime and Delinquency* (1971), 281–288.

[39] Eugene Litwak and Lydia F. Hylton, "Interorganizational Analysis: A Hypothesis on Coordinating Agencies," *Administrative Science Quarterly* (March, 1942), 359–420; Sol Levine, Paul E. White, and Benjamin D. Paul, "Community Interorganizational Problems in Providing Medical Care and Social Services," *American Journal of Public Health* (Aug., 1963), 1183–1195.

its version of the equation can be very different from the values assigned by other divisions as they seek to solve their versions of the equation.

We have also argued that each part of the organization uses different value premises as a means of generating the solution seen as appropriate and other value premises as tests by which to determine whether or not the solution generated meets environmental or organizational restrictions.

We can apply this conception of organizational goal to the correctional policy paradigm rather easily. In some cases, the concern for the community is seen as the generator, and the concern for the offender is seen as the test (reform policy). In other cases, the concern for the offender is taken as the generator of program decisions, and the concern for the community is seen as the test (rehabilitation policy).

In restraint policy the generator is the concern for organizational efficiency, or its ability to structure the interactions of staff and offenders to prescribed rules and regulations. The tests, in this case, are the modification of control strategies so that they do not violate cultural and legal interpretations of basic fairness.

The reintegration policy seeks to generate actions of staff and offenders that will increase the community resources available to offenders and increase the offender's ability to achieve goals in a manner acceptable to community standards. The tests are to avoid programs that exceed offender capabilities and/or that exceed community tolerance for change and disorder.

If we could implement any of these strategies from scratch, the job of seeking organizational solutions that would not fall short of these decision-generating premises or fail these decision tests would be very difficult. But the job is much more complex than that because there are no correctional programs in the United States that can realistically begin fresh. The implementation of any of these policies requires not only meeting its own constraints consistently, but also dealing with the contradictory influences caused by the presence of value premises filtering through the vestiges of other policies and programs. Additionally, the "community," whose value premises must also be considered, is not one monolithic entity consistent in its correctional goals; it is a hodgepodge of competing concerns and interests of the different power blocks, cultures, and scientific disciplines.

These confusing policy conflicts are evident in the examination of internal organizational structure, in the problems of implementing new programs, and in the difficulties of getting different parts of the criminal justice system and the correctional system to cooperate with each other.

CONFLICT IN ORGANIZATIONAL STRUCTURE

A good example of organizational conflict is available in a 1969–1972 study of correctional structure and program change in the Connecticut Department of Correction. An early test of the correctional policy models by means of the *Correctional Policy Inventory*[40] revealed that top management, middle management, and correctional officers all used different value premises as the bases for generating their problem solution strategies. Top management favored the reintegration policy, middle management favored the rehabilitation policy, and officers favored the reform policy.[41] The result, on the level of the offenders, was their belief that the policy of restraint was the most accurate description of organizational decisions.[42]

A later stage in this same program of research revealed that correctional officers tested the satisfactoriness of a policy against its impact on their own job satisfaction and feeling of safety and order, while correctional managers tested the satisfactoriness of a policy against its impact of the social climate experienced by offenders.[43]

Problems in Program Implementation

The experience with closing correctional institutions for juveniles in Massachusetts provides a clear example of generator conflict in program innovation. As new, small residential centers were designed and established by a variety of groups to house the juveniles emerging from the Massachusetts institutions, centers relatively similar in program met with varying degrees of community opposition, depending on the value premises stressed by the new centers as they entered the community. In some communities the stress on rehabiliation of

[40] Vincent O'Leary, *The Correctional Policy Inventory* (Hackensack, N.J.: National Council on Crime and Delinquency, 1970).
[41] Vincent O'Leary and David Duffee, "Correctional Policy: A Classification of Goals Designed for Change," 383–385.
[42] Ibid.
[43] David Duffee, "The Correctional Officer Subculture and Organizational Change," *Journal of Research in Crime and Delinquency* (July, 1974) 155–172.

the juveniles seemed satisfactory. In other communities the stress on rehabilitation raised clear objections that the presence of the treatment program endangered the neighborhood.[44] If all such programs to some extent exhibit the characteristics of reintegration, it is also apparent that the restrictiveness of the community tolerance test is greater in some communities than in others.

Moreover, Scull,[45] Duffee,[46] and others have observed that many "community-based" programs find the community tolerance test easiest to meet in the disorganized and impoverished areas of major cities. If the correctional agency seeks to implement these programs in such neighborhoods as a means of meeting this test, they may fail the other test that sufficient community resources will be available to reduce offender reentry problems.

Problems in Interagency Cooperation

Problems of interagency cooperation take a variety of forms, but the basic conflicts between decision generators and decision tests are visible in many of them. For example, Vincent O'Leary and Donald J. Newman have observed conflicts between probation officers and police over the most important aspects of probation supervision.[47] Duffee, Meyer, and Warner have documented similar conflicts between halfway house staff and institutional counselors as well as parole staff.[48] Studt, Messinger, and Wilson have analyzed the reasons why a milieu program run by outside researchers failed the "decision tests" held by prison administrators, and vice versa, how the decision generators of the administrators conflicted with both the tests and generators chosen by the experimental program staff.[49]

[44] Robert B. Coates and Alden D. Miller, "Neutralization of Community Resistance to Group Homes," in Yitzhak Bakal (ed.), *Closing Correctional Institutions* (Lexington, Mass.: Lexington Books, 1974), pp. 67–84.

[45] Andrew T. Scull, *Decarceration Community Treatment and the Deviant* (Englewood Cliffs, N.J.: Prentice-Hall, 1977), pp. 1–10.

[46] David Duffee, Kevin Wright, and Thomas Maher, *Bureau of Correction Community Treatment Centers Evaluation, Refunding Evaluation Report* (Harrisburg, Pa.: Governor's Justice Commission, Jan., 1975), pp. 55–86.

[47] Vincent O'Leary and Donald J. Newman, "Conflict Resolution in Criminal Justice," *Journal of Research in Crime and Delinquency* (July, 1970), 99–119.

[48] Duffee, Meyer, and Warner, *Offender Needs, Parole Outcome and Program Structure*, Chapter Five.

[49] Elliot Studt, Sheldon L. Messinger, and Thomas P. Wilson, *C-Unit, Search for Community in Prison* (New York: Russell Sage Foundation, 1968), pp. 273–288.

MAKING TESTS AND GENERATORS
CONSISTENT

The above discussion of organizational goal conflict points to a number of crucial issues for correctional managers. (1) Managers probably have a long way to go before they can state that their own conceptualization of correctional programs is consistent and systematic. Managers frequently borrow one program from one set of value premises and another program from somewhere else, and a third program may spring from their own imaginations. Whether these programs fall together, as a synthesis of the same set of decision generators geared to meet the same set of organizational tests, is doubtful.

(2) Correctional organizations, as presently structured, often militate against the adoption of a consistent correctional policy because the functional divisions of the organization are too committed to their own set of decision generators and are too unfamiliar with the rationales behind the programs and structures preferred by other divisions. In this case, it will not do to bring the opposing unit personnel together and "hash things out rationally." Instead, managers must devise new organizational structures that do not divide so strongly the vested interests of different organizational groups.

(3) Given the vast lack of research that would relate one type of behavior or action to one set of decision generators and that would relate another set of actions to a different set of generators, correctional managers have a great deal of difficulty in determining whether or not their staff members are behaving in ways consistent with policy. For instance, does it help or hinder a restraint policy to permit offenders access to lawyers? Does it help the concern for reintegration that halfway houses are frequently located in delapidated buildings in areas in which there are high unemployment rates and high crime rates? Does it help rehabilitation that correctional officers are frequently paternalistic and often ridiculing when managers tell them to relax the rules and regulations and get to know the offenders informally? The lack of specificity in policy can often mean that lower-level staff latch on to behaviors that *indicate* their adherence to policy without actually contributing to the values that managers wish to maximize.

(4) Correctional managers today are in a poor position to determine which of their decision generators are likely to meet the strongest opposition in particular communities or which organization constraints are most likely to present the most rigorous tests as

correctional programs confront their social and political environments. Managers may often have to explain decisions to staff and offenders in one way and to community groups in another. This may not mean that managers have to manipulate the public (and much less that they should). Instead, this observation recognizes the fact that correctional managers may not even know which decision tests they are even facing until they learn how to engage the community in more open and undefensive communication. Doing so may be almost impossible, however, since correctional managers have become defensive and secretive because of the confusion that exists in the community about both generators and tests. Hence, management may have to play the role of clarifier and advocate for certain correctional policies, a role they cannot play well until they obtain a greater wealth of data on actual program consequences and until they rely less on their own beliefs and political leanings as a means of support for particular programs.

It is obvious that these problems cannot be addressed in the same way or in the same place. Which type of problem managers should concentrate on is open to question. It is likely that all such problems need to be addressed simultaneously in any correctional system. The chief executive might delegate specific problems to various subordinates, offenders, outside experts, or combinations of all three. The chief executive would then have to balance the recommendations of various policy task forces against each other and attempt to integrate their various concerns.

In this presentation of management the problems with internal organizational structure will be emphasized first, and the problems of innovation, interorganizational cooperation, and community relations will be covered later. This order of presentation is to some extent arbitrary. Other starting points may be equally good. The working assumption here is that managers will have to take steps to improve the internal organizational operations before the organization is ready to engage in more complex management strategies that cross organizational boundaries or seek programmatic change inside the organization.

5

Consistency
in
Managerial
Directives

(David Duffee, Vincent O'Leary, and Kevin Wright)

Management's role is one of steering or guiding the organization toward its objectives. If the organization were a relatively conventional machine, which once constructed would behave consistently for the purposes that it was built, management would have a relatively easy time of it. Management would merely have to set goals, build a structure that accomplished them, and then go off to lunch or the golf course—the thing would run itself. As was stated in Chapter 1, it is surprising the extent to which organizations do function that way. That is, there is a great deal of self-control and self-organizing capacity in any organization. Officers once charged with a function can often carry it through and employees conform to expectations more often than they do not.

But organizations are more complex than many, if not all, machines, and their guidance and control require more effort than the deus ex machina variety provides. Of course, organizations, like machines, break down, and they need to be repaired. But the attention to maintenance and repair work is not the distinguishing characteristic of organizations. The important differences rest in the nature of organizational goals, which, as we have seen, are complex sets of constraints that change over time and require changing solutions. Moreover, the different parts of the complex organizational goal can change independently. There may, for example, be more than one set of internal solutions or role and decisions structures that will meet a single set of goal tests. If a test of correctional effectiveness is the reduction of crime, this might be obtained by either very effective surveillance work or by getting offenders in some way to alter their motivations or by incarcerating all offenders forever. Any of these strategies might meet the single test of reduced crime, but they would each have very different impacts on the internal structure of the organization.

Additionally, management must be able to determine which goals are most appropriate at a particular time. This determination requires constant interaction with the environment to ascertain how any particular organization output is being received. If there is dissatisfaction with the organizational products, management has complex decisions to make. Perhaps the output itself is not desired, and the organization should be doing something else. Or perhaps the organizational product is of the type desired but it is not delivered in acceptable quality. In this case, management must determine how to do the same thing better instead of change over to something else.

In any case, management needs to read both the extent to which the organization accomplishes policy and the fit of that policy into environmental situations. Divergencies between this reading and what is considered optimum can lead management to do several things. It may be, and usually is, very difficult to change the internal structure of an organization. Hence, one frequent response to the perception of "failure" is to try to convince the environment that the organizational product is fine, and really very important, and that the environment should learn to appreciate it for its own good. This strategy very often works, and commercial enterprises spend millions of dollars convincing people to buy and to appreciate everything from toothpaste to boxing matches.

But no management is foolish enough to think that it can fool all the people all the time. Sometimes, organizations make horrendous errors in calculating environmental demand and produce Edsels. But more often management will read changes in environmental demand with some accuracy and change the internal structure and process of the organization in order to do something else. Sometimes this change is minor and involves making smaller cars instead of different big ones. Other times the change may be major, and a company may divert part of its resources from car production to insurance or from education of undergraduates to community service programs.

When management determines that organizational goal performance does not meet standards or that the goals themselves have to change, then management must alter the organization; management must communicate to subordinates the need to alter behavior. When management must feed back to the organization messages concerning alteration in behavior, it is crucial that the feedback produces the changes that management has in mind. This is a difficult task, and there are a variety of ways of going about it. Sometimes management will assume that it, and only it, knows what changes need to be made and will specify in minute detail exactly what subordinates should do differently. At other times management will assume that it does not know how to solve the problem but that some people in the organization might; these people are given the task of studying the problem and coming up with recommended solutions. At other times management may assume that the needed change is so obvious that it merely screams, "Do it!" The organization, in this case, usually doesn't follow orders.

Management feedback to the organization takes place with different degrees of frequency, but the frequency usually varies according to the type of feedback that is being given. Management rarely waits until everything is falling apart in order to give messages to change things. But the more drastic the change, the less frequent the feedback will be. For example, guards as managers of cellblocks may feed back hourly or more often the requirement that things should be quiet. They may feed back daily the message that the cellblock is messy and needs to be tidied up. Feedback that the organization will engage in group therapy daily and dispense with farm production is rare.

Management does not wait until final results about organizational effectiveness are available to provide feedback. Managers in sales firms use monthly sales figures or perhaps orders as a means of gauging whether or not the sales force is being effective. Waiting to see if the desired profit margin had been reached would be unacceptable because by that time there would be no way to alter inappropriate behavior and correct it in time to reach the desired objective. Similarly, correctional managers do not wait for figures about crimes or revocations to determine if supervision is proper; instead, they use information about staff–offender contacts, rule infractions, etc., as a means of *estimating* whether or not larger objectives will be reached. In other words, managers use subobjectives as indicators that objectives are obtainable, and they use organizational behavior toward those subobjectives as a means of deciding whether or not and what type of feedback is necessary.

Management can run into several difficulties here. The indicators of goal achievement, or the subobjectives, may not be valid indices; they may not have any real connection to the objectives sought or the policy that management has in mind. For example, some correctional practitioners use frequency of internal disturbances as an indicator of how well offenders will do in conforming to legal rules. But there may be a poor connection between conformity to prison regulations or conformity to parole regulations and noncriminal behavior. Managers may use a parole officer's or prison guard's performance with supervision of offenders as an indication of his or her management potential when, in fact, a good front-line officer may not have the integration skills required for management.

In addition to the problem of validity, there is also the problem of reliability. It may be that the data that managers rely on to measure their subobjectives are not accurate. The report that an inmate is free of prison misconducts may not mean that the inmate has conformed to prison regulations, but rather that he or she has not been caught, or that the officer did not report the misconduct, or that the report forms themselves were stolen. As we shall see in later chapters, it is very possible for management to affect the reliability of its own measures by the manner in which it requests data or by the things it does once it has the data. A guard in a cellblock may routinely report all misconducts that he or she has observed in the cellblock until he or she is told by management that he or she has an unruly cellblock and is going to be placed on tower duty until he or she learns how to get along with the inmates. Perceiving that information about not reaching a subobjective may result in punishment, employees (and obviously offenders) often refuse to give accurate accounts of what is going on. Thus, management may fail to achieve policy objectives because the feedback that it has used limited its access to information about organizational performance.

Thus, it becomes very obvious that management needs not only to be careful in setting policy but also to be very sophisticated in the way that it attempts to direct the organization in order to reach that policy. If one intends to reach the tenth floor of a building, the elevator may be the best means of getting there, unless, of course, the electricity is off. If management intends to protect the public through corrections, then reintegration (or any other policy) may be the best way, unless feedback to the organization means the policy is not implemented correctly.

MANAGERIAL CONTROL AND
POLICY IMPLEMENTATION

While correctional theory and practices have been developing along lines suggested by the concepts of total institutionalization and inmate culture, theoretical development has been occuring in the sociology of management and organizations.[1] This second trend focuses on administrative and organizational behavior as it exists on a discrete level that is related to but distinguishable from the substantive activity of any particular system.

This organizational literature describes the variety of controls available to managers in any organization. While one administrator may depend heavily on the reward and punishment system inherent in the hierarchical nature of bureaucracies, another administrator may be democratic in approach and, by involving subordinates in the planning stages of policy, may avoid compliance problems in the implementation phases.[2] It is clear that relationships between organizational members may be dependent on the organizational structure (hierarchical or flat, centralized or decentralized) that management chooses,[3] and it is clear that the means that managers choose to supervise employees can have dramatic impacts on organizational productivity.[4]

Analysis of correctional operations has been relatively devoid of this broader analytical base of management and organizational theory and research.[5] Typically, correctional literature reflects on the problem of institutional control systems that maintain safety and yet are not so rigorous as to militate against therapeutic relationships between inmates and staff. Or it discusses various treatment techniques such as group and individual counseling and the theoretical bases for each. Also, a large body of correctional literature

[1] For a parallel review of the correctional and managerial trend, see Elmer K. Nelson and Catherine Lovell, *Developing Correctional Administrators*, Research Report of the Joint Commission on Correctional Manpower and Training (Washington, D.C.: Government Printing Office, Nov., 1969), pp. 13–16.

[2] Douglas McGregor, *The Human Side of Enterprise* (New York: McGraw-Hill, 1960), pp. 128–131; Rensis Likert, *New Patterns in Management* (New York: McGraw-Hill, 1961), pp. 55–58; and Chris Argyris, *Personality and Organization* (New York: Harper & Row, 1957), pp. 175–191.

[3] Likert, *New Patterns of Management*, pp. 104–116, and Argyris, *Personality and Organization*, pp. 177–187.

[4] Argyris, *Personality and Organization*, pp. 209–228. See also Robert Blake and Jane Mouton, *The Managerial Grid* (Houston: Gulf Publishing, 1964) and Daniel Katz and Robert Kahn, *The Social Psychology of Organizations* (New York: Wiley, 1966), pp. 435–446.

[5] For one exception, see Harold Bradley, Glynn Smith, and William Salstrom, *Design for Change: A Program for Correctional Management*, Final Report, Model Treatment Program, Institute for the Study of Crime and Delinquency (Sacramento: The Institute, July, 1968).

analyzes the variety of correctional goals, such as retribution, restraint, treatment, or general deterrence. But this specifically correctional material does not usually consider the origins of these concerns from an organization perspective, and it does not make full use of sociological concepts to explain the gaps between public policy and actual achievement.

Some of those sociologically identifiable forces are immediately relevant in interpretation of correctional programs that never had, or quickly lose, any therapeutic effectiveness. Several students of organization have identified three core functions common to all organizations: (1) goal-directed activity, (2) internal maintenance activity, and (3) adjustment to environment activity.[6] Using this system's model of organization, we may argue that new treatment and counseling techniques seem to be not so much goal-directed or change-producing activity as they are reactions to environmental forces that seek displays of greater correctional efficiency or more humanitarian treatment. In other words, correctional management may add programs as a means of public relations improvement rather than because of theoretical connections between offender behavior and the programs. Much concern with discipline and control is again not goal-directed activity but activity of internal maintenance, which is by nature a conservative and not a change-producing force.

Moreover, staff–inmate conflicts, much discussed in correctional literature, may not be nearly as unique as they seem in the light of organizational material about echelon conflict in industry.[7] Two recent correctional works[8] have illustrated how administrative behavior may condition the attainment of correctional goals. Studt's work in a California institution was disrupted in its second year when a change in prison administration fragmented a staff she had spent a year developing. Because there was no unified staff, the inmate counterculture reformed, and the integration necessary for milieu therapy dissipated. In a comparative study of six institutions for

---

[6] Philip Selznick, *T.V.A. and the Grassroots* (New York: Harper & Row, 1948), pp. 9–11, 250–253, and Chris Argyris, *Integrating the Individual and the Organization* (New York: Wiley, 1964), p. 319. More complex treatment of organizational genotypic functions are given in Daniel Katz and Robert Kahn, *The Social Psychology of Organizations*.

[7] W. F. Whyte, *Money and Motivation* (New York: Harper & Row, 1955); Michael Crozier, *The Bureaucratic Phenomenon* (Chicago: University of Chicago Press, 1964); and Joseph Bensman and Israel Gerver, "Crime and Punishment in a Factory: A Functional Analysis," in Bernard Rosenberg, et al. (eds.), *Mass Society in a Crisis* (New York: Macmillan, 1964), pp. 141–152.

[8] Elliot Studt, Sheldon Messinger, and Thomas Wilson, *C-Unit, The Search for Community in Prison* (New York: Russell Sage Foundation, 1968) and David Street, Robert Vinter, and Charles Perrow, *Organization for Treatment: A Comparative Study of Institutions for Delinquents* (New York: Free Press, 1966).

juvenile delinquents, Street, Vinter, and Perrow list three "institutiona' models" on a continuum from custody to treatment orientation. It is clear that different formal organizational plans in some way delimit the types of inmate programs that can be run and also influence offender attitudes toward staff.

Nelson and Lovell[9] conducted a survey of correctional administrative practices across the United States. They forecast American corrections as becoming progressively community oriented in philosophy and operations. They then make some assumptions about the type of correctional manager most competent to manage that correctional trend. As correctional programs emphasize the successful return to the community and deemphasize large and remote centers of restraint, Nelson and Lovell hypothesize that correctional administrators will have to be more flexible and democratic and more concerned with the relationship between correctional agencies and the free community. Some measures of administrative philosophy were taken, but no attempt was made to correlate systematically those data with equally specific correctional measures.

Whatever the correctional policy finally chosen by the administrator, he or she faces the task of translating that policy into operational reality. It is in this process that the charge of hypocrisy most often arises. Rhetoric simply doesn't match reality. Despite official claims of "treatment" and "respect for the offender's needs," what is usually produced at the bottom of the correctional organizational ladder is an alienated "society of captives" held in check by coercion and threat. But this fact need not lead to the conclusion that open war between the keeper and the kept is intrinsic to the very nature of the correctional enterprise. Even though the correctional system will always remain coercive, the quality of the interaction among all parties can be significantly altered. Friction across organizational divisions and through hierarchical ranks is common to many organizations. In fact, it is frequent enough to raise the question whether or not the failure to achieve goals may only be partially related to the nature of any specific organizational task and very much related to the extent and character of the discrepancy that may exist between how workers are managed and the tasks they are expected to achieve.

Since the managerial subsystem overlaps all other subsystems of the organization, mismanagement may cause disruptions in other parts of the organization.[10] Many earlier conflict studies have, in a sense, recognized the correlations between managerial practice and organizational stability. In most cases, however, the observation has

[9] Nelson and Lovell, *Developing Correctional Administrators.*
[10] Katz and Kahn, *The Social Psychology of Organizations,* p. 83.

been stated in reverse: that conflict of goals makes correctional organizations unmanageable. Obviously, this statement only makes sense when the criterion of "manageability" is organizational effectiveness.

Organizational effectiveness is a complicated concept that includes not only organizational efficiency (output/input) but also success in cooptation, disbursement of output, increasing productivity, and so on. Techniques have not been discovered to operationalize total facets of the concept. However, one measure of internal effectiveness may well be the degree to which organizational policies originated at top-management levels reach the lowest organizational levels in recognizable form. This measure is obviously incomplete because the lower workers may respond to a policy that is accurately transmitted and received in ways management has not intended. If the policy itself is neither accurately transmitted nor received, chances of expected implementation are certainly dim.

Policy is made at the top levels of the organization and is sent throughout the organization. It can be made and sent, however, in varying forms. Organizational participants are adept in reading many cues from managers and may observe in managerial behavior messages other than the content of policy directives sent along. If, for example, a clerk receives several written memoranda about changes in book-keeping practice but never sees his or her supervisor personally and knows the supervisor does not look at the books, the clerk may consider the changes too unimportant to bother with them. Or, if a parole officer insists he or she wants to "rap" earnestly with his or her parolees because it is therapeutic but turns over information so obtained to police, parolees may not believe the parole officer. In other words, regardless of how important the policy content is to the manager, the manager may miscue his or her transmittal and obtain undesirable results.

This line of reasoning would suggest that to understand staff and offender behavior it is not sufficient to look simply at the goals of a correctional system. And it would not depend solely on explanations that suggest inmate antipathy is the inevitable consequence of imprisonment. This is not to say such factors are not important; it is to say that they should not be stressed to the point that another major determinant of behavior is ignored: the process by which staff are organized and managed, a process which can be analyzed independently of correctional concerns.

Support of this view has been forthcoming from several studies. Most recently Bradley, in discussing designs of a model correctional system, criticized an otherwise creative new program because

. . . the planners adoped a quasi-military organizational pattern which is presently effective within their agency, with no apparent attention to the appropriateness of the new program's treatment goals. In our judgment, the proposal has a built-in but well conceived ticket to failure as an effective treatment program because its organizational features are actually antithetical to the goals of rehabilitation.[11]

Basing his conclusions more directly on empirical data, Piven raised similar questions in another study. He found that probation officers' behavior was much more shaped by the degree to which they were supervised in an autonomous or restrictive style than by their training, education, or ideology. Autonomously supervised officers were much more likely to behave toward probationers in a help-oriented direction than were officers who were given little discretion by their agencies.[12]

The evidence is strong that certain types of managerial behavior are more congruent with specific correctional policies than are others. In order to link specific managerial styles with specific correctional policies, a conceptual scheme is required that provides a fuller set of alternatives than is provided by an autonomy-restrictive scale. One such method of measuring managerial behavior has been developed from the managerial grid of Blake and Mouton.[13] Using this measure not only provides scales with a variety of specific managerial styles, but it also provides a direct link to a rich source of managerial theory and research developed in a variety of organizational settings other than correction.

MANAGEMENT STYLE

Style can be defined as the way in which the administrator attempts to steer his or her organization toward its goals. By conceptualizing administrative behavior along two continua, the concern for people in the organization and the concern for production, Blake and Mouton were able to define different managerial styles as the different relationships between the two dimensions of concern for people and concern for production (see Figure 5-1).[14] Blake and

[11] Harold B. Bradley, "Designing for Change: Problems of Planned Innovations in Corrections," *The Annals of the American Academy of Political and Social Science* (Jan., 1969), 91.

[12] Herman Piven, "Professionalism and Organizational Structure, Training and Agency Variables in Relation to Practitioner Orientation and Practice," unpublished doctoral dissertation, Columbia University, 1961.

[13] Blake and Mouton, *The Managerial Grid*. The grid was also used in the survey by Nelson and Lovell, *Developing Correctional Administrators*, pp. 47–50. The managerial grid has been operationalized in the *Styles of Management Inventory* by Jay Hall, Jerry B. Harvey, and Martha Williams (Houston: Teleometrics, Inc., 1964).

[14] Blake and Mouton, *The Managerial Grid.*

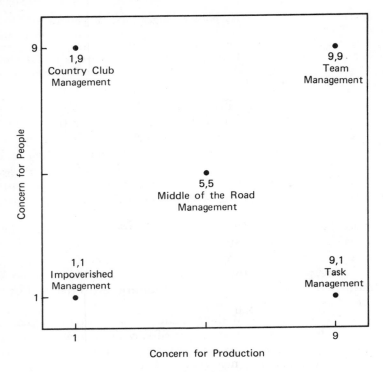

Figure 5.1 **The Managerial Grid**

Mouton suggest that managers may be classified according to the way in which they simultaneously handle the organizational need to complete scheduled tasks and the human needs of persons in the organization. In Figure 5.1, concern for people and concern for production are both represented by axes which range from 1 (or very little) to 9 (or very great) concern. We can identify managerial types in terms of their location on the two-dimensional grid. For example, a 9/1 task manager will demand production at a heavy rate and will tightly organize and control staff and ignore their desire for interest-ing and meaningful work, but a 1/9 manager, arguing that morale is critical, will consider the employee's satisfaction and happiness a primary responsibility and will organize activities without apparent regard for production. Similarly, it is possible for a 1/1 manager, usually found in a highly bureaucratized setting, to default either concern. A common style of management is the 5/5 compromise; here the administrator attempts to balance the two concerns that he or she sees as necessary but conflicting. Management of the newer, problem-solving team approach forms the last corner of the grid. The

9/9 manager attempts to integrate both concerns by enlisting the norms and pressures of the informal social system in a productive direction through democratic and participative techniques.

Black and Mouton assume that most managers will probably use all of these styles at one time or another, so that the question of how one manages is, in their terms, really a question of the relative position of each style in a managerial profile. Blake has used his managerial grid format as the basis for a number of training and organizational ventures and some of them have been highly successful. He has gathered a large amount of data on and experience with the grid as a means of summarizing managerial behavior. He has found that the most *common* profile (i.e., the progression from the style relied on most heavily to the style least frequently used) is 5/5, 9/9, 9/1, 1/9, and 1/1. That is, most managers that Blake tested would compromise between the concerns of production and people first, turn to a team approach second, and default their responsibilities last. Blake also found, however, that the most successful managers ("those who get to the very top in terms of career progress") had a different profile: 9/9, 9/1, 5/5, 1/9, and 1/1. In other words, the most successful managers (using Blake's criteria) had a dominant style of 9/9 backed-up with a task-oriented philosophy. The best managers, then, were generally democratic, facilitating and coordinating the efforts of other people and depending on others to structure tasks and assign specific responsibilities as they saw fit. In order to manage in this way, one would have to be flexible, open to criticism, and trustful that subordinates are technically competent and willing to work. It is also important, however, that this primary philosophy is seconded by the 9/1, the task-management approach. When usually democratic processes fail, the most successful managers step in to assert their own desires strongly.[15]

A review of the literature suggests that the correctional administrator falls short of this ideal profile. Hall, Williams, and Tomaino have suggested that the environment of the correctional field is characterized by a wide divergence of beliefs and practices, that the professional roles are clouded by ambiguity, and that the organizations suffer from the simultaneous pursuit of contradictory goals.[16] These observations are validated by Nelson and Lovell who add that correctional managers frequently attempt changes based on rules of thumb and on hunches instead of on rationally developed managerial

[15] Ibid., pp. 227–248.
[16] Jay Hall, Martha Williams, and Louis Tomaino, "The Challenge of Correctional Change: The Interface of Conformity and Commitment," in Lawrence Hazelrigg (ed.), *Prison Within Society* (Garden City, N.Y.: Doubleday, 1969), p. 327.

principles.[17]   In discussing the problems of planned innovations in corrections, Bradley sets forth several areas of poor management that limit the capacity of the system to change:

1. Plans which specify the elements necessary for a program to be effective are constructed without designs specifying the structure of the program processes;
2. Correctional managers do not create favorable conditions for change, therefore, change cannot be expected;
3. Planning is carried out as things "ought" to be; rather than as things can be, given the existing system;
4. Research concentrates on defining inputs and outputs of the system, rather than identifying how and why the system works as it does;
5. There is a tendency to remain in existing facilities rather than use those more conducive to change.[18]

Bradley sees the five problems as precipitated by the bureaucratic organizational structure that supports the defense of the organization in face of the public demand for safety but that reduces the variety and adaptiveness of the organization that are necessary in the long run if the organization is to keep pace with changing demands.[19]

To summarize briefly, it seems that the correctional administrator lacks the skills, background, and orientation to act as a change agent in an open system. The literature suggests that the correctional administrator is not the modern, scientific manager who would rise successfully in another kind of enterprise, such as business, in which lack of success is usually correlated with some clear indicators of performance that also prompt sactions against the ineffective manager.

STYLES IN CORRECTION AND BUSINESS

The literature paints a dim picture of the correctional administrator as he or she functions today. There is widespread doubt about his or her capability to operate as a change agent in a field in which recent changes in policy make organizational change crucial. Yet, few such studies of correctional management utilize data in the evaluation of the correctional administrator, and attempts are rare to compare empirically correctional administrators to other managers who are considered effective. A broad perspective can aid us in judging the competency of the correctional administrator in relation to

[17] Nelson and Lovell, *Developing Correctional Administrators.*
[18] Harold B. Bradley, "Designing for Change: Problems of Planned Innovation in Corrections."
[19] Ibid, pp. 29–32.

the behavior of managers whose competencies have been studied longer and are more widely recognized. Although it may not be the most rigorous method, from data already available a rough comparison can be made between one group of correctional administrators and a group of "successful" administrators in business, industry, and government.

The measurement device used is a questionnaire called the *Styles of Management Inventory*, which allows managers to compute their individual managerial profiles based on the five styles of the managerial grid discussed above. The items of the inventory are designed to reflect specific behaviors required under each of the five managerial styles. It is assumed that everyone uses all five styles at one time or another; therefore, the inventory is designed to assess an individual's relative preference for each of the styles. A total score is computed for each of the five styles, and subtotals are computed for four different managerial functions: philosophy of management, planning and goal setting, implementation, and evaluation.[20]

The *Styles of Management Inventory* was administered to a group of 56 top-level correctional executives before they attended a national training conference. The group included central office as well as institutional and parole personnel. The scores of this group were compared to a national sample of 378 managers from business, industry, and public administration whose scores were used for the formation of standardized scores on the *Style* instrument. This comparison is interesting (1) in light of what Blake and Mouton say about the "ideal" managerial profile, (2) in terms of how the correctional managers fare against this national group, and (3) in terms of the hypotheses about correctional management (or American management in general) that this comparison suggests.

Analysis of the standardized scores for the correctional sample demonstrated that these managers were above average on 9/9 and 5/5 styles, almost exactly average on 9/1 and 1/9, and slightly below average on the 1/1 style. An analysis of the standardized subtotals for the different managerial functions showed again that correctional managers relied slightly more on 9/9 and 5/5 styles than did the sample of business managers, and they relied less on the 1/1 management by default style. There was, however, a slight tendency for the correctional managers to place more than normal emphasis on the 9/1 task-management style when they were concerned with implementation.

It is clear from the comparison of both the totals and subtotals that

---

[20] See Jay Hall, Jerry Harvey, and Martha Williams, *The Styles of Management Inventory*.

correctional managers are not very different from the 378 managers in business, industry, and other types of public administration. If anything, the correctional managers are slightly stronger than the base group in their team orientation, and they are evidently slightly weaker in their 1/1 style than are most managers.

The fact that there is little difference between these two groups would appear very significant, given the expectations or the widely accepted perception that American management *in general* is effective but correctional management is ineffective. In terms of managerial style, there is little evidence that the correctional managers behave very differently from other managers, even if their training and experience are somewhat different.

It is true that the profile of the correctional managers does not match the ideal profile described by Blake. The difference is that the correctional managers emphasize the 9/9 style more and the 9/1 style less than Blake's "best" managers. How welcome would be the problem of making people *more* directive, *more* task-oriented, and less concerned with the goals of their personnel! Increasing the "directiveness" of correctional managers, however, is exactly the route that Nelson and Lovell,[21] O'Leary and Duffee,[22] and others recommend *against*.

While these data only allow tentative conclusions, the lack of difference between correctional and business managers raises some interesting questions and suggestions. One is that, under the circumstances, perhaps corrrectional managers are really fairly effective. While Nelson and Lovell have not found them to be professionally trained managers, they seem to stack up fairly well against a broad sample of managers in different American enterprises in terms of the styles they use. Nelson and Lovell also praised the managers they studied for their willingness to take the blame for ineffective correctional organization. Nelson and Lovell state that these managers had a "voluntaristic approach" to correctional management and really believed that they could bring about significant changes in corrections if they planned and implemented correctly.[23] Perhaps Nelson and Lovell should have been dismayed at such foolish arrogance, insisted that these managers were performing as well as could be expected, and pointed a finger at contradictory goals for corrections and other constraints under which even effective managers may founder.[24] Correctional managers apparently *do employ* the

[21] Nelson and Lovell, *Developing Correctional Administrators.*
[22] Vincent O'Leary and David Duffee, "Correctional Policy: A Classification of Goals Designed for Change," *Crime and Delinquency* (Oct., 1971), 373–386.
[23] See Nelson and Lovell, *Developing Correctional Administrators*, p. 43.
[24] Donald Cressey, "Contradictory Directives in Complex Organizations: The Case of the Prison," *Administrative Science Quarterly* (March 1959), 1–19.

sets of interpersonal and organizing skills that are recommended by managerial experts, but at the same time they have been criticized for being traditional, unprofessional, and too autocratic. Academicians have always reserved for classroom chuckles the observation that academically trained men such as Donald Clemmer, O. W. Wilson, and Richard Korn confronted many problems as administrators, but perhaps the inability of surprisingly good men to make criminal justice agencies "run like a business" should key us into a verity that correctional experts frequently dismiss lightly. It may simply be true that correctional organizations *cannot* run well.

The difficulty with this conclusion, as logical as the data and past commentary may make it seem, is that the consequence of its acceptance is one of certain failure. Some correctional managers, who may actually require change or replacement, can hide behind the claim that they are doing an impossible task, while the good managers will probably leave to take up more rewarding pursuits. In other words, one would suspect that liberal reformers would reject the inevitability of correctional failure simply to gain entry for "progressive" interventions. There is, however, a hidden danger in this gallant rejection of the pessimistic option. If managerial improvements and correctional reform are really a jousting with windmills, then to what reality will managers and reformers be abruptly returned and with what unsettling consequences?

Another possible interpretation of these data is that correctional managers really are rather bad and that other American managers are just worse than Blake, Mouton, and others have suggested. Perhaps the success criteria that make the 9/9, 9/1, 5/5, 1/9, and 1/1 profile ideal are shortsighted criteria that have, for example, allowed successful managers to run out of energy, sell dangerous products, and make inflationary profit. Because correctional managers deal directly with ultimate human payoff, correctional managers have not had the luxury of short-run success and long-run failure.[25]

It is possible that American corporations are just now beginning to reap the harvest of improper management. We might even say that industry and business are suddenly faced with contradictory directives of their own: reap a profit *and* contribute to the social and physical health of the community.

A third possibility is that the measurement device (the *Inventory*) is a faulty way of measuring management practices or organizational concerns. There is little doubt about reliability and little doubt about certain kinds of validity. What seems questionable is whether or not the things measured as managerial style by various researchers

[25] Richard Korn, "Of Crime, Criminal Justice and Corrections," *University of San Francisco Law Review* (Oct., 1971), 45–72.

really get at the heart of correctional management. The grid model describes concerns and activities recognized by managers, lower personnel, and inmates, but it does not address fundamental issues such as the status differences between the keeper and the kept or the social rift between the proponents of retribution and the proponents of effective offender change. Thus, it might be arguable that the device is valid in industrial or business organizations but that the concept of managerial style is inapplicable to the situation of the correctional manager. For example, it is difficult for correctional managers to agree about the "production goals" that the grid model assumes will be emphasized to some degree. Similarly, it is possible that the status and role contrast between inmates and staff is so vast that this class conflict overwhelms the manager's "concern for people" in his or her organization.

Finally, it is possible (and perhaps the way out of the above three dilemmas) (1) that correctional managers today are indeed *ineffective*, (2) that other managers are relatively effective, and (3) that the measurements are valid and sensitive even to the most crucial correctional problems. In other words, it is *possible* that the profile that is effective for other enterprises is not effective in correctional work (although the organizational concerns remain the same). Perhaps, correctional organizations as "people-changing organizations" need "deviants" at the helm rather than "average managers." The deviance needed, it would seem, is an emphasis on team management so strong that in other types of organizations it would be extremely unlikely or perhaps even dysfunctional. The last possibility is undoubtedly the most emotionally if not intellectually satisfying because it allows correctional reform and managerial change to continue along the same path as they have.

RELATIONSHIP OF POLICY AND STYLE

It is obviously not enough to examine correctional policy or correctional management style separately in order to make determinations of effective management strategy. Obviously, what is needed is some way to relate policy and style systematically and to examine the effects of one on the other.

Using the *Styles of Management Inventory* and the *Correctional Policy Inventory*, it was possible to set up a matrix between grid styles of management and correctional policy. The first phase consisted of a series of studies examining the relationship between the two; 56 correctional administrators completed both questionnaires.[26]

[26] More than half of these responses were collected at a Correctional Management Institute conducted by the National Council on Crime and Delinquency at The Pennsylvania State University in December, 1970. The other half was collected from a group of correctional administrators in a single state.

Table 5.1 Predicted Positive Correlations Between Style and Policy

Policy	Style				
	9/9	5/5	9/1	1/9	1/1
Reintegration	+				
Rehabilitation		+		+	
Reform		+	+		
Restraint			+		+

Based upon the assumptions underlying these instruments, correlations in the directions summarized in Table 5.1 were hypothesized.

1. Reintegration and 9/9. It would seem to take a highly flexible and creative manager willing to take risks and be open both with employees and inmates to implement the demanding reintegration model.

2. Rehabilitation and 5/5 and 1/9. It was hypothesized there would be positive correlations between this correctional policy and both of these managerial styles. The identification mode of correctional influence should be compatible with the nonassertive 1/9 style or the stronger, more manipulative 5/5 style.

3. Reform and 9/1 and 5/5. The reform model of corrections calls for a highly production–supervision-oriented manager who keeps both employees and inmates under tight schedule during the habit-instilling process. It would seem to require the 9/1 style of close supervision and low staff participation to achieve this model. The 5/5 managerial style with its qualified emphasis on production should also be associated with a reformist policy.

4. Restraint and 1/1. The restraint policy, in which change seems impossible or accidental, should correlate with the 1/1 managerial style, which also implies a lack of planned effects.

5. Restraint and 9/1. The restraint philosophy, to the degree that it contains the strongly moralistic philosophy of corrections as retribution and loyalty to the prison organization, may correlate positively with 9/1 management. Even without change-oriented goals, the restraint philosophy may require high production in tasks of institutonal maintenance and order.

The results supported most of the proposed relationships, but there were three exceptions (see Table 5.2).

1. The relationship between the 5/5 managerial style and a reform policy, although very pronounced, was not sufficient

Table 5.2 Correlation of Style and Policy Means for Correctional Managers

Policy	Style				
	9/9	5/5	9/1	1/9	1/1
Reintegration	.4980*	.1517	−.2533	.1842	−.1300
Rehabilitation	.2242	.4619*	.1316	.1360	.2291
Reform	.1874	.2540	.3986*	−.0395	.0883
Restraint	.1883	.0877	.4307*	−.0037	.1926

$N = 56$.
*$P = .01$

to meet the test of statistical significance (.01) used here.

2. Rehabilitation was not correlated with the passive 1/9 style. The uneasy balance between custody and treatment seemed most associated with the production-oriented but compromising 5/5 style.

3. The correlation between restraint and a 1/1 managerial style was not significant; apparently there were too many overtones of productive efficiency in the restraint policy. As expected, the correlation with a 9/1 managerial style was significant.

Clearly, specific managerial styles appear related to correctional policies. The data suggest, for example, if a manager elects a reintegration correctional policy, the manager is also likely, other things being equal, to select a 9/9 managerial style. A reform or restraint program appears to be most strongly related to a 9/1 managerial style. Conversely, the probabilities of finding managers who prefer a reintegrationist policy and a 9/1 style would appear to be smaller. These data do *not* say that a compatible managerial style *alone* is sufficient to implement a given type of policy. But the relationships between policy and style might be a starting point in explaining faulty implementation. What would happen, for example, if a 9/1 manager chose to implement a reintegration policy or a 9/9 manager chose to implement restraint policy?

STYLE AND POLICY CONFLICT

Policy statements in too many correctional programs seem to remain rhetorical and do not appear to affect programs. The style–policy correlations suggest one source of this divergence. The administrator's unspoken but very visible managerial style may symbolize for employees and inmates an organizational policy of its own. If policy and style are inconsistent, then subordinates are given a choice between official policy content and the messages or cues they receive from managerial behavior. If the behavior and policy are not congruent, the subordinate has an important decision to make. Whether the subordinate opts to respond to the enunciated policy or the behavioral cues depends on the anticipated rewards for the individual's reaction. In other words, the effectiveness of policy implementation depends on the anticipated rewards of various alternatives. This includes both positive additions or improvements in the individual's situation and the avoidance of unpleasant repercussions.[27]

There is considerable evidence in organizational literature of the importance of the individual's immediate supervisor to the formation of his or her behavior. In the stratefied hierarchical system, rewards and punishments of the lower echelons are generally administered by the level above. The subordinate therefore has in his or her policy choice to decide which message "belongs" to his or her immediate superior.

Most generally in prisons a subordinate will interpret his or her immediate manager's behavior as the "real" policy transmitted for him or her to follow. If a subordinate must judge his or her superior's commitment to an official policy statement, he or she is likely to make the judgment on the consistency of the managerial behavior with the structural patterns implied in policy statements. When the supervisor's rejection of policy (conscious or unconscious, spoken or unspoken) seems particularly strong, the subordinate may even logically consider that punishment will attach to his or her adopting the behavior demanded by the public policy.

Managerial styles compatible with either reintegration or rehabilitation are not widely used by lower-system administrators, and hence the kind of correctional policies that top-level administrators would tend to endorse are largely unrecognizable in the elaboration of organizational structure as the policy is filtered downward through the communication network. Public policy statements that concern the rehabilitative programs of the organization will be seen by employees as hypocritical but necessary public relations statements. They may be seen by inmates as sincere but ridiculous in the face of the actual situation. If policy makers themselves have any accurate

[27] When the style and policy are inconsistent, we can conceptualize the receiver's dilemma in terms of listening to a radio broadcast. In the original state, the listener is bothered by considerable noise, since he or she is receiving transmission from two frequencies simultaneously. The listener is likely to tune one out and the other in, and in making a choice the listener weighs the value of each program against the other. The reward value of A is compared with the reward value of B. They may not be the same rewards the sender intended to transmit. Of course, the receiver may turn the radio off completely, analogous to a common occurrence, it seems, in our prisons.

information about the distortion of policy as it reaches lower levels, they, too, may cease to think of policy as having structural effects and think of its formation as a "public relations" function; it quiets political muckrakers and it seems generally harmless to the organizational status quo.

While there are not enough managers tested to make these conclusions final, data from the correctional system in one state do support these suggestions. Table 5.3 describes the scores from the *Styles of Management Inventory* recorded by the top and middle administrators in the department of correction. Clearly, top administration expressed a strong personal preference for a 9/9 style of management followed by a distant second choice of a 5/5 style. Middle managers expressed a 9/9 first choice to a much less degree, with an almost as strong second choice style of 9/1.

Table 5.3 Management Styles by Level in One Department of Correction

Level	Style				
	9/9	5/5	9/1	1/9	1/1
Top Administration (central office and superintendents)	92.9	74.7	70.6	61.9	35.6
Middle Managers (captains and case-work supervisor)	78.6	66.4	77.8	55.8	40.0

In Table 5.4 the distribution of scores on the correctional policy questionnaire is shown for the same groups. In addition, correctional officers were asked what policy they perceived in operation and 88 offenders were asked what kind of correctional policy they saw in effect in the system.

Administrators clearly preferred a reintegration policy; their second choice was a rehabilitation policy. Middle managers opted strongly for a rehabilitation policy. Officers reported that their behavior was consistent with a reform policy. Offenders said that the organization was little concerned with reintegration or rehabilitation and was somewhat more concerned with reform. Above all, offenders saw the staff most interested in the restraint concerns of "do it by the book" and "don't rock the boat." The offenders perceived the officers' reaction to them as being more consistent

Table 5.4 Policy Means by Level in a Northeastern State*

Level	Policy			
	Reintegration	Rehabiliation	Reform	Restraint
Top administration (N = 30)	80.0	76.8	57.7	48.2
Middle managers (N = 27)	69.8	80.3	66.0	56.2
Officers (N = 42)	55.2	68.4	77.7	61.5
Offenders (N = 88)	59.7	57.0	80.0	90.9

*Mean differences between groups are significant at the .01 level.

with the 9/1 managerial style by which the officers were supervised than by the policies enunciated by higher-ranking officials.

It is obvious that the correctional policy preferences of the top administrators are hardly recognizable at either the officer or inmate levels. Several explanations are possible for these data, but certainly not to be minimized is the fact that managerial styles at lower levels tend toward a rigidification of procedure and a decrease in participation. As a consequence, policy perceived and implemented at lower levels appears to reflect more closely the managerial cues of superiors than the policy statements of top administration.

An administrator working in these circumstances would certainly conclude that there was conflict in the system, but he or she would be likely to blame the nature of correction (goals are incompatible) instead of perceive that policy content and manner of transmission may be inconsistent. While the latter alternative seems at least as plausible as the first, systematic feedback on managerial practice has been slow to develop, and perhaps it is harder to accept by managers than assertions of goal conflict inherent in the system.

The conclusion is clear. The performance of managerial functions not only has relevance to the amount and quality of correctional production, but to a significant degree it may also determine the *kind* of correctional policy that actually is operational. This is especially important in the planning and implementation of change in corrections and in criminal justice as a whole. If practices are determined by implied or explicit policies, corrective and control systems are limited by the men who must implement legislative mandates and the implications of research. Concomitantly, and fortunately, managerial behavior is not an uncontrollable variable.

Managers can be trained in new methods of operation, and organizations can be restructured to increase the possibility of more effective behavior patterns.

Today's management development courses are constructed largely to expand administrators' awareness of the assumptions upon which they operate. Techniques of planning, evaluating, implementing, and controlling organizational activity can be improved without integration of those techniques and the purposes of the specific organization. This cannot be the case in the training of correctional administrators. In organizations whose very material of production are people, or changes in people, the tasks of production and internal maintenance of the organization are so intertwined that separating them can be disastrous. For example, when a correctional manager decides to open planning sessions to lower staff echelons, he or she is implicitly stating something about the way the lowest echelon offenders should be managed by front-line staff. Indeed, to "liberalize" a management style without including a similar change in the handling of offenders may increase the offenders' (and staff's) perception of institutional hypocrisy. And, vice versa, to liberalize a correctional policy without changing the management styles of supervisory staff may reduce correctional change to word games.

6

Social
Climate
in Correctional
Organizations*

The correctional policy and managerial style "surround" the correctional situation that the manager is trying to control. The situation itself exists between the manager's manipulation of input (or the managerial style) and the manager's demand for output (or the manager's correctional policy). The correctional situation is all the activity within the organization that is important to the accomplishment of goals. The situation is the "throughput" of the correctional system, the area in which the inputs are transformed in order to become outputs. It is this part of correctional activity that has for many years been treated as a "black box." We have frequently studied outputs from it or inputs to it. Very few observations of the processes *between* those two viewing points of the "box" have helped to alter significantly the output that the organization delivers.

*Adapted with permission of the publisher from David Duffee, *Correctional Policy and Prison Organization* (Beverly Hills, Calif.: Sage-Halsted, 1975). Chapter 8, "Measures of the Correctional Situation," pp. 155–185.

THE SITUATION AS STRUCTURED BY POLICY
AND STYLE

The internal situation of the correctional organization has not been frequently studied, probably because it is difficult to define. It is much easier to talk about the organization in its entirety (including managerial practice) or to talk about one segment of the organization at a time. The "situation" that needs examination, however, is *not* the externally visible organization, not "what it feels like to be an inmate," not "what it feels like to be an officer," or not "what it feels like to be a parolee." The internal organizational situation is the social interactions among all organizational participants as they are affected by managerial strategies.

One definition of this situation has been called the "character" of the organization.[1] It was one attempt to explicate the felt differences between the internal atmospheres of different juvenile institutions. Trying to raise to a rational level the reasons for these usually intuitive and emotional assessments of institutions was difficult. The argument was made that, analogous to individuals, organizations may have "character," which is an overall effect of the organization on any particular observer or participant. The major variables influencing character are relationships with the environment, organizational goals, staff–staff relations, and staff–inmate relations.

A similar description of the organizational situation is given by Street, Vinter, and Perrow. They speak not of character but of organizational "climate."[2] They suggest that although each institution has a unique climate, each institution may not have unique goals or unique executive strategies for the implementation of goals.[3] The climate is not only the result of executive action, it is also a result of staff and inmate responses to executive directives, action initiated by staff or inmates, and executive responses to these actions. The climate might be called the total effect of living and working within the organization. It is important to distinguish the concept of climate from any particular activity or set of activities (such as a managerial style) because the climate is the accumulation of these activities over time and is thus a variable in its own right.

The claim that an organizational climate is "unique" will be modified as the study of climate progresses. In order to treat climate as a variable, it obviously must become known as having a set of

[1] Mayer Zald, "The Correctional Institution for Juvenile Offenders: An Analysis of Organizational 'Character,' " in Lawrence Hazelrigg (ed.), *Prison Within Society* (Garden City, N.Y.: Doubleday, 1969), pp. 229–246.

[2] David Street, Robert Vinter, and Charles Perrow, *Organization for Treatment* (New York: Free Press, 1966); see, for example, pp. 26–39.

[3] Ibid., pp. 21–22.

values that can be specified.[4] One attempt to quantify the organizational climate variable has been Rudolph Moos' work with the "environmental press" of an institution.[5] According to Moos, the analysis and prediction of behavior have too often emphasized personality factors and too infrequently studied the environmental factors that affect behavior. Recent psychological studies, especially those concerning institutional behavior

all . . . strongly indicate the importance of the setting and the person's interaction with the setting in accounting for the behavioral variance (and) suggest that systematic assessment of environments might greatly increase the accuracy of behavioral predictions.[6]

In the formulation of the Social Climate Scale, Moos presented himself with the following problem:

Which of the items identifies what might be characteristic of an environment which exerts a press toward affiliation or toward autonomy, etc.? What might there be in an institutional environment which could be satisfying to, or would tend to reinforce or reward, an individual who had a high need for affiliation or for autonomy, or spontaneity, etc.?[7]

Moos was seeking to measure the ways in which the social environment of an institution may press an individual toward certain kinds of perceptions and certain kinds of behaviors. He was concerned that correctional officials too frequently consider that inmate behavior is explained in terms of the individual's psychological characteristics. He made the countersuggestion that much behavior in a correctional organization may be socially induced by pressures that affect all organizational members.

The existence of such an environmental press toward particular kinds of human interaction would be crucial to the formulation of correctional policy. Reform, rehabilitation, and reintegration policies all seek to change offender behavior in one way or another. Either the behavior is a direct target of change or alterations in behavior are treated as indications of variation in an internal change-target such as an "attitude." Since the correctional goal is implemented through policy and managerial style, or through structuring the internal situation in certain ways, that situation of structured interaction is the medium in which inmate reactions take place and are observed.

[4] See the discussion in Leslie Wilkins, *Evaluation of Penal Measures* (New York: Random House, 1969), pp. 25–26, on the resolution of the argument of "uniqueness" and measurement.

[5] Rudolph Moos, "The Assessment of the Social Climates of Correctional Institutions," *Journal of Research in Crime and Delinquency* (July, 1968), pp. 174–188, and *Evaluating Correctional and Community Settings* (New York: Wiley, 1976).

[6] Moos, "The Assessment of the Social Climates of Correctional Institutions," p. 175.

[7] Ibid., p. 177.

The discovery in correctional organizations of such a medium, or climate, would support the policy of reintegration as a correctional goal, since it is this policy that attempts to change the interactions among inmates and staff rather than change something within the inmates themselves. In contrast, reform and rehabilitation policies that focus on internal attitudes or conditions, rather than on interconnections between people, would be less viable alternatives to the extent that the organizational environment is a determinant of behavior.

This kind of consideration is beyond the scope of this chapter. We are not presently concerned with the consequences of particular climates, although this is obviously an important problem for future investigations.[8] We want to study climate as a consequence of two major aspects of the managerial role: policy formulation and feedback (or style). If it is possible to show that changes in managerial behavior are accompanied by changes in the social climates of institutions, then our system model may really provide us with methods of altering the throughput of an organization and hence the effectiveness of correctional organizations in changing offender behavior.

CLIMATE AS THE INTEGRATING CONCEPT IN THE STUDY OF CORRECTIONAL ORGANIZATIONS

If the social climate is really a variable of cumulative interactions in an organization, then this environment should change when the structure of the organization is altered. In particular, we would expect that the environment should press toward social health or harmony when style and policy indicate managerial concern for congruence between individual and organizational goals, and the environment should press toward social ill health and discord when style and policy indicate managerial lack of concern for congruence in organizational life. For example, if an organization had a managerial policy of reintegration and a managerial style of 9/9, the climate should be relatively healthy. The 9/9 managerial style indicates simultaneous concern for goals of organizational members and goals of the organization itself; the policy of reintegration indicates a simultaneous concern for offenders and community. At the opposite extreme, an organization with a managerial style of 9/1 and a policy of restraint should be relatively unhealthy. The 9/1 style would indicate that managers are not willing to consider

---

[8] Wright has recently examined the impact of organizational climate on recidivism. See Kervin Wright, "Correctional Effectiveness—The Case for an Organizational Approach," unpublished doctoral dissertation, Pennsylvania State University, 1977.

employee goals while they are trying to achieve organizational goals, and the restraint policy would indicate lack of concern for both offenders and community. The first example demonstrates maximum concern for congruence in the organizational matrix; the second example demonstrates minimal concern for congruence in the organizational matrix.

In Chapter 5 it was demonstrated that both of these combinations of policy and style are compatible. That is, the 9/9 style is the feedback technique most likely to be used in the implementation of the reintegration policy. Similarly, the 9/1 style is most likely to be used in the implementation of the restraint policy. Although, in this sense, both pairs are examples of "congruent" or consistent style and policy, only the first example should produce a healthy organizational climate because only the first pair (9/9 and reintegration) indicates the manager's *conscious* use of the tendency of organizational members to achieve congruence. Or, as it was stated in Chapter 1, only certain correctional administrators utilize the natural tendencies of human systems in their attempts to manage them.

It may also help to understand that the organizational climate is *not* a desired end product of the correctional organization; it is only a *means* to that end. Some goals require a healthy climate while other goals require an unhealthy one. To carry through, the goal in the first example above is, by definition, returning changed offenders to the changed community. The organizational climate, or the medium in which that goal is achieved, is one of harmonious social interactions. The goal in the second example above is, by definition, maintaining the organization for its own sake, that is, holding offenders out of an unchanging society. The social climate, or organizational medium, in which that goal is effected is one of discord and disharmony.

THE SOCIAL CLIMATE SCALE

Moos originally decided to measure 12 separate dimensions of the environmental press.[9]

[9] The number of dimensions has been revised from time to time, depending on statistical analyses of the questionnaire items. The 12-dimension scale, which is described here, was later collapsed to 9 dimensions. See Ernst Wenk and Thomas Halatyn, *The Assessment of Social Climates in Correctional Institutions* (Davis, Calif.: National Council on Crime and Delinquency Research Center, June, 1973). Wright's more recent use of the Social Climate Scale includes a strong argument for further revision. See Wright, "Correctional Effectiveness—A Case for an Organizational Approach." In this chapter the original 12-dimension Social Climate Scale is introduced because the research relating policy and style to climate utilized that version. All later research supports the basic thesis put forward here. See the following Chapter 7 in this book, Wright's dissertation, and David Duffee, Peter B. Meyer, and Barbara D. Warner, *Offender Needs, Parole Outcome and Program Structure in the Bureau of Correction Community Services Division* (Harrisburg, Pa.: Governor's Justice Commission, 1977).

1. *The Dimension of Spontaneity.* Ten questions on the Social Climate Scale ask organizational members whether or not they can do what they feel like doing in the organization. How often do people do spur-of-the-moment things? How often are there ulterior motives and hidden goals behind activities? Presumably we would not find much spontaneity among officers or offenders in a reform organization. We would probably find much more in a rehabiliation organization. We would expect spontaneity if there were an emphasis on developing and expressing feelings. Similarly, managerial styles of 1/9 and 9/9, and to a lesser degree 5/5, should encourage spontaneous behavior, but 1/1 and 9/1 managerial styles would not.

2. *The Dimension of Support.* Ten questions on the scale measure the amount of encouragement and positive reinforcement or lack of challenge one feels in the organization. How often does one feel confidence in oneself, trusting that someone else is not waiting to betray or punish? The rehabilitation policy should generate a supportive atmosphere, as would 1/9 and 5/5 management. In contrast, reform and restraint policies and 9/1 and 1/1 management would tend to create defensive behaviors and aggressive, nonsupportive climates.

3. *The Dimensions of Practicality.* Ten questions on the scale deal with the degree to which the organization or people within the organization deal with problems or have goals that appear to have payoff for the organizational member. Are correctional programs make-time or useful? Would a prison leave an inmate unprepared when released or would the inmate be prepared to start parole on solid footing? The two policies that would generate practicality would be reintegration and reform. Both of these policies are deeply concerned with the completion of tasks and the pragmatic consequences of these tasks. For offenders, there is a heavy emphasis on vocational training in both policies. Practicality should also be influenced by 9/9 and 9/1 management, since there is heavy emphasis on the usefulness of activity in the accomplishment of goals.

   There may, however, be a somewhat surprising show of practicality in some organizations with a rehabilitation policy, if the ideology of treatment is particularly pervasive. To the extent that such an ideology is an accepted principle by staff and offenders, then the "therapeutic" atmosphere would seem practical, since people would perceive changes in internal attitudes as leading to reduction in criminality.

4. *The Dimension of Affiliation.* Ten questions ask how many friends one has in the organization. Are there many forces that tend to keep people apart or is comradeship rewarded? This environmental dimension should be positively influenced by the reintegration policy and by 9/9 management. It is a goal of that policy to facilitate intergroup communication, and it is a technique of that style to work through groups in order to accomplish goals. Rehabilitation policy that emphasizes the milieu approach and change via identification should also strengthen this dimension.

5. *The Dimension of Order.* Ten questions ask about physical order. Are rooms neat or messy? Do people keep appointments or are they constantly canceling them? How much of the daily activity is predictable? This dimension does not ask about relative regimentation. It is possible for an organization to maintain order and remain fairly flexible, and it is possible for an organization with emphasis on mass treatment or regimentation of people to be disorderly. Nevertheless, order should correlate with reform policy because neatness and punctuality are treated as virtues to be instilled in offenders.

6. *The Dimension of Insight.* Ten questions ask how often people look for motivation and reasons behind another's or their own behavior. How superficial or how deep are relationships? Insight obviously should be characteristic of an environment structured by the rehabilitation policy. In this policy the motivations and reasons for behavior are emphasized.

7. *The Dimension of Involvement.* Ten questions ask to what degree people are committed or involved in events in the organization. Do they participate in decision making or not? Do they carry out orders in the letter or the spirit? There is most likely a press toward involvement in an environment structured by 9/9 management and reintegration policy; 9/9 management requires that the group responsible for a task assign roles to its members as the members analyze the problem presented to them. The activity of the group binds the members to the goal and makes them interdependent. Reintegration policy demands that various information sources be pooled and that the various skills possessed by the members of the organization be integrated.

8. *The Dimension of Aggression.* Ten questions ask how much open conflict and visible anger are present in the environment. Are people always shouting? Are there many fights or threats of fights? Do people cooperate with each other or are group tasks disrupted and difficult to manage?

It is difficult to predict which policies will correlate with a press toward aggression. It is hard to say that more aggression will be felt when a policy such as rehabilitation encourages spontaneity or a policy such as reform represses it. Rehabilitation and reintegration policies work to resolve aggressions and therefore deal with conflict openly. Reform and restraint forbid expression of aggression and therefore alter the ways in which it is expressed.

The managerial style that probably increases a press toward aggression is the 9/1 style, which makes a high demand for production and uses manipulation of rewards in order to achieve it.

9. *The Dimension of Variety.* Ten questions ask how many different things there are to do in the organization. Is the organizational routine tedious and monotonous or is it varied and complex?

Variety should be increased by policies that treat change as a complex activity and by the 9/9 management style that uses a variety of maintenance structures in order to support production. It is the reintegration policy that views human behavior as most complex. Therefore, the reintegration strategy calls for an increase in opportunities for offenders. As these opportunities increase, the alternatives open to staff should also increase.

10. *The Dimension of Clarity.* Ten questions ask how clear and understandable the organizational goals are. Do things make sense in the organizational scheme or are the reasons for orders, activities, etc., hidden?

Clarity may be a product of consistency between policy and style. Ignoring these possible interactions for the time being, it would seem that the reform policy should influence a press toward clarity because the rules and regulations are constantly emphasized. Similarly, a 9/1 management style may influence the clarity dimension because 9/1 managers set out their rules, rewards, and punishments in advance. On the other hand, the 9/1 manager is not so open about his or her goals and may produce some confusion about the reasons for the sanctioning pattern that he or she enforces. In this sense, reintegration policy and 9/9 management should produce a higher press toward clarity.

11. *The Dimension of Submission.* Ten questions ask how frequently people are forced to do things one way and how often they knuckle under and have no means to appeal decisions.

The press toward submission should be produced by managerial strategies that limit the behavioral alternatives. Reform and restraint policies offer staff and inmates the fewest choices to make on their own and the fewest opportunities to exercise discretion.

The managerial styles that should press toward submission are 9/1 and, to a lesser extent, 1/1. A 1/1 style is probably a symptom rather than a major cause of submission, but a 1/1 style asks others to submit to the regulations, and it does not reward innovation.

12. *The Dimension of Autonomy.* The last dimension is measured by the ten questions about the amount of activity one could do on one's own. How much self-determination is present? How many times must someone ask for advice or permission?

The rehabilitation policy emphasizes self-expression and may to some extent press toward autonomy. But the kinds of decisions that the rehabilitation policy would allow a client to make on his or her own are limited. The reintegration policy obviously should press toward autonomy in the climate because change through internalization asks the offender not only to adopt behaviors that he or she personally values but also to practice new behavior in the external environment. The 9/9 managerial style should also increase a press toward autonomy, since this style operates to include subordinates in planning and decision making.

Moos tested his scales in 16 California Youth Authority institutions with small resident and staff populations. He found little correlation between the climate dimensions and background characteristics of inmates (such as age and length of stay), relative lack of correlation among the scale dimensions themselves, and predictable correlations with objective data (resident to staff ratio, frequency of aggressive behavior) and certain dimensions of the scale.[10] Results of the questionnaire accurately distinguished institutions from each other, whether inmate and staff scores for each institution were compared separately or combined. Moos concluded that the dimensions measured by this questionnaire may be at least as important as the more readily available objective indices such as number of residents, number of staff, types of security and custody precautions, or amount of physical space available.[11]

---

[10] Moos, "The Assessment of Social Climates of Correctional Institutions," pp. 180–182.
[11] Ibid.

SOCIAL CLIMATE MEASUREMENT
IN A SYSTEM FOR ADULTS

The administration of the Social Climate Scale in a variety of correctional settings took place between 1969 and 1972.[12] One part of this national survey took place in Connecticut during a training program for Department of Correction Central Office and top institutional staff. In the time between the first and second conferences for top managers the trainers and administrators were looking for a way to demonstrate the effects of policy and style as they had been measured at the first conference. Although the wardens, especially, were somewhat anxious about the probable results, the group agreed that seeking such data was important.

Samples of 20 percent of the inmates and staff were selected by pulling every fifth personnel and inmate file within each of the six institutions in the state. These six were as follows:

1. Somers Prison. This prison was built in 1961 and has a capacity of 1000 inmates. At the time of the survey the inmate population was 900. Somers is a maximum security operation, and until 1969 it was the only formally recognized prison (Enfield was a satellite managed by the Somers warden and his assistants). Relative to other maximum security prisons, Somers was widely recognized for its positive social and physical condition.

2. Enfield Prison. Enfield was recently separated from Somers. It is called a minimum security institution but in other states it might be classified as medium security. It has a capacity of 400, and the population has fluctuated wildly, probably because of changes in the classification of minimum security inmates and because of the change in its status to a separate institution.

3. Cheshire Reformatory. This institution was built in 1911 for offenders from the ages of 16 to 21. It is basically a maximum security unit and it has a variety of school and vocational programs. There were several administrative changes in rapid succession at Chesire, and there was general consensus at the beginning of the study that Chesire had had for years an overly punitive regime.

4. New Haven Correctional Center. This is a large, local jail taken over by the Department when counties were abolished in the state. The building was in disrepair at the time of the study; and, with roughly 200 convicted and detained inmates, it was probably overcrowded.

[12] Wenk and Halatyn, *The Assessment of Social Climates of Correctional Institutions.*

5. Bridgeport Correctional Center. This is a large jail that holds approximately 300 inmates and detainees. Although the facility has one modern wing, even the new addition was built without toilet facilities in the cells.
6. Niantic. This is a complex of institutions for approximately 125 women. There are maximum, minimum, and jail units on the grounds. Niantic was organized on a cottage-counselor principle similar to traditional training schools instead of along traditional prison lines.

THE SOCIAL CLIMATE OF ENFIELD PRISON

In the other institutions the Correctional Policy Inventory and the Styles of Management Inventory could not be extensively used. The top managers in the other institutions responded to both inventories in conjunction with the first training conference. There were some middle managers from each institution present at a middle-management training conference in which the inventories were also used. But only from Enfield was a large enough delegation of middle managers selected that their scores on policy and style could represent the entire middle level for the institution. No more than two or three managers from other institutions were sent to the conference. Hence, only at Enfield is the picture of managerial strategy in terms of policy and style inventories very complete. Therefore, before examining the climate data for all institutions, it may be helpful to examine the Enfield climate.

The Enfield managers had a rehabilitation policy, but the policy was not effectively implemented at the time. The middle managers, particularly, depend very heavily on a 9/1 managerial style. Although it has not been called their "managerial style" to this point, officers reported that their behavior most frequently supported a reform policy.

In terms of climate, the initial emphasis on rehabilitation may affect somewhat the environmental press dimensions such as spontaneity, support, and insight. However, most of the effect of the rehabilitation policy of managers must surely be negated by the 9/1 style of the same managers and, at the lower levels of the organization, by the shift in policy to reform and restraint.

We would expect relatively high scores (over 5) on the aggression and submission dimensions and relatively low scores (under 5) on all the other dimensions. (Moos' subscales run from a low of 1 to a high of 10.) In field interviews it was found that officers, particularly, complained of close supervision and lack of goal definition. We might then expect particularly low scores on the dimensions of clarity and autonomy. In general, we should expect the climate to be relatively "unhealthy," in the sense that someone choosing a social environment to live in would probably desire aggression and submission to approach 1 and the other dimensions to approach 10. Furthermore, since the policy data distinctly demonstrated a low perceived concern for the inmate, we should expect that the environment press at the top of the Enfield organization would be much healthier than the press at the bottom of the oganization.

The data in Table 6.1 tends to bear out these expectations. The two highest dimensions were aggression (6.74) and submission (8.20). Clarity (3.12) was rather low and autonomy (2.39) was the lowest of the 12 means. Spontaneity (2.62) was also rather low. The dimensions of practicality and order both had means over 5, which may indicate the strength of 9/1 management and the de facto

Table 6.1 The Social Climate of the Enfield Institution Reported as an Average for the Entire Sample and Separately for Managers, Officers and Inmates

Level	Social Climate Dimension					
	Spontaneity	Support	Practicality	Affiliation	Order	Insight
Manager (N = 6)	4.50	5.50	7.50	7.83	8.00	5.00
Officer (N = 40)	3.67	5.55	5.83	6.45	7.20	4.63
Inmate (N = 88)	2.02	2.65	5.03	3.42	4.01	3.11
Grand Mean (N = 134)	2.62	3.56	5.38	4.51	5.06	3.64

Level	Social Climate Dimension					
	Involvement	Aggression	Variety	Clarity	Submission	Autonomy
Manager (N = 6)	5.80	6.18	5.83	6.83	7.17	3.17
Officer (N = 40)	3.43	6.15	5.27	4.98	7.18	3.25
Inmate (N = 88)	3.48	7.04	4.53	2.03	8.74	1.94
Grand Mean (N = 134)	3.56	6.74	4.73	3.12	8.20	2.39

reform policy in the institution. It is also important to note that the social climate was considerably healthier toward the top of the institution than it was toward the bottom. Managers did not feel the same environmental press as inmates did or even as officers did. Under these circumstances, managers may have difficulty understanding officer and inmate behaviors that are affected by the unhealthier climate.

IMPACT OF GOALS AND MANAGEMENT ON SOCIAL CLIMATE

If the Social Climate Scale is at all useful, it should be able to discriminate among prisons. The variance of social climate scores among institutions should be greater than the variance for individuals within each institution. If this is not true, then the scale does not measure social or organizational environments. If the scale does measure prison differences, then it would seem to be sensitive to something about organizations. Since we have argued that correctional policy and managerial style are important determinants of organizational behavior, these variables should go a long way toward explaining organizational climate differences.

Unfortunately, it was not possible to use managerial style and correctional policy inventories in all institutions. Therefore, it is necessary to divide the Social Climate Scale scores by other variables that are known to have certain associations with the policy and style variables. One variable that is known to vary with policy is the hierarchical level in the organization. A variable that varies with managerial style is the amount of choice a person perceives himself or herself to have in decision making. Another variable is how frequently the person's opinions are sought by decision makers, and another variable is the accuracy of the records that are kept, since the more autocratic the management, the more inaccurate the information seems to be. It was possible to pool some of these variables into an "organizational profile" questionnaire that was administered to all staff along with the Social Climate Scale. Therefore, after investigating the usefulness of the Social Climate Scale for distinguishing organizations, it is possible to see whether or not the organizational variables we have deemed important do make a difference in the internal situation as measured by the Social Climate Scale.

Table 6.2 provides a summary of the analysis of variance performed on the 12 climate dimension scores for the six institutions. In every case except the dimension of aggression, the scores vary

Table 6.2 Correctional Policy and Prison Organization: Summary of One-Way Analysis of Variance Performed on Social Climate Dimensions for Six Correctional Institutions (November, 1969)

Social Climate Dimensions	Variations Among Levels		Residual		Variance	
	D.F.	Mean Square	D.F.	Mean Square	Ratio	P
Spontaneity	5	33.65	698	6.51	5.16	.01
Supoport	5	47.58	698	9.63	5.08	.01
Practicality	5	136.80	698	12.49	10.95	.01
Affiliation	5	50.03	698	12.13	4.12	.01
Order	5	51.97	698	9.52	5.42	.01
Insight	5	32.73	698	6.48	4.12	.01
Involvement	5	39.90	698	10.10	3.95	.01
Aggression	5	20.58	698	22.97	.90	.10
Variety	5	45.49	698	7.08	6.42	.01
Clarity	5	34.06	698	7.77	4.38	.01
Submission	5	75.88	698	23.86	3.18	.01
Autonomy	5	34.43	698	4.80	7.17	.01

significantly from institution to institution. Thus, the Social Climate Scale would seem to be sensitive to *something* about differences among institutions.

The usefulness of the Social Climate Scale will depend on our ability to predict the ordering of the prisons as they are differentiated by their social climate dimension means. One could make this prediction based on a clinical assessment of the climate in the institution. Moos suggests that his scale is a quantification of the vignettes and informal observations about organizational character. If it is, there should be a general agreement between the Moos' subscale scores and the general assessment of climate by a trained observer. This approach, however, is not as useful for our purposes as a prediction based on types of managerial strategy.

Because there was no questionnaire by which to measure goals in five of the institutions, an assessment of policy was made from the policy questionnaires of the top managers, interviews with the top managers and officers, and informal observations about the structure of the organizations as they were influenced by goals. If one assesses policy in this manner, one is likely to rate two institutions as rehabilitation-oriented, two as reform-oriented, and two as restraint-oriented.

The Niantic institution had a *rehabilitation* policy. The top two officials at Niantic both reported rehabilitation as their strongest policy preference. Interviews in the institution demonstrated a high concern for inmates and considerably less concern for changing the community. Most importantly, the Niantic institution was structured along the lines of a traditional training school. The institution was organized into cottages and most decisions about inmates were made by the professional staff in charge of each cottage. The treatment staff at Niantic equaled the custodial staff in number, and nearly twice as much money was spent yearly on each inmate at Niantic as at Somers. Niantic probably came as close as we can find to a protoype rehabilitation institution.

Chesire Reformatory also had a *rehabilitation* policy. Chesire was a maximum security institution, which certainly detracted from the strength of the rehabilitative atmosphere. But the two top executives at Chesire reported that rehabilitation was their first choice of policy. Interviews in the institution underscored the fact that Chesire had not always been a rehabilitation institution. A very harsh regime was reduced quickly by the first commissioner of corrections, and the commissioner's newly appointed superintendent had, in his first six months of office, impressed many people with his emphasis on changing the institution. Structural changes were also visible. The school program and vocational training program had been expanded and between June and December 1969 a dozen new counselors were hired. With a long-term adult population, these changes may not have made too much difference, but with a short-term youthful offender population the change in policy should have been reflected in climate because the short-term inmates should have been less affected by previous prison climates.

The Enfield institution had a *reform* policy. Much more was known about Enfield than about the other institutions. Judging from questionnaires, interviews, and daily operating patterns, reform was probably a fair compromise when balancing the rehabilitative policy of managers against the perceptions of restraint by the inmates.

The Somers institution had a *reform* policy. The warden at Somers was almost a personification of the reform policy. When he was appointed, the departmental paper claimed that he was "firm but fair." According to the Inventory results, three of the four top managers of the Somers institution preferred reform policy. The interviews at Somers underscored the closeness of the supervision and the strict adherence to rules and regulations. To bolster the intended policy, which was to instill accepted community attitudes in the inmates, there were many vocational training and work programs at the maximum security institution.

The Bridgeport Correctional Center had a *restraint* policy. According to the Inventory results, the warden of Bridgeport preferred a reform policy, but interviews in the institution quickly highlighted despair and deceit on the part of the officers and concern for image rather than substance on the part of the warden. In addition, there were no programs and there were no possibilities for training that would suggest anything but the goals of restraint.

The New Haven Correctional Center had a *restraint* policy. This institution, much like Bridgeport, had no social and physical facilities to boast about. Unlike at Bridgeport, the warden's position at New Haven changed hands three times in 1969. Even though the third of these wardens was to prove one of the more capable administrators in the department, the climate in New Haven was probably affected by changes in leadership and two riots as much as by the newest warden. The general attitude was that, for the present, officers merely seemed glad to still have jobs and an institution in which to do them.

In Table 6.3 the 12 social climate dimension means for the six institutions are presented. The institutions are listed in the order in which they were described. Niantic, with the most rehabilitative policy, is listed first and New Haven, with the most restraint-oriented policy, is listed last. If climate is affected by goals, all dimension means except aggression and submission should descend in value from Niantic to New Haven. Aggression and submission should ascend in value from Niantic to New Haven.

It is clear that the prediction of means in terms of institutional goals was fairly successful. The extremes were correctly predicted. Niantic seemed to have the healthiest climate and Chesire the second healthiest. The New Haven climate is the least satisfactory. The dimensions of aggression and submission do not conform to the prediction at all. It would seem from the data on those two dimensions that the maximum security factor, rather than goals, increased the aggressiveness and submissiveness felt in the institution. It is also obvious that whenever it was difficult to distinguish the policies of the institutions with the methods available, the prediction was less successful. Enfield, Somers, and Bridgeport are occasionally misordered, as on the dimension of spontaneity, and are sometimes correctly ordered, as on the dimension of practicality. But in all cases, the means of these institutions are rather close together. In general, it would be fair to say that the social climate differs as expected, being relatively healthy in institutions with a rehabilitation policy and relatively unhealthy in institutions with a restraint policy;

Table 6.3 Social Climate Scale Means for Six Correctional Institutions

	Social Climate Dimension					
Institution	Spontaneity	Support	Practicality	Affiliation	Order	Insight
Niantic (N = 75)	4.23	5.32	6.04	6.09	5.43	5.21
Chesire (N = 130)	3.53	4.49	6.36	4.89	4.80	3.90
Enfield (N = 135)	2.62	3.56	5.38	4.51	5.06	3.64
Somers (N = 167)	2.88	3.70	5.07	4.66	5.03	3.61
Bridgeport (N = 102)	3.37	3.62	4.07	4.23	3.85	3.75
New Haven (N = 95)	2.86	3.53	3.35	3.82	3.62	4.23

	Social Climate Dimension					
Institution	Involvement	Aggression	Variety	Clarity	Submission	Autonomy
Niantic (N = 75)	5.17	6.53	5.21	4.07	5.89	4.07
Cheshire (N = 130)	4.04	7.28	4.53	4.11	6.68	2.75
Enfield (N = 135	3.56	6.74	4.73	3.12	6.32	2.39
Somers (N = 167)	3.64	7.34	5.42	3.41	8.13	2.53
Bridgeport (N = 102)	3.80	6.39	4.10	2.77	6.92	2.97
New Haven (N = 95)	3.16	6.54	3.78	2.93	7.03	2.01

climates in institutions with a reform policy fall between these extremes.

The preceding chapters on correctional policy and managerial style attempt to draw out the consequences of decision alternatives that range from the preset and predetermined to the undetermined and nonjudgmental. Taken together, the Enfield data have shown that a policy of rehabilitation implemented in a 9/1, task-oriented managerial style can be associated on lower organizational levels with increasing interpersonal polarization and increasing divergence from a recognition of the original policy. If the Enfield data are similar to policy–style relationships in the other prisons, then the differentiation on social climate dimensions may be seen as the end result of progressive polarization in the playing of organizational roles. As the organizational members rate their own roles, managerial positions should be more open and flexible than officer positions and officer positions should be more open and flexible than inmate positions.

In order to test this hypothesis, an "organizational profile" questionnaire was devised and administered to staff along with the Social Climate scale. The questionnaire was originally designed as a "reversed managerial grid" by which employees would rate their supervisors on the dimensions of (1) concern for employees and (2) concern for production. The 15 questions for each dimension did not prove independent, for there was a high intercorrelation between items supposedly demonstrating concern for employees and items supposedly demonstrating concern for work. Therefore, the Blake–Mouton grid format was discarded and a simple continuum was substituted.[13] Although the questionnaire does not measure concern for personnel and concern for organizations separately, it does seem to measure personnel's perception of their manager's tendency to achieve goal congruence or to maintain a fragmented structure.

The original questionnaire consisted of 30 items. When it was seen that the two dimensionality was not achievable, the decision was also made to choose the 10 items of the 30 with the highest correlation to the total score. Each item consisted of two statements about a specific organizational activity, and below each item there was a five-space scale. Each respondent was asked to put a check mark in the space that he felt represented the behavior of the organization on that activity:

1. The records which are kept on the organization fail to reflect the real work which is being done.

Records which are kept in the organization really measure how well the job is getting done.

:_____ :_____ :_____ :_____ :_____ :

The items were scored from 0 at the item extreme that represented the perception of organizational insensitivity, inaccuracy, and

[13] The continuum and the questionnaire are very similar to those developed by Rensis Likert, *The Human Organization* (New York, McGraw-Hill, 1967), pp. 197–211.

closure to 4 at the item extreme that represented the perception of organizational sensitivity, accuracy, and openness. The scores on the ten-item questionnaire then ranged from 0 (completely closed) to 40 (completely open).

Table 6.4 shows that the managerial level is, indeed, perceived as the most open by the role incumbents and that the officer level is perceived as the most closed by the role incumbents. The organizational profile mean for managers is 22.29; the mean for officers is 16.91. The hypothesis that the perception of distance from other organizational members increases at lower organizational levels is, therefore, supported. Table 6.5 shows that the profile differences between hierarchical levels are significant at considerably better than .05.

Since the organizational profile questionnaire seemed to distinguish from autocratic feedback patterns, it seemed usable as a substitute for the managerial style questionnaire as a measure of managerial feedback. In order to see if the profile would delineate distinct social climates, employee groups were classified by their organizational profile scores. The groups were separated by whether they were within or outside two standard deviations from the organizational profile mean. Three employee groups were thereby distinguished:

Table 6.4 Organizational Profile Means for Four Prison Hierarchical Levels (November, 1969)

Group	N	Mean
1. Managers	31	22.29
2. Counselors, etc.	45	20.07
3. Supportive service	14	20.71
4. Officers	181	16.91

Table 6.5 Analysis of Variance for Organizational Profile Scores of Prison Staff Classified by Hierarchical Level (November, 1969)

Variance Among	Degrees of Freedom	Mean Square
Staff Levels	3	354.60
Residual	267	105.43

Variance ratio 3.36 significant at .05.

1. A group perceiving the organization as very open (scores of 28.5+);
2. A middle group perceiving the organization as average (scores from 7.5 to 28);
3. A group perceiving the organization as very closed (scores of less than 7).[14]

The analysis of variance performed on the social climate dimensions for these profile groups yielded significant differences on all dimensions except aggression and submission (see Table 6.6).

In all cases in which there is a difference of significance, the comparison of social climate means demonstrates the impact of open system management (see Table 6.7). For example, personnel who felt that they were managed in an open manner had a mean support score of 7.15, but the average group had a mean of 5.95. The group that felt it was managed in a closed manner had a mean of 3.92. The open group had a practicality mean of 7.60; the mean for the closed group was 4.18. In other words, the group that felt it was managed openly also felt that the prison social climate included a consideration for the accomplishment of specific practical goals. Personnel who were managed in a closed fashion felt that the prison had little practical value. In the same way, the group managed openly

Table 6.6 Variation Among Profile Score Levels (High, Average, Low)

	Profile Variance		Residual Variance			
Dimension	Degrees of Freedom	Mean Square	Degrees of Freedom	Mean Square	Variance Ratio	P
Spontaneity	2	15.18	268	3.52	4.31	.05
Support	2	136.90	268	4.00	34.20	.01
Practicality	2	157.49	268	5.25	28.54	.01
Affiliation	2	107.70	268	4.13	26.06	.01
Order	2	53.77	268	6.45	8.34	.01
Insight	2	12.91	268	3.90	3.30	.05
Involvement	2	123.31	268	6.18	19.97	.01
Aggression	2	27.31	268	30.14	.91	.20
Variety	2	31.47	268	10.15	3.10	.05
Clarity	2	190.00	268	7.30	26.02	.01
Submission	2	4.10	268	3.36	1.22	.20
Autonomy	2	41.32	268	3.87	10.68	.01

[14] These three groups may be considered analogous to Likert's System III, II, and I management patterns, respectively (*The Human Organization*, pp. 3–12).

Table 6.7 Social Climate Means for Three Organizational Profile Levels
for Staff in Six Prisons

Social Climate Dimension	Profile Group		
	Low (Closed) $N = 51$	Medium $N = 168$	High (Open) $N = 52$
Spontaneity	3.65	4.36	4.69
Support	3.92	5.95	7.15
Practicality	4.18	6.37	7.60
Affiliation	4.94	6.80	7.75
Order	5.73	6.76	7.77
Insight	4.27	4.91	5.25
Involvement	2.75	4.48	5.83
Aggression	6.90	5.94	6.83
Variety	4.75	5.57	6.31
Clarity	3.45	5.27	7.29
Submission	6.63	6.58	6.15
Autonomy	2.84	3.74	4.63

felt it was easier to make friends on the job (affiliation mean of 7.77) than the group managed in a closed fashion (affiliation mean of 4.94). Similarly, the open group felt more spontaneity, order, involvement, variety, clarity, and autonomy in the prison climate.

It seems clear that the way in which people perceive themselves to be managed had considerable effect on the kind of social situation that they found themselves in. In general terms, the openly managed group lived in a healthy atmosphere, and the closed group lived in an unhealthy and strained one. The effects then that management can have on the probability that personnel will act in an open and considerate way with inmates are certainly great. For example, it would seem much more likely for officers who feel great amounts of spontaneity, support, and practicality in their work situation to extend the much greater effort that is needed in order to make inmates perceive and react to reintegration and rehabilitation behavioral patterns than to reform and restraint patterns.

SOCIAL CLIMATE SCORES AND ORGANIZATIONAL LEVEL

The social climate data analyzed prison by prison demonstrated that prison social climates do indeed seem to differ. In prisons in which the college-educated counseling staff of "treatment" personnel were obviously superordinate and in which rehabilitation ideology had evidently had some structural effects, the environmental dimensions such as spontaneity, support, affiliation, clarity, and autonomy were relatively high and the dimension of submission was relatively low. In prisons in which there was a lower concern for the inmate, the reverse was true. Using general information about the policies of the prisons, we see that it was possible to predict, roughly, the ranking of means on the Social Climate Scale. Ranking staff by their scores on the organizational profile questionnaire, we were able to distinguish social climates across prisons.

A variable that would seem to differentiate both the correctional policy and the organizational profile would be the one of hierarchical level. We have seen in Enfield that the policy intended by managers becomes increasingly less recognizable until a totally different policy is perceived at the inmate level. We have also seen that the organizational profile scores are higher at the top of the organization and lower at the officer level. As we descend toward the inmate level, the behavior of the immediate supervisor seems to increase the amount of conflict the subordinates feel and the amount of fragmentation in the organization. A separate advantage of using hierarchical level as an independent variable in the analysis of variance is that we can include inmate scores. In general, the higher organizational levels should have the higher social climate means and the lower organizational levels should have the lower means, except in the cases of submission and aggression, where the reverse should be true.

To test this hypothesis, the respondents to the social climate questionnaire were divided into five groups: (1) wardens down through lieutenants; (2) counselors, maintenance supervisors, and teachers; (3) supportive services such as clerical or secretarial; (4) officers; and (5) inmates. The means on each of the 12 climate dimensions are presented in Table 6.8. Divided into status positions (from 1 to 5), the groups report rather different social climates. However, unless the custody positions are compared separately, a U-curve appears in the comparison of group means. In many cases, group two (counselors, supervisors, and teachers) and group three (supportive services) are higher than group one (wardens through lieutenants). On the submission and aggression dimensions, groups two and three are considerably lower than the managerial group (compare the means in Table 6.8). By eliminating these two groups and comparing the means of managers, officers, and inmates, the U-curve disappears except on the dimensions of spontaneity and submission. There are probably two related reasons why the managerial group feels less spontaneity, support, practicality, affiliation, etc., and more aggression and submission than groups two and three.

Table 6.8 Social Climate Dimension Means for Five Prison Hierarchical Levels

Dimension	Warden–Lieutenant $N = 32$	Counselors Teachers $N = 46$	Clerical $N = 14$	Officers $N = 182$	Inmates $N = 430$
Spontaneity	4.03	5.02	4.50	4.13	2.45
Support	5.84	6.87	7.07	5.41	2.79
Practicality	6.44	7.22	6.64	5.88	4.38
Affiliation	6.69	7.35	7.29	6.39	3.39
Order	6.94	7.63	7.29	6.51	3.33
Insight	5.09	5.46	5.21	4.65	3.36
Involvement	4.62	6.09	5.93	3.84	3.44
Aggression	6.13	5.46	5.50	6.62	7.24
Variety	5.97	5.13	5.57	5.59	4.13
Clarity	5.41	6.33	5.93	5.02	2.16
Submission	7.16	5.67	5.93	6.66	7.23
Autonomy	3.56	4.39	4.86	3.52	2.13

First, the managers must feel a subordination to their superiors (lieutenant to captain; warden to deputy commissioner) that the two staff groups do not feel. Second, both groups two and three were perceived in all institutions, with the exception of Niantic, as having limited scope and responsibility in the prisons. They, above all, did not have direct responsibility for keeping order in the institution. Thus, it is very likely that these groups may have felt less pressure and few of the effects of fragmentation than the managers who have responsibility for maintaining internal order. On the dimensions that might be associated with an integrated climate, inmates do have the lowest of the five means; and, on the dimensions associated with a fragmented climate, inmates do have the highest of the five means.

The analysis of social climate scores by hierarchical level suggests very strongly that the social climate of instiutions differ rather significantly from position to position. The traditional break between inmates and staff is certainly visible; the greatest difference in means in most cases occurs between officers and inmates. Nevertheless, there are also differences among staff groups. While the inmate–staff split may be an exacerbated hierarchical break, it is not a unique one. While many critics of prison organization claim that the major hinderances to rehabilitation are the formation and maintenance of the inmate counterculture, the social climate data suggest that the problem is essentially an organizational one. The positive feedbac] loops in the fragmented prison generate a number of different climates. Over time these climates may lead to different perceptions of reality.[15] As a consequence, the communication of information for joint problem solving breaks down. Different organizational groups emerge with group-specific methods of problem definition and solution. Problem-solving and reward systems of one group may be irrelevant or in conflict with the problem-solving and reward systems of other groups. In the long run, about the only things that these structurally bound groups value in common are the competition against each other by which each group reinforces its own destiny and the physical space of the facility itself which becomes a playing field for misunderstandings.

Perceptions about organizational integration can be changed. The seemingly unwieldy and unyielding prison organization may be changed. The internal social situation will vary as management alters goals and changes the way in which it relates to lower levels of the organization. The dimensions of social climate that would presumably measure organizational health will be felt more strongly when management is democratic than when it is autocratic, that is, when it involves people in decision making instead of treating people like means to an end. Altering the patterns of management in a prison is a large undertaking, but it can be more optimistically addressed if we know that not all prisons must have the characteristics of "total institutions" or the atmosphere of concentration camps.

Indeed, we could conclude that the concept of "total institution" lacks validity when we compare one prison to another. These organizations may be very different internally, and it may well be these internal differences allow us to change them so that they more effectively achieve the goals that are espoused by correctional executives, legislatures, and the public alike. Key variables in the creation of change would appear to be managerial policy and managerial style, which, taken together, apparently explain to a great degree the internal differences between correctional organizations.

SOCIAL CLIMATE IN OTHER CORRECTIONAL ORGANIZATIONS

Organizational climate is a characteristic of organization rather than a characteristic merely of corrections. The climate of an organization refers to the psychosocial dimensions of organizational behavior that very naturally will be found in any system that binds individuals to related statuses and interacting roles. In the above

---

[15] For a general description of this process, see Leslie Wilkins, *Social Deviance* (Englewood Cliffs, N.J.: Prentice-Hall, 1965), pp. 88–95.

research, a means of measuring social climate in correctional institutions was elaborated in an attempt to demonstrate its relationship to organizational goals and managerial behavior. Attention to social climate and understanding how other organizational variables may influence it are equally significant steps to be taken in the effective management of other types of correctional organization.

Of course, it should be anticipated that the climate created in an organization will differ significantly as other parts of the organization change. Size and staffing patterns, the types of offenders supervised, the types of interaction and the frequency of the interaction with the community, and the physical setting of the organization will all have some impact on the resulting social climate.

Furthermore, we might expect that the importance of the organizational climate itself will vary considerably depending on the extent to which the organization controls the life-space of its members. For example, in prisons we might expect that the organizational climate has greater impact on the behavior of inmates who reside in the organization than it has on the behavior of staff who work there and go home. On the other hand, we would expect that the climates generated in probation and parole organizations will have greater impact on the behavior of staff who are full-time employees than they will have on the behavior of offenders whose involvement in the organization is much more sporadic and is usually mediated by a field agent. Social climates under conditions of partial confinement, such as found in halfway houses and work release centers, should fall somewhere between these two extremes.

In relatively closed institutions the behavior of organizational members toward each other might be explained in great measure by the similarity of differences they experience in the climate or climates associated with their various organizational positions. In correctional field settings, however, explanation of staff–offender interaction would depend more heavily on the extent to which the staff members' organizational climate allows staff to relate effectively to the offenders as they experience very different social climates at work, in their families, and so on.

For managers, an examination of social climate can be a crucial factor in determining whether or not organizational policy is being implemented effectively. Social climate research would indicate that managers must be aware of the actual sociopsychological milieu that their program and program structure generates for staff and offenders. It is common now that correctional managers seek community alternatives to the use of large institutions for a variety of reasons. One of the reasons has to do with the belief that the environment of institutions is detrimental to therapeutic staff–offender relationships; another reason is that large institutional climates are so dependent on external control systems that offenders lose the ability to experiment with new behavior and staff lose the ability to be flexible in their reactions to offenders. Community settings for correctional work are seen as organizational means to alleviate these problems and make the correctional organization more effective.

While there may be some theoretical strength to these assumptions, most correctional managers are rather inattentive to the sources of the organizational dysfunctions that they are attempting to remove. Hence, when community programs are established, many of them are administered, staffed, and operated exactly like institutions, but on a smaller scale. The new community programs have the same social climates as the prisons that they were to replace and they exhibit the same organizational problems.[16] There is no reason to expect noninstitutional correctional programs to be more effective (either for reducing crime or for simple matters of internal control) than institutional corrections, unless the organizational structures that implement these programs are indeed really different.

In probation and parole programs and in some other field options, a variety of other managerial concerns become important. Although it may be true in these least structured, or least intrusive, correctional alternatives, that management cannot directly affect the social climates that are of greatest salience to the offender, management of the organization is certainly going to influence the behavior of field agents. Sigurdson et al.,[17] Sullivan,[18] and others have made suggestions for altering the organizational arrangements of probation and parole service so that staff could have a greater impact on the social milieus that do influence offenders. For example, Sullivan offers reintegration and new careers models for field team work that would allow correctional officials to have greater impact on work, family, and educational settings.[19] Duffee, Meyer, and Warner found that offenders returning to the community from prison depended most heavily on family, friends, and other community contacts for the solution to their emotional and relational problems and that

[16] These observations have been widely reported by now. See Wright, "Correctional Effectiveness, A Case for an Organizational Approach," Rudolph Moos, *Evaluating Correctional and Community Settings* (New York: Wiley, 1975).

[17] Herbert R. Sigurdson, A. W. McEachern. and Robert M. Carter, "Administration Innovations in Probation Services," *Crime and Delinquency* (July 1973), pp. 353–366.

[18] Dennis C. Sullivan, *Team Models for Probation* (New York: National Council on Crime and Delinquency, 1971).

[19] Ibid.

correctional staff should pay more attention to correctional supervision impacts on these relationships if the rate of problem solving is to increase.[20]

Finally, in terms of the social climate *within* probation and parole organizations, a manager's policy setting and feedback roles may have great influence on the social milieu experienced by their subordinates. Research from other kinds of organizations would suggest that certain organizational environments can impede the productivity of workers, and vice versa, other environments can increase the workers' commitment to the organization and their productivity levels.[21]

In conclusion, it is important to understand the way in which organizational policy and patterns of supervision influence the quality of life in the organization. Some years ago Chester I. Barnard argued that the ability of the organization to integrate its individuals' goals with its productivity goals was the basic measure of organizational efficiency.[22] While there is no reason to suspect that efficient organizations are necessarily effective, it would seem true that highly efficient organizations can provide both management and staff with more time to examine the issues important to effectiveness. Or, if we use Simon's distinctions about types of goal constraints,[23] if the internal tests of organizational solutions are easier to meet because the organizational members interact effectively, then the organization has a greater chance to attempt to meet the external tests of organizational solutions.

[20] Duffee, Meyer, and Warner, *Offender Needs, Parole Outcome and Program Structure.*
[21] Rensis Likert, *New Patterns of Management* (New York: McGraw-Hill, 1961).
[22] Chester I. Barnard, *The Functions of the Executive* (Cambridge, Mass.: Harvard University Press, 1968).
[23] Herbert Simon "On the Concept of Organizational Goal," *Administrative Scienc Quarterly* (June, 1964), 1–22. See also the discussion in Chapter 4 of this text.

7

Organizational Structure and Decisions about Offenders

(David Duffee, Joseph P. Briggs, and J. Jackson Barnette)

Correctional managers not only must manage a system that has the purpose of controlling or changing offenders; they also must manage a system that makes decisions about offenders in terms of who the offenders are, what programs or routines they will be subject to, how much deprivation of freedom they will suffer, and so on. At first glance, this distinction may seem unnecessary. Of course, in order to treat, punish, or control, officials will decide how best to do that, and how offenders will be distributed over the available punitive options in order to accomplish these tasks. But it can be helpful in examining correctional management to distinguish between two semidiscrete functions: (1) the organizational routines that are established in order directly to control or act on the offender and (2) the organizational routines that are established in order to determine which offenders receive which kinds of action.

In traditional correctional terminology, the distinction is often made between the tasks of classification, assessment, or evaluation and the tasks of "treatment" or "program." This distinction is most commonly made in institutional corrections in which there are reception and classification centers separate from the main body of the prison (either as designated separate units on the same grounds or as completely separate facilities). Brief reflection, however, will demonstrate that the disposition/distribution function and the direct program/supervision function are found in all aspects of the correctional system. Sentencing, for example, is probably the major disposition unit for the system, for it is there that determinations are made between probation and incarceration and between the use of state or county facilities. The same functional split is also observed in probation and parole departments where the activities of presentence reports or preparole investigations are very distinct from the field officer's case supervision duties. The parole board itself is another major classification unit. Similarly, halfway house centers, work release centers, and other partial confinement options have both referral/acceptance functions as well as supervision functions.

Formal organizations whose primary function is to change people have sometimes been called "people-changing" organizations. Street, Vinter, and Perrow note that these organizations deal with people "not only by working with or through people, but also on them."[1] In contrast, another general organizational type might be termed "people-processing" organizations. Hasenfeld states that "people-processing organizations are defined as attempting to achieve changes in their clients not by altering basic personal attributes, but by conferring on them a public status and relocating them in a new set of social circumstances."[2] Hasenfeld notes that the general difference between the two types is that people-changing organizations strive for behavioral change through socialization and resocialization techniques that require the presence of the "client" in the organization for a relatively long period of time, while people-processing organizations strive to alter status through classification/disposition decisions in a relatively short period of time.[3] Thus, people-changing and people-processing organizations vary in type of product, the type of technology used, and by the relative duration of staff-client encounters.

Hasenfeld coined the term "people processing" in the examination of organizations that did only that, such as social referral agencies, courts, employment agencies, and so on. But he notes that people processing and people changing are often two separate functions

[1] David Street, Robert Vinter, and Charles Perrow, *Organization for Treatment* (New York: Free Press, 1966), p. 3.
[2] Yezekiel Hasenfeld, "People Processing Organizations: An Exchange Approach," *American Sociological Review* (June, 1972), 253.
[3] Ibid.

within the same organization or system. "As people-changing organizations increase in size and complexity, these processing functions are likely to be delegated to distinct subunits or organizations."[4]

While classification, or processing, and correctional programming may become increasingly distinct functions, and at times even distinct, separate organizations, they are definitely not *independent* functions. Purpose, accuracy, and speed of classification will always be major constraints, or determinants, of correctional program and structure, and vice versa, the various structural and program options available will always have a major impact on the kinds of processing decisions that precede or follow from them. For example, the decision to place a great many or only a few individuals in prison rather than on probation can have drastic effects on both probation supervision and on conditions in prison.[5] The belief that prisons are overcrowded or injurious to the offender can and has influenced processors such as judges and parole boards to keep more people from going to or remaining in prison. Classification functions and program functions should be coordinated, but they often are not. Classification centers that concentrate on the intrapsychic problems of offenders may produce distribution patterns of offenders that are not synchronized well with either security-conscious or reintegration-conscious program staffs.

The potential impact of the decision-making process in correctional people-processing is extremely great, and hence the study of how and why decision makers make the decisions they do is extremely important. It should be clear that in corrections we are dealing not only with behavior about offenders, but also with the judgments about that behavior. Indeed, no offender ends up in the correctional system for his or her "objectively" described behavior alone. Although the offender's behavior provides cues for the initiation of the decision-making process, the offender is convicted not on his or her behavior but on judgments about that behavior. All people-processing decisions, from sentencing through revocations and terminal releases, similarly entail not only the behavior of the offender but also the behavior of officials. Thus, if the correctional system is to be managed, it is not only offender behavior that must be predicted and controlled, but also the behavior of the decision makers.

Emphasizing the importance of this fact should take only a few examples. One of the clearest examples, and one that is getting much attention today, is the research by Gottefredson and others about

---

[4] Ibid., p. 256.
[5] See Paul Lerman, *Community Treatment and Social Control* (Chicago: University of Chicago Press, 1975).

parole-granting decisions.[6] This large study of parole board behavior examined the factors taken into consideration by parole board members and how various pieces of information influenced their decisions to release or hold in prison. The material was later developed by the SUNY-Albany group for use in sentencing, and it is now being implemented in several states. The main point is that major changes in criminal justice dispositions are being made not by altering the behavior of offenders, but by altering (in this case, by providing guidelines) the behavior of decision makers. Institutional classification seems equally open to variation caused by changes in or constraints placed on the decision makers rather than the offenders being processed. Shover cogently argues that prison counselors who remain in prison work beyond their probationary period are those who make decisions or classifications based on factors of self-protection rather than on factors of "treatment."[7] And perhaps the most startling study of the importance of the decision makers demonstrated that the California Community Treatment Project was not "more successful" than traditional institutional programs because offenders' behavior changed, but only because the parole agents and board engaged in revocation less frequently.[8]

These and other studies demonstrate that it is imperative for managers of correctional action to be cognizant not only of how organizational strategies influence the interaction patterns of staff and offenders but also of how organizational structure may change the type of decision making engaged in by staff. Although it is true that managers cannot predetermine all the factors that staff will take into consideration, and much less how they will value those different factors, nevertheless, managers can take major strides to assure that the type of decision-making structures they shape are consistent with their aims and that the types of information systems they put together in order to provide input to decisions do not change the nature of the decisions made.

GENERAL AND ORGANIZATIONAL MODELS OF THE JUDGMENT PROCESS

In England in the mid-sixteenth century, religious groups and political philosophers led a prison reform movement to end the

[6] D. M. Gottfredson, L. T. Wilkins, P. B. Hoffman, and S. M. Singer, *The Utilization of Experience in Parole Decision Making: A Progress Report, Summary* (Davis, Calif.: National Council on Crime and Delinquency Research Center, Parole Decision Making Project, June, 1973).
[7] Neal Shover, "Experts and Diagnosis in Correctional Agencies," *Crime and Delinquency* (Oct., 1974), 347–358.
[8] Lerman, *Community Treatment and Social Control.*

mistreatment and corruption in prisons. They recommended that "neophytes should be separated from hardened offenders, and that prisoners should be separated by sex, age, and type of offense."[9] These initial efforts at management by segregation are early evidence of the present-day classification/disposition process. Around the mid-nineteenth century, variables of race, mental or physical condition, and particularly the seriousness of the offense became the bases in determining whether incarceration should be in local jails (misdemeanors) or specialized state institutions (felons).[10] One problem with the classification criteria used was that the processing of offenders by organizational *maintenance* criteria alone led to "custodians having the right not only to issue and administer the orders and regulations which are to guide the life of the prisoner, but also the right to detain, try, and punish any individual accused of disobedience—a merging of legislative, executive, and judicial functions which has long been regarded as the earmark of complete domination."[11] However, even with the high-power position held by the custodians, complete control was impossible to achieve. Since the primary goal of most inmates is to "get out" of prison, and with the knowledge that their fastest exit is through the ability to become "reclassified," the people-processing function has been readily corruptible. Sykes notes that "the lack of a sense of duty among those who are held captive, the obvious fallacies of coercion, the pathetic collection of rewards and punishments to induce compliance, the strong pressures toward the corruption of the guard in the form of friendship, reciprocity, and the transfer of duties into the hands of trusted inmates—all are structural defects in the prison's system of power rather than individual inadequacies."[12]

The "treatment model" of correction emerged out of a discontent with classification/disposition variables that could not eliminate management tension and could not aid in the constructive development of character and fulfillment of individual needs. Stimulated by advances in the social sciences, the treatment model brought on a significant elaboration of the people-processing function. Corrections became concerned not only with educational and vocational skills and training, but also with measures of the inmate's personality, personal preferences, and intelligence. Under this system, offenders were generally processed from a specialized central diagnostic/classification center to an institution for treatment.

[9] National Advisory Commission on Criminal Justice Standards and Goals, *Corrections* (Washington, D.C.: Government Printing Office, 1973), p. 198.
[10] Ibid.
[11] Gresham Sykes, *The Society of Captives* (Princeton, N.J.: Princeton University Press, 1958), p. 41.
[12] Ibid., p. 61.

More recently, considerable disenchantment has been generated about the treatment model. The National Advisory Commission suggested that the multiplicity of problems begins with the neglect of basic social work principles of voluntarism and self-determination.[13] Street, Vinter, and Perrow emphasize that the treatment model was a "unilateral strategy" based largely on the belief that people-changing practices could be effective despite the inmate's deprivation of freedom and removal from the community. The built-in weakness of the prison as a social system, described clearly by Sykes, is apparent within the processing technology that operates under the treatment model. Biases toward maintenance and control are reinforced by a treatment staff which tend to shift their subjective opinion of inmates when it is administratively convenient.[14] Furthermore, the National Advisory Commission stated that the inmate "is likely to be judged less on his behavior than on his 'attitude,' his demeanor, his degree of 'contrition,' his 'desire to change,' or some other subjective factor."[15] The treatment model may have signified some movement toward a more individualistic approach to correctional processing than was true of nineteenth-century classification systems, but the degree of improvement is questionable.

More recently there have been moves away from the classification of people based on the psychological factors stressed by the treatment model and moves toward classifications that once more stress security and inmate management factors. The National Advisory Commission has recommended such a shift based on the assessment of our knowledge about treatment. The Commission argued that our technology for assessing why offenders behave as they do and how to correct undesirable behavior is so rudimentary that it is frequently inaccurate and is frequently used for ulterior purposes, such as internal control. Hence, the Commission argued that a simpler classification scheme based on security and management factors was more fair.[16] Obviously, this recommendation is consistent with recent moves toward determinant sentencing because determinancy will remove from the correctional release decision determinations about treatment stage and treatment needs.

Although it is clear that people-processing technology has changed over time, why and how it changes are not so clear. Perrow stresses a variable which he calls "the nature of the raw material" in the prediction of how decision makers will handle or process the people

[13] National Advisory Commission, *Corrections*, p. 199.
[14] Ibid.
[15] Ibid.
[16] Ibid., pp. 202–204.

under consideration. For example, he suggests that in some "custodial institutions" the *perceived* nature of the raw material (inmates) is uniform and stable.[17] He observes that in other correctional organizations (to which he refers as a cottage type) the perceived nature of the raw material is unstable and nonuniform.[18]

In a similar manner, Thompson has provided a typology of assessment situations in organizations. He stresses that (1) the decision makers believe they possess a "complete knowledge" about cause and effect relations relevant to assessment decisions and have "crystallized standards of desirability" about the persons being considered or (2) the decision makers feel that their cause and effect knowledge is "incomplete" and that they operate under "ambiguous standards of desirability."[19]

Perrow's variable "perceived nature of the raw material" is very similar to Thompson's variable "belief about cause and effect knowledge." Also, with Perrow's statement that "organizations uniformly seek to standardize their raw material in order to minimize exceptional cases,"[20] one sees that Perrow's "variability of material" is similar to Thompson's "standards of desirability."

Street et al. also recognize the importance of the perception of human material and the trade-offs of responsibility to the organization (bureaucratization) and to the individual (particularization). They state that

> On the one hand, persons and behaviors may be perceived as mostly non-uniform resulting in a proliferation of non-routinized, individualized modes of operation, with consequent difficulties in organizing operations. On the other hand, events may be defined principally in gross categories of inmate characteristics and behaviors, with resultant difficulties in predicting individual behavior.[21]

It seems that some authors (Thompson, Perrow, and Street et al.) imply that organizational variables such as size (large vs. small), amount of discretion, and degree of centralization may be important influences on the decision maker's perception of certainty (belief in cause and effect knowledge or belief in perceived nature of raw material) and desirability (perceived standards of desirability and variability of material).

Since a number of organizational experts have identified similar if

---

[17] Charles Perrow, "A Framework for the Comparative Analysis of Organizations," *American Sociological Review* (April, 1967), 194–204.
[18] Ibid.
[19] James Thompson, *Organizations in Action* (New York: Wiley, 1967), pp. 86–87.
[20] Perrow, "A Framework for the Comparative Analysis of Organizations," p. 197.
[21] Street, Vinter, and Perrow, *Organization for Treatment*, p. 5.

not identical variables that contribute to the kind of decision made, these variables should play a crucial role in our analysis. But, before looking at classification judgments in an organizational context, it may be helpful to examine a more general model of the people-distributing process. This model has been provided by Leslie Wilkins.[22] Wilkins begins by noting that *size* is not necessarily a significant independent determinant of organizational perception of certainty or desirability. Referring to studies on incarceration rates of large and small social systems, he notes that important interacting variables lie within the "informational feedback loop which changes the experience set with which members of the system operate and which influences the definition of deviance."[23] His general theory of deviance could serve to illustrate the relations between previously mentioned variables (size, centralization, etc.) and the perception of certainty and desirability by the classification/disposition decision makers.

He argues that in any society the frequency of actions will be distributed relatively normally. Toward the tails of this normal distribution will be relatively infrequent actions, some of which are perceived as exceptionally "good," or functional for society, and some of which are perceived as exceptionally "bad," or dysfunctional for society. He suggests that since people who behave in a dys-functional manner are judged "bad," they are frequently separated from the normal society and live in cultural "pockets" or subcultures where normal activity is perceived very differently from activity perceived in the parent distribution (see Figure 7.1). Wilkins provides a brief orientation to the model:

The modification of the information available within the truncated sections of the distributions will generate forces which will force the two distributions apart. The norms of the distributions cut off will no longer be the same as the norms of the distributions from which identification has been severed (i.e., the parent distributions). That is to say, instead of a centripetal force toward the general (parent) norm of the culture, the norms of the truncated parts of the distribution will reveal characteristics of a centrifugal force.[24]

From this he proposes the following feedback system:

Less tolerance leads to: more acts being defined as crimes, more action against criminals, more alienation of deviants, more crime by deviant groups, less tolerance of deviants by conforming groups . . . and round again.[25]

[22] Leslie Wilkins, *Social Deviance* (Englewood Cliffs, N.J.: Prentice-Hall, 1965).
[23] Ibid., p. 86.
[24] Ibid., p. 91.
[25] Ibid., p. 89.

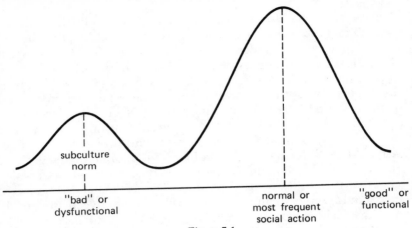

Figure 7.1

Through the evolution of decreasing information and tolerance, the normal curve develops subcultural normal curves. For purposes here, the subcultural curve to the left (which theoretically evolved from dysfunctional elements in society) can serve to illustrate correctional populations. The offender population, having been rejected by middle-class norms, in turn, rejects the standards of "respectable" society and generates its own subculture. This sub-culture develops its own normal curve with exceptional cases to this subculture at its own ends (see Figure 7.2).

Exceptional cases may be viewed differently by offenders and classification staff, because of their different references. The staff might generally view an inmate who has a record of high institutional achievement and perfect conformity to rules as exceptionally good,

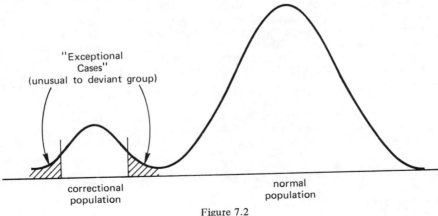

Figure 7.2

while offenders might view the same person as exceptionally bad (i.e., square john). The staff might see an absconder or escapee as exceptionally bad, but offenders may see him or her as exceptionally good. An offender who shows little or no aggressiveness in prison but whose record denotes a high degree of violent and aggressive behavior on the streets might be considered an "all-right" guy by inmates but still exceptionally bad by the decision makers.

Although it is important to draw the distinction between the different levels of perception, the inmate's perception is not of particular relevance here. The way inmates view other inmates and themselves in relation to their subculture is important to the classification/disposition function only to the extent that it may be observed or communicated to the classification staff.

It is hypothesized that most classification staff see certain types of exceptional cases falling under the categories of *security risks* and *personal attributes* (see Figure 7.3). A description of these various types, and the kind of information that is sought (focus of search) and the time it takes to discuss it (degree of search time), can be found in Table 7.1.

Now that the conceptual framework has been presented, there is a need to address three questions that have been raised. (1) How does the classification staff's perception of certainty/desirability characteristics of the offender relate to processing decisions? (2) In addition to the cultural/environmental variables, how do the variables of

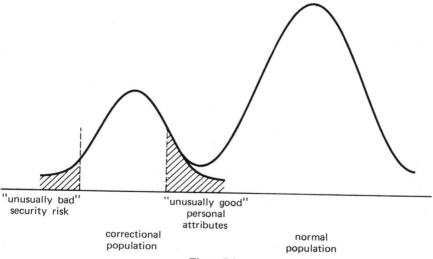

Figure 7.3

Table 7.1 Exceptional Cases

	Security Risks		
Types	Definition	Focus of Staff Decision	Degree of Decision Time*
Escapes	Attempted to escape Escaped Potential to escape	Escape potential Physical limitations of prison Security status; job vocational eligibility	High (resident is considered otherwise "all right" or "likable")
Manipulator Aggressor Victim of aggressor	Persuasive residents Organizers, leaders, aggressors, victims	Reports, requests, interviews recounting such behavior	Medium to high (Factors: persuasion by counselors and psychologists; staff respect of, not necessarily confidence in "professional" opinion)
	Personal Attributes		
I.Q. Education Vocation	High I.Q., high in education and vocational skills	Potential for legitimate success	High (lecture by caseworkers)
Community environment Family relations	Ability to "make it" Effective communications with parents and siblings	Presentence investigation report, letter writing, visiting record	Medium
Institutional achievement Friendly disposition	Constructive involvements Good personality	Relations in prison with different groups, positive aspects of attitudes and reasons for it.	Medium

*Is dependent on the type of institution.

organizational structure interact with each other and relate to the staff's perception of certainty/desirability characteristics of the inmate? (3) How does all of this relate to the Wilkins model and to the two types of exceptional cases that have been described?

(1) Standards of desirability and variability are likely to be influenced by the *decision-processing mechanism* that is used, most notably, who is included in the decision-making process and what skills they bring to the classification task. The interest in the nature of the offender reached its zenith with psychometric testing and the use of psychologists and psychiatrists to make classification decisions. These experts were typically located in high-prestige positions in centralized reception and classification units. They rarely saw offenders out of the classification unit and rarely dealt with front-line staff. Moreover, these experts were not likely to seek inputs to decisions from either front-line custodial workers or from offenders. They believed that offenders were "sick" and could not themselves contribute significantly to the classification decision. Moreover, the correctional officer was merely to guard the offender, not to participate in treatment, and was not seen as having the expertise to determine dispositions.

Offenders were seen as complex individuals, true, but the removal of the decision from the front-line and the dependence on measurement of personality attributes rendered the "material" as rather stable and uniform, in the sense that offenders were labeled or categorized into relatively discrete treatment categories. Offenders were treated as if there were relatively complete knowledge about them and as if the nature of their problems were relatively stable and uniform.

As was indicated previously, correctional practitioners are now less than enthused about the validity of these classification methods. The departure from psychometric testing and diagnosis of pyschological problems demonstrates a shift in correctional beliefs toward the feeling that offenders are not uniform and that standards of desirable behavior are not crystallized and certain. In terms of organizational implications, the shift indicates accommodation to the fact that correctional experts can never fully control, predict, and change the behavior of offenders.

As these beliefs have changed and as doubts have increased about the certainty and uniformity of "material," we have begun to see other personnel engaged in the classification process. Classification decisions now frequently include front-line staff, and in some places offenders. Discretion in the classification decision is no longer reserved for a small group of clinical experts near the top of the organizational hierarchy. By delegating greater discretionary power to lower-level staff, the organization is implicitly stating that the upper-management levels cannot easily control inmates or do not even know how to handle them. In admitting that offender behavior tends toward nonuniformity, correctional people-processing functions can become less bureaucratized and more particularized because fewer decisions require centralized decision making or decisions by a small and high-paid professional staff.

The decentralization of decision making provides for more democracy in the allocation of offenders to various programs and options because not one but many angles of evaluation are considered important and because a variety of different staff roles are included in decision making.

From the offender's point of view, this shift in the locus of classification decisions can have positive or negative effects. It may be bad from the offender's point of view because the offender's behavior is more visible to lower echelon staff, and therefore the offender's chances of going wrong may be increased. On the other hand, lower-level staff may also give more credit for kinds of offender behavior that would rarely be reported to a central classification committee, and this new positive information may balance out what might otherwise be a poor record.

In general, the decentralization of classification would decrease the reliance on measured indices of behavior and would increase the reliance on directly observed behavior. This shift in the "focus of search" for classification information should lead toward a middle ground on the notion of uniformity of material and toward more tolerance in standards of desirability. As this trend continues toward uncertainty in beliefs about cause and effect and toward ambiguity in what is desirable, correctional classifications are less likely to emphasize a single set of community standards by which to judge offenders or toward which to direct them. Consequently, staff are less likely to treat offenders as exceptionally bad, and staff are less likely to treat offenders as belonging to a separate "subculture."

(2) The size of the organization and the kind of information flowing through it are also likely to influence classification decisions. Large organizations are more likely to have well-developed and entrenched maintenance subsystems than are smaller organizations. As the maintenance dynamic toward stability and predictability increases, the organization seeks to formalize or institutionalize all aspects of organizational behavior, that is, to find a "standardized operating procedure which has been legitimated for all relevant

human behavior in the system."[26] Organizations with these characteristics tend to rely heavily on external, mechanistic controls of both staff and offender behavior. They typically do so by highlighting "negative variance" in organizational routine, such as very disruptive behavior by offenders, or classification decisions with negative consequences by staff. Mistakes are punished, but positive behavior is not always rewarded. Such control systems tend to produce threat and generate conditions for dishonesty in both staff and offenders. Offenders will attempt to fool the classifiers, and the staff will attempt to make safe rather than accurate decisions. Organizational management will attribute decision errors to staff rather than to problems in the system of knowledge, and staff will attribute deviance to individual offenders rather than to the structure of the situation.[27]

Hence, large organizations having rather rigid and highly vertical information systems that rely on external, rule-bound control systems will usually be rife with inaccurate information and self-defensive action. Moreover, such systems have tremendous difficulty in generating a sense of equity for the decisions made and the sanctions that are allocated. "Equity is determined not by those who administer extrinsic rewards but by those who receive them. The perception of equity on the part of (organizational members) is the crucial factor."[28] When carried to the extreme in correctional classification, the consequences of these conditions, have led in one system to broad judicial intervention in the entire classification process. The correctional managers who attempted to control offenders and staff through a rigid and autocratic classification process have in turn lost considerable power to the courts where equity in the allocation of offenders to various programs is determined by legal principles instead of administrative convenience.[29]

In contrast, the internal information flow is likely (but not always) to be better and to be less reliant on external sanctions and rules in decentralized organizations and in relatively small organizations. In such systems there is likely to be somewhat more congruence between the perception of offenders and staff.[30] The better the information flow, and the smaller the size of the organization, the more an organization-processing staff are likely to be able to cope with less

[26] Daniel Katz and Robert Kahn, *The Social Psychology of Organizations* (New York: Wiley, 1966), pp. 88–89.
[27] Douglas McGregor, *The Professional Manager*, ed. by Caroline McGregor and Warren G. Bennis (New York: McGraw-Hill, 1967), pp. 123–124.
[28] Ibid., pp. 142–143.
[29] *Morris* v. *Travisano*, 310 F. Supp. 857 (D.R.I., 1970).
[30] David Duffee, *Correctional Policy and Prison Organization* (Beverly Hills, Calif.: Sage Halsted, 1975), pp. 157–180.

certainty in their perception of the material being processed. The staff are not as likely to behave defensively, and decisions are more likely to be group processes rather than individual decisions. Hence, there is less likelihood of "finger pointing" if something goes wrong, and the group, as opposed to the individual, is more likely to remain committed to its decision once it is made rather than back down in order to conform to rules.

(3) Finally, the relative degree of centralization, the type of information flow, and the size of the organization are likely to influence the staffs' tolerance for a wider range of behavior and hence their judgments about whether the offender is seen as inside or outside the "normal population" of society. In Wilkins' illustration (Figure 7.1) the normal population develops a subculture population (at the left in Figure 7.1) as judgments about unusual behavior are utilized as a means of segregating some people from the community. This subcultural population will have its own set of exceptional cases (see Figure 7.3).

This situation will place many offenders (whose behavior is seen to fall between the norms of the subculture and the norms of the parent population) in a difficult position. These offenders will find themselves caught between the norms or rules of the offender group and the norms of larger society. These persons are in a situation analogous to the highly productive factory worker who is accepted neither by management nor by his or her own group because he or she is a "rate buster." Much like the foreman supervising the rate buster may treat the rate buster in ambivalent fashion, classification staff will treat these offenders in ambivalent fashion. The factory worker may be recognized as a highly productive person, but the foreman who has to judge the worker's performance must also recognize that the worker's behavior may be disruptive because it is looked upon negatively by other factory workers. Similarly, the classification staff, when dealing with such an offender, may be forced to judge the offender by standards applicable to other offenders who conform more rigidly to the subculture than they are to judge the offender by standards applicable to the general society. Hence, we can hypothesize that in some correctional organizations offenders who possess personal or social attributes that would seem to make them capable of "making it" in the community are considered deviant by the organization and may have a more difficult rather than less difficult time obtaining the positive social sanctions (including release) that the organization has to offer.

From our above discussion on points one and two, it seems to follow that the smaller the organization, the more decentralized, and the better the information flow, the more the staff will be able to cope appropriately with the ambiguity and uncertainty of the "offender in the middle" for several reasons. First, there will be less defensiveness on their part. Second, there will be a smaller or less dominant subculture. Third, the community norms will be applied less ritualistically.

In conclusion, as organizations move progressively toward decentralization, the more irrelevant highly standardized classification information will seem and the less it will be used. As organizations move away from decentralization, the less ambiguous and the more manipulative (and manipulated) will the classification information become, and the less valid will decision making be with both community standards and the inmates' value system. These relationships are summarized in Table 7.2.

Table 7.2 Organization of Classification

Organizational Characteristics		
Structure	Decentralized	Centralized
Size	Small	Large
Information flow	Adequate	Inadequate
Perceptions of Classification Staff		
Understanding of causal knowledge	Incomplete Not well understood	Complete Well understood
Standards of desirability	More ambiguous Nonuniform and varying	More crystallized Uniform and stable
Staff/inmate perception	More congruent	Less congruent
Percentage of exceptional cases	Low	High
Policy most likely to be implemented	Reintegration	Restraint, rehabilitation, reform
Inmates' characteristics as perceived by:		Security Risks	Personal Attributes
The community	Questionable to good	Bad	Good
The staff	Suspicious, but acceptable	Bad	Bad
Staff decision as perceived by inmate	Good	Bad	Bad

PROBLEMS IN GETTING INFORMATION
TO DECISION MAKERS

The major point that we have made so far is that judgments about offenders can be altered rather dramatically by changing the belief structure of staff and by changing the organizational structure of the decision-making process. Throughout this discussion it has been necessary to speak not only of the action of making judgments but also of the action of systematically gathering information. However, the problems of creating an information system is worthy of in-depth coverage itself.

The techniques of information gathering, processing, and analysis have dramatically increased in sophistication in the last 20 years. Within the last decade many aspects of information system hardware, software, and utilization have been applied within the field of criminal justice. Benefits have been attained by administrators, researchers and planners, front-line personnel, offenders, and the public at large. At the same time, there have been many difficulties, and the new information systems have created their own by-product dysfunctions, such as the ethical/legal question of the right to privacy. Some of these problems have been recognized and steps are being taken both to anticipate and to solve them. However, some relatively less visible problems in the operation of offender process-ing (that have plagued correctional administration for years) are now looming with new intensity.

In correctional systems, information about the offender is used for a number of purposes: policy making, program implementation and evaluation, allocation of resources, security and treatment decisions, and so forth. Although this information is frequently processed and analyzed in automated fashion, the information is still generated by people, i.e., offenders, correctional officials, and agents in related organizations. These persons, through the quality of interaction with each other, can and do have a significant impact on the quality and quantity of information generated. New information guidelines and automated technology have probably reduced considerably both the unreliability and the systematic bias present in the information about offenders and program operation. Nevertheless, a growing body of research on classification and information points to some sources of information error and bias that reduce the effectiveness of the correctional information system, even if the system has been automated.

This section outlines several people-related variables that mediate between any data source about correctional offenders and the entry of data in an automated or manual information system. It is demonstrated that ideology of the personnel responsible for gathering the information and the style in which these personnel are supervised may impact significantly on the willingness and/or ability of correctional personnel to conform their data gathering to the requirements of an information system. Finally, suggestions are made for increasing the accuracy of the information by modifying the interaction of correctional personnel. But there will be no easy solutions: Correctional managers will have difficult decisions to make.

Problems with Delivery of Information

Information is defined in relation to its uses. That an inmate has curly hair or a widow's peak is probably irrelevant to a parole board, but it may be highly significant to the prison barber. To the former, the data is not information because it is irrelevant to the purpose; to the latter, the data is information because it sets constraints for the task at hand. Since information is tied to purpose, one problem with correctional information systems is likely to be related to the age-old problem of correctional goals.

The current literature on correctional goals is labyrinthine, but there seems to be a general consensus that goals are vague or ambiguous, multiple, and frequently contradictory. While it may be true that the acts of structuring an information system and initiating requests for data that conform to system requirements lead to some greater goal clarity in most organizations, there is some reason to suspect that the introduction of rigorous information systems in corrections may not serve this function. There are several reasons for this inconsistency.

Correctional goals, unlike goals in many profit motivated and even other service ventures, tend to hinge on basic moralistic assumptions such as, "It is good to punish wrongdoers." The "information" supporting this assumption is not tied to an empirical base, and any information gathered about the operation of the agency has an arbitrary connection to the basic motivation of the system in the first place. Because questions of morality are unresolvable within an empirical sphere, they tend to be handled in a bureaucratic setting not by resolution but by delegation. The several possible moral imperatives for guiding correctional practice are merely established as partners in an uneasy separation of staff into different groups responsible to different moral rationales. In other words, goal ambiguity may be functional in a correctional system because it allows the coexistence of unresolvable differences, all of which must be accommodated.[31] But this accommodation is likely to mean that data are relevant to different, coexisting purposes. Hence, the same data are treated as information by some staff but as noise by other staff or, even worse, as different information altogether.[32]

A second reason for pessimism is that traditional correctional goals have seldom implied much need for information and indeed have tended to inhibit its flow and use.[33] Correctional workers and administrators have generally been trained in disciplines whose understanding of data is antithetic to its systematic and uniform collection and analysis.[34] Correctional staff who have line authority are likely neither to be competent to design information systems nor to be concerned critically with the outputs of such systems. While the growing complexity of correctional organization has led to pressing demands for information collection and analysis, it is very likely that information experts and information systems will be imported from other disciplines. The need for this borrowing of personnel is not a criticism of the information systems that they develop, but it partially explains a feeling that many correctional systems designers and analysts must have: that the informational "order" imposed through their initiative rests like an ill-fitting template on the organizational behavior that exists below. In short, the information experts may continue to be outsiders whose objectives of validity and reliability are blocked by an inadequate bridge between themselves and the front line rather than by problems internal to the information system itself.[35]

The third problem for information system development generated by correctional goal ambiguity is suggested by studies of goal preference distributions within the hierarchy of correctional organizations. As we have seen in Chapter 4, there are several correctional goals that direct different divisions of the correctional organization, and there are also significant differences in the priority given to any one goal at

[31] Gresham Sykes, *Society of Captives* (Princeton, N.J.: Princeton University Press, 1971), pp. 10–12; Donald Cressey, "Contradictory Directives in Complex Organizations: The Case of the Prison," *Administrative Science Quarterly* (March, 1959), 1–19.

[32] Leslie Wilkins, *Evaluation of Penal Measures* (New York: Random House, 1969).

[33] Elmer K. Nelson and Catherine Lovell, *Developing Correctional Administrators*, final research report, Joint Commission on Correctional Manpower and Training (Washington, D.C.: Government Printing Office, Nov., 1969).

[34] Ibid., Chapter Three.

[35] Leslie Wilkins, *Social Deviance* (Englewood Cliffs, N.J.: Prentice-Hall, 1965), Chapter One.

different levels of the organization. In other words, not only may custodial, treatment, and maintenance divisions have different purposes and require different information, but also top, middle management, front-line staff, and even offenders frequently must cope with different organizational constraints.[36] For example, the dimensions of correctional supervision that apparently explain a parole agent's relationship to his or her superiors may be invalid as explanation of behavior between the officer and the parolee.[37] Consequently, information requirements specified at a central office level for programmatic and managerial purposes are not likely to capture or constrain, to a significant degree, the interactions of front-line staff and offenders.

Sanctions Retarding Upward Information Flow

While information system experts have made remarkable headway recently in specifying the data requirements and system linkages necessary to track the flow of offenders through a correctional system, the study of decision maker preferences and of constraints on decision makers is still in its infancy. There are, however, several relevant studies concerning the characteristics of organizations that produce accurate information.

Wilensky, for example, suggests that organizations that rely on covert operations are unlikely to receive or process valid information. His study of intelligence operations in foreign affairs indicates that covert data are generally dangerously biased by the fact that secrecy between informer and receiver does not provide the information user with sufficient means to check on validity.[38] Beer adds that highly bureaucratic organizational structures can be equally dysfunctional for information flow because the accuracy of information is often judged by the position of the information giver in the hierarchy rather than by the information giver's competence. Common divisional conflicts in bureaucracies make it difficult to get complete information flowing upward. Subdivisions are likely to hoard information and other resources for their own direct benefit or merely to make it more difficult for another division to complete its work.[39] Wilkins

---

[36] Nelson and Lovell, *Developing Correctional Administrators*, Chapter Six; Street, Vinter, and Perrow, *Organization for Treatment*; Vincent O'Leary and David Duffee, "Correctional Policy: A Classification of Goals Designed for Change," *Crime and Delinquency* (Oct., 1971), 373–386.

[37] John Irwin, *The Felon* (Englewood Cliffs, N.J.: Prentice-Hall, 1970), pp. 149–173.

[38] Harold Wilensky, *Organizational Intelligence* (New York: Basic Books, 1965).

[39] Stafford Beer, *Decision and Control* (New York: Wiley, 1966) and Edward E. Lawler III and John Grant Rhode, *Information and Control in Organizations* (Santa Monica: Goodyear, 1976), p. 99.

distinguishes between objectives that require consensus and objectives that do not, and he suggests that a collegial or peer arrangement is more satisfactory than a hierarchical one when consensus is necessary.[40]

Consensus would apparently be recommended for many correctional decisions in which diverse information sources need to be drawn upon and several actors will be involved in completing the processing of one offender. There are aspects of correctional organization, however, that militate against both the achievement of a true consensus and a means of recording the consensual outcome. Donald Cressey argues that an open sharing of information about correctional operations on particular offenders is nearly impossible to achieve. Correctional structures, he argues, are coercive, not only in their handling of offenders but also in their handling of staff. Staff and offenders are each governed by particularistic, prescriptive rules and regulations. Adherence to rules is demanded as a duty to the organization, and nonconformity to directives is interpreted as disobedience. The sanctions for disobedience are punitive, and most staff and offenders attempt to avoid such sanctions even if they are not committed to the rules or do not understand the objectives that obedience to rules supposedly achieves. Cressey points out that in such circumstances an official or offender who is requested to supply such information always evaluates the content of what should be said on the probability of being punished for saying it.[41] This climate is not conducive to accurate information because information sharing is seen as a risk instead of an opportunity for learning. Valid information concerning the rationale and outcomes of various correctional processes would require an educative instead of a punitive climate. This is a prerequisite that administrators are not able to achieve within the present social environment of correction, which presses for the control of disobedience.

In addition to the problem that the coercive organizational climate is not conducive to the sharing of information, other organizational characteristics impede information flow and analysis. Correctional field agencies such as probation and parole are geographically dispersed and decentralized in authority structure to the extent that a central office staff, including research and information system units, are relatively dependent on the good will and cooperation of these individuals in order to obtain information. Front-line staff can usually answer information requests by saying that the additional desk time interferes with the "therapeutic process." Correctional

---

[40] Wilkins, *Social Deviance*, Chapter Two.
[41] Cressey, "Contradictory Directives in Complex Organizations."

institution staff are hampered by conflicting divisional goals, shift work, and shortages of manpower to the extent that it is frequently impossible to hold a "staffing" in order to bring all information sources together. In Pennsylvania, for example, the attempt to include correctional officers in prerelease classification decisions and in the disposition of minor misconducts has been hamstrung by the inability to relieve officers from their posts in order to have them attend decision meetings.

Rewards for Poor Information

Researchers frequently have lamented the poor quality of the case files in corrections. Many have suggested that research based on case files is invalid because the files themselves appear to be irrelevant to correctional operations. Since it is hard to conceive of an information system that would bear any closer resemblance to correctional operations than case files achieve, an examination of the reasons for vague and incomplete files is relevant to the design and operation of information systems.

In addition to the organizational research briefly described above, some answers to the problems of getting valid data into an information system are provided by a structural-functional analysis of case processing in the criminal justice and mental health fields.

Sudnow's analysis of the use of case files in a public defender's office suggests that officials do not consult files for specifics about cases and they do not expect to find specific information recorded. Instead, they research only to determine if the case is a "normal one," that is, one fit for normal processing, or whether or not oddities of the offender's status, resources, or crime suggest special processing.[42] In the situation of a "normal crime," the prosecutor and the defender rarely resort further to either the file or the legal code because decisions on cases appropriate for plea bargaining are constrained by the informal, normative standards of negotiation rather than by the specifics of the case. In this situation, an accurate information system, that is, a data processing system that would render in black and white the particular circumstances of the case, might actually be disruptive to the normal processing routine.

Arlene Daniels found a rather similar pattern in the use of files in military psychiatric diagnoses.[43] Her analysis concludes that officials responsible for entering diagnoses in records consider not

[42] David Sudnow, "Normal Crimes: Sociological Features of the Penal Code in a Public Defender Office," *Social Problems* (Winter, 1965), 255-276.

[43] Arlene Kaplan Daniels, "The Social Construction of Military Psychiatric Diagnoses," *Recent Sociology*, No. 2 (New York: Macmillan, 1970), pp. 192-205.

only the present symptoms of a patient but also the possible consequences such information may have in the future career of the patient. Since it is frequently difficult for the diagnostician to predict how future contingencies will influence the interpretation of any recorded information, military psychiatrists were likely to record only vague, jargon-coded labels that would have to be returned to them for interpretation vis-à-vis new circumstances as they unfolded. Contingencies to which the diagnosticians were particularly sensitive included the requirements for receiving medical disability benefits, i.e., determining whether the individual or the Army should bear the cost of incompetent or inappropriate behavior. This situation clearly parallels some correctional situations in which the persons responsible for entering information about an offender in a file are responsive to potential feedback from other agencies or other bureaucratic subdivisions, especially over politically sensitive matters such as parole release and revocations.[44]

Neal Shover, speaking specifically about the correctional classification process, goes a bit further than Daniels by suggesting that in addition to organizational constraints on the *language* entered in the file, correctional organization delimits the *kinds of personnel* who become responsible for diagnostic work, file creation, and file maintenance.[45] The socialization of the correctional counselor, reports Shover, includes the lesson that "The worker has a stake in finding something wrong with *everyone* . . . [and in not] finding anything seriously wrong with anyone."[46] The counselor also learns that reports on individual offenders are rarely taken seriously, "except as *ex post facto* rationalization for decisions presumably made on the basis of other criteria."[47] Shover suggests that counselors rapidly grow cynical about the entire process and either quit or remain on the job for security reasons. Those who do remain beyond the initial learning process become more adept at "beating the system" by finding ways to present information that probably cannot rebound to their own discredit or demerit. They favor an information system that will ease the flow of the correctional process rather than one that will retain relevance to the task of behavior change.

Garfinkel and Bittner's study of records in a psychiatric clinic supports the above findings, but it goes further by suggesting the existence of a fundamental conflict between the functions of the

[44] Ibid., p. 204.
[45] Neal Shover, "Experts and Diagnosis in Correctional Agencies."
[46] Ibid., p. 354.
[47] Ibid., p. 355.

self-reporting forms used as a data base for the information system and the characteristics of the people-changing task.[48] Garfinkel and Bittner argue that clinical records are frequently criticized for being inaccurate, duplicative, or incomplete in their relation to their "actuarial function," or their validity for predicting behavior in the future. They suggest, however, that the deficiencies of the information for research and management decisions about the future of offenders are related to the fact that the same information serves another organizational function. As well as being used to build classification decisions, the record also serves as a "contractual" record of transactions that have already taken place between staff and patients. In this latter sense, every record is *always* complete and accurate because it is constructed in such a way that the entries (and the absence of entries) can change in meaning over time as a method of explaining and justifying the current state of negotiations between the staff and the patient. Garfinkel and Bittner conclude that it is this second use of the information that is of *primary* importance to front-line staff and that the demands for actuarial precision needed in proper processing will be resisted because such demands constrain the fluidity of meaning that data entries must retain within the people-changing subsystem of the organization.

TESTING THE HYPOTHESIS OF PROCESSING- CHANGING CONFLICT

In the course of evaluating the classification process and information system in one department of correction, the authors conducted several data collection and data manipulation efforts, the objectives of which were the formulation of recommendations leading to a more efficient offender processing system and an information system that would be more helpful in making decisions about offenders. One aspect of this evaluation was a formal testing of the Garfinkel–Bittner hypothesis that the information recorded about offenders served two purposes: that the recording of information performed one function for front-line staff and another function for the officials concerned with the management of the department and with the accuracy of the classifications. From the point of view of both managers and researchers, recorded information about offenders should both explain or predict the decisions made about offenders as well as enable an evaluation of the appropriateness of the matches made

---

[48] Harold Garfinkel and Egon Bittner, " 'Good' Organizational Reasons for 'Bad' Clinic Records," in Harold Garfinkel (ed.), *Studies in Ethnomethodology* (New York: Basic Books, 1967), pp. 186–207.

between types of offenders and types of programs. From the point of view of the counselors and other front-line staff who initiated program decisions and delivered different services to correctional clients, the recorded information seemed to perform different functions that ranged from protection of the Bureau if an offender created havoc after release, to "licensing" the offender as appropriate for a change in status, to a bother or protective barrier that kept staff busy in paper work and removed from direct contact with offenders.

The format for entering information in the case files and the policy on what information to gather were controlled by the central office, but the recording of information was delegated to the front-line staff. It was our hypothesis that, taking any significant correctional decision, the recorded data would *not* predict the decision made or, in other words, the data would not discriminate between those who were chosen for a particular correctional option and those who were denied that option. The decision we chose to examine was the decision to refer and accept an offender into the halfway houses operated by the department. In 1974 data were collected from three institutions concerning the decision to refer an offender to the centers and data were collected statewide on the decision to accept an offender into the halfway house program. Approximately 30 items of information concerning the offender's demographic characteristics and the extent and nature of participation in institutional programs, as well as the kinds of evaluations received by different staff groups, were used as predictor variables. Both univariate and multiple regression analyses were conducted in an attempt to predict referral and acceptance. Our expectation was that if the recorded data were in fact contractual or justificatory in nature rather than classificatory, the data would be relatively impotent as predictors of the placement decision. The analysis was very supportive of this hypothesis, with only five variables yielding significant chi-square values and only one, the outcome of a home furlough, remaining significant in the multiple regression analysis. The status of the home furlough outcome as a significant predictor is interesting because furlough, like the halfway houses, is part of the prerelease program and is itself a decision proximate in time to placement in a center.

While such a finding is rather exasperating to a researcher and cannot provide managers with an evaluative data base, it does not, in our opinion, suggest that front-line officials are indiscriminate in these placement decisions. On the contrary, it suggests that the fixed items of information requested of the front-line staff for entry in the record are either not utilized in the decision or are utilized in a different way. Our later observations of staffing meetings in several institutions confirmed this suggestion. Consistent with Daniels, Shover, and Garfinkel, recorded data as utilized in staff meetings are neither ignored nor explanatory of the decisions made. The recorded data elements simply served as "punctuation points" or coded signals in treatment decision negotiations, the content of which was not recorded but retained by front-line staff.

ORGANIZATIONAL STRUCTURE
AND ATTITUDES TOWARD CLASSIFICATION

As a subsequent step in the above research, we administered a lengthy questionnaire to all staff (from the commissioner down to all counselors and classification unit custodial officers) involved in the departmental classification system. The survey had several components. Relevant to this discussion are the results from *Correctional Policy Inventory* (described in Chapter 4) and results from the Organizational Profile Questionnaire described in Chapter 6.

The distribution of policy preferences was particularly relevant because of the relationship between information and purposes. Variations in goal perception, especially between management and staff responsible for recording information, could help to explain the conflict between the people-changers who provide information and the managers concerned with processing. The measurement of the managerial climate, or organizational profile, was relevant to the concern of Cressey and others. Where correctional organizations are prescriptively managed, lower staff are alienated from upper echelons and therefore, information is recorded in a fashion that will allow for defense from negative sanctions in its transmission.

The data from the correctional policy survey demonstrated that management concern with the correctional policy of reintegration was significantly higher than front-line concern on this objective. On the objectives of restraining, reforming, and rehabilitating, management and front-line staff were about equal. Since it is only in the process of reintegrating the offender to a community that concern for offender performance after release becomes paramount, only in relation to the reintegration objective is that information concerning change of offender's behavior after release seen as important. Given the managerial concern with reintegration, the demand for actuarial precision in information about offenders is understandable. But given front-line staff's relatively stronger concern with provision of services and maintenance of surveillance within the institution, one should expect less attention to, or outright resistance to, information requests that are theoretically relevant to predicting future behavior or evaluating program effects on performance of offenders when released. Those staff concerned with reform, and therefore with surveillance, are likely to respond to recorded information as Sudnow's public defenders and prosecutors did: The record serves to indicate the ordinary disciplinary case from the not so ordinary, and subsequent data entries will record and justify the sanctions administered, but the record will not capture *why* an offender was handled as he or she was. Those staff concerned with rehabilitation are those most likely to confront the recording of information as did the clinicians in the studies by Daniels and Garfinkel. Information describing the offender will be kept purposefully vague so that the clinicians can retain some control over how future events should change the meaning of what is recorded. To the extent that restraint is of importance, records should serve as a means of defending the organization from outside complaints about the state of operations. The information that best does this will, as Shover suggests, ascribe sufficient problems to every inmate that inmate idiosyncracies can be blamed for future disruptions but will not suggest critical problems that would have required specialized or individualized care for many offenders.

The scores on the organizational profile questionnaire tended to support Cressey's contention that the climate at the lower end of the correctional hierarchy militates against the educative uses of information. Significantly more so than managers, the front-line staff perceived the organization as autocratic, relatively unresponsive to information generated at the front line, and relatively more likely to engage in punitive behavior for information about undesired events. This perception by front-line staff may be in part a valid observation that managerial practice is inconsistent with the managerial goal of reintegration, but it is also fostered by the front-line concern for correctional goals that are not systematic in scope and are more concerned with matters of internal organizational routine than with behavior of offenders in the community.

IMPLICATIONS FOR CORRECTIONAL MANAGEMENT

The analysis of correctional people-processing and people-changing functions have several important implications for correctional management. Managers should be aware that the way in which they organize personnel for the task of making judgments about offenders will influence the type of judgments made. The decision structures used for reform or restraint policies, for example, are not appropriate for rehabilitation decisions, and the structures that developed for the rehabilitation policy are not relevant to the implementation of reintegration programs. Managers should also be aware of potential conflict between the means that they use for controlling staff behavior and the quality and accuracy of information that are generated in their organizations. Finally, there is a potential conflict between the people-processing and people-changing functions, at least under some correctional policies. The uses that people-changers make of information are not necessarily the same as the uses of information made by people processors. Consequently, if managers expect the *same* staff to do both functions, at least in large organizations, the information system is likely to be inaccurate for one purpose or the other. Hence, in large and complex systems it may be functional to separate these functions. If, however, the classification and changing functions are separated, then problems of coordinating the separate units should be expected to increase.

PART THREE

MANAGING INNOVATION IN CORRECTIONS

INTRODUCTION

Managerial responsibility for change has been mentioned continuously throughout Parts one and two of this book for the simple
reason that the managerial control function *includes* the role of
changing the organization. Managers are continually working for
change in organizational structure. Sometimes they attempt to re-
direct divergent organizational behavior toward already set and
established organizational policies and standards; at other times they
attempt to change entire sets of policy and the organizational structures that go with them. Since the ability to produce and direct
change is a fundamental managerial responsibility, it has been only
recently taken up as a separate topic; all managers are engaged in the
activity of a change everyday.

Nevertheless, the activities of management that facilitate *lasting* and effective change in organizations have become an increasingly important topic in managerial literature lately. There are several reasons for this. Probably most important is that managers have been too concerned with the implementation of minor, or day-to-day, changes in organizational behavior in order to effect policy, and they have been underconcerned with major changes in policy and entire organizational designs. As a consequence, changes in the environment of organizations have not been met with equal change in the goals and functions of the organizations. Related to the first problem is the fact that organizational environments are changing much more rapidly than used to be the case. Consequently, managers must develop new skills in understanding and predicting the vagaries of their environment and applying this understanding to internal operations. Third, our American culture has changed significantly, and with it the perception of legitimate change and control tactics, whether they be applied by insurance executives to their accounting department or by the city police in a ghetto. Because there have been marked shifts in beliefs and ethics about how managers can undertake change, their battery of techniques for changing and controlling the organization needs an overhaul.

Discussions of planned change in organizations are lengthy and involved and worthy of book-length treatment on their own. This part of this book does not attempt to cover all of the relevant change techniques or the complete explorations of the ethics and philosophies of planned change. Instead, the following three chapters attempt to focus on three recurrent problems that will face correctional managers as they attempt to undertake change in their organizations. Chapter 8 deals with the prelude to change itself—the difficulties involved in creating an adequate information base to analyze the problems of the organization accurately. This problem may be compounded by the difficulties that we discussed in the last chapter on implementing information systems in correctional organizations. When information is purportedly going to be used to change how things are done, the resistance to giving and using the information may increase. As Chapter 8 will make evident, it is extremely important to look at every aspect of a problem situation before undertaking change programs, not just the perceptions of one or two groups.

The focus of Chapter 9 is rather narrow, but it is one that has broad applicability across a variety of correctional organizations. The problem addressed is how to actually implement a change project that will bring front-line staff and higher correctional management closer together in their perception of correctional goals.

Finally, Chapter 10 examines the relatively gargantuan problems that arise when a correctional system undertakes a process of fundamental change. Can correctional policy and operations actually be radically altered? What are the roadblocks to fundamental change in our bureaucratic social control organizations? To what extent should a movement such as deinstitutionalization be interpreted as a major change in correctional operations and goals?

8

Developing Relevant Data for a Correctional Organizational Development Program

(Vincent O'Leary, David Duffee, and Ernst Wenk)

Correctional institutions in the last several years have been under sharp attack from several quarters. While the sources of criticism have been disparate, the conclusions have been similar: Prisons fail to rehabilitate, they are inhumane, and they should be used as little as possible as correctional measures.[1] The force of these arguments is that community-based alternatives should largely supplant prisons. Both the ideological assumptions and the data supporting deinstitutionalization pose a dilemma familiar to the reformer: To what degree should efforts be made to improve prisons at all? One runs the risk that improvement efforts will have no more than cosmetic effects that will simply prolong the general use of such institutions. Balancing this concern is the hard fact that few of the even most outspoken critics of institutions realistically expect that most prisons

[1] American Friends Service Committee, *Struggle for Justice* (New York: Hill & Wang, 1971) and National Advisory Commission on Criminal Justice Standards and Goals, *Task Force on Corrections* (Washington, D.C.: Government Printing Office, 1974).

for adults will be closed in the near future.[2] Continued public concern with crime in the streets and demands for increased criminal penalties make it further unlikely that prisons will be soon eliminated. Thus, efforts directed toward the improvement of prisons will be needed for some time to come, and organizational developers who neglect this problem will have served neither the deinstitutionalization movement nor the incarcerated offender.

This chapter describes an effort to develop a set of techniques that were used in change efforts within an existing prison. The research took place in Connecticut over a period of 2 years and involved six prisons, a parole staff, and a wide range of allied community services. It concentrated primarily on the managers in that statewide system and the staff and inmates in one prison that became the focus of a set of experiments in intervention. The central aim of these efforts was to discover the means by which to modify the network of human and organizational relationships in that correctional system which, to an important measure, fixed the scope and quality of programs in that state. This chapter describes how certain research instruments were used in that process, some of the things that were learned about them, and some ways such instruments can be used as tools of change.

Organizational intervention has grown rapidly as a subject of study in the last few years. Early studies of organizational management were largely concerned with treating and arranging workers in such a way that the results were best for the enterprise.[3] Whether the studies recommended training workers, an improved chain of command, or the building of morale, the emphasis for a number of years was on factors of individual personality that were presumed to sum to an organizational total.[4] As this line of inquiry matured, however, interest grew about factors operating at a different level. Scholars, particularly those with a system approach, argued that organizational variables could not be reduced to psychological variables and, therefore, change-relevant variables must deal with patterns of social arrangements instead of with individuals.[5] Hence, the search for the "right man for the job" was transformed into a search for the best organization of human resources. A growing number of specialists are

[2] It has been demonstrated that state juvenile correctional systems can be operated with extremely limited use of incarceration. See Yitzhak Bakal (ed.), *Closing Correctional Institutions* (Lexington, Mass.: Lexington Books, 1975).

[3] Frederick Winslow Taylor, *The Principles of Scientific Management* (New York: Norton, 1967).

[4] Chris Argyris, *Personality and Organization* (New York: Harper & Row, 1957).

[5] Daniel Katz and Robert Kahn, *The Social Psychology of Organizations* (New York: Wiley, 1966), pp. 499–551.

concerned with discovering means by which organizationally relevant variables may be manipulated to increase an organization's effectiveness and its capacity to enhance the lives of those who are involved with it.[6]

One group of these specialists has developed a distinctive change technology which has been termed "organizational development." Heavily influenced by a tradition that emphasized experimentally based learning techniques, organizational development (O.D.) practitioners have typically stressed a collaborative relationship between themselves and members of the "client" organization and have been committed to the development of data collection systems that include a good deal of information on social and psychological dimensions as well as those relating to the "producing" activities of an organization. A major part of an O.D. strategy is to make available these data to organizational members under conditions that will permit them to examine freely the implications of the data for organizational change and to take appropriate steps to achieve that change. Organizational development has a clear bias in favor of more open and humane organizations; the further assumption is usually also made that such organizations are likely to be more proficient in problem solving and thus more "effective."[7]

Although an O.D. approach has been undertaken in a variety of settings—education, industry, research centers—few attempts have been made to apply that technology to a correctional setting. When Commissioner Ellis C. MacDougall invited O'Leary, who was subsequently joined by Duffee, to undertake a series of training programs in his agency, an opportunity to test the feasibility of that technology in a prison for adult male felons became available.

STUDIES OF THE PRISON ORGANIZATION

Though the prison has had little formal attention from organizational development specialists, it has been an enterprise that has long attracted researchers concerned with understanding the nature of this formal organization if not, at least explicitly, with methods of changing it. Sociologists, especially, have laid claim to the prison as a microcosm of society in which variables of a holistic rather than an aggregate nature can be isolated and studied in a useful way.

Clemmer, in his pioneering work, used the term "prisonization" to refer to the socialization of inmates into an alienated prison

---

[6] Rensis Likert, *New Patterns of Management* (New York: McGraw-Hill, 1961); Douglas McGregor, *The Human Side of Enterprise* (New York: McGraw-Hill, 1960).

[7] W. Burke (ed.), *Contemporary Organization Development: Conceptual Orientation and Interventions* (Washington, D.C.: National Training Laboratory, 1972).

world after which the probabilities of successful community living were decidedly diminished.[8] Sykes, elaborating Clemmer's thesis, emphasized the deprivations experienced by all prisoners, regardless of their individual differences, that generate a distinctive prison culture.[9] And, while Irwin has raised doubts about the primacy of the prisons in generating the inmate culture, he has strengthened the thesis that a series of criminal justice organizations systematically affect the behavior of the inmates in their perception of the world. He has demonstrated that even those individuals who were relatively isolated from the effects of prisonization, as Clemmer defined it, saw themselves as distinctly different from normal citizens because of their unique institutional experiences.[10]

Other studies have shown the power of organizational variables as they operate within the prison. In an ecological study of the large maximum security prison, Wallace has demonstrated that the ostensible goal of modifying an inmate's behavior as a criterion of cellblock transfer is, more often than not, an administrative rationalization and that an individual's behavior after such transfer is more related to the status of the cellblock within the institution to which he is assigned, than to any traits he may possess as an individual.[11] Wilson also reports that inmate adaptation patterns correlate with types of institutional management rather than with individual personality classifications.[12] Additionally, Street, controlling for individual differences, has found that inmates are less "prisonized" and more cooperative with staff in a "treatment" rather than a "custodially" organized prison.[13]

The utility of studying a prison as a set of complex interdependencies was furthered by Studt and her colleagues who began a treatment project in a California prison under the assumption that their experimental cellblock within the insitution could be sufficiently isolated so that concomitant changes in the rest of the institution were not needed. After several years of study, they concluded that the variables relevant to the success of the program in the one cellblock were systemic in nature and not only the prison, but also the entire departmental administration, would have to make significant

[8] Donald Clemmer, *The Prison Community* (New York: Holt, Rinehart and Winston, 1967).

[9] Gresham Sykes, *Society of Captives* (Princeton, N.J.: Princeton University Press, 1971).

[10] John Irwin, *The Felon* (Englewood Cliffs, N.J.: Prentice-Hall, 1967).

[11] Robert Wallace, "Ecological Implications of a Custody Institution," *Issues in Criminology* (Spring, 1966), 47–60.

[12] Thomas Wilson, "Patterns of Management and Adaptation to Organizational Goals: A Study of Prison Inmates," *American Sociological Review* (Sept., 1968), 146–157.

[13] David Street, "The Inmate Group in Custodial and Treatment Settings," *American Sociological Review* (February, 1965), 40–55.

changes before a "community for treatment" in a cellblock would be viable.[14]

While inmates have been more often the focus of study than have prison staff, Studt and Cressey both conclude that organizational variables impinge on staff behavior as well as on inmates. For example, officers were found to be evaluated differently and were more or less satisfied with their job depending on the perception of inmates advanced by officials in the institution.[15] Further, staff effectiveness with inmates varied depending on whether staff were organized by bureaucratic divisions (i.e., custodial or counseling) or by task (i.e., roles determined by competence).[16]

IMPLICATION FOR ORGANIZATIONAL CHANGE

Implicit throughout the prison organization literature, but rarely directly broached, are issues of planned change. If the behavior of organizational members is significantly shaped by organizational constraints, changing those constraints may have a concomitant effect on behavior. While organizational change is difficult, its central role in any hope of prison reform has been made abundantly clear in repeated studies and attempts at amelioration. More than that, organizational interventions may also, to some degree, overcome an offender's entry characteristics which make the offender prone to recidivism.

As indicated, O'Leary and Duffee were concerned with the study of systematic change, specifically the technology associated with organizational development, in a state correctional system for adults. Their central concerns were to understand more fully the manner in which prison organizational forces impinge on its members and to uncover means by which those forces might be modified to alter the world in which the keepers and the kept find themselves.

The primary "unfreezing" technique used was the survey feedback technique notably associated with Floyd Mann.[17] In the most familiar form of this process, selected organizational groups are

[14] Elliott Studt, Sheldon Messinger, and Thomas Wilson, *C-Unit: The Search for Community in Prison* (New York: Russell Sage, 1968).

[15] See Studt, Messinger, and Wilson, *C-Unit*, and Donald Cressey, "Limitations on Organization of Treatment in the Modern Prison," in *Theoretical Studies in Social Organization of the Prison* (New York: Social Science Research Council, Pamphlet 15, 1960), pp. 78–110.

[16] Studt, Messinger, and Wilson, *C-Unit*.

[17] Floyd C. Mann, "Studying and Creating Change: A Means to Understanding Social Organization," in Conrad M. Arensburg et al., *Research in Industrial Human Relations* (New York: Harper & Row, 1957), pp. 144–167.

presented data on organizational goals, activities, and attitudes as seen by various constituencies of the organization. The source of unfreezing behavior lies in the discrepancies between the expected patterns in goals, activities, and attitudes and the patterns that actually exist. If the data are relevant to the group—and relevance is the key ingredient—the disconfirmation occasioned by the discrepant information begins a process of alternative search that is crucial for beginning a planned change effort.[18]

A key question that arises with this approach is the kind of data which are most useful to the change effort. The writers had been impressed by the work of Murray and others who had developed and used the notion of "environmental press" in analyzing the behaviors of persons within organizations, and particularly the application of this notion by Rudolph Moos.[19] Moos had developed a set of scales by which institutional climates could be charted according to specific dimensions. These scales had been originally developed in mental hospital settings, and with the collaboration of Wenk at the National Council on Crime and Delinquency Research Center, they had been adapted into a Correctional Institution Environmental Scales and tested in a number of correctional settings (see Chapter 6).

A choice that inevitably faces the organizational change practitioner who is using a survey feedback technique is whether to use such instruments as these, which have been developed carefully over a long time span, are subjected to appropriate and rigorous statistical tests, and are linked to a body of theory that permits the results to be generalized to issues beyond the immediate set of information. The advantages are obvious, but the disadvantages are equally obvious. The change literature is replete within many instances, demonstrating that when data are shaped, both in form and content, by the person or group controlling the means of change, the data are much more likely to be seen as relevant—and change potent—than are data that were not initially chosen by that controlling group.[20] The practical difficulty that faces the interventionist who develops scales "on the spot" is the lack of time and resources to shape instruments of sufficient scope and reliability to which he or she can address with much certainty issues beyond the very immediate change setting. One sacrifices precision and depth for present potency.

[18] Edgar H. Schein, "The Mechanisms of Change," in Warren G. Bennis, Edgar Schein, Fred Steele, and David Berleu (eds.), *Interpersonal Dynamics* (Homewood, Ill.: The Dorsey Press, 1964), pp. 342–378.
[19] Rudolph H. Moos, "Changing the Social Milieus of Psychiatric Treatment Settings," *Journal of Applied Behavioral Science* (Oct./Nov./Dec. 1973), 575–593.
[20] Chris Argyris, *Intervention Theory and Method* (Reading, Mass.: Addison-Wesley, 1970), pp. 89–127.

The gains to be achieved by using the Correctional Institution Environment Scales (especially their power to describe reliably various correctional institutions, an important consideration when dealing with the top managers of the system) swung the decision to the use of these scales. The issue was how to make them most change inducing, especially at the institutional levels. The effort began with

Table 8.1 Correctional Institutions Environment Scales (CIES), Form C Description of Subscales

1. Involvement	Measures how active and energetic inmates are in the day-to-day functioning of the program—i.e., interacting socially with other inmates, doing things on their own initiative and developing pride and group spirit in the program.
2. Support	Measures the extent to which inmates are encouraged to be helpful and supportive toward other inmates and how supportive the staff are toward inmates.
3. Expressiveness	Measures the extent to which the program encourages the open expression of feelings (including angry feelings) by inmates and staff.
4. Autonomy	Assesses the extent to which inmates are encouraged to take initiative in planning activities and take leadership in the unit.
5. Practical Orientation	Assesses the extent to which the inmate's environment orients him toward preparing himself for release from the program. Such things as training for new kinds of jobs, looking to the future, and setting and working toward goals are considered.
6. Personal Problem Orientation	Measures the extent to which inmates are encouraged to be concerned with their personal problems and feelings and to seek to understand them.
7. Order and Organization	Measures how important order and organization are in the program, in terms of inmates (how they look), staff (what they do to encourage order), and the facility itself (how well it is kept).
8. Clarity	Measures the extent to which the inmate knows what to expect in the day-to-day routine of his program and how explicit the program rules and procedures are.
9. Staff Control	Assesses the extent to which the staff use measures to keep inmates under necessary controls—i.e., in the formulation of rules, the scheduling of activities, and in the relationships between inmates and staff.

Source: Ernst Wenk and Rudolf Moos, *Journal of Research in Crime and Delinquency*, July, 1972, p. 141.

the administration of the Correctional Institution Environment Scales to a random sample of 704 staff and inmates in 6 correctional institutions in the state system under study. The version of the questionnaire that was used measured 12 dimensions, which were later combined into 9, of the environmental press existent in those correctional institutions[21] (see Table 8.1).

Inmates and staff answered a series of true-and-false questions about climate dimensions in their institution. For example, a press toward involvement was inferred from "Inmates on this unit care about each other." A press toward expressiveness was measured by statements such as, "People say what they really think about here." And a press toward practicality was derived from such statements as, "Inmates here are expected to work toward their goals." Each of the dimensions was measured by ten true-and-false questions. Several methods were used to administer the test, including a tape recording for illiterate inmates and translations for those inmates who spoke Spanish or other languages.

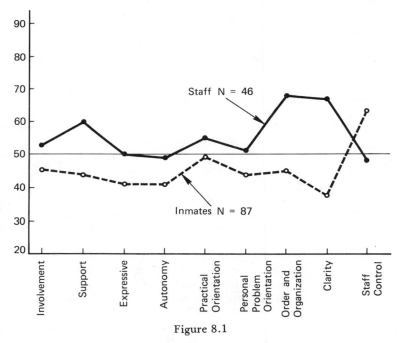

Figure 8.1

[21] Ernst Wenk and Rudolph Moos, "Social Climates in Prisons: An Attempt to Conceptualize and Measure Environmental Factors in Total Institutions," *Journal of Research in Crime and Delinquency* (July, 1972), 141.

As expected, the scales differentiated strongly between the inmates' and staff's view of a correctional institution. For example, the results from the prison that became the primary locus of major organizational development efforts in this study are shown in Figure 8.1.

With the exception of the dimension of involvement, staff and inmate scores were significantly different at the .01 level on all items. Importantly, inmates rated the institution significantly less on all the characteristics measured, except for measures of staff control, which they perceived as being considerably higher than did the staff.

Many other comparisons were feasible with these data. For example, in Chapter 6 we compared staff and inmate scores across all institutions as measures of departmental uniformity or as indicators of critical institutional differences, and we used the climate scores as a dependent variable showing the effects of different management styles. It was also possible to contrast total departmental staff and total inmate scores as a sign of the extensiveness of the inmate culture. But ultimately, in any of these comparisons, questions arose as to their importance. Is there an ideal institution? What would it look like? Do test scores allow us a better understanding of the obstacles to change? These are the questions that immediately arose when these data were used as feedback to departmental personnel.

THE USE OF DATA IN TRAINING

A central question that remains to be answered in most cases where data are developed for feedback is: "What is the ideal profile those receiving the data want to achieve in a given situation?" Obviously, there are some limits on the options available, since the items selected for inclusion in the test instrument almost always reflect to a degree some concepts about a desirable state as perceived by the test designer. Thus, while scales may be presented as "objective" measures against which judgments are to be made, they inevitably have some statement of value contained within them. For example, the Correctional Institution Environment Scales did not contain "corruption" or "racism" dimensions which one could argue are as badly needed as measures of prison life as "practicality" or "support."[22] Beyond this type of question there is the related issue of the extent to which one dimension "should" be rated higher or lower than another.

Before scales can be fruitfully used in a feedback setting, some specification of the goals to be obtained—the direction in which one

[22] For a critical comment on this problem, see E. Currie and Jerome Skolnick, "A Critical Note on the Conceptions of Collective Behavior," *Annals of the American Academy of Political and Social Science* (Sept., 1970), pp. 34–45.

is to move—is needed. And the selection of a goal is a complicated process that inevitably brings with it a host of questions. Not only is the character of the goal involved, but the level of generalization becomes important as well. Almost any set of goals relates to a larger set of goals. For example, a warden of a prison might easily select a goal of security for an institution. But the selection of that goal carries with it implications about more general goals of a correctional institution in our society.

More often than not, goal questions are not explicitly addressed; they are assumed. This may not be a significant problem provided there is an underlying, even if unarticulated, agreement about the purposes an organization is to serve. When there is a high degree of consensus about desirable norms—goals and the methods to achieve them—there may be difficulty in getting people to accept and act on data that indicate that the goals are not being reached, but this problem is of a different order when there are differences about how to judge the meaning of data. Moos describes, for example, how in a mental hospital setting staff and patients who were viewing scale profiles were able with some facility to decide on concrete action steps.[23] Very similar scales fed back to prison personnel did *not* evoke the same responses.

Those who were participating in the feedback session had participated in several full-scale training conferences lasting over 2 weeks and the principle of instrumented feedback had been introduced and was well accepted. Those previous experiences had created a fairly open stance on the part of administrators and staff and they were eager to see the result of the social climate survey.

The eye of the administrator, however, is not the eye of the researcher. When the Correctional Institution Environment Scales were presented, there was a good deal of interest in the results, but it was difficult to stimulate the prison staff to think of ways in which to use the results for planning further activities. They readily accepted the various information that was presented on the scales as statistical confirmation of what they had long felt intuitively. But when they were asked what might be done to improve the lot of all those who lived in the prison only a few suggestions arose. It was pointed out to them that the different perceptions of the climates between staff and inmates could have administrative significance. However, no matter how the data were elaborated, they remained largely of significance to the research function of the enterprise. The problem was that the managers had not previously used such measures of organizational

---

[23] Moos, "Changing the Social Milieus of Psychiatric Treatment Settings."

behavior, and initially they saw no connection between these data and the managerial roles of goal setting and organizational feedback.

Richard Steinert, the superintendent of the prison in which the data were presented, asked if a specific profile could be chosen as a goal and activities planned to achieve it. His central concern was whether any change would benefit the institution and what specific actions were needed to change the profile. He wanted to know which direction to take and precisely what had to be done in behavioral terms on the part of institutional employees to change a profile in a desired direction. His concern, like most administrators, was in the direction of action needed to the attainment of a specified tangible goal.

The researchers suggested that it might be possible to have the group draw an ideal goal profile.[24] This was attempted, but a good deal of dissatisfaction among the staff was expressed in the process. Arguments arose over the meaning of the dimensions and their relationship to the pace and life of a correctional institution. In a variety of forms two questions, which indicated deep disagreements about the ends of the prison and the means to achieve them, were posed by the group: 1. What was the basis on which to make a judgment on what would be an ideal profile? 2. What were the behaviors that related a profile to specific programs?

Clearly, the Correctional Institution Environment Scales were useful in stimulating a set of questions at a general level, but it was also apparent that another set of questions needed to be answered before the forces of change could be channeled and mobilized. For this purpose, a scheme was needed which more directly dealt with the issues in correctional terms.

RELATING POLICY AND SOCIAL CLIMATES

Since the correctional policy theory has been developed with correctional employees and accepted by them as a sensible way of understanding various correctional alternatives, the next step was to link the correctional policies scores to social climate dimensions. In order to work out these relationships, a version of the *Correctional Policy Inventory* was devised that would measure the kind of policy in effect in an institution as revealed by the reported behaviors of staff. The inventory was given to 30 inmates and 18 employees to describe the situation prevailing in the test institution. The questions asked were designed to illustrate the kinds of behaviors various kinds

---

[24] A similar procedure was used by Moos in his mental hospital change experiments ("Changing the Social Milieus of Psychiatric Treatment Settings").

of policies might manifest. For example, if there were an inmate complaint about a rule, a "restraint" officer would be expected to stress the need to obey the rules fixed by higher authority. A "reform" officer would be concerned with being seen as firm, fair, and directly involved. A "rehabilitation" officer might be willing to listen to complaints of inmates but would tend to refer them to counselors. A "reintegration" officer would tend to listen to complaints about rules, and if the rules seemed to require change, to entertain that possibility. The same group of inmates and staff was asked to complete the social climate scales and resultant intercorrelations (Table 8.2) were developed.

Table 8.2 Intercorrelations Between Policy Scales and Social Climate Scale

Social Climate Scale	Reintegration	Rehabilitation	Reform	Restraint
Expressiveness	.27	.45†	−.28*	−.56†
Support	.22	.42†	−.03	−.48†
Practical Orientation	.32*	.31*	.18	−.13
Order and Organization	.26	.26	.05	−.30*
Personal Problem Orientation	.38†	.37†	−.19	−.39†
Involvement	.14	.14	−.03	−.08
Clarity	.16	.18	−.09	−.35*
Staff Control	−.08	−.37†	.17	.54†
Autonomy	−.02	.35†	−.28*	−.58†

$N = 48$
*P .05 = .28
†P .01 = .37

As might be expected, the reintegration model, which provides the opportunity to test alternate behavior patterns, correlated with dimensions of practicality and personal problem orientation. The rehabilitation model showed a somewhat similar relationship, but the emphasis on personal relationships of the classic treatment type appeared in correlations with expressiveness, support, and autonomy and a negative correlation with staff control.

The reform model showed negative relationships, as might be expected, with expressiveness and autonomy, but the strongest negative correlations were generated by the restraint model in which concern for individual and community were both lacking. There, one can also see a strong positive correlation with staff control.

In order to test further the relationship of the Correctional Institution Environment Scales with correctional policies, the data from two institutions other than the test prison were examined. No example of an institution with a pronounced reintegration stance could be located, but two prisons, one with strong rehabilitation and one with strong restraint policies were subjected to analysis. Institution A clearly had a rehabilitation policy. For example, extensive interviews with its administrative staff demonstrated their high concern for providing treatment programs for inmates. They showed considerably less concern for community change, as one would expect in a reintegration stance. Institution A structured itself along the lines of the traditional treatment prison. The institution was organized into cottages in part to foster a benign atmosphere; decisions about inmates were made by professional staff in charge of each cottage. The professional staff complement at this institution equaled the number of custodial staff, and the per capita costs per inmate were twice as high there as at Institution B. In brief, Institution A came as close as could be found to the prototypical rehabilitation prison in the state.

On the other hand, Institution B was clearly restraint-oriented. In most respects, it operated very much like a jail. Physical facilities and programs resembled most modern prisons for adults—adequate physical care, minimal "treatment" staff, and an overriding concern with custody and control. The general attitude was that they were glad to have their jobs and an institution in which to do them. There was little concern for change. The staff of Institution B was concerned with keeping a quiet ship and an efficient operation.

Table 8.3 contrasts the environment scores of these two institutions. The table uses the five social climate dimensions which were shown to be most highly related to rehabilitation and restraint correctional policies as shown in Table 8.2. It will be recalled that those results were obtained from questionnaires administered to staff and inmates in the test institution. These findings inevitably (and too quickly) lead to the conclusion that once a correctional policy could be settled upon, a desirable social climate profile could be drawn and used as an index of progress at least somewhat independently of other measures being used. Thus, if an "expressiveness" dimension was highly associated with a reintegration policy, for example, the higher the scores on that dimension, the more the desirable policy was being implemented.

Table 8.3 Correctional Institution Environment Scores by Selected
Dimensions in Prisons A and B

Social Climate Dimensions	Prison A N = 75 Rehabilitation Oriented	Prison B N = 95 Restraint Oriented
Expressiveness	4.23	2.86
Support	5.32	3.53
Personal Problem Orientation	5.61	4.23
Staff Control	5.89	7.03
Autonomy	4.07	2.01

All significant at .01.

At a prior meeting of the top correctional policy makers of the state a decision had been made that a reintegrative policy with rehabilitative elements was to be implemented on a statewide basis. And since now the relationship between those policies and the Correctional Institution Environment Scales was charted, it appeared to the researchers that the Correctional Institution Environment Scales could be used as an effective feedback device. The Scales, indeed, served that purpose, but the relationship between perceived climate and perceived desirable behavior was more complicated than these descriptions of simple profile relationships.

To begin with, correctional officers had a very different view of the characteristics of a desirable correctional policy for the state than did the top managers of the system. For example, prior research by O'Leary and Duffee had shown sharp differences among correctional policy preferences by staff at various organizational levels in the state's six prisons and the policy actually in effect as seen by the inmates of those institutions.[25]

There was little question that correctional officers preferred policies that featured high staff control and dominance—the policies of reform and restraint. And until these issues were confronted and resolved, describing a profile jointly desired by officers and managers posed a major dilemma.

The attempt to develop a higher degree of agreement among prison staff on the appropriate correctional policy turned into one of the major issues of the intervention activity in that prison system.

[25] See Chapter Five of this text and Vincent O'Leary and David Duffee, "Management Behavior and Correctional Policy," *Public Administration Review* (Nov./Dec., 1971), 603–616.

What is of relevance here is how the Correctional Institution Environment Scales were useful in diagnosing problems and in the design of change tactics.

One feature of the session in which correctional staff viewed the results of the Correctional Institution Environment Scales was their apparent agreement at times on the desirability of certain climate dimensions, even when differences in other attitudes appeared. "Order," for example, seemed desirable no matter who was asked. However, although there might be agreement on the desirability of a high or a low score on certain dimensions, there were very different views about the perceived behaviors of staff that were associated with those dimensions.

Further, while correctional officers, expressed support for policies that featured high staff control and dominance, the sources of that preference were unclear and were initially accounted for by the researchers through a variety of explanations: social distance, cultural attitude, or individual biases. While each of these seemed to be a contributing factor, during the course of extensive interviews with these officers it became clear that a much more dominant concern was the "control" of the institution.

One might succeed in changing attitudes toward inmates or lessen prejudices among correctional officers, but at base there remained an overriding preoccupation with maintaining the stability of the prison. Even though the institution in which the intervention was taking place was classified as a minimum security facility, a good deal of the technology of that institution was aimed toward controlling inmates.[26] Stability and order were obviously central concerns of correctional officers, concerns that were heightened during the course of the study when a group of inmates attacked a group of officers at another but nearby institution during a baseball game and severely wounded several of them.

Support, expressiveness, and a personal problem orientation might be, and indeed were, important to clinicians and caseworkers, but to the correctional officers a stress on order and low aggression were desirable features of a correctional institution. Most important, the officers associated a restraint correctional orientation as the way to achieve them. "Be detached" and "enforce the rules" were the watchwords of many correctional officers, but in actual practice such behaviors were often diluted and compromised. Officers' behavior was also supportive of reform and restraint because over time these

[26] David Duffee, *Correctional Policy and Prison Organization* (Beverly Hills, Calif.: Sage-Halsted, 1975), pp. 106–123.

behaviors had become associated with a social environment desirable to the officer group. Consequently, changed management behavior, and the managers' providing officers an opportunity to participate in reintegration activities, met with resistance on the part of the custodians. By the time of the change effort they had evolved a cultural predisposition to aloofness, to a militaristic chain of command, and to the withholding of discretion and opportunity testing from offenders. In contrast, offenders apparently perceived their own group needs better met within the behavioral context consistent with the managers' newly espoused reintegration policy. This situation also seemed to explain the inmates' proclivity (previously thought peculiar to us) to dissociate top managerial levels from their otherwise general criticism of the correctional system.

As the intervention process continued, involving a series of sessions with inmates and staff, two central obstacles (technology and the perceived climate in the organization) emerged that had to be overcome if the goal of a more generally "reintegrationist" style of institutional life had any hope of fruition.

The technology that fixed the character of correctional officers' activity and ultimately their perceptions had to be altered. It is important to emphasize that not all officers were in favor of a restraint policy or were opposed to reintegration. Often they were very confused about policy either because they received contradictory messages from their superiors or they found their prescribed roles in conflict with the espoused goals of the organization. They were, under the circumstances, safer if they operated in ways that supported a restraint or reform regime.[27] If alternative behaviors were to be induced, prison managers had to alter their managerial practices and modify expectation about correctional officers' duties and behaviors.

But even with such technological interventions, it was also apparent that somehow officers' concerns about security and order had to be resolved to the extent that these interests involved vested interests of the officers as a group. It was at this point that the Correctional Institution Environment Scales provided several important insights and suggested tactics of change interventions.

It is easy to forget that prisons can be dangerous places for inmates, and their concern for "law and order" may be even greater than that of most guards. Indeed, it is a fear of the disorganization and violence that occur during times of riots which may be one of

---

[27]David Duffee, "The Correctional Offender Subculture and Organizational Change," *Journal of Research in Crime and Delinquency* (July, 1974), 155-172. And see Donald Cressey, "Contradictory Directives in Complex Organizations: The Case of the Prison," *Administrative Science Quarterly* (June, 1959), 1-19.

the chief reasons why there is not more disorder in many prisons of the country, even though brutalizing and inhumane conditions may exist. Through the process of meeting with inmates in a variety of settings the researchers were reminded that the inmates' concerns for low aggression and order were no less than those of the officers. Not surprisingly, inmates were also very much concerned that an institution fostered realistic opportunities to develop the means to cope successfully with the world outside—the dimension of practicality. What did not become clear until inmate Correctional Institution Environment Scales scores were separated from those of correctional officers and correlated with correctional policy scores was the difference of perceptions between the two groups concerning how to achieve the climate objectives which both groups saw as desirable.

Table 8.4 shows the relationships among three critical Correctional

Table 8.4 Correlation Between Selected Correctional Policies and Correctional Institution Environment Dimensions by Officers and Inmates

Social Climate Dimensions	Reintegration		Restraint	
	Officers	Inmates	Officers	Inmates
Practicality	.08	.67	.42	−.20
Order	.11	.43	.50	−.22
Aggression*	−.15	−.43	−.57	.25

Officer N = 18.
Inmate N = 30.
*The "aggression" dimension was not included in the final form of the Correctional Institution Environment Scales, but it was included in the early forms which were used in this study and is included here because of its special relevance.

Institution Environment Scales dimensions and two correctional policies. Although the sample size was small because of the difficulty in getting all the necessary forms filled out by the common groups of officers and inmates, the pattern of correlations was clear and was confirmed by subsequent feedback sessions with officers and inmates.

Clearly, inmates saw practicality and order as positively related to a reintegration regime in prison. They also perceived a negative relationship between aggression and that policy. The views of the officers were diametrically opposite. They saw aggressive behavior as much more negatively related to a policy of restraint. Practicality and order were positively associated with that policy for officers.

It was apparent that if one wished to shift officers from a restraint focus, it would be necessary either to give them the opportunity to discover that order and low aggression may not be as important as they saw them (a difficult task indeed) or to discover that these features can be associated with a reintegrative program. Inmates, to some degree, already held that view. The officers needed some credible evidence that these elements, which were basic to their well-being in the prison setting, could arise out of a different social-technical system.

To restate the change problem, it became clear only after considerable change effort in the prison that our original change strategy was ineffective because our original understanding of the prison as a complex system was incomplete. It was only through using several research instruments simultaneously and our elaboration of the original diagnostic research design that the crucial "unfreezing" points in the change strategy became clear. The problem was far more difficult than aligning managerial behavior with chosen correctional policy and then watching the rest of the prison tumble into place.

The domino theory of implementation was insufficient to our needs because there existed in the prison not simply a disagreement about means, but also a disagreement about ends. Officers behaved in ways that produced reform or restraint-oriented interactions with inmates *partially* because of the managerial behaviors that were not totally consistent with the professed goal of a reintegration policy. But the officers also behaved in ways supportive of reform and restraint policies because these behaviors had become associated over time with a social climate that was linked to the very basic needs of the officer group. Consequently, changed management behavior, and the provision by managers to officers of an opportunity to participate in reintegration activities, met with resistance on the part of the officers. By the time of the planned change effort they had evolved a cultural predisposition to aloofness, a militaristic chain of command, and a withholding of discretion and opportunity testing from offenders. In contrast, offenders apparently perceived their own needs as being met within the behavior context consistent with the managers' newly espoused reintegration policy.

A number of activities were undertaken which included shifts in job definitions in the institution and opportunities for inmates and officers to review organizational activities.[28] In addition, a special action research unit consisting of officers and inmates were established.[29]

[28] Richard Steinert, "Postscript," in Duffee, *Correctional Policy and Prison Organization*, pp. 205–208.
[29] David Duffee, *The Use of Correctional Officers in Planned Change*, final research report, National Institute of Law Enforcement and Criminal Justice, NI-71-115 P6, Sept. 30, 1972.

As important as these action steps was the demonstration that, given institutional officials with sufficient courage and commitment, the techniques of organizational change that are today so commonplace in many other settings can be applied to what appears to be the most intractable of all institutions—the prison.

The project also demonstrates that an important contribution to theory and technique can be made in such a setting. Certainly, for example, this intervention underscored the necessity of recognizing the complex relationships that exist among sets of behaviors, technology, and perceived climates in an organization. These realizations are particularly crucial to an enterprise that is concerned with purposeful change. An increase in an apparently "desirable" climate score can be made almost impossible to different sets of actors behaving in almost contrary fashion because the way each seeks to achieve the desired climate may be in flat contradiction. The experiences from this effort in using these types of instruments in a planned change effort are not that they are ineffective; to the contrary. The availability of a reliable and sophisticated measure of climate permitted the completion of a series of diagnostic steps that were very important to the design of feasible interventions in a type of organization that has a reputation for its militant slowness at purposeful change.[30]

[30] This chapter is revised and abridged from Vincent O'Leary, David Duffee, and Ernst Wenk, "Developing Relevant Data for a Prison Organizational Development Program," *Journal of Criminal Justice* (Summer, 1977), 85-104.

9

Breaking the Barriers to Change: The Reutilization of Front-line Staff

(David Duffee, Richard Steinert, and Robert Dvorin)

In Chapter 8 we examined some of the problems in developing indicators and measurements for use in implementing new correctional policies. A particularly difficult part of that development had to do with facing the resistances to change within the front line of the organization. Dealing constructively with that resistance entailed several different attempts to perceive the problems of correctional work from the perspective of front-line staff and then developing methods of change that included resolving the problems of disagreements that these people had with the new policies. In this chapter we will examine in detail some of the activities undertaken in the Connecticut Correctional Institution at Enfield in an attempt to involve officers and inmates more directly in the policy changes desired by management.

While this chapter, then, deals specifically with altering the behavior and attitudes of correctional officers, the techniques used, and the theoretical explanations of their effectiveness, are not limited to prison work. There is ample evidence that front-line staff in a variety of organizations face the same problems with management and managerially initiated change that the correctional officers in this prison faced. Whyte and others have convincingly demonstrated the distance and alienation of factory workers from management and the organizational factors impinging on the front-line staff that militate against their cooperation with management.[1] McCleary has made similar observations about front-line parole staff,[2] and Skolnick, Toch et al., and Rubenstein about police officers.[3] Hence, the material presented here should be widely applicable across correctional organizations and represents a key problem in any massive policy change effort in correctional systems.

THE CORRECTIONAL OFFICER SUBCULTURE AND ORGANIZATIONAL CHANGE

It is not a radical suggestion that correctional officers might have their own subculture. The police, who face many similar problems, have been called the "blue minority," and research has found police to be a very cohesive group, both on and off duty.[4] Other analogies might be made with foremen in industry,[5] noncommissioned officers in the military, and orderlies and nurses in hospitals.[6] Like the others, correctional officers are caught in the middle. They must enforce the rules and control those under them. Usually they are not given the necessary tools to do this job; often, full employment of the tools at their disposal causes disorder rather than order. They spend 8 hours each day among men and women they might not like. They are not supposed to fraternize with these men and women, but often they can identify with the offenders' complaints about their superiors. Like the inmates, they enjoy identifying dishonesty and hypocrisy in those above them, and like the inmates, they feel alienated from middle-class society which has asked them to do its dirty work and

[1] See particularly William F. Whyte et al., *Money and Motivation* (New York: Harper & Row, 1955).

[2] Richard McCleary, "How Structural Variables Constrain the Parole Officer's Use of Discretionary Powers," *Social Problems* (Dec., 1975), 209-225.

[3] Jerome Skolnick, *Justice Without Trial* (New York: Wiley, 1966); Hans Toch, Douglas Grant, and Raymond Galvin, *Agents of Change: A Study in Police Reform* (New York: Schenckman Halsted, 1975); Jonathon Rubenstein, *City Police* (New York: Ballantine, 1973).

[4] Skolnick, *Justice Without Trial*, pp. 42-70.

[5] See Joseph Bensman and Israel Gerver, "Crime and Punishment in the Factory: A Functional Analysis," in Bernard Rosenberg et al. (eds.), *Mass Society in Crisis* (New York: Macmillan, 1964), pp. 141-152.

[6] On the similarities in a variety of "total institutions," see Erving Goffman, *Asylums* (Garden City, N.Y.: Doubleday, 1961), pp. 1-25.

then ignores them completely or condemns them as brutal and inhuman. Like inmates, correctional officers feel relegated to the same position in the organization for their entire life stay and explain the selection for the infrequent promotions as owing to "pull" and "politics." Again, like inmates, they feel that the rewards of the job are inconsequential and the punishments unavoidable. So why work? Much like inmates, officers have very little idea of the continuity of corrections. What becomes of inmates after release from prison has only a passing connection with their job. Parole is seen in terms of the inmates who return from it, and "the street" is irrelevant because it is so far away.

Correctional officers, of course, are not inmates. They have a great deal of power over a large number of human beings and they can leave the prison every day. The facts that they spend a lot of time with inmates and that they have a similar perspective on many aspects of prison life are not in themselves sufficient to generate a subculture. A subculture becomes likely when the officers' situation as described becomes problematic.

Because the formation of a subculture is generally a group response to commonly felt conflict, the officer subculture, if it exists, is probably rather recent. While guards may have had a tense, low-paying job 50 years ago, they also had a rather clear-cut role. Officers were in power and inmates were not. Officers told inmates what to do and the inmates obeyed or were punished. When there was a confrontation, the administration assumed that a guard's story was true and an inmate's was a fabrication.

As the image of the inmate has changed considerably in the last 50 years, and he or she is treated in a considerably different manner by prison administrators, so, too, have the image and treatment of the correctional officer changed. While 50 years ago correctional officers guarded people perceived as subhumans and misbehavior against them was excusable, whenever it was even recognized, today correctional officers are responsible for the management of individuals perceived as human beings and whose word clinically and legally may stand up against their own. More importantly, most correctional officers openly agree that a change in correctional policy is for the better. There may be some regrets about losing the clear-cut rules of yesterday, and there are certainly many complaints about the lack of power and respect today, but most correctional officers do not and would not care to deny that inmates are fellow human beings who should be "getting a better shake." It is only after this fundamental shift in the generally perceived humanity of inmates that the officer subculture has come about. The correctional officer subculture, more than anything else, is born of the frustrating belief that inmates on the whole deserve better treatment than officers (or anyone else) are capable of giving under present circumstances. Just what correctional officers expect of themselves or correctional organizations is not always clear, but in keeping with the new view of inmates, *they expect something more than and different from mere order.* As one officer expressed it: "I'm not sure what I'm here for; I know it is not security. Let's face it—the joint's secure. No, I must be good for something different."[7]

In part, much of the officer value complex may be built on this flight from ambiguity: that officers have discarded the goal of punishment and find in its place only the competing claims of professors, researchers, politicians, managers, counselors, and inmates, none of which they are willing to accept. Officers are in the anomic position of working for a goal that is negatively defined as the absence of punishment and is manifested by no acceptably measured results and is mediated by no reliably correlated means.[8]

EMPIRICAL INVESTIGATIONS OF THE OFFICER SUBCULTURE

Although there has been an increasing amount of research on correctional processes and correctional organization, we still know rather little about the men who make up the largest bulk of correctional staff.[9] Much more of the research effort has been expended on the study of the offender. If the behavior of the offender is perceived, reported, and responded to by staff, this research emphasis is fatally inadequate. If the treated are interacting with the treaters, we must also obtain systematic information on the treaters. This lack of information also makes it difficult to make any inferences about one segment of that group. It will be difficult to say officers belong to a subculture unless we can see the divergence between their values and those of their superiors. Hence, we must also have data on the values of correctional managers.

Several kinds of information about correctional personnel can be gathered. For example, we can seek to know age, educational level,

[7] The quotation is taken from interviews conducted in a minimum security prison, which will be described momentarily. The sentiment expressed was representative of the feeling of roughly half of the officers in the institution.

[8] See Donald Cressey, "Nature and Effectiveness of Correctional Techniques," *Law and Contemporary Problems* (Autumn, 1958), 754–771.

[9] John J. Calvin and Loren Daracki, *Manpower and Training in Correctional Institutions,* Joint Commission on Correctional Manpower and Training, Staff Report (Washington, D.C.: Government Printing Office, Dec., 1969), p. 11.

father's social status, number of previous jobs, number of cars owned, kinds of magazines read. Differences between managers and correctional officers on these kinds of variables might point to differences in value, but they would not give us any direct information about the way staff at any level perform in the correctional institution. These background data, of course, might help us to explain some of the differences between values, if we found some. However, the change program reported here was based on the assumption that organizational variables would have more effect on organizational performance than other kinds of variables would. We assumed, for example, that an inference about a warden's treatment of offenders is more safely built on a knowledge of his or her correctional goals than on a knowledge of the university he or she attended. Similarly, to know how an officer behaves, it is more important to know the officer's values and beliefs about corrections than his or her father's social status or the level of the officer's income. Also, in terms of alternatives of planned change, it seems more likely that interventions can be made to help clarify and influence the officer's views of corrections more easily than can interventions be aimed at changing the officer's social status or his income level.

The Program Site

The program was conducted in the Connecticut Department of Corrections. Entree was gained during a management training seminar. Before attending the seminar the top managers of the Central Office and of each of the major institutions in the department responded to questionnaires measuring their correctional policy and their managerial behavior. During the course of the seminar it was decided jointly by the managers and the consultants that additional data were desirable about the consequence of managerial strategies. Questionnaires measuring social climate and supervisory behavior were then administered to a random sample of 20 percent of all staff and inmates in the department (see Chapter 6).

Additionally, Superintendent Steinert suggested that the Enfield Institution might be used for more in-depth study on the correctional officer and inmate levels. A battery of interviews was conducted at this minimum security prison in order to validate the questionnaire findings and to fill in gaps in our knowledge of the process of policy formulation and implementation. The diagnostic phase of the activity in Enfield has been reported in Chapter 8. Our data demonstrated that correctional officers were effectively cut off from the world of correction as perceived by both management and offenders by the fact that the officers' individual goals were achieved by means associated with policies that management no longer espoused and wanted to change. It was clear that the front-line staff would have not only to alter their behavior if a new policy were to be implemented effectively, but also that the means of obtaining the personal goals of officers would have to be made congruent with the means of obtaining the organizational goals. But such a step cannot simply be ordered. It requires changes in attitudes as well as changes in knowledge about corrections.

Implications for Training

While we now seem aware that changing an inmate is a much more complex, time-consuming, and challenging activity than a high-flown lecture on morality and civil duty, most training for correctional officers (where any is offered) amounts to little more than simple lecturing. In the course of an orientation class, or within the framework of a training academy, correctional officers may be given several hours lecture on such things as "Role of the Counselor," "Human Behavior," and "Leadership and Employee Attitudes." Although the goal of such training is admirable and its implementation is long overdue, the process used to convey the content is not always compatible with the kind of behavior desired in correctional officers as a result of the training. The most common format of these sessions is the straight, stand-up lecture given by selected departmental personnel and outside consultants who have some functional relation to the topic to be covered. Lectures may be broken by films and on-site visits, and there is generally some time for question and answer discussion sessions after the formal talk.[10] In other words, the "courses" in the training academies often tend to be taught in the style of a several-period lecture on the freshman level in a university.

It is likely that one or two hours of lecture on a specific subject has a miniscule effect on even the best students listening to the best professor in a good university. Such lectures are *only* effective as they counterpoint carefully selected readings and occur within the peculiar university atmosphere where foreign ideas, even in the least interested students, enjoy some prestige. Such is not the case in a correctional training academy where many officers have little respect

---

[10] Trainees at two academies with which the author is personally acquainted usually select the discussion periods as the most rewarding.

for "book learning,"[11] or for the men whose learning is from books rather than the real life of the cellblock.

In spite of these problems, the usual educational techniques may be of some value *so long as the goal of the educator is to impart information.* It is true that our schools and colleges do change the behavior of the students who attend, but it seems likely that changes in behavior can be attributed to the forceful socialization processes that occur in the institutions of education, not to the content of lectures. A quantum of information itself *may* change a person's behavior, but it is likely to change his or her tactics *within* a preset perspective and pattern of behavior.[12] The information *itself* is likely to be received and interpreted within that mental and emotional framework. Within somebody else's circumstances, that piece of information may bring a very different response. In correctional training in which courses have been devised in order to change correctional officer behavior, it is very possible that the wrong design is being used. If the major goal is to change behavior (i.e., to increase cooperation between custodial and treatment staff), a more effective design would be one that could cut through the ideological differences between the people involved. An analogous problem occurs when a counselor tries to break through the values of the inmate caste in order to reach the individual inmate.

We would no longer plan to change an inmate subculture by lecturing to inmates on the advantages of "doing your own time" or the virtues of obeying the rules. On the contrary, we are aware that such a subculture breaks down when it ceases to have payoff, as, for example, when new careerists take on paraprofessional roles and learn new ways of gaining status, prestige, and money.[13] Similarly, the typical training program conducted for correctional officers

---

[11] The lack of respect, of course, may be caused by a number of other factors such as envy and anger at those who are educated, threat to self-image for not being educated, anger and resentment at economic demands that precluded education, or disenchantment with college or academy programs that do not reflect the realities of custodial supervision. Also, the suggestion was made elsewhere that traditional university education is only effective in the context of the campus culture. When training or retraining is to provide trainees with information and the ability to use it in non-university settings, considerably more attention must be paid to the process (as opposed to the content) of training. See Roger Harrison and Richard Hopkins, "The Design of Cross-Cultural Training: An Alternative to the University Model," *Journal of Applied Behavioral Science* (Oct./Nov./Dec. 1967), 431–460.

[12] Within the "ideology," as that term is used by John Griffiths in "Ideology in Criminal Procedure or a Third Model of the Criminal Process," *Yale Law Journal* (January 1970), 359.

[13] See, for example, *Ex-offenders as a Correctional Manpower Resource*, the proceedings of a seminar of the Joint Commission on Correctional Manpower and Training (Washington, D.C.: Government Printing Office, 1966).

ignores the problem that information received by officers in the course of training will be interpreted in terms of the values that they consider important. If the goal of officer training is to change officer behavior (i.e., to make it compatible with a certain policy), then methods of training should be used that can change the weight that officers place on certain kinds of information.

Changing the Officer Subculture

There is no reason why the method most recently used and most successful in breaking down the inmate culture might not also be used in undermining the officer value set. This strategy involves "use of products of a social problem in coping with the social problem."[14] The basic notion in this mode of change is that people will accept as trainees or colleagues information and behavior that they would not accept as changees. Toch has had success both with violent inmates and violent policemen when they were enlisted in a project to study and change violent behavior in others.[15]

The problem to be confronted by this technique used with correctional officers is not to reduce violence, but to reduce the pressures on the officer that lead the officer to be comfortable with reform and restraint behavior patterns and to increase the factors that would lead the officer to be comfortable with a reintegration policy.

The target of the particular phase of the program reported here was the variables within the organization that were assumed to narrow an officer's role and limit the officer's perspective on correctional goals. Approximately 30 percent of a staff of 150 were affected directly. Approximately 400 inmates indirectly felt the impact of one or another aspect of the program.

THE DESIGN OF THE CHANGE PROGRAM

The three major components of this phase of the program at Enfield were planned and developed in the first part of 1971 and

---

[14] Department of Health, Education and Welfare, *Experiment in Culture Expansion*, Report of Proceedings of a Conference on "The Use of Products of a Social Problem in Coping with the Problem," held at the California Rehabilitation Center, Norco, Calif., July 10, 11, and 12, 1963, and see Donald Cressey, "Social Psychological Foundations for Using Criminals in the Rehabilitation of Criminals," *Journal of Research in Crime and Delinquency* (July, 1965), 44–55.

[15] Hans Toch, *Violent Men* (Chicago: Aldine, 1970) and Hans Toch, J. D. Grant and R. Galvin, *Agents of Change: Study in Police Reform*. This type of change strategy is generally traced to Kurt Lewin's war work in changing buying habits of civilians; see Lewin, *Resolving Social Conflicts* (New York: Harper & Row, 1948) and "Group Decision and Social Change" in T. Newcomb and E. Hartley (eds.), *Readings in Social Psychology* (New York: Holt, Rinehart and Winston, 1974).

were initiated in June of that year. Interestingly, the three components developed independently in the minds of two different people.
For a year or so the superintendent had been thinking of using a
modified treatment team approach at Enfield that would replace the
centralized classification committee. This approach had been used
previously in several federal institutions[16] and was instituted in
Enfield after the superintendent studied the team operation at the
federal Reformatory in Petersburg, Virginia. The superintendent had
been thinking of ways in which the treatment teams could be more
than a classification and program review committee. So that such
teams could monitor the daily interactions of inmates and staff on a
more regular basis and receive continually updated information on
the feelings and perceptions of the inmates on the team caseloads,
more information was needed. Thus, the superintendent decided
that in order to increase the immediacy of information and to
decrease the distance between staff and inmates, inmate discussion
groups of eight to ten men should begin shortly after the decentralization of classification. Each discussion group was led by a volunteer
correctional officer who received some minimal but necessary training in group processes, how to handle problems of confidentiality,
and so on. The goal was to have the entire caseload of each treatment
team participating in a discussion group. Discussion leaders could
then bring generalized information (if not the identity of individual
speakers) to the attention of treatment team members and to policy
makers.

While this planning had been going on, Duffee, who had participated in management training at Enfield in previous years, became
concerned with the lack of officer participation in the institutional
planning and problem-solving processes and with the apparent
ineffectiveness of traditional modes of officer in-service training.
Analyzing available data on the administrators' correctional policy,
the failure of officers to follow that policy in operation, and the
differential social climate perceived in the institution by organizational participants at different hierarchical levels, he concluded that
an occupational subculture did exist at the officer level. This hypothesis, which was supported by the data, provided an explanation
for the ineffectiveness of policy implementation, in that while
receiving information from superiors about how they should perform,
officers were interpreting this information in terms of their own
value set. The strategy of change in this case was the creation of an

---

[16] See Daniel Glaser, *The Effectiveness of a Prison and Parole System* (Indianapolis:
Bobbs-Merrill, 1964) and Charles R. Hagan and Charles F. Campbell, "Team Classification in Federal Institutions," *Federal Probation* (July 1968), 30-35.

officer study group that would meet weekly to discuss problems in the organization as members of the group perceived them. The rationale was that the small group dynamics approach that had been effective in breaking down certain value sets and then changing behavior with both inmates and police could be effective in changing the correctional officers' perception of "what counted" and could improve the probability that they may adopt behaviors congruent with new institutional policy.

We emphasize the independent development of these two change projects from the resulting activity, because there appears to be important practical and theoretical implications to be drawn from the parallel but separate thinking of an administrator and a researcher. First, we must emphasize that these two men had known each other for 2 years prior to this undertaking. They both knew the system in question in some detail but from different vantage points. And they had different specific motives but a similar ultimate goal. Perhaps the motives in question are the most interesting aspects. The project of management training and organizational research that had previously brought Duffee to Enfield had ended some 6 months before the announcement of these separate plans. Duffee had returned to school to finish a dissertation based on that research, and Steinert was again alone at his institution after having experienced a short spurt of university interest. The researcher was wondering about his first professional role and how to begin his research career. The superintendent was left with something of a dilemma—whether to accept the management training program for what it had been or to continue in some way these new developments in his institution without outside support or advice.

The researcher's goal, in terms of the officer "research" team (as it was called), was to test a hypothesis about a value-changing technique. The superintendent's goal, in terms of the treatment teams and officer-led inmate discussion groups, was to begin, at a modest level, the reorganization of his prison along lines suggested by the management training and research which had demonstrated to him that existing policy was not as effectively implemented as it should have been and that there were principles of "democratic" management that might be useful in reducing the policy-implementation gap.[17]

[17]The management training conference, conducted between June, 1969 and July, 1971, was led by Professor Vincent O'Leary of the State University of New York at Albany. Information supplied to managers in the whole department included McGregor's notion of X and Y theories of management, Likert's notion of the "linking pin," and Blake and Mouton's managerial grid. In addition, O'Leary devised and O'Leary and Duffee finalized in Connecticut a typology of correctional policies that clarified correctional managers' concerns about the community and the offender and demonstrated certain operational

The researcher obtained funding for the officer project, and a meeting of the commissioner, deputy commissioner, superintendent, and others was convened in Hartford to discuss implementation.[18] In addition, the superintendent outlined his own plans for the decentralization of classifying the treatment teams and the discussion groups.

Some problems were immediately apparent. The superintendent welcomed the researcher's project, but he did not see it as compelling for his present organizational goals as the other two activities. The researcher wanted to proceed with his project, but he did not want to interfere with the administrative plans which had obvious merit. Interference seemed likely, however, because neither Steinert nor Duffee could predict at that moment how the institutional personnel and inmates would respond to either planned change. Furthermore, since both were pilot efforts, both plans required a certain number of volunteers. If we could predict only a limited number of volunteers (both men expected the number of initial volunteers to be small), there was the obvious chance that one project or the other would run short of manpower.

There was also the methodological disadvantage that the team efforts planned by the superintendent might interfere with the evaluation of the officer research effort, since the environment of that group would be changing at the same time that changes were being induced within the group. If change occurred, it would be very difficult to partition out, even subjectively, how much change might be attributed to the different processes, which could apparently have interdependent effects.

There were, however, some obvious practical and theoretical advantages to the initiation of both sets of activities simultaneously. Practically, it was possible, we thought, that the two programs announced simultaneously might draw more volunteers than either program might alone, because the planned expenditure of effort and the demonstration of administrative and outside commitment would be larger.

---

characteristics of the different policies. See Douglas McGregor, *The Human Side of Enterprise* (New York: McGraw-Hill, 1960); Rensis Likert, *New Patterns of Management* (New York: McGraw-Hill, 1961); Robert Blake and Jane Mouton, *The Managerial Grid* (Houston: Gulf Publishing, 1964); and Vincent O'Leary and David Duffee, "Correctional Policy: A Classification Designed for Change," *Crime and Delinquency* (Oct., 1971), 373–386.

[18] The officer research project was titled "Using Correctional Officers in Planned Change," N171-115 PG. (NTIS 1972). The fact the LEAA funds supported parts of this project does not imply that the National Institute of Law Enforcement and Criminal Justice agrees with the opinions expressed herein.

Financially, there were possible rewards also, since the kinds of training the various groups would receive in the beginning phases would be similar, and the kinds of issues each group would confront (openness of communications, feedback, confidentiality, etc.) would be similar. Consequently, it would be possible to train a larger number of volunteers for about the same cost, since the type of trainer to be hired and the number of trainer days would be the same whether there were 7 trainees or 30. The fact that both projects had mutually supportive goals would mean that weakness in the budget of one project could be bolstered by strengths in the other, and vice-versa.

Theoretical advantage clustered around the notion of system–environment exchange and the consequent impact on the *intensity* of change. Several organizational theorists have suggested that the most significant changes in a system are frequently externally induced.[19] Perceiving each group as a system and each other group as part of the environment of that system, we logically predicted greater changes within each group if the others operated simultaneously. Because of supportive changes in each group environment, such as competition among groups and the greater cohesion within groups that this might produce, plus the knowledge in each group that they were not alone in volunteering "to be different," we expected that change influences might "take" faster and be longer lasting than if the projects were independently initiated.

Lastly, for the research group project, the administratively initiated changes provided some valuable substance to the planned weekly discussion sessions. In other words, rather than wait for correctional officers to pull issues together completely on their own (a skill that they developed over time), it became their initial charge to provide a peer evaluation of the treatment teams and discussion groups. This task, we thought, might serve to get them off the ground, because the substantial structural change alone—in decentralizing classification—would provide examples of issues about lower staff participation, feedback patterns, and decision-making structure that would later have significance in their own right.

It was decided in Hartford that both projects were desirable, that they would support each other, and that the gains for the institution would be greater if the interaction effects we expected would occur. It was also decided that these benefits outweighed the disadvantages. This chapter examines this year-long undertaking. Major emphasis is on the officer research team, because formal evaluation was not

[19] See Daniel Katz and Robert Kahn, *The Social Psychology of Organizations* (New York: Wiley, 1966), Chapter 13.

required of the officer-led discussion groups and team treatment operations. Nevertheless, evaluations are made of the overall set of activities because the other groups interacted with the research group, they were trained with them, and they were supposed to be informally evaluated by them. As such, we have a narrative of the way in which administrative and research plans can cohere with extra payoff. In addition, we have, in the case of the research team, a narrative of a process that to our knowledge has not been attempted frequently in this context. We were applying a technique previously used with deviants (violent offenders, assaultive/assaulted police) in a *normal* situation; and we expected changes that were less dramatic and more routine, but perhaps for both these reasons more fundamental to correctional processes and organization.

From a broader perspective, it is necessary to see the activities taken by management and researchers here as based on the data and theory presented in the last eight chapters. The changes attempted in the Enfield organizational structure were consistent with that research. The positive evaluation of this activity led to the possibility of its expansion, in which the entire correctional system could be altered to implement the reintegration policy.

METHODS OF THE CHANGE PROGRAM

The entire training program utilized two related training techniques. The first, pioneered by Floyd Mann, is the survey feedback technique and has been used previously in the departmental management training program.[20] Within this change strategy, an organization is divided into task-relevant families or clusters, goals are formulated for each cluster, a measure is taken of the present organizational state, and strategies are taken to close the goal-implementation gap. On the officer level, this process involved dividing the men into working units. Then in small groups the nature of the managerial and policy material was explained, and the officers' preferences, opposed to those of other echelons', were reported. The men were asked to account for their preferences, and they also met with administrators to explore mutually acceptable means of negotiating differences.

At this point, the information feedback system was relaxed, while officers were selected as trainees who were to be responsible for research and change activity with fellow officers. The attempt was made to include a number of volunteers with strong preferences for

[20] Floyd Mann, "Studying and Creating Change," in W. Bennis, K. Benne, and R. Chin, *The Planning of Change* (New York: Holt, Rinehart and Winston, 1961), pp. 605-615.

the traditional custodial policy of compliance with rules and regulations and punishment for deviation. Under the supervision of Duffee and Steinert's top management team, who had received management training already, this small group of officers was responsible for research into those variables that affect policy preferences from the officers' viewpoint.

Much of the trainee activity took place while officers were performing their various custodial duties. More intensive training took place in scheduled conferences under the leadership of Dvorin, a skilled small group and management consultant. The first of these conferences lasted 3 days. During the conference, training material was used in several exercises designed to (1) inform trainees of the use of feedback, (2) measure and improve team communication, and (3) review correctional policy and available Connecticut data. A second 1-day conference was structured on planning for the achievement of goals and methods of in-service, observer–participant research. Laboratory techniques that enabled trainees to study themselves and the processes of communication were frequently used. Additional 1-day conferences were scheduled during the winter as program developments warranted.

In addition, the trainees met weekly so that activities on the different shifts could be coordinated. A tape recorder was used in these sessions so that officers could have immediate feedback on discussions of policy, inmate relations, and their ability to work together effectively. Trainees also had a tape recorder available for their own use during the week. The schedule of program time was roughly designed to be congruent with prison activity fluctuation. Prison population and officer activity were highest in the summer and the information feedback sessions were scheduled at the beginning and end of the program. Officer free time was highest from fall to spring, and it was during this time that extensive trainee work took place.

THE NEW WORK GROUPS

Of the 13 different staff teams that were formed during the summer of 1971, Duffee was directly responsible for one: the research group. Because this group trained, operated, and was evaluated with the other 12 groups, it is impossible to speak only of the research team. The consultants and the superintendent decided to gear the first training conferences of the summer for the entire pool of staff volunteering for participation in the program. Individuals were selected later for specific groups.

In the middle of June a memorandum was distributed with staff paychecks describing the origination of the ideas and the specific opportunities open to staff in terms of the new team positions. The superintendent spent the last 2 weeks of June collecting the names of volunteers and describing the proposed program in greater depth to both officers and inmates. During this period Steinert was in the institution talking to staff and offenders from 12 to 16 hours a day. By the beginning of July there was a volunteer list of approximately 40 names, most of whom were correctional officers. This number far exceeded original expectations, and the fear of a manpower shortage rapidly dissipated.

A first training conference was scheduled for July. Present were 16 persons to be split into 4 treatment teams, 6 persons who were to lead inmate discussion groups, 7 who were to form a research team, and several alternates. The training during the first conference had two related goals: (1) to impart some information about different ways of communicating and (2) to practice the art of communication within the new groups. The key substantive points made were that (1) supervisors' dysfunctional behavior may be supported by certain actions of subordinates, (2) subordinates can give accurate feedback and be critical without fearing reprisals, (3) the most desired communication style among the group was developmental and democratic while the most commonly found styles were either controlling or relinquishing,[21] (4) that inmates very likely desire the same kind of developmental, give-and-take communication. In terms of practice, the trainees were given various tasks to complete as teams so that they could get practice working as teams. Some of the tasks involved the description of developmental methods of handling controversy between staff members or between staff and inmates. The trainees left the session in anticipation of conferences in August and September that would relate specifically to the tasks of the different groups.

The groups formed had the following make-up and functions:

1. Four Team Treatment Groups. These were mixed groups. Included in each were a correctional officer, a work supervisor, and a counselor. These groups were to take over all functions of the classification committee for all inmates with more than

[21] It should be noted that these findings on a "training" instrument reinforce the research findings that officers desire democratic supervisors but often find them autocratic. The training instrument was Educational Systems and Designs, Inc., *Management Models: The Communication Process* (Westport, Conn., E.S.D., 1967). The research concerning administrative styles utilized the *Styles of Management Inventory* by Jay Hall, Jerry Harvey, and Martha Williams (Austin: Teleometrics, 1964). The research is reported in Vincent O'Leary and David Duffee, *Public Administration Review* (Nov./Dec., 1971), 603–616, and in Chapters 5 and 6 of this book.

9 months' sentence to serve. In addition to tasks previously done by the classification board, a treatment team would meet more frequently with the inmates on its caseload and work out specific contracts with inmates, the performance of which could earn a recommendation for release to the parole board.[22] The treatment teams served the additional functions of decentralizing important decisions, expanding the roles of work supervisors and correctional officers, and crossing the barrier between treatment and custody. These four teams were later expanded to six teams.

2. Six Discussion Groups. All discussion leaders were correctional officers specifically selected and trained by a group process expert. Each officer had from eight to ten inmates in his discussion group. The inmates for these groups were selected from the caseloads of the treatment teams.

3. One Research Group. This group originally consisted of six correctional officers and one correctional sergeant. It was their task to evaluate the activity of the other groups, analyze the problems of the minimum security prison that kept it from running as it should, and foremost, to analyze the goals of the prison and the role of the correctional officer in achieving them.

The activity of the three groups was to be coordinated by the counselor supervisor.

THE RESEARCH TEAM

The original method suggested for selecting members of the research team was that they be officers who had a traditional custodial orientation, considerable leadership ability, and rapport with other officers. The superintendent had been dubious about selecting only officers and in June suggested that the group should be a mixed one that included other kinds of staff personnel. However, after the selection of treatment team members and discussion leaders, the superintendent was left with seven correctional officers. Since he had selected, particularly for the discussion leader role, the youngest and most liberal volunteers, the research team members generally had the most years in service and the most conservative outlooks of the volunteer group. All seven were, however, energetic

[22] Richard Steinert put considerable effort into attempting to obtain from the parole board an agreement that Enfield inmates who completed their prison contract successfully *would* be paroled. This attempt, however, predated the national interest in "contract parole" by several years and was not successful. Steinert's idea was successfully implemented in some institutions several years later.

and dedicated, somewhat doubtful about the possibility of significant change, but rather tired of the status quo—they were amenable to change.

On the whole, it was a highly intelligent, verbal, and volatile group. Leadership was rapidly assumed and stability continually provided by the correctional sergeant. The sergeant was one of the men with the most service behind him. He had started his career in the maximum security prison at Wethersfield and had served at the new Somers maximum security unit before coming to the Enfield minimum security prison. He had been promoted to sergeant shortly before the start of the progam. Although he held rank over the other men, his group leadership was clearly not dependent on his formal status. He was quiet spoken and reserved, and he continually returned other members in the group to the point at hand. He seemed to have a natural ability for continually trying to pull the good points out of either side of an argument. In this way, he played a moderator role between the more conservative approaches of four of the officers and the more liberal approaches of the remaining two.

Policy Conference

A 2-day conference was organized for August, 1971, during which the research team was introduced to the theory and data that lay behind the program and was given an opportunity to wrestle with the specific goals set out for the research team. The group already noted at this time a certain negative aura had sprung up around the term "research." The discussion leaders and treatment teams were somewhat anxious about being evaluated by another staff group, and officers who had not volunteered for the program at all were treating the group as a bunch of "oddballs." Although the group was taking most of this pressure in good humor, it certainly increased the anxiety level. Most of this emotion appeared as dubiousness about their skills to tackle the stated goals. Duffee and Dvorin noticed at this point that they had made one particular mistake. There was an evident need to very specific tasks, the completion of which would have given the group an early sense of accomplishment. Although the group devised on its own some tasks of this type later in the year, no small but valuable exercises had been provided early on. It was, therefore, thrust on the members of the group rather prematurely that they were suddenly out on a limb both socially and scientifically. The consultants knew of no other correctional program in the country where correctional officers had been asked to perform in this manner before. To add to this fear of being in unchartered waters, the group had anxious feelings about how other officers felt about the idea. Fortunately, the group dynamics was working very well within the group. A very visible cohesiveness and esprit de corps balanced and was perhaps partly generated by the ambiguous relationship of the group to the rest of the prison and to the outside world.

Substantively, the August meeting had several specific goals: (1) to present the idea of correctional policy and to have the group decide its goal in relation to the prison policy, (2) to see the idea of policy as it is related to the ideas of communication techniques (including managerial style) that had been presented in July, (3) to select a leader, (4) to decide on a regular procedure and time of meeting, and (5) to select some first items of business.

The conference was fairly successful with the exception of the fifth goal. The group never really defined for itself specific topics for its first weekly sessions. The greatest impact on the group, although partly negative, was the presentation of the policy and managerial data. The group responded with surprise and interest that questionnaires and figures could be used to demonstrate complaints in the correctional work that it had vaguely verbalized. The group could see in more objective terms that the goal of reintegrating offenders into the community, which was the written policy of the Central Office, was not perceived on the operational level by inmates.

This discovery may have had some negative impact in that the consultants were not prepared for how quickly the officers would interpret these data, which indicated disagreements about goals among all echelons, to mean that top correctional officials were hypocritical. The suggestion by the trainers that correctional officers *also* had a role to play in the failure to implement chosen policy did not strike home completely. The trainers were successful, however, in getting the officers to relate the policy material back to the general communication material presented in July. Some members of the group at least made the *intellectual* admission that all levels were involved in the distortion of policy. The *emotional* commitment to that admission was to come later. Perhaps the greatest surprise of the conference was that no officers questioned the validity of what the inmates reported seeing. The officers seemed to accept that inmates were accurate in their portrayal of staff behavior as supportive of traditional custodial goals, despite the fact that few staff members consciously desired these goals. In other words, they felt the inmates were essentially correct in reporting that the organization's chief concern was with the smoothness of internal operation rather than with some lasting positive effect on the inmates. The fact that the officers accepted the data demonstrated how open to change they were, because the easiest way out of any change effort would have been to reject the data.

The remainder of the conference was used in trying to spin out a correctional policy unique to the institution. The group undertook this task when most of the members decided that there were good points in all the policy models presented by the researcher. The distance the group moved in the next 9 months is measurable in terms of an action proposal that the group finally wrote. This proposal involved the formation of officer–inmate teams to increase productive interaction between the prison and the surrounding community. Without ever stopping to peg the policy type into its proper category, they had devised a completely collaborative, community-oriented project. Nine months previous to their decision about this proposal, the group's major concern appeared to be how managers and inmates unconsciously made life impossible for officers. The group's perception of system relationships and their commitment to changing these relationships changed markedly over the year.

The Attica Uprising

On August 20, 1971, the Enfield Officer Research Team began meeting weekly on Thursdays from 3 p.m. to 5 p.m. The first three meetings were not recorded on tape because there were technical difficulties. The team dealt with procedural matters such as membership, meeting time, and report procedure.

The Attica riot in September, 1971, halted the regular agenda for much of the month for officers and their families across the country suddenly became concerned with the role and status of correctional custodial personnel in the correctional enterprise. On September 28, 1971, Duffee traveled to Connecticut for a special meeting on Attica. The basic goal of that meeting was to analyze the Attica riot as it was and was not relevant to the Enfield Institution. The contrast was emphasized between New York and Connecticut correctional systems and between maximum and minimum security situations. The generation of riots was analyzed in terms of the communication model that had been used during the summer training sessions. The group, with the exception of one officer, reached the consensus that the Attica riot should not dissuade officers and other correctional officials from undertaking development projects such as this one. The Attica riot, in short, was deemed relevant as a manifestation of the dysfunctions in traditional prison organization that had to be replaced with more rational policy and implementation.

An interesting contrast with reaction of the officers to Attica was their reaction 8 months later to a minor uprising very much closer to home. A couple weeks prior to the conclusion of the project the Enfield staff were confronted with two refusals of the inmates to eat. Two days before the second sit down, eight inmates from the maximum security prison attacked the correctional officers on duty at an interprison softball game. The reaction of the officers in the research group at that time was that the offenders were maximum security inmates, not Enfield inmates. They refused to generalize from one group to the other and continued with their present group tasks.

Research Group Work on Institutional Goals

The first major category of activity that the research group undertook was to define Enfield correctional goals from the officer's perspective and to discuss the ideas on training and development that can help to achieve these goals. The group began wrestling with the problems in August by introducing the correctional policy data. In terms of final products, this may not have been their most successful endeavor, but it was perhaps the area of greatest impact on themselves.

From the beginning the group had difficulty deciding on what kind of goals its attention should be focused. The members' discussion seemed to take three major tracks: (1) the goal of producing change in people, (2) the goal of the superintendent or other official definers of the situation, and (3) the constraints built into organizational function by physical arrangements, planners' designations, or kind of inmate incarcerated. They would jump in their discussions of organizational dysfunctions from identifying variables that hindered the reintegration process to second-guessing the superintendent's or commissioner's desires to searching for a "natural path" or line of least resistance for the organization to follow in the unfolding of its activity. In other words, they would frequently shift from a planning and change-oriented focus to an analytical but actionless focus. At some points they sought to understand the organization as an entity directed toward some future goal that they themselves would be instrumental in achieving. At other times, they sought to understand the organization as an entity designed from the beginning for a specific, unalterable purpose which it was their job to discover. Internally, the group shifted in correlation to these approaches to the prison. Alternately, the group felt powerful, resourceful and the initiators of activity, and the men impotent, bewildered, and the followers of other's directives. In many ways, the training conferences for managers, conducted a year earlier demonstrated the same fluctuations on the higher level.

There was, however, a greater and likely a longer lasting decision made about goals than appeared in any overt attempts of the group to influence others. This greater effect was a reflexive one felt by the group itself. While the group spent most of its time considering the correctional goals of the organization as a whole or for all officers in general, the greatest differences were found visible in the group's own behavior. The group completed its project year by writing a proposal that it hoped would be funded by an external source. The draft was written by one officer and an inmate member who joined the group in March. It was a collaborative effort by an officer and an inmate about a project that would be a collaborative effort between correctional staff, inmates, and citizens of the surrounding community.

In smaller ways the same unspoken decision about the group's own goals was visible elsewhere. One officer in one of the last sessions related a story about his personal change. He had started addressing inmates as "Mr." and was surprised both with himself and with the favorable reaction of the inmates. Another officer said that previous to the project if he found an inmate sleeping with his television set on, he would wake the man up with his foot and yell at him to turn the television off. Now he said he would turn the set off himself, turn off the inmate's light, and let him go on sleeping.

Perhaps even more important, the implicitly chosen reintegration goal of the group was visible in the way the members treated each other. A constant theme throughout the fourth quarter of activity was how much each member of the group appreciated knowing the other men in the group. A change in their relationships had taken place that they had not expected. They all found a new respect for correctional officers and for each other's thoughts. As one member of the group said, "I thought all the rest of you were pretty dumb guys until we had an opportunity to hash things out." The new feeling of working as a team is most important to a reintegrative correctional policy. If it is desired that staff and inmates should collaborate on an offender's future, then staff must function as a cohesive and open group. If there are fractionalization and dissension among staff, inmate leaders of the old inmate subculture find partners in some staff members who are willing to undermine the new collaboration.

Research Group Work on Organizational Problems

From its own viewpoint, the research group had most success when dealing with specific organizational problems that were correctable at its own intervention. Some of the problems the group perceived and dealt with were resolved or corrected by the time the project year was over, some were being actively attacked, and some had merely been identified, but all were correctable with limited resources and limited skills. For example, the group initiated the offering of the Red Cross first-aid training course for officers; the first trainee was graduated shortly before the project concluded. The group was also instrumental in having the Correctional Department school system initiate courses in English as a foreign language for Spanish-speaking inmates and in Spanish for correctional officers. The group unsuccessfully tried to arrange longer and more convenient commissary hours, but the group was defeated by a broken payroll machine and the lack of clerks to man the commissary. The group did manage to have channel locks placed on dorm televisions to reduce unauthorized channel switches and the resultant squabbles that kept dorm officers away from other duties.

Perhaps the group's most important contribution involved procedures for receiving inmates back from weekend furlough. Because the number of men on furlough made urinalysis for each returnee out of the question, the Correctional Department had the policy of spot checking individuals at random. Part of this policy was that the randomly selected men would have to spend the time between taking of the urine sample and receipt of test results in administrative segregation. At times this necessitated men being assigned to administrative segregation for 48 hours. The inmates interpreted this procedure as punishment, although the Correctional Department stated it was a precautionary measure to ensure that a surprised inmate would not try to escape between the taking of the urine sample and receipt of positive test results. Both officers and inmates understood that there was some sense in this precaution, once the reason for it was explained. But the research group took the inmates' side that this procedure was unfair to the randomly selected but innocent inmate. The officers won a change in procedure so that a urine sample was only taken when staff suspected an inmate had indulged in drugs during furlough. The inmates seemed satisfied that inmates relegated to administrative segregation were there under suspicion for behavior on return (i.e., mannerisms that demonstrated the influence of drugs) rather than under bad luck of the draw.

The research group did not begin to tackle problems such as the ones above until November. From November to June the number of problems selected and the percentage of those dealt with successfully is nothing short of impressive. The members of the group proved themselves to be effective problem solvers when the problems were of a short-range nature and when all the boundaries of the problem could be fairly well defined. While the problems solved were clearly definable, an outsider should not think that the group did not have very important decisions to make. While there is a difference between dealing with ambivalent or ambiguous situations (such as the definition of correctional goals) and dealing with well-defined situations (such as the impossibility of certain inmates being able to reach the commissary when it was open), decisions have to be made in either case. The group made decisions well and was not afraid to take the inmates' side in controversial issues (i.e., the furlough case).

Under the constraints of functioning for only one year, the group proved much more successful, in its own eyes, on this short-term problem basis than as goal setters or policy makers. This finding is certainly not surprising. About the only training the group received relevant to goals was the project training during the summer. However, it can be safely said that short-term problem solving is what correctional officers are trained for (to the extent that they receive training at all). In any event, it is successful short-term problem solving that is one of the most recognized assets of correctional officers who are highly rated by their superiors. Hence, it may be said that the group was most successful at doing the kind of activity it had been doing as officers all the time.

There are many differences, however, between the problems the group worked with and the way in which they worked and the kinds of problems and the methods available to a single correctional officer during a tour of duty. (1) The group met on a continual basis and had some power and responsibility to see a problem through. An individual officer is usually only a suggestion source whose changes in work assignments and/or shift will reduce the time and interest he has in following a problem through. Furthermore, the individual does not have the resources that the group has to make sure a job gets done. (2) The group was rewarded for its accomplishments by the mutual satisfaction and praise of various group members. This group reinforcement was sometimes a sole reward and sometimes a reward in addition to administrative recognition and praise. There is no doubt, however, that the group members strove to gain that group approval as an end in itself. In contrast, an individual officer has no group approval to seek if he successfully solves an organization problem. In fact, he would likely be seen by his peers as a "brown noser" or "rate buster" and would lose rather than gain respect. In short, the group created a work-oriented climate in which the values were to improve the organization. This climate can be contrasted with the climate felt by the individual officer who is usually under pressure to keep his activity at the status quo. (3) The group shared its resources in problem identification and problem solution and, therefore, was more successful than an individual would probably be if he were given the same task of organizational problem solving. (4) The group attacked more complex and more controversial problems than an individual would likely tackle on his own. While correctional officers are problem solvers, the group was also motivated to be problem seekers. As the individual group members gained confidence by earning the praise and respect of other group members, and as the group earned respect by being successful with its first problems, the group began to attack more controversial and complex problems. The result was that the group generally dealt with problems traditionally relegated to middle managers. Because the individual officer does not have sufficient positive feedback to spur on his problem-solving efforts, he is likely to deal with even shorter-term problems (such as inmate rule infractions), the solutions to which are needed so that he can complete his 8 hours rather than to improve the organization. (5) Because the group dealt with problems usually relegated to middle managers, middle managers were freer to consider more important things (such as goal implementation or policy decisions) that were traditionally left to the highest prison management. This one group did not have that effect, but it seems clear that many such groups effectively operating could free correctional top managers to work on problems that are rarely addressed these days, for example, integration of the agencies in the criminal justice system. (6) If we consider this same group activity in terms of the benefits it gives the correctional officer, the fact that the group process increases the complexity of problems handled has the effects of (a) broadening the officer's perspective on the organization and (b) integrating his job more completely with the overall goals of the organization. At the level where the individual officer normally operates, he does not have sufficient contact with organizational goals and functions to make him appreciate and respond to the daily opportunities to expand his role and have more impact on organizational outcomes.

Research Group Work on Project Evaluation

The last responsibility to the research group was to act as a lay evaluation unit to assess the effectiveness of the other groups that began operating with the research team. The group was to try to evaluate the treatment teams and the discussion groups (or at least the officer leaders of the discussion groups). It was on this assignment that the research group was probably least successful. There were several reasons for this failure: (1) The group felt somewhat unqualified to evaluate other groups who were also struggling with a new venture. (2) There was definitely some group conflict and group competition that may have increased the productivity of any one group but decreased the flow of information and cooperation among groups. (3) In addition to this group rivalry, the treatment teams and discussion leaders were anxious about being evaluated, especially by another group of officers. (4) The confidential nature of *all* the actual meetings of the discussion leaders with other groups and *some* of the meetings of treatment teams with their caseloads necessitated that much of the research evaluation be done from second-hand information anyway. (5) Different ideas existed elsewhere about their responsibilities and mandate. (6) Time pressures for officers who did this work in addition to their shift duties were intense and they had limited resources.

Because of these difficulties facing them, evaluation activity became the least likely task of the three for the research team to undertake at any given time, partly because the team was very frustrated whenever it attempted it and partly because it became the least possible task to undertake. As a result, the research group evaluation of the other groups remained unformalized, unfinalized, and beclouded with complaints of frustrating secretiveness of the other groups. Nevertheless, the research group consensus about the other groups accurately reflected the major inmate and staff complaints about the groups one year after initiation. The major points were that (1) the treatment teams did not always manage to meet, (2) the treatment teams did not have enough authority to make the completion of the contract arranged with each inmate really rewarding (see footnote 22), (3) inmates considered the contract process itself rather inflexible and autocratic, (4) inmates viewed both treatment team members and discussion leaders underqualified for their tasks, (5) inmates participating in discussion groups during the first year were unclear about the kinds of discussion topics to be addressed or the priority of such topics, such as prison operation vs. personal problems. All of these points were raised by inmates and other staff in the final evaluation sessions reported in the next section. At the same time, all staff and inmates recognized that all teams had made significant contributions to changing prison climate and structure.

The research group information seemed to be accurate, but the evaluation process was not carried on in such a way that the other groups could use the criticism to make adjustments in procedure before the year was over. Much of this problem, however, must be attributed to problems external to the group, such as adequacy of group linkages provided in the action design. Such problems bring us to a final evaluation.

EVALUATION OF THE GROUP PROGRAM

Evaluation of the project will be done in two steps. First is an evaluation of the research group as a method for breaking down an officer subculture and building officer acceptance of inmate-oriented correctional policy. Second is an evaluation of the context within which the research group operated. This material is incomplete but sufficient to indicate certain directions in group work with correctional staff. It is particularly relevant as it reflects a change in the organizational environment within which the research group operated and as such represents a change in the conditions about which the research group was proposed as an antidote.

Evaluation of the Research Group

The evaluation of how the research group addressed the specific changes that were set for it has been discussed above. The assessment is certainly relevant to how the group performed in the course of a year, but the evaluation criteria of primary interest here pertain to the performance of this group along the dimension of the program goal rather than any specific goals on which the group chose to concentrate. How did this group function as a technique to make correctional officers internalize the correctional goals that show high concern for inmates? What happened to the correctional officers in the group itself? How did they differ in behavior toward inmates and toward administration at the end of the project compared to the beginning of the project? Could any different procedures have been more effective in directing change in the desired direction?

Because of the small number of people involved, there are no statistical evaluations possible. Because the available questionnaires would have been unreliable for an evaluation of the changes (if any) in the behavior of these seven men, other indices of change were sought. The selection criterion upon these other indices was that they should have been planned in advance rather than discovered at the end of the project, because a post hoc evaluation can be biased by the desire among project personnel for success. Four of these indices, although none of them terribly exact, were planned. They were (1) the voluntary invitation of the group for particular inmates to participate in the group activity; (2) the group's ability to communicate productively with other groups and other parts of the prison; (3) the group's ability to communicate productively with the superintendent; (4) the group's ability to produce the draft of an action proposal and the goals of that proposal.

Voluntary admission of inmates to the team was used because it was thought to demonstrate the officers' openness with inmates on the dimensions of concern to officers most directly related to the officer subculture. In the group sessions the topics ranged from open criticism of the superintendent to open criticism of inmates and included analysis of the performance of correctional officers. In a June, 1971, planning meeting the superintendent and the researcher decided that inmates should be introduced to the group. We decided to introduce the possibility of inmate membership so that the group would know of the opportunity but we decided to leave the decisions to invite and whom to invite completely up to the group.

The possibility for inmate membership arose as the group began seeking a member in October to replace an officer who dropped out because of personal problems. The first candidates included a counselor and a school teacher who had been the group's first guests in their problem-seeking sessions. Duffee acknowledged these choices as possible and suggested that the group also consider one ex-inmate who was employed by the Correctional Department as a prerelease counselor and Alcoholic Treatment Program coordinator. The suggestion was made October 27, 1971, but it was met with little enthusiasm and outright objections from two officers who said they did not want an ex-inmate listening to their conversations. Duffee left the session saying the decision was completely up to the group. The following week the ex-inmate was invited as a "guest" and in the second session in November he was welcomed as a permanent member. From November until his death of a heart attack in March, the ex-inmate was a very vocal and active member of the group. The six remaining officers fully accepted him as one of the group and looked to him for guidance on many topics. He became with the sergeant a second leader. After his death, the group, acting out of complete consensus, invited an inmate to take his place. The inmate was a full member from April until his parole on June 2, 1972. The inmate chosen behaved in the group much as the ex-inmate had. He was just as vocal and just as much a leader. He did much of the drafting of the proposal that the ex-inmate had started.

On the criterion of inmate involvement, the group can be rated a mild success. It is true that the test was somewhat watered down because Steinert and Duffee decided to suggest an ex-inmate first. But it is also true that the group then invited the inmate without even a suggestion and without waiting for anyone's approval. On the other hand, the inmate chosen was the highly educated inmate librarian who had been convicted of a white-collar crime. Nevertheless, the inmate, once a member of the group, took "liberties" during group sessions that were fairly surprising for any inmate. He frequently berated officers for being cynical, not seeing the whole picture, or for being hasty in their judgment.

Although the success on this criterion is definitely qualified by the nature of the choice, it is important that it was a voluntary invitation. It is very possible that the group could have accepted a different kind of inmate if a higher authority had insisted upon it. But pulling rank to force action was contrary to the goals of the project. In summary, the inmate and the ex-inmate behaved as peers in the group—even as leaders—which is behavior that officers in June, 1971, would probably never have accepted.

Communication with other groups was used because reintegrative policy requires team work and collaboration. The goal is to use all resources available from staff or inmates to increase the chances of an inmate's successful reentry to the community. In this regard, the group was somewhat successful. The members proved rather definitely in the number of short-term problems that they solved or helped to solve that they could communicate effectively with other parts of the organization. On two occasions they had seriously hostile reactions to deal with—once involving the commissary and once involving the counselor supervisor who coordinated the teams. In both cases, they dispelled animosity with more diplomatic second efforts.

They were less successful in dealing effectively with the discussion group leaders and the treatment teams. The reasons for this have already been covered. It seems very possible that the project design did not provide for sufficient among-group meetings and adequate among-group coordination. The group coordinator had many other pressing duties as a counselor supervisor, and the groups only met together in June, 1971, for training, and in June, 1972, for evaluation.

Communication with the superintendent was treated separately because of the importance of the officer's relationship with the institutional executive, since the problems they researched were often of immediate concern to the superintendent. Indeed, they often dealt with problems that previously had been handled unilaterally by the superintendent or one of his close subordinates. In addition, the officer–superintendent relationship raises in its ultimate organization form the issues of power and authority.[23]

---

[23] Ultimate when we consider the organization to end with the superintendent. It is possible to consider relationships with the commissioner also if we think of departmental organization.

Approaching the superintendent was a key issue for the research group from the time of the August training conference on policy. At that time, the group began to think about the goals of the institution. As it did so, several officers became concerned that any statement of institutional goals that they might formulate could be countermanded by word of the superintendent. Several officers suggested that they should call the superintendent into the meeting and discuss their conception of institutional goals with him. Several other officers, however, thought that this action was premature. They argued that the group should have a clearer interpretation of its own perception of the operations before it should seek debate with the superintendent.

Although the reasons for the assumption were never entirely clear, the group definitely expected that its first meeting with the superintendent, indeed every meeting, would involve serious disagreements if not a cut and dried veto by him of their plans. When asked for reasons why the group expected this, the group was always ambiguous. The safest but not necessarily the most accurate conclusion is simply that the correctional officers had considerable fear of the superintendent because he was traditionally perceived as inaccessible. In other words, according to the traditional chain of command as they knew it, officers reported to captains instead of to "the boss." A part of this fear may have been reflexive and generated by the new program rather than traditional and generated by the superintendent's superior status. In terms of the program, the officers were uncertain and anxious about their participation in an untried project. They were uncertain how their participation was affecting their status in the prison or how it was related to their role as correctional officers. At the same time, they enjoyed a sensation of elevated status because they were in close and continual contact with university professors, professional training consultants, and the upper echelons of the prison. Lastly, they very strongly desired to do a good job, although they were at times doubtful about their competency as well as the objectives they had taken on. The superintendent's reactions stood as the greatest threat to all their hopes and the most visible manifestation of all their doubts.

In reality, although the group relationship with the superintendent improved remarkably over the course of a year, it never lost a certain edge of apprehension. The group did not formally meet with the superintendent until December 20. Some of the material discussed was fairly well developed by October 27 and ranged from the issue of grooming regulations for officers to the officers' desire to make inmate disciplinary procedures more adversary in nature. Most of this material the group prepared as "ammunition." Duffee and Steinert left totally to the group the task of inviting the superintendent to a meeting, but this task was continually put off. Almost 2 full months went by between the final session on supervisory problems in October and the meeting with the superintendent on December 20. When the meeting did take place, the group did not use the material prepared and instead began a general meeting on research group goals in which the group looked to the superior for guidance. Disappointed with the outcome of the meeting, Steinert suggested at that point that a method be invented to keep him informed on a regular basis of the group's activity. Beginning in early January the group began to keep formal minutes of the meetings in addition to tape recording each session. Copies of the minutes were sent to the superintendent and the counselor supervisor who was coordinating all the new groups.

Over the second half of the project the group communicated regularly with the superintendent in both oral and written forms. The group gradually learned that he had no intentions of flatly refusing to listen to suggestions or veto proposals. The relationship never developed to the extent that it might have had a full-time consultant or change facilitator been present in the institution. It seems that the variable of authority in the prison is so important among staff, as well as between staff and inmates, that changing authority relationships among staff subordinates and their superiors requires the utmost attention. This relationship was *more* difficult for the group to handle than changed relationships with inmates, but inmates are indeed closer to the officers, organizationally and normatively, than upper administration is.

From the superintendent's point of view, the most difficult and trying portion of the relationship was his own apparent inability to instill in the research team the fact that the opening of communication within the institution was meant to include the superintendent. He had an easier time combating the militaristic, hierarchical communication patterns with inmates and on the inmate to officer level than on the level from officers to himself. It appeared to him that the members of the research team were actually in a quandry about choosing whether to accomplish a task or to refrain from ruffling the feathers of the "boss."

He was never sure during the length of the project whether this apparent dilemma was because of an image that he actively projected or because of the fact that the opportunity for input by officers into problem solving and policy matters was so new and unusual that their hesitancy was caused by inexperience and fear of failure. Historically, the Enfield Institution placed correctional officers, as key-turners, in a position of infallibility since all decisions were made above them and they had merely to follow orders. When the time came to parcel out the opportunity to make decisions and delegate responsibility to front-line workers, most employees did not see this change as advantageous to themselves, to the institutional community, or to the inmates. When the team was formed and the superintendent actively began seeking out problems, assistance, and answers, many institutional personnel and inmates thought that the change could only be window dressing for the general, demanding, and inquisitive public and/or the new commissioner of correction. The members of the research team wondered how far out on a limb they could go before they found that they had misread cues and were to be held solely responsible for their own and others' errors.

The superintendent had doubts that such anxieties were ever completely dispelled, but he could see inroads made because of the project. Additionally, he had personal questions to resolve: Should he really relinquish absolute control, and could the institution survive and succeed in face of a possible failure initiated by him? This risk of failure is crucial in an institution in which both many inmates and many staff are going to live and work for extended periods of time and in which their memory of failure could negatively affect other new and "weird" ideas in the future. Hence, the acceptance of risk by both lower and upper staff is crucial to organizational change.

The action proposal written by the group was chosen as a criterion of evaluation because it offered an opportunity to examine how the group functioned on an extended project in which the members had to arrive at a consensus on the one problem in the institution most worthy of extended effort by themselves and others. The proposal also gave the group an additional opportunity to exclude or include inmates in activity planned by staff and in planning activity. Furthermore, the proposal, being a written document, afforded the evaluators a more objective criterion than did criteria two and three.

The grant proposal activity was fairly successful. The officers began consideration of topics in January. For several meetings they were vaguely searching for ways of furthering (and for rewarding) correctional officers. Several members of the group rather actively opposed any proposal that might be primarily beneficial to inmates. The inmates received too much, they said. It was time that extra programs for the advancement of correctional officers were established.

Objections were made to this attitude by one officer, the ex-inmate, and the sergeant. These three suggested that there might be projects that would have beneficial effects for both officers and inmates. After considerable discussion, the other officers agreed to this point and the group finally achieved consensus on a project that would involve both officers and inmates. The project was chosen from three criteria: (1) that it be important to the institution, (2) that it have continuity with officer training already underway, and (3) that it have continuity with the superintendent's plans for the organization as a whole.

The project chosen, the project that the group decided met all these criteria, was the formation of officer–inmate teams to meet with community groups in the surrounding town in order to explore additional avenues of institutional–community cooperation that would aid offender reintegration in the community. The project was to include three major phases:

1. The continuation of internal development activity in the institution to establish officer–inmate teams capable of attacking commonly established goals.
2. Contact and initiation of negotiation with the community about the expansion of the institution's role in the community;
3. Community–institutional activity to achieve a more effective reintegration organization.

Given that outline, one officer and the ex-inmate met on their own time to draft a rough proposal. Following the death of the ex-inmate two weeks later, the officers went forward immediately and invited an inmate to join the group. During the March 2, 1972, meeting the inmate was briefed on the purpose of the group, the kind of activity it engaged in, and the proposal outline. He took on the responsibility of joining the officer in continuing to draft the project.

The project that the group finally decided on was directly related to the trends the superintendent had in mind for the institution, although the group and the superintendent had not consulted each other about the specific project. In addition, the project was basically sound and its implementation appeared to serve the needs of organizational development in the institution for the coming years. Furthermore, as mentioned previously, the proposal content definitely demonstrated a change in the attitude of the group. The group had moved from a desire to use programs to reward correctional officers for previous duty to a project oriented toward democratization of the prison, flattening of the bureaucratic hierarchy, and reintegration of the offender into the community.

Overall Evaluation

The process of organizational redevelopment that relies on the redistribution of work tasks and the reordering of the organizational social structure has had a long and varied history. Emery and Trist reported a tremendous increase in productivity of textile mills that reorganized responsibilities so that teams rather than individuals were the basic work unit.[24] Floyd Mann has used "natural work groups" as a basis for organizational change by collecting data relevant to the operation of each group and its superior and subordinate groups and then having the groups plan ways to reduce the gap between goals and the measured operational achievement.[25] Rensis Likert warns that groups themselves are not a panacea and that there are many cohesive groups with high morale whose goal is to work *against* the organization. Likert is careful to point out that there is a difference between groups who work in an organization but remain informal appendages to the planned structure and groups that *are* the organizational structure.[26]

In correctional work, experimentation with groups has been slow to develop. Hagan and Campbell[27] and Glaser[28] reported a rather successful transition in federal prisons from the use of classification boards for the entire prison population to the use of treatment teams with caseloads of approximately 80 inmates. In addition to the greater concern and time the teams had for inmates, the group approach had the advantage that a greater variety of personnel became familiar with and responsible for the treatment operations in the prisons. In some Pennsylvania institutions this concept has been altered so that each inmate has a unique team whose members' skills are matched to the inmates' diagnosed needs. These teams include a "community sponsor" who is willing to meet with the inmate when he is in prison and aid him later when he is on parole. In addition to the treatment team idea, correctional officers have been used in several states as leaders in inmate discussion groups, and in New Careers and similar projects correctional staff and/or outside professionals and selected inmates have been joined in teams to accomplish special tasks, for example, the study of violence.[29]

[24] F. E. Emery and E. L. Trist, "Socio-Technical Systems," in F. E. Emery (ed.), *Systems Thinking* (Baltimore: Penguin, 1969), pp. 281–296.
[25] Floyd Mann, "Studying and Creating Change."
[26] Likert, *New Patterns of Management.*
[27] Hagan and Campbell, "Team Classification in Federal Institutions."
[28] Daniel Glaser, *The Effectiveness of a Prison and Parole System*, pp. 137–138.
[29] Hans Toch, *Violent Men* and H.E.W., *Experiment in Culture Expansion.*

As far as we know, this minimum security institution in Connecticut is the only prison in the United States that has used a team-building approach as a complete program of organizational redevelopment. The project reported here is just a small portion of that program. It was not, however, an insignificant part of that program. In all the correctional literature that reports redevelopment activities we have not found another group reportedly given so much freedom to roam over the issues of greatest daily importance to an institution as was true of this officer group. Many other groups in other places have been successful, but these groups often involved new ways of handling inmates rather than new ways of organizing the prison as a whole. The most thorough change in organizational structure reported elsewhere is the team treatment programs wherein considerable authority over inmate classification is decentralized. The research group here was much different in that it had no direct power to reorganize any of the prison components, although many of its recommendations were carried out. But more importantly, it is very rare indeed for a subordinate group that includes inmates to be given official recognition and approval as it attempted to question the most central issues in the institution—its goals and operational policy.

APPLICATION TO OTHER CORRECTIONAL SETTINGS

While the front-line correctional officer certainly faces situations unique to his position and enunciates his problems and constraints in a language specific to that situation, there are generalizations to be drawn from this experience that have wider applicability. In many ways, the organizational problems that confront correctional officers may be more similar to those faced by city police than to other correctional staff, and the change techniques that were used in Connecticut with correctional officers have indeed been applied to police departments with varying degrees of success.

However, we should not overlook the findings of this research as it would apply to halfway houses, parole and probation offices, and other correctional organizations. Management in any of these correctional units is frequently confronted today with front-line staff's resistance to changes in organizational policy and structure, even when there may be agreement, on a very general level, between management and front-line staff about the functions of corrections.

In the above case example, we can see that the new organizational policies chosen by management were generated primarily upon their concern for more effective delivery of service to offenders and/or change in offender behavior upon release. The decision tests that management and outside researchers were primarily concerned with meeting as new policy was generated involved community acceptance of the new efforts, economic feasibility of the undertaking and adherence to valid organizational theory. But the decision tests applied to the same policy by the front-line staff involved whether or not the new policy helped them achieve a greater sense of satisfaction from the job, a greater sense of order and clarity in their routine, and freedom from coercion in how they should do their work. On these decision criteria held by lower staff, the new policy failed until greater effort was expended in linking the new policy to these front-line goals and engaging a significant portion of the front-line staff in the job of making that link explicit.

The majority of new thinking about correctional policy and change in management behavior in correctional organizations stresses the need for managers to include lower-level staff in the planning of change and to depend on work groups or teams as the basic organizational unit instead of on the individual employee. Many of these suggested shifts in managerial strategy will necessarily take place whether or not corrections in general continues on a course of reintegration, reverts to restraint, or implements portions of both simultaneously. For example, even if correctional policy widely switches to determinate sentencing, disengages treatment and educational participation from release decisions, and abolishes parole per se, these changes will not be effectively implemented unless managers can involve staff in making the switch a reality. It will be as difficult to change "treatment-oriented" institutions into restraint-oriented ones as it has been to accomplish the opposite.

While it has been and will be difficult for more reasons than are relevant here, certainly one of the major problems has been the relative isolation of the front-line staff from the formulation and elaboration of policy at the upper organizational levels and the attempts by management to implement unilaterally newer policies without interacting with front-line personnel in any significant way. Ironically, managers have even attempted to implement more "democratic" correctional policies in an autocratic manner. This is a good example of how narrowly focused we can become and how rapidly we can tune out discrepancies between our daily actions and what we say we want.

This situation does not suggest that managers are hypocrites, liars, or fools. But it does demonstrate that the normal, traditional patterns of power and authority are so ingrained in American bureaucracy that they are frequently retained even in heroic attempts to over-throw tradition in other aspects of the system. Bradley remarked with surprise that one innovative California community-based pro-gram was scuttled because the program designers included traditional power relationships and role descriptions such as "guard" and "counselor" in a program whose very objectives included doing away with bureaucratic designations and treatment/custody conflict.[30] Duffee, Meyer, and Warner have noted a similar problem in an eastern state in which a widely dispersed halfway house system was administered under the same principles that were used in large and isolated prisons.[31] Gilbert Smith has observed similar problems in probation and parole settings.[32]

Similar problems are likely to have similar solutions. This does not mean, of course, that a program identical to the one used in a prison can be transplanted for use in field and halfway house settings or that the programs will always be implemented by similar cadres of people. It is very interesting, for example, that the kind of collabora-tive change effort described above has also been utilized by judges as well as by management and management consultants. In systems in which management has refused to change the manner in which it relates to the frontline and offenders judicial intervention has initi-ated such change. Moreover, we should not expect such change to be limited to relationships among management, front-line staff, and offenders. New probation and parole concepts prescribe the inclusion of various community groups in the correctional task, and institutions at Vienna, Illinois, and Enfield, Connecticut, among others, have been noted for similar involvement of outsiders in prison activity.[33]

While many of the distinctions in the kind of change effort applica-ble to noninstitutional as opposed to institutional settings will have to await experimentation, some basic differences can be suggested. First, in small halfway houses and similar settings, involving front-line staff in policy decisions may be expected to involve offenders even more directly than is the case in institutions. The distance

[30] Harold Bradley, "Designing for Change: Problems of Planned Change in Corrections," *The Annals of the American Academy of Political and Social Science* (Jan., 1969), 89–99.

[31] David Duffee, Peter B. Meyer, and Barbara Warner, *Offender's Needs, Parole Outcome, and Program Structure in the Bureau of Correction Community Services Division* (Harris-burg, Pa.: Governor's Justice Commission, 1977).

[32] Gilbert Smith, *Social Work and the Sociology of Organizations* (London: Routledge & Kegan Paul, 1970), pp. 94–102.

[33] David Fogel, *We Are the Living Proof* (Cincinnati: Anderson, 1975), pp. 105–107, and Richard Steinert, "Postscript," in Duffee, *Correctional Policy and Prison Organization*, pp. 205–208.

between front-line staff and offenders in such settings is much less, usually, than is true of prisons, and the atmosphere is much more informal. Hence, managers will probably need to seek ways of involving offenders and staff *together* in policy changes. In probation and parole settings, whether agents are deployed in teams or in the casework model, implementation of new policy will involve not only new staff behavior but also new behaviors from external community groups. Hence, a greater sharing of power and the inclusion of greater numbers of people there must mean not only new roles for staff, but also new organizational roles for groups who were previously outside the organization. Such change is likely to be even more threatening to our standard ideas about bureaucracy and organization than have been any recent changes in prisons.

Perhaps in all of these other correctional settings a major distinction (but perhaps not a necessary one) between the new roles for staff in field settings and institutions is that front-line staff in field settings will have to function much more as managers and referral agents than they do now and they will have to leave much more of service provision and "change" work to outside agencies and groups. This is true regardless of whether management selects reintegration or restraint options for correctional policy. Hence, while the change practices used in prison, as reported here, are useful beginnings in thinking about change in other correctional settings, the change in these other units may be more complex. Not only will we have to learn new ways for management and front-line staff to interact, but front-line staff will also have to adopt new attitudes toward outsiders as well as toward offenders.

10

Fundamental Change in Corrections: Is it Really Happening?

(Joseph P. Briggs, David Duffee, and Peter B. Meyer)

In the past decade there has been increasing frustration with the functioning of the traditional correctional system. Consequently, various task forces and other important groups have called for fundamental change. Community mental health centers, community-based correctional centers, and juvenile diversion through youth service bureaus have emerged as replacements for institutional services. The purposes of this chapter are to examine the extent to which these trends signal real change in the system and to identify problems confronting management during implementation of change.

In the attempt to analyze change in the correctional system, it is important to take into account the fact that organizational change of open systems often leads to consequences that were not originally intended.[1] Since the main responsibility for change lies with traditionally unchanging systems (prisons, juvenile courts), an immediate difficulty must be faced: the administrators' inability to perceive the institutional role within an open system framework. In these isolationist-type systems, unexpected outcomes appear even more probable as each system struggles to understand and adapt to its turbulent environment. Within such an operational context, one must be skeptical about proposals to implement fundamental change. Despite the fact that massive subsystem change involves great risk and uncertainty, very little, if any, attention has been devoted to answering some very basic questions about the conceptualization and implementation of fundamental change. Some key questions that need to be answered are: How much and in what direction has each system changed? Have we really achieved fundamental change? What would we consider to be a fundamental change? What criteria could be used to describe and compare fundamental change?

Not only do we lack empirical knowledge about this subject, we are also hard pressed to conceptualize the problems of fundamental change. Some attention has been devoted to the study of "large" or fundamental *decisions*.[2] But little time has been dedicated to the consequences of such decisions. This is why many authors have recently stated that studies of implementation are so important yet are also so rare or nonexistent.[3] One author expressed his surprise at the lack of literature (referring to divorce rates, anti-poverty programs, etc.) concerning things that are initially agreed upon but do not work out the way they were expected to when implemented.[4]

What are the impediments that block successful implementation? What are some common conditions that influence many different fundamental changes? What stage of change is most crucial toward achieving successful implementation? These and other questions, long ignored by social scientists, are the main focus of this chapter. An effort will also be made to avoid the traditional "tunnel vision" or intradisciplinary approach. Instead of analyzing a program's problems from a narrow lens angle, the emphasis here will be on comparing the problems of several programs (or general movements) from various perspectives.

More specifically, this endeavor will analyze and compare the

[1] Daniel Katz and Robert L. Kahn, *The Social Psychology of Organizations* (New York: Wiley, 1966); Paul Lerman, *Community Treatment and Social Control* (Chicago: University of Chicago Press, 1975).

[2] David Braybrooke and Charles Lindblom, *A Strategy of Decision* (New York: Free Press, 1963).

[3] Jeffrey Pressman and Aaron Wildavsky, *Implementation* (Berkeley: University of California Press, 1973).

[4] Seymour Sarason, *The Creation of Settings* (San Francisco: Jossey-Bass, 1972).

juvenile justice diversion movement and the correctional deinstitutionalization movement. These two movements will supply the social problem substance for the application of two general conceptual developments:

1. The development of specific criteria to aid in conceptualizing and judging whether or not (or the degree to which) a movement deserves to be called a fundamental one.
2. The development of fundamental change stages and the potential obstacles encountered within each stage of the fundamental change process and within key areas of organizational and interorganizational relations.

FOUR CRITERIA FOR FUNDAMENTAL CHANGE

A. A fundamental change must contain a shift from one ideology to another ideology.

Perhaps it is most appropriate when searching for criteria for fundamental change that the first dimension lie in the nature and definition of the problem. The definition of a problem logically depends on one's philosophy about the source of that problem. A change in the definition of a problem makes a huge difference in societal reaction and sanction of behavior. It will make a difference in specific theoretical justifications and programmatic responses. For instance, if the source of the problem is perceived as lying in the individual (various psychological and some sociopsychological theories), then the solution of the problem might be direct services (counseling, group therapy, etc.). If the source of the problem is perceived to rest in the organizational and institutional structure (differential opportunity structures, Marxian analysis, etc.), then the solution of the problem might be indirect services (manpower projects, training, negative income tax programs, etc.). If the source of the problem is the way society labels and processes people (labeling theory), then the solution might be the redefinition of criminal (and deviant) acts (decriminalization legislation, changing the social climate in many institutions that perpetuate the labeling process).

If public policies (or the beliefs of a majority of key influential leaders) shift dramatically from any one of these ideologies to another, then the first conditions for fundamental change will be fulfilled. It will be shown later that both diversion and deinstitutionalization movements have been affected by an ideological shift from an individual orientation to either a community focus, or labeling focus, or some combination of both orientations.

B. A fundamental change must contain a dramatic shift in operations and programming that reflects the ideological shift.

A fundamental change cannot exist in a shift in philosophy alone; it must be demonstrated or implemented. This is a major fundamental change dimension and is often the key stumbling block. It is a very difficult process to change traditional agencies and bureaucracies in any dramatic way. It will be shown later that diversion and deinstitutionalization have included paradigmatic or ideological shifts. But the outcome of this change in philosophy has not brought about any fundamental change because it was not implemented in the same spirit.

C. A fundamental change must contain a dramatic shift in the role of production workers.

Production workers can be defined as those people who work on things or work with clients to produce or achieve organizational outputs (and goals). This definition applies to anyone affected by a change in programming that springs from a basic change in ideology. Their roles are likely to change dramatically because the source of the problem has been redefined through a change in organizational goals and operations. Industrial workers might switch from routine assembly-line work to work in which they essentially start and finish the product. Professional service providers might change their basic emphasis from direct to indirect preventive/advocate types of service delivery. Very often workers already familiar with programmatic changes will have to be hired in place of traditional workers who are intensely resistant to change. When resistant workers hold key positions and are influential in administrative matters, fundamental change becomes highly contested and is rarely fully achieved. Such leaders have become instrumental in slowing down and even diverting the direction of fundamental change in the areas of diversion and deinstitutionalization.

D. A final important dimension to fundamental change is that in order to implement the change, the best possible means will be the most acceptable administrative procedure (and it will be that which is closest to achieving the ideological objectives).

The question of *jurisdictional rights* will not be limited to traditional delivery systems, but rather to any variety of alternative patterns and authorities. For instance, the social control function of communities might be better achieved outside some fixed boundary of the justice system. Closing down prisons and moving into alternative community-based correctional centers, all under the authority or financial support of a justice system espousing a traditional ideology, are highly unlikely to achieve fundamental change. However, if, for instance, community services, preventive care, and restitutional funds for victims were provided, then the justice system could keep jurisdictional control and achieve fundamental value changes. The main idea is that it is not necessary for traditional service agencies to maintain jurisdictional rights. In fact, it is sometimes detrimental to fundamental change. Diversion and deinstitutionalization may simply be extensions of an old ideology and expansions of boundary and jurisdiction with a new public image (under organizational decentralization).

Having set forth the four basic criteria for fundamental change, this framework can now be applied in a brief analysis and comparison of diversion and deinstitutionalization.

THE APPLICATION OF FUNDAMENTAL CHANGE CRITERIA

Perhaps the single most important factor in raising doubts about diversion as fundamental change is to see its relationship to the Child Saving movement which led to the establishment of the Illinois Juvenile Court in 1899. Both movements seem to have had similar philosophical changes. The original objectives of the juvenile court were not achieved, and deinstitutionalization is also unlikely to achieve its operational goals. Like the juvenile court, it is doubtful that diversion through Youth Service Bureaus will be an effective nonjudicial social service approach. Since its implementation is unlikely to achieve its ideological objectives (focus on the needs of youth rather than on the offense), then it cannot be considered a fundamental change according to our definition. As one of the fundamental change dimensions, *jurisdiction* can be focused on as the keystone for success or failure of diversion. Diversion away from the traditional justice system must be voluntary and devoid of stigmatization. For this to be achieved, diversion should somehow take place outside the jurisdiction of the justice system. It must be pointed out that the definition of diversion within the jurisdiction of the traditional justice system, however, would most likely become coercive in character and lead to less due process rights, greater encapsulation of youth, and probably less fulfillment of individual needs.[5]

Deinstitutionalization in corrections, at least its main thrust,

[5] Thomas Blumberg, "Diversion: A Strategy of Family Control in the Juvenile Court Process" (Florida State University School of Criminology, 1975) and especially Andrew Scull, *Decarceration* (Englewood Cliffs, N.J.: Prentice-Hall, 1977).

centers on the output of community correctional centers, special probation and parole programs, and other means of handling offenders *in lieu* of incarceration. These alternatives can provide a convenient focus for deinstitutionalization along the four dimensions of fundamental change.

Like the Youth Service Bureaus, the call for community programs was an ideological shift at the outset. Both movements developed mainly out of frustration and the failure of traditional clinically oriented activities within an institutional context. Some community programs, which provide indirect rather than direct services, have made larger ideological shifts than other programs. However, the methodology for achieving change has been unclear. The role of the direct service provider (psychologist, psychiatrist, counselor) has not been delineated or distinguished from the same roles in institutions. Consequently, the battle between the traditional service providers and more recent community organizers is being won by traditional service providers.[6] This more entrenched group, as Bloom notes, "rarely undertook genuinely innovative programs and rarely documented the effectiveness of their services."[7] In the mental health area, the lack of accountability and competing demands for federal funds have led to a vast drop in federal support. Bloom estimates that only about 25 percent of the community mental health centers originally called for will be established by 1980.[8] Delaying the growth of this movement, however, may be for the better. Sarason emphasizes that one of the unanticipated consequences of community centers is that they tend to vastly increase the readmission rate to state hospitals. He states:

> There are fewer patients in the state hospitals, their stay is shorter, but their number of stays has increased. The community mental health center virtually guarantees the continued existence of the state hospital even though its initial rationale was opposed to that of the state hospital! It could hardly have been otherwise because these centers were conceived within the same traditions of professional practice and theory—the same nomenclature, administrative hierarchical structure, professional preciousness, and professional responsibility—that are the basis for the state hospitals.[9]

Similar problems have occurred in at least some community correctional programs. Lerman's incisive analysis of the highly regarded California Community Treatment Program demonstrated that the youths on intensive probation in lieu of incarceration

[6] Paul Lerman, *Community Treatment and Social Control*, pp. 1–10.
[7] Bernard C. Bloom, *Community Mental Health: A Historical and Critical Analysis* (Montclair, N.J.: General Learning Press, 1973).
[8] Ibid.
[9] Sarason, *The Creation of Settings*, p. 188, and see Rudolph Moos, *Evaluating Correctional and Community Settings* (New York: Wiley, 1975), pp. 248–251.

actually committed more offenses than youths processed through the traditional system.[10] In Minnesota the state planning agency has placed a moratorium on all halfway house programs after their evaluation demonstrated no benefits from the new program.[11] Martinson's survey of correctional program evaluations raises similar doubts about the efficacy of the new programs, although he suggests that they may be *equally* effective and probably cheaper, if nothing else.[12] Lerman, on the other hand, raises doubts about cost savings as well.[13]

Concerning the four-dimensional fundamental change framework, only the dimension of ideology may have changed. The programmatic implementation, professional personnel, and jurisdictional rights have not changed.[14] Jurisdiction, again, does not necessarily need to change, but its change often facilitates fundamental change. The power of traditional service providers is probably the biggest impediment to change.

In addition, the philosophical change reflected in community correctional programs may not be as great as it first sounds. The emphasis is still direct service to an offender who needs change. there is an underlying body of support, however, for massive organizational and institutional change in communities, with particular emphasis on prevention. Also, as the *Report of the Task Force in Corrections* points out, the movement away from traditional professional service providers (psychologists, psychiatrists, counselors, etc.) is manifested by an emphasis on the utilization of community services (housing, welfare, employment, etc.) and the responsibility of involved citizens (as educator, reformer, policy maker, and direct service provider).[15]

---

[10] Lerman, *Community Treatment and Social Control.*

[11] Evaluation Unit of the Governor's Commission on Crime Prevention's Control, *Residential Community Correction Programs in Minnesota* (St. Paul, 1970).

[12] Robert Martinson, "What Works? Questions and Answers About Prison Reform," *The Public Interest* (Spring 1974), 22–54.

[13] Lerman, *Community Treatment and Social Control.*

[14] One may argue that the jurisdictional rights have changed in some programs. For example, in Massachusetts the state contracts to private agencies for the direct supervision of many youth in the new community programs established by Jerome Miller. However, it can still be argued that the jurisdiction for these programs still remains with the same state bureaucracies, since they pay the contract service providers, and it is only through the legal jurisdiction of the state over delinquent youth or adult criminals that service is provided in the first place. According to Scull, *Decarceration*, and others, the essential similarity between the new and old programs is that both deal with the technologies of social control rather than change in any fundamental way the power and resource distribution between the treaters, the state, and the "client." See also Alvin Gouldner, "The Sociologist as Partisan: Sociology and the Welfare State," *American Sociologist* (May 1968), 103–116.

[15] National Advisory Commission on Criminal Justice Standards and Goals, *Corrections* (Washington, D.C.: Government Printing Office, 1973).

As an improvement over prison, most administrators and academicians would agree that community programs are the wave of the future. However, certain key issues on the question of fundamental change remain. To what extent should correctional agencies be involved with this movement? Jurisdiction remains unresolved and often unaddressed. The role of professional service providers or the training of new providers, as well as the issue of what determines appropriate programmatic implementation, have been neglected. Consensus on these dimensions of fundamental change does not exist. And as more and more community programs become operationalized without a strong ideological and programmatic distinction from prisons, then fundamental change is not likely to be achieved.

To this point, we have specified the essential fundamental change criteria and have briefly analyzed why diversion and both deinstitutionalization movements do not fulfill these criteria and should not be considered fundamental change.

Now attention can be turned to the development of fundamental change stages and potential obstacles encountered within each stage of the fundamental change process. This will better enable us to analyze key barriers to the implementation of diversion and deinstitutionalization movements. It will also aid in the conceptualization of roadblocks to organizational innovations in general.

STAGES OF AND OBSTACLES
TO FUNDAMENTAL CHANGE

The basic stages in a change process can be thought of as unfreezing, changing, and refreezing the behavior of human systems.[16] Similarly, organizational innovation can be thought to consist of the following stages: initiation, implementation, incorporation, and effects.[17] For our purposes, it is also important to analyze obstacles from the *antecedent conditions* prior to organizational innovation. It should be pointed out that the incorporation and effects stages of diversion and deinstitutionalization movements have already been addressed and their failure to become fundamental changes has been demonstrated. In our analysis, this stage need not be included except to mention that the effects of both movements need continued evaluation, analysis, and guidance for their redirection. As it stands now, diversion through Youth Service Bureaus is likely to

[16] Kurt Lewin, "Group Decision and Social Change," in Macoby et al. (eds.) *Readings in Social Psychology* (New York: Holt, Rinehart and Winston, 1958).
[17] Neal Gross, Joseph Giacquinta, M. Bernstein, *Implementing Organizational Innovations, A Sociological Analysis of Planned Educational Change* (New York: Basic Books, 1971).

continue to lead to encapsulation and abuses of individual rights. It also seems that both deinstitutionalization movements will only lead to an expansion of boundaries with changing *physical* structures but not changing *social* structures.

Presenting the stages of change in their most logical order is not meant to imply that all change efforts follow this smooth pattern. Many plans are never implemented, and much implementation takes place without planning.[18] However, it is convenient and helpful to use a framework here in order to conceptualize and to analyze systematically some of the obstacles in each stage. The objective is to recognize and categorize problems similar to various movements so that (1) solutions can be found, (2) better planning and implementation can take place, and (3) communication can open up between various service sectors with the better understanding that they seek to resolve common problems.

Stage One: Antecedent Conditions

Ignorance of historical conditions produces naive assumptions and a general inability to think critically about basic issues.[19] Yet it is not uncommon for many large-scale planned change studies to ignore historical influences. A review of the literature on *successful* implementation of organizational innovations shows a generally positive association with the variables of external pressures and internal tension,[20] a previous atmosphere of change,[21] and an outside expert with a positive image.[22] These variables apply to the deinstitutionalization and diversion movements.

For both movements, there appears to be a high level of external pressure and internal tension. In corrections, the external pressure comes from many sources. Presidential reports, evaluation research, civil and individual rights movements, etc., have generally increased the system's level of anxiety, its search for relief, and its susceptibility to change. Internal pressure mainly comes from inmates constantly affected by the destructive institutionalization and mortification process of total institutions.[23]

---

[18] Aaron Wildavsky, "If Planning is Everything, Maybe It's Nothing," *Policy Sciences* (June 1973), pp. 127–55.

[19] Stephan Thernstrom, " 'Yankee City' Revisited: The Perils of Historical Naivete," in M. Aiken and P. Mott, *The Structure of Community Power* (New York: Random House, 1970).

[20] Larry E. Greiner, "Antecedents of Planned Organizational Change," *Journal of Applied Behavioral Science* (Jan./Feb./March 1967), pp. 51–86.

[21] T. B. Burns and G. M. Stalker, *The Management of Innovation* (London: Tavistock Publications, 1961).

[22] C. I. Hovland and W. Weiss, "The Influence of Source Credibility on Communication Effectiveness," *Public Opinion Quarterly* 1951

[23] Erving Goffman, *Asylums* (New York: Anchor Books, 1961).

Similarly, external and internal pressures for juvenile diversion have been influenced by the increased concern about the harmful effects of labeling, the high cost and ineffectiveness of institutionalization, the increased rights of juveniles, and discrimination within the juvenile court.[24] (Wealthier clients are referred to private social services or have the advantage of private lawyers.) Some external and internal obstacles to change are: (1) society probably tends to resist innovative strategies which call for an increase in local community tolerance and responsibility for deviants; (2) fundamental change of one organization is often resisted by another organization because of domain consensus problems such as the fear of competition;[25] and (3) professional personnel and staff fear that any organizational innovation or fundamental change will cause a major overhaul of the system and bring psychological distress and potential loss of jobs.

Most criminal and juvenile organizations have a very low level of innovation. Correctional organizations, particularly, have traditionally closed themselves off in order to defend themselves from public criticism. Consequently, their staff have not been asked to make frequent changes in their work habits and are less likely to be capable of implementing innovative changes. Similarly, it would seem logical that juvenile court judges, who are often elected or appointed for long terms on the bench, are particularly threatened by deinstitutionalization and diversion-type changes. Other actors who are usually connected with and threatened (at least, politically) by these movements are local school board members, county commissioners, the child welfare director, the chief probation officer, the detention home director, and police department officials. All parties effectively resist change and produce a prevailing status-quo atmosphere in the juvenile courts.

Another obstacle to change having a past influence on these systems is the neglect or incapability to use a dynamic open systems model for analyses. Previous change efforts in the criminal justice, juvenile justice, and other similar fields have used closed system analysis and many staff are aware that an overall change can result in a more negative state of affairs for all parties' purposes. It has been pointed out that such interventions stemming from a closed system analysis in a complex environment become no better than intuition and result in many unanticipated consequences.[26]

[24] N. Klapmuts, *Diversion from the Justice System* (Hackensack, N.J.: National Council on Crime and Delinquency, 1974).
[25] M. Zax and E. L. Cowen, "Early Identification and Prevention of Emotional Disturbance in a Public School," in E. L. Cowen, E. A. Gardner, M. Zax (eds.), *Emergent Approaches to Mental Health Problems* (New York: Appleton Century Crofts, 1967).
[26] J. W. Forrester, *World Dynamics* (Cambridge, Mass.: Wright Allen Press, 1971).

The final antecedent-to-change variable advances the notion that a change agent with a positive image is most likely to be successful in obtaining change. Although it is difficult to determine how often corrections and juvenile courts have sought to obtain leaders who have the prestige and expertise, the answer is probably not very often. Certainly Pennsylvania's Governor Shapp has brought in Jerome Miller[27] to improve the chances of deinstitutionalization and diversion movements. Whether this has increased support or consolidated resistance is debated, but both outcomes seem likely. Resistance to Miller's mission in Illinois was sufficiently strong that the legislature did not confirm his appointment by the governor.[28]

On the whole external pressure and internal tensions are the strongest antecedent influences for change. The weakest forces for change are its lack of a previous atmosphere for change and its inability to seek and/or find experts who have a positive image.

Stage Two: Initiation of Change

Organizational change literature predominantly supports human relations training (group dynamics, sensitivity, or T-groups) in order to decrease resistance, develop a commitment to change, and improve communications and problem-solving skills.[29] Although such training is potentially helpful, it is also likely to be ignored shortly after trainees return to their jobs. Often it serves only to frustrate further the "hopeful" people at the lower ranks of the organization if blockage of communication channels continue. Indeed, if change agents are successful in initially correcting injustices, revamping service delivery patterns, and redistributing power, then perhaps one of the obstacles to implementation is that, at this latter stage, the change agent often does not participate.[30]

[27] Andrew Rutherford has documented Miller's role; see Andrew Rutherford, "The Dissolution of Training Schools in Massachusetts," Academy for the Study of Contemporary Problems: Paper presented at the Battell Institute, Seattle 1973. R. Richard Ritti, Daniel Katkin, and Bruce Bullington are presently analyzing Miller's role in Pennsylvania.

[28] Similar resistance was encountered by Larry Barker who was selected by Allyn Srelaff to lead the adult community program in the Pennsylvania Bureau of Correction. Evidently the elements that make such a figure positive to some groups guarantee the opposite by other groups. See David Duffee, Kevin Wright, and Thomas Maher, *The Evaluation of Community Treatment Services in the Pennsylvania Bureau of Correction: Final Evaluation Report* (Harrisburg, Pa.: Governor's Justice Commission, January, 1975).

[29] Chris Argyris, *Interpersonal Competence and Organizational Effectiveness* (Homewood, Ill.: Dorsey, 1962); Kenneth D. Benne and Max Birnbaum, "Change Does Not Have To be Haphazard," *School Review* (Autumn 1960), pp. 283–93; Kurt Lewin, "Frontiers in Group Dynamics," *Human Relations* (June 1947), pp. 5–41; Katz and Kahn, *The Social Psychology of Organizations*.

[30] W. Bennis, "Theory and Method in Applying Behavioral Science to Planned Organizational Change," *The Journal of Applied Behavioral Science* (Oct./Nov./Dec. 1965), pp. 337–60; and George W. Fairweather, David H. Sanders, and Louis G. Tornatzkv, *Creating Change in Mental Health Organizations* (New York: Pergamon, 1974).

Outside change agents with expert knowledge are thought to be more competent to stimulate change than are members of the target organization. In general, although there have been scattered instances in which outside change agents and sensitivity training have reportedly been effective in increasing staff participation, morale, fulfillment of need, and commitment to change, a review of the literature suggests no systemic use of such approaches in either the deinstitutionalization or diversion movements.

Stage Three: Implementation of Change

The major explanation found in the literature on the implementation of organizational innovations is that success or failure depends on the ability of management or a change agent to overcome members' initial resistance to change.[31] And the best method to unfreeze resistance is based on a number of assumptions (not empirically proven) contained in the power-equalization concept.[32] It basically assumes that resistant personnel must help formulate the innovation in order for these personnel to be committed to its implementation.

The main point that needs to be raised is not so much the shortcomings of this method as much as it is the fear that the enthusiasm it generates masks other more basic problems of implementation. In addition to overcoming initial resistance to change, we also need to pay attention to other conditions that are critical to successful implementation.

Gross suggests that

1. Nonresistant members may face obstacles to implentation;
2. Management must help staff overcome these obstacles;
3. Obstacles will frustrate attempts to implement and will increase resistance.[33]

In each case, the obstacles concern clarity of role, competence to implement, adequacy of resources, and organizational compatibility with the innovation. An illustration of the relationship of these obstacles to our innovative movements when members are not originally opposed to change can be shown (see Table 10.1).

The table shows that role requirements, skills, resources, and organizational arrangements were unclear and inadequate from the

[31] Warren G. Bennis, *Changing Organizations* (New York: McGraw-Hill, 1966) and Gross, Giacquinta, and Bernstein, *Implementing Organizational Innovations.*
[32] Harold J. Leavitt, "Applied Organizational Change in Industry: Structural, Technological and Humanistic Approaches," in J. G. March (ed.), *Handbook of Organizations* (Chicago: Rand McNally, 1965).
[33] Gross, Giacquinta, and Bernstein, *Implementing Organizational Innovations.*

Table 10.1 Implementation of Innovative Movements

Members not Opposed to Change Encounter Obstacles	Adult Deinstitutionalization	Juvenile Diversion
Degree of clarity about new role model	Programs are unclear	Concept is unclear
Possession of skills and knowledge to implement	Low; knowledge of community and determination of risk to community is inadequate	Low; interorganizational relations are a key problem
Availability of required materials and equipment	Low; physical facilities and services are inadequate	Alternative pro-programs for youth are still developing
Compatibility of organizational arrangements with the innovation	Low; leads to ineffectiveness resulting from the lack of community relations and the intensity of stigma	Low; leads to coercion and abuse of due process rights

start of each movement. Management and feedback mechanisms can be said to be ineffective. And as each of these problems continues to go unresolved, resistance to innovation increases. Most significantly, it seems that these obstacles intensify the constraints on the more progressive developments of each movement. Programs such as out-residency or extended furlough in corrections and diversion programs *outside* the jurisdiction of the justice system incur much stress and fear of extinction.

Before concluding, a final distinction needs to be made. The *interplay* of unclear roles, inadequate training, resources, and organizational arrangements can better be conceptualized in a short discussion of (1) organizational and (2) interorganizational barriers to implementation.

Organizational literature documents the problems of implementing innovative changes within bureaucracies. Organizational survival and expansion, rather than concern for individual needs, are typical dilemmas of even small human service agencies. This notion is intensified for large-scale justice organizations that usually operate with an overload of cases, conflicting goals, and inadequate resources. Such organizations are generally forced to categorize routinely and to process hastily youth in order to maintain organizational control. With the inclusion of the innovative diversion program, the court's control mechanisms are often adjusted to the court's own advantage and to the disadvantage of both justice and the individual needs of youth. Thomas Blumberg studied this control adjustment process and concluded:

> The diversion programs influenced the administering of control in two ways: First, the programs initiated a displacement process whereby youth formerly viewed as suitable for a previous form of control are judged within a less constrained framework of control alternatives, suitable for diversion. This displacement was evidenced by the marked decrease in 1972 youth arrests, probation referrals, and juvenile court petitions which provided youthful clients for the diversion programs. Second, new clients previously not considered for control are now judged suitable for diversion. This was demonstrated by the indirect referrals of siblings as well as parents into diversion's Family Intervention programs. Together these findings tentatively indicate that diversion's goal of limiting the scope and jurisdiction of the juvenile court has not been achieved. Instead, diversion appears to have accelerated the scope and jurisdiction of the juvenile court system and the proportions of population under its control.[34]

A similar arrangement takes place in the deinstitutionalization movement. Corrections organizations make a meager attempt to change their ideology and programmatic strategy as they move into the community. At the same time, institutional populations seemingly continue to expand. Little real change is made on either front.

On the interorganizational level, successful deinstitutionalization and diversion, even when administered by the justice system, are largely dependent on the cooperation of community social service agencies. Mandell has delineated a number of barriers to criminal justice–social service agency cooperation that can be applied to diversion: (1) Stigma of the justice system clients is feared to be contagious. This notion, then, impedes the performance of their service function. (2) Most human service agencies with a shortage of money and work force prefer to concentrate on clients who "can be helped." Juveniles and adult offenders usually are not thought to fall into this category. This compels the courts and correctional agencies to develop their own programs or to become self-sufficient. (3) Judges or other public officials (police, probation officers) are expected to make decisions about complex educational, psychological, and employment issues. Then, without training, they are to refer to agencies with which they may have poor communication. (4) The feedback from the police, media, and community in general is negative and discouraging. The courts resent public criticism and negative research evaluation, and they generally react defensively.

---

[34] Blumberg, "Diversion: A Strategy of Family Control in the Juvenile Court Process."

This, of course, only compounds the problem of interagency co-operation.[35]

The conceptual framework of fundamental change is shown to be helpful in the analysis of complex organizational change movements such as the implementation of deinstitutionalization and diversion. It is pointed out that although these change movements were originally intended to be fundamentally different from traditional operations, the implementation of such progressive change has been greatly impeded. It is suggested that we must recognize the deviation from the original planned change in terms of criteria, stages, and obstacles to fundamental change. It is hoped that this framework will enable the identification of problems within a conceptual context, whereby we can begin to overcome roadblocks in the overall fundamental change process.

ALTERNATIVE EXPLANATION OF PROGRAM CHANGE

If the diversion and deinstitutionalization movements do not signal fundamental changes in the way that youthful or adult offenders are handled, then what is going on? Even if the change is not a harbinger of significant shifts in social structure or in the basic social reactions to deviance, it is certain that massive alterations in the structure of organizations and the provision of services are taking place. Even if basic social change is absent in these movements, managers of existing and emergent social agencies for handling adults and juveniles are being involved in both initiating and reacting to change on a scale that *they* perceive as challenging, threatening, and at times radical.

In an effort to examine these remaining questions, we would like to examine briefly two competing ideological stances toward these movements and then move to a third explanation, one that focuses on the *organizations* that are undergoing change. It is our feeling that it is within this third perspective of organizational analysis that we can gain a firmer and more accurate understanding of the changes that we are experiencing in corrections today. It would seem to us that the basic social control strategies have remained the same but that some organizations are losing public confidence and others are gaining more, so that the root explanation of change lies not in *what* is being accomplished, but rather in *who* will accomplish it. Stated in

[35] Wallace Mandell, "Making Corrections a Community Agency," in Gary Perlstein and Thomas Phelps (eds.), *Community Alternatives to Prison* (Santa Monica: Goodyear, 1975).

other terms, some organizational managers in the correctional area have been more successful than others in obtaining for their organizations a greater share of the public resources (from basic confidence to financial and personnel) that enable them to accomplish their tasks.

HUMANE CORRECTIONS OR LOW-COST SOCIAL CONTROL?

The rapidly growing network of community corrections programs offered as alternatives to incarceration is an area in which useful questions may be raised about the changing scope of the criminal sanction and the nature of social control. The debate over community corrections has not been about *facts* so much as it has been over interpretation of the social and political significance embodied in those facts. To venture a simplified version of a multidimensional argument, we have the concern on one hand for both the supposed greater humaneness and the greater potential effectiveness of community correction (at least as compared to institutional supervision). On the other hand, we find the claim that deinstitutionalization merely provides a more subtle form of social control by which power elites make their dominance less obvious and at the same time manage to reduce the economic costs of supervision.

Data on a variety of programs and efforts at promoting community corrections and community delivery of services to correctional clients are readily available. We have chosen not to pursue quantitative analysis of these data; instead, we have chosen to draw on the information available to us for purposes of review of the issues which must be raised before such analysis is conducted. In doing so, we will be drawing on data from two studies of community corrections efforts: a completed evaluation of one state's development of a community corrections system and partial data and findings from a national study of nonjustice system providers of services to corrections clients in community settings.[36]

Nicholas Kittrie suggests that a major subtrend within the growth of the welfare state is the "divestment of the criminal justice system."[37] He observes that the responsibility for both large clusters of social problems and large groups of people perceived as problems is being transferred to other agencies. One of his concerns with this trend is

[36] David Duffee, Peter B. Meyer, Thomas Maher, and Kevin Wright, *Products, Issues and Problems in a Community-Placed Correctional System* (Harrisburg: Governor's Justice Commission, Nov. 30, 1976; update report, Community Services Evaluation Df-76-E-9D-9-740); and materials gathered by Meyer while working under grant 75 NI-99-0118 from the National Institute of Law Enforcement and Criminal Justice.
[37] Nicholas Kittrie, *The Right to Be Different* (Baltimore: Penguin, 1973).

that the due process safeguards guaranteed (even if poorly implemented) in the criminal process are not even guaranteed in the more
generalized "social welfare system" because procedural rights are not
deemed applicable to persons being "helped" rather than "punished."

Concentrating on the criminal process, rather than on its emerging
alternatives, Herbert Packer suggested that there were limits to the
criminal sanction.[38] Packer argued that the scope of the criminal
sanction should be narrowed to objectives it could feasibly accomplish. Van den Haag's recent justification for retribution and deterrence as the feasible objectives of the penal system is very similar.[39]
While his book has been roundly criticized by radicals, many of
van den Haag's arguments essentially support the radical interpretation
of the criminal justice functions. Van den Haag admits that a system
of penal justice can only protect or maintain the predominant system
of distributive justice. In other words, the criminal sanction is
effective only for the control of "marginal criminality" in a stable
social system.[40] To the extent that criminal behavior is a consequence
of an awareness and resentment by certain groups about discrimination in distributive justice, then sweeping changes in the distribution
of social resources are required rather than modifications in any
system of penal sanctions. David Fogel has advanced a "justice model
of corrections" aimed at the just administration of correctional
organization.[41] The justice model includes the abolition of coerced
participation by offenders in treatment programs and a return to flat
terms matched to the severity of the offense.

While Packer, van den Haag, and Fogel, on the one hand, and
Kittrie, on the other, are observing the same trends in the different
processing of American citizens, their policy recommendations and
evaluative assumptions differ considerably. The three analysts who
concentrate on the *internal* administration of the criminal justice
system as it stands argue for a shrinking of its claimed goals, the
scope of human behavior with which it should be concerned, and the
rational restructuring of its remaining responsibilities. All three say,
albeit in very different ways, that the system can be fairer to the
convicted offender (and provide more valuable output to the social
system) if it tackles the culturally unpopular mission of retribution
in an evenhanded manner rather than trust either our competency
or motivations toward "improvement" in the person or condition of

[38] Herbert Packer, *The Limits of the Criminal Sanction* (Stanford: Stanford University Press, 1968).
[39] Ernest van den Haag, *Punishing Criminals* (New York: Basic Books, 1975).
[40] Ibid., pp. 5–15.
[41] David Fogel, . . . *We are the Living Proof* . . . (Cincinnati: Anderson, 1975).

the offender. It is perhaps not too farfetched to suggest that they would provide the criminal process with something akin to the ambivalent prestige provided the person of the ancient, hooded executioner—respect for efficient dispatch in a loathed but necessary set of skills. Ironically, all three apparently display trust in the broader set of social institutions to which their reforms of the criminal process will return many sorts of "welfare" activity. This trust is ironic because it either dispenses competence by fiat to other bureaucracies suffering from problems paralleling those of corrections or it assumes that these other structures are more voluntary or less social control-oriented than the one they hope to "clean up."

Kittrie is far more ambivalent. His observation that the criminal justice system is being divested does *not* suggest that the social control function is simultaneously crumbling, or even that the normative interpretation of "coercion-as-help" is a less viable technique than it used to be. One can easily argue that the divestment of the criminal process in fact represents an *expansion* of the social control network from the confines of one set of agencies to a broader, more diverse set of agencies and groups. From this perspective, the apparent return in the criminal process to retribution and deterrence is not a significant policy shift, but rather the old skin of a much more subtle snake which has moved off to entwine with other agencies.

We find the above arguments and related discussions concerning correctional "reform" and expansion and diversification in social control to be incomplete and carried on at a level of abstraction that is suspicious in its own right. Probably the greatest problem is that such arguments adopt, to some degree, the traditional juridical paradigm for analysis, which proposes to consider different courses of action by contrasting the wants and rights of the "individual" citizen with those of "the state" or "society." The constructs of "individual" and "society," on which this paradigm relies, have apparently been useful to judges and legal scholars who have taken the individual defendant in court as the model of "individual" and the rules he has broken and/or should be applied to him as manifestation of the "state" or "society." These abstractions are not very helpful, however, in either resolving debates about community corrections or understanding why community corrections is elaborating as it has. We suggest that juxtaposing an individual to a set of rules is inadequate because it ignores the questions of various group processes and values within which an individual exists and will operate and ignores the alternative sets of rules (and organizations legitimated by them) to which all individuals are and will be subjected

In other words, the state and the individual, even assuming they exist as discrete entities for some decision objectives, are, for our purposes, contained within and mediated by groups and complex organizations. Furthermore, it is an unsubstantiated act of faith to assume that groups are merely individual needs, wants, and goals writ large or that complex organizations are simply a reflection of the state or society. We will concern ourselves in the rest of this chapter with issues on the complex organizations that administer social and penal sanctions.

Many arguments for and against community correction focus on its humaneness for offenders or its effectiveness and/or efficiency for the state. It is also possible, however, to question the behavior of the organizations involved in community corrections and the extent to which *their* behavior is *itself* pivotal in explaining deinstitutionalization on the one hand and the reascendancy of retribution and general deterrence on the other. Regardless of whether one perceives correctional organizations as "instruments of the state" or not, this inquiry would seem essential to understanding the community corrections trend and to informing social policy for either criminal justice or welfare agencies. The basic justification of this search is relatively simple and can be derived from either historical analysis or systems theory. There are numerous historical examples of instances in which correctional organizations did not or could not implement the types of programs or reach the types of objectives set for them by the "state." Whether the organizations were to administer theologically based reformation or the sternest, punitive regime, they simply have not achieved the goals expressed in legislative mandates or reformist oratory. Approaching the same divergence of expressed social policy from organizational reality from a systems perspective, one might say that complex organizations, as systems, are semi-autonomous from their environments. They perform on their inputs certain operations which are only *partially* constrained by factors external to themselves. Simply stated, appreciating correctional organization as an aspect of the state is necessary but *insufficient* to informed conclusions concerning the functions of correctional structures and processes.

Simon states that whether the actual organizational goals are functional or suicidal for the social system that constrains them is an empirical question.[42] There can be no a priori proofs that the bureaucracies of a capitalist state are as functional for the suppression of the working classes as a conscious power elite might want

[42] Herbert A. Simon, "On the Concept of Organizational Goal," *Administrative Science Quarterly* (June, 1964), 1–22.

them to be.[43] Nor are there any logical, deductive procedures by which to demonstrate that social welfare, or individual reformation, or any other manifestly beneficent objective will be delivered unaltered within the internal constraints of the complex organizations responsible for their delivery.

There are undoubtedly a variety of useful points from which to begin the inquiry about the organizational activities which explain deinstitutionalization. Our key concern is *why* the apparent shift in responsibilities from one set of organizations (traditional prisons, probation and parole agencies) to another set of organizations (emerging subunits of the traditional public correctional enterprise, such as state-run halfway houses, work release facilities, etc., or other public organizations, such as welfare, mental health agencies, or even private organizations, newly established or taking on new responsibilities concerning convicted offenders). Given this concern with the *exchange* of functional responsibilities, one useful approach is to examine the patterns of organizational exchange and to infer from those patterns the organizational goals at play.

ORGANIZATIONAL DOMAINS

Whether new organizations are assuming old social control functions (e.g., the criminal justice system is expanding) or old welfare functions are now being housed in agencies more competent to deliver (e.g., the scope of the criminal sanction is being limited) is a question effectively posed within organizational theory. What factors influence organizational expansion and contraction?

Marshall Meyer suggests an examination of organizational "domains" vis-à-vis the resources available both to expansion and to delivery of goods or services of sufficient quality to justify legitimacy over the domain claimed by the organization.[44] The term "domain" has been used frequently in organizational theory to refer to that set of resources, functional processes, and environmental demands over which an organization has control. Organizational domain is easily measured for profit-making units in which share of the market or other such measures can be used to indicate the nature (diverse, specific) and size of the domain in question. Domains are less easily

---

[43] For example, Scull argues in *Decarceration* that the capitalist system has necessitated decarceration because it is cheaper rather than more humane or more effective. He ignores the fact that the community programs subjected to greatest scrutiny proved more rather than less expensive and that the correctional organizations rather than the state seemed to benefit from the change. See Lerman, *Community Treatment and Social Control.*

[44] Marshall W. Meyer, "Organizational Domains," *American Sociological Review* (Oct., 1975), 599–615.

indicated in public organizations in which goals are usually more ambiguous and outcomes more diffuse.[45] As an alternative to organizational domain when dealing with public organizations, Meyer suggests the term "claimed" and/or "perceived" domain. His analysis of three types of public finance bureaus (e.g., comptroller's offices, financial offices, and offices of administration) concludes that an organization's expansion or contraction in both size and function is directly related to the organization's claimed domain and the effectiveness with which the organization communicates that claim to its supporting environment.

Meyer found that financial bureaus that claimed very narrow domains of essential core functions remained very small but stable over time. Other bureaus with more expansive claims (e.g., to planning and evaluation as well as bookkeeping) either expanded or contracted over time, depending on whether their technical resources, such as computerization, and their products or services could legitimate the original claims. The units which he found to be most unstable, and most vulnerable to contraction over time were, surprisingly, the financial offices that had made "middle-range" claims rather than the offices of administration that had the most diverse and expansive set of claims to functional competency. Comparing the actual activities conducted by financial offices and offices of administration, Meyer found little difference, thus suggesting that one resource facilitating the maintainence of a large domain was a claim to sufficient diversity so that the claim itself became a power resource in the negotiation of additional manpower, materials, and functions.

THE DOMAIN OF CORRECTIONAL ORGANIZATIONS

The community corrections trend seems analogous to the trends Meyer observed in the case of public financial organizations. Services, rather than products, are rendered, and the share of the public service domain captured by one agency rather than another is difficult to measure except as the external domain is reflected in internal organizational changes. The domain claims of traditional, public correctional agencies seem similar to those of financial offices: They have been *middle-range claims*, being functionally diverse (rehabilitation, deterrence, retribution, etc.) but not terribly expansive (concerned only with convicted offenders). Over time, the legitimacy of those middle-range claims has clearly withered to the extent that

[45] Ibid., p. 600.

some functions and some organizational members (both staff and offenders) are now being transferred to other organizations and auspices. The rising trend in correctional policy (e.g., toward flat terms for "hard core" offenders deserving fairly administered retribution) may be seen as a contraction of organizational domain to essential core services (analogous to those claimed by comptrollers' offices). As the domain of traditional correctional agencies contracts (or, in the case of parole, possibly is abolished altogether), other organizations assume the domain space once occupied by the correctional agencies.

These castoff functions, such as education, vocational training, alcohol and drug counseling, reintegration services, etc., are being assumed under remarkably varied auspices. While these correctional functions are being assumed in some areas by relatively small organizations having narrow and specialized claims (such as a private, single-unit halfway house for alcoholics), in other areas the organizational units assuming correctional functions have expansive and diverse claims (such as junior chambers of commerce, service branches of religious organizations, private corporations operating with public funding, and neighborhood or community civic improvement groups, etc.).

Whether their domain claims are narrow and specific or expansive and diverse, one characteristic of most of these organizations that distinguishes them from the traditional correctional agencies is their ability to structure their budget so that the costs of direct correctional supervision are either reduced or rendered less visible than they would be if the same services were rendered under the auspices of traditional correctional agencies. In the case of organizations with narrow domains, this usually means that the apparent cost is for rendering a special service, such as counseling or treatment of alcoholism, rather than for the supervision of convicted offenders (who make up only a small percentage of the total caseload). In the case of the more diverse organizations, costs of client supervision may be diffused throughout other types of activity. Finally, the nature of some of these units (such as junior chambers of commerce and religious organizations) allows for normative rewards to "staff" rather than remuneration. Volunteer services cost these organizations nothing, although the time volunteers expend in supervision of offenders rather than in other pursuits should be considered a social cost. Indeed, many noncorrections agencies have been successful in obtaining services and financial payments from the offenders themselves.

One stark instance of the mechanisms of lower-cost supervision provision may be cited. An upper middle-class voluntary organization in one major city founded a program of supervision for convicted misdemeanants. Volunteers from the organization were used in supervisory roles. Administration of the program and office space thus constituted the only identifiable costs of the social control. The 1975 cost per week for supervision of one person thus amounted to a meager $6.00 on average. However, the program of supervision included a behavior modification system of incentives which rewarded community volunteer work *on the part of the convicted offender.* If the work rendered by the persons supervised, constituting a minimum of 3 hours per week, is considered as restitution to the community for the actions for which they were convicted, then, at a nominal valuation of $2.00 an hour, the persons supervised in effect paid for the total cost of the program!

As this example illustrates, the organizations that are now assuming correctional functions are able, because of the nature of their domains, to assume the costs of administering punishment (i.e., they are supervising convicted offenders) with less direct drain on public money or they are able, because there is less direct evidence that punishment is taking place, to control the resources (volunteer energy, offenders, participation) that are less available to traditional correctional agencies.

SOCIAL CONTROL AND SOCIAL COMPLEXITY

To those who would ask if the above shift in domains represents a lower cost, less visible means of social control, we would probably answer yes. To those who would ask if this situation is more humane, we would also answer yes. Some people may consider this double affirmative a paradox, while others may simply suggest that all benefits have attendant social as well as financial costs.

The contrasts between the new, diverse network of community correctional agencies and the traditional correctional bureaucracies are analogous to the contrasts between the performance of the social control function in village and urban cultures. Both Banton and Wilkins suggest that the apparent effectiveness of the small British village in controlling deviance compared to the control in urban centers is that the village structure manifests a *more complex* rather than a simpler system for the reaction to deviance.[46] Banton argues that since the village has a higher "social density" than a city does, all village members play more interdependent roles. Consequently,

[46] Michael Banton, *The Policeman in the Community* (New York: Basic Books, 1964); Leslie Wilkins, *Social Deviance* (Englewood Cliffs, N.J.: Prentice-Hall, 1965).

deviation from expected (or appropriate) roles is less frequent and less extreme. By contrast, urban structures are less integrated or more fragmented, and the social control function is delegated to specialized agencies, within which the apprehended person is locked into the deviant role rather than steered toward conformity. The village, because its social control function is performed in a diffuse manner, obtains a higher degree of conformity at less expense (or less visible expense), but the village structure also provides less room for individual freedom and innovation.

We conclude with a simple finding that is based on this village–city comparison. The emerging community corrections network, while raising system complexity and social interdependency, may well provide less visible and less costly corrections services that are simultaneously less humanly brutalizing than the incarcerative alternatives. However, in a manner precisely analogous to the pattern exhibited by village social control systems, the development of such "alternatives to incarceration" augurs a future in which our society will "provide less room for individual freedom and innovation." The new alternatives to incarceration will not only provide lower cost and more humane corrections, but they will also provide more pervasive, more intrusive social control. Whether such a level of control is tolerable in our complex, diverse society is a matter that is open to serious question.

PART FOUR

MANAGEMENT AT THE BOUNDARIES

INTRODUCTION

We have examined a general theory of organizations as applied to correctional agencies and have reviewed some of the issues involved in the internal management of these organizations and some of the issues concerning adaptation and change. As any examination of change in correctional organizations demonstrates, an increasingly important topic in correctional management is the management not of the internal organization, but instead the management of relationships with the correctional environment—from the capacity to deal effectively with other, specific organizations that affect the correctional task to the capacity to adapt and to change the general perception of corrections in society. We will approach the first of these management tasks here; the concentration will be on interorganizational relations. In the last part of this book we will attempt to examine general public attitudes toward correction and their effect on correctional policy.

The field of interorganizational relations is considerably newer than the field of organizational management. The practical need to study fields of interorganizational interaction, as opposed to actions generated internally in an organization or by one organization upon its environment, has arisen only lately as organizations and social structure have grown more complex. For example, Geoffrey Vickers gives an insightful, historically rooted account of the growing complexity of the economic sphere in which he points out that it has only been in this century that understanding the economy requires an examination of the industrial–union–government complex. Previously, it may have been sufficient to understand the isolated machinations of independent entrepreneurs.[1] Dahrendorf makes similar observations about power and authority in the twentieth century. He argues that the frequency of polarized conflict between countries and between classes of people is less likely now than previously because it is less likely that one group is dominant in all spheres of life and that all groups are more interdependent than has previously been the case.[2]

If general political economic systems have become more complex, it is certainly true that organizational environments have done the same. Emery and Trist have suggested that organizational environments have gone through four stages of evolution: from placid to reactive to interactive to turbulent.[3] Organizational management in a turbulent environment is drastically different from that in less complex ones because the turbulent environment changes rapidly, and spontaneous events in the environment, ones that managers neither planned for nor tried to affect, may have drastic consequences for the organization. Shirley Terryberry utilized Emery and Trist's conceptual scheme in an attempt to predict how organizational management would have to change under conditions of turbulence.[4] She suggests that, under today's rapidly changing conditions, managers of organizations must concentrate on creating conditions beneficial to their organizations not by focusing on internal problems, but by focusing on how several diverse organizations can support each other. It will become commonplace in turbulent times, she suggests, for organizations having very different goals to band together and for organizations to diversify in their own goals considerably in an attempt to pacify or control a greater portion of their environment.

[1] Geoffrey Vickers, *Making Institutions Work* (New York: Halsted, 1973).
[2] Ralf Dahrendorf, *Class and Class Conflict in Post-Industrial Society* (Stanford: Stanford University Press, 1955).
[3] F. E. Emery and E. L. Trist, "The Causal Texture of Organizational Environments," in F. E. Emery (ed.), *Systems Thinking* (Baltimore: Penguin, 1970), pp. 241–58.
[4] Shirley Terryberry, "The Evolution of Organizational Environments," *Administrative Science Quarterly* (March, 1968), 590–613.

While international firms whose octopus-like branches produce everything from raisins to concrete are now commonplace, this growing intraorganizational and interorganizational complexity is not limited to financially motivated enterprise. Warren and his colleagues have recently argued that the entire social service sphere of communities must be analyzed as an interorganizational field rather than as political or organizational endeavors.[5] Regardless of whether social policy is formulated by an elitist group or by some pluralist structure, policy makers and program implementors have to have access to a network of social service organizations whose actions are determined by their interrelationships rather than their own internal goals.[6]

Correctional organizations may be less interdependent on outside organizations than is presently true of other organizations in the "human services." Corrections, of course, was not always seen as a human service, and like mental hospitals, correctional organizations have had a long tradition of attempting to provide within themselves all of the services that an offender needed or was deemed worthy of enjoying. But this perspective has changed drastically in recent years. The ascendancy of "treatment" instead of punishment may have been legally inaccurate, but it probably aided somewhat the perception of correctional organizations as part of the human service "family," and therefore as organizations that could enter into interorganizational relationships with other service organizations. In the 1960's the emphasis on reintegration in correctional work stressed the need to link offenders with a variety of human resources, from jobs and education to counseling and better medical services. Hence, it became part of policy that correctional managers had to discover how to engage other organizations in the supervision and treatment of offenders. Moreover, changing perspectives on the offender as a citizen reduced the ability of other organizations to fend off correctional clients. Offenders, like other citizens, were supposed to have available the types of services that other agencies were mandated to provide. Finally, Morris,[7] van den Haag,[8] and others have recently argued for the divorce of punishment from treatment and that all treatment or service provision to offenders, either in prison or on the street, should be provided by outside agencies.

---

[5] Roland L. Warren, Stephen M. Rose, and Ann F. Bergunder, *The Structure of Urban Reform* (Lexington, Mass.: Lexington Books, 1974).

[6] Ibid., and Roland L. Warren, "The Interorganizational Field as a Focus for Investigation," *Administrative Science Quarterly* (Dec., 1967), pp. 396–419.

[7] Norval Morris, *The Future of Imprisonment* (Chicago: University of Chicago Press, 1974).

[8] Ernest van den Haag, *Punishing Criminals* (New York: Basic Books, 1975).

For these and other reasons, the management of correctional organizations is increasingly concerned with the management of organizational boundaries, and with gaining services as well as giving services, to other organizations. The following chapters will concentrate on three important facets of interorganizational relations in corrections. In Chapter 11 we will examine in detail the interaction between one correctional organization and an outside organization and we will concentrate on conflicts that arise when new interorganizational relationships are established. In Chapter 12 we will examine the relationship of correctional organizations to human service agencies and the impact of that relationship on resolution of problems for offenders as they reenter the community from prison. Finally, in Chapter 13, we will review the impact of the courts on corrections and will concentrate on the interorganizational dimensions of the new legal changes in corrections.

11

Interorganizational Conflict in Corrections

(Robert Sebring and David Duffee)

According to Bennis, a win–lose conflict in organizations involves cognitive distortions, entangled issues, and resort to personality combat. Win–lose battles frequently escalate and become independent of their initiating causes. Therefore, such conflict is one of the most difficult problems for an organization to control and it "probably dissipates more energy and money than any other single organizational disease."[1] In a business organization the toll can be measured in terms of production, efficiency, absenteeism, turnover, and morale. The price paid by individual organization members, according to Harvey and Albertson, can be measured in terms of misery and loss of self-esteem and confidence and may ultimately be reflected in the company's profit–loss balance sheet.[2] In a human service organization, such as a correctional institution, however, the losses may

---

[1] W. G. Bennis, *Changing Organizations* (New York: McGraw-Hill, 1966), p. 57.
[2] J. B. Harvey and D. R. Albertson, "Neurotic Organizations: Symptoms, Causes, and Treatment," in W. W. Burke (ed.), *Contemporary Organization Development: Conceptual Orientations and Interventions* (Washington, D.C.: NTL Institute for Applied Behavioral Science, 1972).

be more difficult to measure, more diffuse, and have more destructive human consequences; while organizational pathologies in industry may well take their toll in human terms, pathological staff behavior in prison has immediate impact on the involuntary residents whom the staff are to manage.

This chapter describes the case of a particularly vicious and costly organizational conflict that developed among prison staff in a state correctional institution and the prison personnel and an outside educational agency that was funding the prison's vocational education program. Once the conflict began, the spiteful and invidious nature of the interpersonal and intergroup behaviors created an organizational paranoia that was very contagious and difficult to treat. What makes this case even more serious is that it is not atypical in its dynamics when compared to other cases of conflict in correctional institutions.[3] However, there is very little information about how to deal with such conflict. Until more is known about this kind of organizational problem in human service organizations, a great deal of public employee time, energy, and commitment, in addition to taxpayers' dollars, will continue to be wasted on inefficient and ineffective programs.

One purpose of this case study, therefore, is to increase managerial understanding of the politics and dynamics of win–lose organizational and interorganizational conflict. The other is an attempt to make recognizable the characteristics of the organizational climate that result when such conflict has been ongoing for some time. Understanding these dynamics is an essential prerequisite to diagnosing conflict and selecting an appropriate social intervention. This study examines the background of the organizational and interorganizational conflict in one correctional facility, the symptoms of organizational paranoia, and the organizational consultants' approach to alter the win–lose conflict. Several recommendations are made concerning the problems of implementing planned change strategies within this type of situation.

SETTING

The correctional facility is located just outside a small farming community. From the highway the ivy-covered administration building, well-kept lawns and buildings, open, spacious grounds, red brick

[3] Richard McCleery, "Correctional Administration and Organizational Change," paper presented at the annual meeting of the American Political Science Association, Washington, D.C., Sept., 1972. Mayer Zald, "Power Balance and Staff Conflict in Correctional Institutions," *Administrative Science Quarterly* (June, 1962), 22–49. G. H. Weber, "Conflicts Between Professional and Non-professional Personnel in Institutional Delinquency Treatment," *Journal of Criminal Law, Criminology and Police Science* (May–June, 1957), pp. 26–43.

dormitories or "cottages," surrounding corn fields, and the tall, poplar-lined drive leading to the "sign-in" building give the institution the appearance of a small liberal arts college. It is only after one signs in, enters the grounds, and experiences the glares and "sizing up" of the residents that one realizes it is a prison.

Until a few years ago the facility was a correctional institution for women. Today, although it has been "integrated" with a few male prisoners, the inmate population still remains predominantly female. Approximately 70 percent of the residents are urban, black, working-class females, and 25 percent are white, rural and urban, working-class females. Black males and white males make up the remaining 5 percent. Some years ago the institution was notorious throughout the state for overt lesbianism, corrupt guards, shakedowns and hustles by inmates against each other, interracial strife, and political patronage jobs. Today, however, the relative cooling of racial tensions in the country, the introduction of new treatment programs, community work release, experiments in inmate self-government, integration of several male prisoners, a furlough system, a paraprofessional teacher aide program for inmates, and implementation of vocational education programs have helped to improve the prison climate.

Despite these innovative programs, many problems and tensions continue to exist. Recently, for example, intergroup conflict developed within the education program. On the surface, what apparently began as a philosophical disagreement between the education director, a black woman, and one of her staff, a white woman, over how to teach home economics to the predominantly black women residents led to a personality clash which ultimately divided the institution staff into two groups. The pro-administration forces—superintendent, home economics teacher, and several other teachers—formed one group; the educational director and several of her teachers made up the pro-education director group. As the conflict worsened, it affected a regional education program that was funding the vocational education program and culminated in a political struggle between the state department of corrections and the state department of education over control of vocational education funds for prison educational programs.

On the surface, the conflict in the prison apparently originated because the education director believed that the recently hired home economics teacher was teaching "old-fashioned" home economics in order to make inmates "good domestics." The home economics teacher admitted that she had quarreled with the director over this and other related problems. Subsequently, according to the home economics teacher, she had been trying to teach students the latest consumer-oriented home economics, but she felt that the director had never forgotten their earlier "run in" and held a grudge against her. There were repeated open and heated clashes between the home economics teacher and the prison education director. Apparently, after each confrontation each contestant gathered social support for her side, thereby developing a loyal cadre of supporters among the teaching staff. Consequently, cliques formed and, according to one education staff member, "Gossip became the delight of the day." This problem and other critical organizational incidents involving the education director persuaded the prison administration (superintendent and the deputy superintendent) to side with the home economics instructor and her supporters.

A great deal of political intrigue, backbiting, and unprofessional behavior developed within this organizational context. One teacher said, "People are trying to hurt each other instead of trying to help the residents." Another staff member added, "We're here to help people and not bicker. It's uncalled for." Still another said, "One begins to wonder who is doing what to whom."

ORGANIZATIONAL PARANOIA

People in this environment believed it was necessary to "cover" and defend themselves; memos were copied; and the education director, using her shorthand skills, took notes during meetings, and then, according to the superintendent and deputy superintendent, used the notes later to embarrass them publicly. As a consequence of these behaviors, people were very guarded and suspicious of everyone's behaviors, motives, and questions. Defensiveness replaced the ability to listen or receive help. In addition to such feelings, each group accused the other of acts of sabotage. For example, the administration accused the education director and some of her teaching staff of purposely trying to undermine the deputy superintendent's new teacher aide program in which inmates were used as teaching assistants to help their fellow classmates. The education director and her supporters, on the other hand, charged the administration with deliberately deemphasizing the educational program and overemphasizing competing rehabilitation programs and work detail in order "to make the education director look bad." They also believed the administration, especially the deputy superintendent, was using the teacher aides to spy on the education director.

Each side accused the other of going around the group to enlist the aid and political support of central office correctional officials and elected state officials. Each side denounced the other's "dirty tricks" and norm-breaking behavior and "unprofessionalism" but then engaged in the same behaviors. As a result, no one was "clean," each side had its own "facts" and its own "truth," and each described the other in terms of negative stereotypes while blaming the other side for all the wrongdoing. The situation supported the statement that in time of crises what people believe to be true is more important than the "truth" of events.

Organizational paranoia reached the point where each group saw the other side as the enemy. For example, the education director believed the newly appointed home economics teacher was better educated and better politically "connected" (the home economics teacher's brother-in-law was a state senator and was the chairman of the higher education committee) and, therefore, had been hired to replace her. The superintendent believed the education director was trying to get his job; and some of his supporters claimed that the education director had started rumors about the superintendent and deputy superintendent's private lives with the objective of having them fired. According to some education director supporters, the administration was now "out to get" the education director in retaliation for such rumors. The administration, of course, denied these charges and insisted the stories were false. They asserted that the education director had done a good job, but they felt she was now beginning to develop a serious case of paranoia. This paranoia, the administration claimed, was seriously interfering with her ability to carry out her assignment.

Furthermore, the superintendent heard reports from central office officials that the education director was going around him to develop political support with several important and influential black political leaders and central office officials. The administration saw this political maneuvering as the education director's attempt to fabricate a racial incident at the correctional institution in order to save her job and possibly get his job. In the administration's eyes, the education director was unfairly using the fact that she was black and a woman to her advantage. To further complicate matters, in this zero-sum situation some of the inmates were trying to divide the staff by playing one side against the other. Other inmates simply withdrew from the conflict, became disillusioned with the education program, and stopped attending class. At one point 7 teachers were instructing only 27 students out of a total 300 inmates.

BUREAUCRATIC CONFLICT

It would seem that the tensions within the education program resulted from the larger, more serious administration—education director conflict and that they represented what L. R. Pondy[4] has called the "bureaucratic conflict model" characterized by superior-

[4] L. R. Pondy, "Organizational Conflict: Concepts and Models," *Administrative Science Quarterly* (September, 1967), pp. 296-320.

subordinate conflict along the vertical dimension of the organization hierarchy, both between the administration and the education director and between the education director and the home economics instructor. Put differently, the conflict at the higher bureaucratic level was diagnosed as recycling itself at the education program level. It was hypothesized that until the education–administration source of the conflict was resolved, no significant change could occur anywhere else in the organization. Any organizational interventions would have to begin at the top and then work down to the education staff level.

INTERORGANIZATIONAL CONFLICT

Figure 11.1 shows the human services matrix in which the dispute occurred and the areas of interorganizational conflict. Beginning at the top of the hierarchical structure, the figure illustrates that the state governor, with the approval of the state senate, appoints the secretary of the department of education, the attorney general, and the commissioner of corrections. In addition, the state legislature approves budget allocations and performs oversight functions for these departments. At the state prison level, the prison education program director is subordinate to the chief of vocational education programs but reports directly to the prison superintendent and deputy superintendent. In turn, the home economics teacher is subordinate to the education director, but her salary, along with that of six other vocational teachers, is paid with vocational education funds channeled through the regional education department.

The regional education department is a relatively new public organizational structure located within the state department of education. Developed in 1971 in response to the consolidation of schools, regional education departments replace the former county superintendencies and provide specific pupil, personnel, and educational services for their member school districts.

Regional education department policy and budget are formulated and approved by a board of directors made up of local school board representatives. Each representative school district board must also approve the regional education department's budget. School district chief administrators (principals and superintendents) advise the regional education director on policy and program planning matters. Regional education department funding is set according to formulas and policies established by state law.

Within this bureaucratic matrix, Figure 11.1 demonstrates that one source of interorganizational conflict existed between the commissioner of corrections and the state secretary of education; another

STATE GOVERNMENT

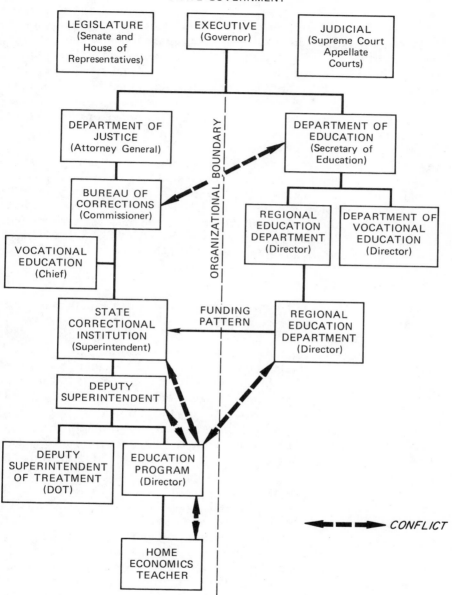

Fig. 11-1

conflict existed between the regional education director and the prison education director.

The department of corrections–state department of education conflict grew out of the local dispute and developed because of the department's "strain toward maximizing its autonomy."[5] The local conflict, in other words, had caused the state department of corrections to grow cautious about participating in organizational exchanges with the department of education; it was reluctant to allow "outsiders" to evaluate or otherwise exercise any leverage or control over its inside operations.

The local conflict between the prison education director and the regional education director developed because of unclear supervisory, program planning, and reporting responsibilities regarding the vocational education program. This dispute can best be understood by examining the organizational characteristics of the correctional institution and the regional education department which contributed to the conflict and by analyzing the linkage relationships between the two organizations along four key dimensions.

The Correctional Institution

There are a number of organizational characteristics that contribute to the paranoid climate and frequency of a win–lose conflict in prisons. First, imprisoning large groups of people against their will and attempting to supervise them closely with comparatively few staff have led to a "strain and conflict-producing system."[6] According to Erving Goffman, this system with its competing and incompatible interests between inmates and staff and distinct staff and resident castes all help contribute to the suspicious, distrustful, hostile, and aggressive prison climate. In this environment, "moving on," "conning," and "setting someone up" become modes of organizational behavior among both staff and residents and contribute to the organizational paranoia.

Another conflict-producing organizational characteristic is that, compared to business and industrial organizations, prisons have more difficulty measuring their efficiency and effectiveness. The intangible nature of prison reform and rehabilitation goals make it difficult for correctional managers to measure the impact of their treatment programs on changing inmate behavior and to demonstrate the marginal utilities of one more dollar spent here or there, or of one more inmate hour spent in class, on work detail, or in therapy groups. As a result, interdepartmental conflicts often develop over competition

---

[5] Alvin Gouldner, "Reciprocity and Autonomy in Functional Theory," in Llewellyn Gross (ed.), *Symposium on Social Theory* (New York: Harper & Row, 1959).

[6] Erving Goffman, *Asylums* (New York: Doubleday, 1961).

for the inmate's time. Conflicting staff philosophies on prison goals and objectives also make it difficult for prison management to achieve valid consensual evaluative standards for the several bureaucracies that they oversee.[7]

A related characteristic, according to Street, Vinter, and Perrow, is the disagreement among the taxpaying public, elected officials, criminologists, and penologists about appropriate ways to change inmate behavior. As a result, correctional managers are sensitive to outside criticism and any attempt to interfere in the prison.[8]

In addition, Donald Cressey argues that prisons contain at least three separate bureaucracies: one for custody, one for treatment, and one for service or maintenance.[9] Frequently, there may be more than three sets. Prison education programs, for example, may have direct or at least strong secondary ties to the state educational system. Compared to industrial top management, therefore, these three characteristics—the intangible nature of treatment goals, differing and conflicting philosophies on appropriate ways to change inmate behavior, and multiple bureaucracies—often produce interstaff and interdepartmental conflict and make it difficult for prison management to achieve staff integration.

Another organizational characteristic that contributes to the paranoid climate and frequency of win–lose situations is that prisons often experience rapid turnover of top management and "political" appointments of high-level executives. The rapid turnover in attorneys general, commissioners of corrections, and prison superintendents, for example, often lead prison staff members to develop departmental "fiefdoms" and to establish political power bases with central office bureau staff, state politicians, and, in this case, black activist groups, in order to buffer themselves and their staff from capricious changes and accompanying job insecurities.

In this case, the state has had three attorneys general and three commissioners of corrections, and the prison has had three different superintendents and two deputy superintendents in 2 years. As a result, when organizational problems develop and there are inadequate structures or procedures to help manage the conflict locally, department heads often go around the superintendent and complain to central office officials.

Also, because prisons have a high degree of functional independence, autonomy, and strong extracommunity relations, superintendents have traditionally developed "unilateral strategies for setting

[7] Jerome Skolnick, *Justice Without Trial* (New York: Wiley, 1966).
[8] David Street, Robert Vinter, and Charles Perrow, *Organization for Treatment* (New York: Free Press, 1966), pp. 1–22.
[9] Donald R. Cressey, "Contradictory Directives in Complex Organizations: The Case of the Prison," *Administrative Science Quarterly* (March, 1959), pp. 1–19.

organizational policies and have depended very little on outside agencies for organizational exchanges to accomplish their goals and objectives.[10]

Within this organizational framework the relatively inexperienced, reform-minded superintendent had been assigned to clean up institutional corruption. To help him carry out these reforms, he hired a strong-willed, experienced, and rather autonomous education program director. With her in charge, he hoped he would be able to devote more time to supervising and reforming other parts of the prison. Because he was busy working on prison reform and was inexperienced in interorganizational relations, he did not supervise the education director and did not meet with the regional education director to work out the details of the organizational exchange.

The Regional Education Department

The regional education department was struggling to develop its legitimacy as a viable addition to the education community. As a newly established organization, the regional education department was devoting a great deal of time and effort to establishing new programs for its member school districts. Because the regional education department was busy with these tasks and was under-staffed and inexperienced in working with correctional institutions, it did not supervise the vocational education program or meet regularly with the prison staff. Furthermore, the interviews, observations, letters, and memos exchanged between the regional education director and the prison superintendent demonstrated that considerable confusion and role ambiguity existed regarding supervisory and program planning responsibilities. As a result, neither organization supervised the education program or took the time to standardize or formalize the organizational exchange. These responsibilities were not adequately spelled out until after the organizational conflict had developed.

These organizational structural characteristics and their effects on interorganizational relations are summarized below along four key dimensions for analyzing organizational exchanges: formalization, intensity, reciprocity, and standardization.[11]

[10] Street, Vinter, and Perrow, *Organization for Treatment,* and Elmer K. Nelson and Catherine Lovell, *Developing Correctional Administrators* (Washington, D.C.: Government Printing Office, 1969).

[11] H. Aldrich, "Cooperation and Conflict Between Organizations in the Manpower Training System: An Organization Environment Perspective," in Anant R. Negandhi (ed.), *Conflict and Power in Complex Organizations: An Interinstitutional Perspective* (Kent, Ohio: Comparative Administration Research Institute Center for Business and Economic Research, Kent State University, 1972).

Formalization. Formalization is defined as the degree to which exchanges between organizations are given official sanction and are agreed to by the parties involved and the extent to which an intermediary coordinates the relations. The data gathered for this study revealed that, up until the conflict, there were very few formal or informal interactions between the two organizations. Each organization was too busy handling other problems ever to formalize their relationships.

Intensity. Intensity refers to the frequency of interaction required by the size of the resource invested. Preoccupation with other programs and problems, the relatively small amount of money invested in the educational program ($30,000), and the inexperience of both organizations in handling interorganizational relations all led to a low-intensity level of interorganizational relationships. Infrequent interactions among organizational intermediaries and no formal structure (interagency staff meetings) for handling interorganizational problems also contributed to the win–lose conflict.

Reciprocity. Reciprocity involves the direction of the exchange (unilateral, reciprocal, joint) and the extent to which terms or the basis and conditions of the exchange are mutually reached. Because the regional education department had "inherited" the vocational education project from one of its school districts, the terms of the organizational exchange were never mutually agreed on. In fact, a mutual organization exchange agreement was never developed until the home economics teacher–prison education director conflict developed. After the conflict intensified, the regional education director developed a specific set of program-planning guidelines for the prison education director to follow in order to apply for vocational education funds. As it turned out, however, this last-minute attempt to standardize relationships only aggravated the relations between the two education directors and heightened the tensions and paranoia within the prison.

Standardization. Standardization refers to some reliable determination or fixedness of the units of exchange and procedures for exchange between the organizations. Because of the organizational characteristics already mentioned, no standardized procedures for the unilateral exchange had been developed. Only after the conflict had gotten out of hand were there any attempts to formalize and standardize exchange relationships between the correctional institution and the regional education department.

A PLANNED INTERVENTION

The staff at the prison were worried, frustrated, insecure, and depressed. They were all aware of the upset and wanted things to change, but they were frozen into dysfunctional, paranoid patterns of behavior. So much interpersonal and intergroup history and so many critical organizational incidents had occurred, and the issues had become so entangled in personalities and emotional conflict, that it was difficult for outsiders to know whom to believe. Within this dehumanizing struggle, several correctional staff members actually wondered who were the real prisoners. As one staff member put it: "This place is sick. We're all becoming paranoid. We're the real prisoners."

Despite these problems, the state department of education notified all regional education directors that prison vocational education programs were to receive high priority. Pending regional education board approval, therefore, the $30,000 per year prison vocational education program was to be increased to $100,000. However, the regional education director was concerned about the prison's educational staff problems. The home economics teacher had reported to him about the "intolerable situation" at the correctional institution. Therefore, the regional education director hired two organizational consultants to obtain more information about what was going on inside the prison and to see, as he put it, "if he was getting his money's worth." Before he recommended increasing vocational education expenditures, he felt he had a responsibility and an obligation to his board of directors, the funding source, and to the public to investigate the education program and its organizational problems. Consequently, with the approval of the correctional institution superintendent, consultants were hired to carry out an assessment.

The Process-Consultation Approach

The consultants decided to use a "process-consultation" approach[12] in order to involve actively the correctional institution staff members themselves in the early planning, data gathering, assessment, and diagnosis and goal-setting stages. In other words, rather than have the organizational participants accept the diagnosis and prescription for organizational change from outside experts, an attempt was made to include correctional institution staff members in the analysis and problem solving. The main thrust here was that if

[12] E. Schein, *Process Consultation: Its Role in Organization Development* (Reading, Mass.: Addison-Wesley, 1969).

the correctional institution staff were to be able to handle their present and future problems, then they, as clients, would have to learn to see the problem for themselves, take part in the diagnosis, and be actively involved in developing a solution.

To carry out the process-consultation approach, a meeting was first held with the correctional institution superintendent and the regional education director in order to clarify their aims and objectives, obtain the superintendent's commitment and sanction of the project, and to gain an understanding of the superintendent's perspective of the organizational problems.

Next, because a great deal of the discussion revolved around the superintendent's problems with the educational director, a joint meeting was held in the regional education director's office, this time with the superintendent, the correctional institution education director, and the regional education director. The main purposes of the second meeting were: (1) to hear both sides of the story and to discuss a preliminary plan to evaluate the educational program and assess the organizational problems, (2) to test the main participant's "mutual motivation to reduce conflict,"[13] and (3) to obtain the prison education director's input and commitment to the project.

The next step involved a meeting with the correctional institution education program staff. At this meeting the superintendent, the education director, and the regional education director explained the reasons for the evaluation and asked for staff's cooperation. After this, the consultants explained the assessment procedures, answered questions, and then developed an interview schedule. For the next 3 days 1-hour, in-depth interviews were conducted with all educational staff members, including the home economics instructor, the educational director, the superintendent, and the deputy superintendent. In all, a total of approximately 30 hours were spent interviewing. The questions focused on the following areas:

1. The problems facing the organization.
2. The kinds of things causing the problems.
3. The perceived organizational strengths that could help to solve the problems.

After gathering and analyzing the data, it became apparent to the consultants that if something did not happen soon to alter or reverse the situation, the vocational education program and several staff members' jobs and professional reputations would be in jeopardy. The problem for the consultants, of course, was to know just what to

[13] R. Walton, *Interpersonal Peacemaking: Confrontations and Third-Party Consultation* (Reading, Mass.: Addison-Wesley, 1969).

do. After the consultants analyzed the situation, they found that there seemed to be two alternate and conflicting diagnoses:

1. The staff and main participants to the conflict were distressed with the situation and wanted it to change, but they did not know what to do about it and were not skilled in handling interpersonal and intergroup conflict. Therefore, an outside arbiter was needed to develop institutional mechanisms to deal with the conflict and to help teach the staff appropriate interpersonal and intergroup confrontation and problem-solving skills and techniques.
2. The conflict had gone too far for any resolution at the local level, and it had actually reached the point where it became functional for each side to drive the other out. In other words, two paranoid systems were purposely "feeding one another" in an attempt to cause the other to reach the breaking point.

The challenging questions confronting the consultants, therefore, were: Was there a "synchronized readiness for dialogue and confrontation" and was there a "mutual motivation to reduce the conflict" between the two groups?[14] Or was one party ready to compromise and work out a mutually agreeable solution and not the other? Or did both groups want to continue the win–lose conflict until the bitter end?

To help determine the answers to these questions, individual meetings were first held with the superintendent, the deputy superintendent, the education director, and the regional education director. One purpose of these meetings was to present personal feedback to the key executive leaders that would help them carry out their assignments and organizational responsibilities more effectively. These individual sessions were also used to see if the key organizational leaders were willing to move to the next step: the group feedback session.

Since there seemed to be sufficient mutual motivation and readiness to move ahead, a group feedback session was held in the superintendent's office. The purpose of this meeting was to confront the institution's staff leaders very straightforwardly with the "hot" organizational issues that had to be resolved immediately. Since the organizational problems were diagnosed as both bureaucratic and interorganizational conflict, and since the source of the education staff conflict was identified as originating between the administration (superintendent, deputy superintendent) and the education director, these individuals and the home economics instructor, the regional

[14] Ibid.

education director, and the director of treatment (D.O.T.) programs were present. It was felt that if the feedback sessions, and ultimately the organizational change efforts, were to be successful, these key organizational leaders had to reach a consensus on the issues, set priorities for action planning, and be committed to solving the problems. If there was such a commitment, then the consultants were prepared to assist the staff in their problem-solving efforts.

The director of treatment programs was invited to attend these sessions at the education director's request, because the education director regarded the D.O.T. as a neutral party and as one that could be trusted. Consequently, this request was implemented so that the education director would not be outnumbered by her enemies. Walton has shown that symmetry of situational power between the principal parties is an important determinant in helping to resolve conflict.[15]

Another important factor in resolving conflict is the "organizational norms supporting the expression of differences."[16] Unfortunately, in highly political, highly regimented, closed bureaucratic systems like prisons, organizational norms do not promote openness. In fact, as has been shown, there is a growing body of evidence to demonstrate that uncooperativeness, disloyalty, dishonesty, aggressiveness, and paranoia are characteristic properties of the organizational environment.[17] Because of the seriousness of the conflict and the reluctance of any of the participants to move toward any compromise, it was necessary for the consultants to establish an "optimum level of tension."[18]

At the first feedback session, therefore, the consultants confronted the staff very straightforwardly with the serious organizational issues and the stakes involved in continuing the conflict. Loss of jobs, professional reputations, possible mental and physical illness occurring among the staff, and the threat of losing $100,000 or more in federal funds for vocational education programs were all explained as possible consequences of continuing the conflict. After answering several questions about the data, the consultants divided the participants into three problem-solving groups to discuss the findings and to identify what steps could be taken to improve the situation. After about an hour each group reported back to the larger group.

It was clear from the discussion that no one had any real suggestions for improving the situation. Each staff member was still denying

[15] Ibid.
[16] Ibid., p. 147.
[17] Goffman, *Asylums*; Cressey, "Contradictory Directives in Complex Organizations."
[18] Walton, *Interpersonal Peacemaking*.

any real responsibility for the situation and continued to accuse the other side for all the wrongdoing. Attempts had failed to develop mutual motivation to reduce conflict, synchronized readiness for dialogue and confrontation, reliability of personal communications, and organizational norms supporting the expression of differences.

At the second meeting the director of treatment was absent, and an asymmetry of power existed. The education director, who had originally agreed to the second meeting, announced that over the weekend she had had second thoughts about proceeding and subsequently announced that she would not participate at any more meetings until at least one or two staff members from the correctional central office were present. When the superintendent denied this last-minute request, the education program director withdrew from the meetings, at which time the regional education director exploded and announced he would not put "another cent" into the vocational education program at the correctional institution while the present education director remained in her position.

At the end of this meeting the consultants were approached by both the superintendent and deputy superintendent to write the report to support their side. The consultants responded that the education director's behavior would be noted but that the consultants would write the report as objectively as possible and "let the chips fall where they may."

Throughout this project the consultants were under a great deal of pressure to take sides and to write their report to support one group against the other. Strategies were also used by both groups to "divide and conquer" the consultants and to play one off against the other. For example, phone calls were made to one consultant's college department and to correctional officials with whom the consultant had worked to check up on his "credentials" and to find out more about his "political leanings." In short, win–lose strategies being used inside the prison were being used against the consultants. And, interestingly enough, these actions caused the consultants to develop cautious and "covering" kinds of paranoid behaviors, such as making sure to say the same thing to both groups and to interview all staff members for the same length of time, making sure not to be seen talking to a member of one faction for any length of time, being careful about whom they ate lunch with in the cafeteria, carefully writing out their notes and sending copies of the report to all the principal parties on the same date and by registered mail.

A couple of weeks later copies of the report describing the situation at the correctional institution were mailed to all the participants. The report concluded that because of the interstaff conflict and the fact that so few inmates were benefiting from the education programs and were actually being "harmed" by the organizational conflict, the consultants recommended that all vocational education funds be withheld from the prison until the correctional institution program staff problems were resolved. In addition, the report included the following seven alternative recommendations:

1. Split up the personalities involved in the conflict.
2. Fire one group (the superintendent and deputy superintendent or the education director) and support the other group.
3. Fire both groups, "clean house," and start over.
4. Support the administration and their actions and not allow the educational director to go around or above the administration.
5. Take the problem to third-party arbitration and make the contending parties work out a settlement agreeable to both— but mainly one that the correctional administration can support.
6. Implement staff development programs like those begun during the intervention, but with support and participation by central office officials.
7. Along with staff development programs, psychological evaluation and therapy are recommended for certain staff members.

Several weeks after submitting the report the consultants were requested to present their findings and discuss the case with the director of the state department of vocational education and the department of correction's vocational education director.

At this meeting the report corroborated each director's previously gathered data on the conflict and underlined the seriousness of the problems at the correctional institution. Consequently, the central office officials used the "outside objective" report to force the commissioner of corrections, who had repeatedly refused to deal with the problem, to take some action to "resolve" it.

A month later the superintendent at the correctional institution was appointed director of group treatment facilities in another region of the state, and a new superintendent was appointed. The deputy superintendent and the education program director remained in their same positions. The home economics teacher was removed to the regional education offices. At last report she was working as a librarian in an area public school. Vocational educational funds were cut off, and all vocational education programs were ended. The basic education classes are still poorly attended while large sums of unspent public monies remain available for vocational educational programs in correctional institutions. At the state government level, the department of education and the department of corrections reportedly continue their political struggle for control of these federal education funds. Also, the governor appointed a new corrections commissioner, and attempts were being made to get another regional education department to fund the vocational education program at the correctional institution.

A year after these developments the new superintendent and the deputy superintendent were fired and new appointments have again been made. The state legislature has held hearings to investigate the "problems and irregularities" at the institution. Throughout it all, however, the prison education director has remained. This fact prompted the regional education director to state that she had "won" and that the superintendent, deputy superintendent, the home economics teacher, the residents, and the taxpayers had lost.

SUMMARY

In summary, two bureaucracies that normally would have little contact or reason to relate to each other, were attempting, because of funding patterns, to work together. Because of the unique organizational characteristics and the important tasks facing their executive leaders, they were unable to cooperate and develop effective interorganizational relationships. In fact, the problems of one organization began to impinge on the other. Further complicating these issues were the interpersonal and intergroup organizational conflicts within the correctional institution. The commonly accepted norms of organizational behavior, conduct, and morality that governed staff interpersonal and intergroup relations had long been broken and the resultant stress and paranoia had impaired the staff's perceptive and cognitive processes to the point where everyone suspected each other's motives. Each group held a simplistic, stereotyped view of the other group.[19] The dimensions of the conflict, the centrality of the issues, the number of issues involved, and the rigidity and interdependence of these issues all made this case extremely difficult to resolve through any traditional organizational development procedures.

CONCLUSIONS

Because of the complexity of these problems, consultants need time to untangle and unravel the conflict issues and break them down into their component parts. In order to help do this, it may

[19] M. Deutsch, *The Resolution of Conflict* (New Haven: Yale University Press, 1973), p. 355.

be helpful to begin the change interventions with the symptoms at the lower organizational level and then work upward toward the interdepartmental and intergroup sources of the conflict. Using this "bottom up" approach will not only allow the consultants more time to develop trust, build a base within the institution, and gain some success, it will also help to develop the much needed interpersonal confrontation skills on the part of staff and help to build organizational norms of openness and mutual motivation to resolve the conflict. In addition, this approach will help avoid beginning the change program at the point of greatest stress in the system.[20]

Second, while working on these interpersonal peace-making interventions, the consultants could begin to improve staff meetings and to develop organizational structures to manage the conflict and facilitate a better integration of the prison's various "bureaucracies."[21]

Third, because of the prison's organizational structure and the staff's self-protective strategy of developing political power bases and loyalties with central office personnel, attempts should be made to involve central office staff members and other interested parties to the conflict in the planning for its resolution. For example, when the prison education director announced at the second meeting that she would not proceed further unless several central office staff members were present, the consultants should have acted more forcefully and demanded that her conditions be met. This action would have ensured a symmetry of organizational situational power and could have enhanced the prospects of successful conflict resolution. In retrospect, central office officials should have been actively involved in the early planning, data gathering, diagnosis, and action planning stages of change.[22]

Fourth, to help prevent future interorganizational conflicts between the regional education department and the prison, mutual agreements on expectations about lines of supervisory authority should be established, regular interagency staff meetings should be held, and all interorganizational exchanges should be structured to promote *formalization, standardization, reciprocity,* and *intensity.* This increased program review and evaluation by the outside agency would also help prevent the win–lose conflict and paranoia from festering so long within the closed prison system.

Fifth, more organization development interventions are needed

[20] K. D. Benne and M. Birnbaum, "Principles of Change," in K. D. Benne, W. G. Bennis, and R. Chin (eds.), *The Planning of Change*, 2nd ed. (New York: Holt, Rinehart and Winston, 1969).
[21] P. R. Lawrence and J. W. Lorsch, *Organization and Environment* (Cambridge, Mass.: Harvard University Press, 1967).
[22] Benne and Birnbaum, "Principles of Change."

to help improve human service organizations. The knowledge gained in business and industrial organizations needs to be adapted and applied to the specific organizational characteristics described in this chapter. Correctional managers have to recognize the usefulness of organizational development in improving their system—hopefully before conflict reaches a zero-sum situation.

If these cooperative, consensus approaches to change do not work, drastic measures, such as "cleaning house" and removing entire groups of people or key actors, are recommended. Traditional piece-meal or halfway measures such as transferring and reshuffling personnel are only temporary solutions. Organizational conflict will continue if the parties remain in functional interdependence. Consultants, therefore, must use their written reports, expertise, and "objective" knowledge of the situation to help correctional central office officials act decisively to implement their recommendations for change. For example, in this case, the consultants should have insisted on helping the commissioner of corrections arrive at a decision on the prison conflict situation. In other words, outside consultants cannot be disinterested parties "above the battle."

In serious win–lose conflicts like the case just described in which no one speaks the truth or trusts anyone and in which both sides are putting a great deal of pressure on consultants to support their group's point of view, there is a point where traditional collaborative, consensus approaches to change are not effective and conflict and power-coercive approaches must be used. To facilitate this approach, it is helpful for consultants, especially those working in human service organizations like prisons, to consider the residents and tax-payers as the clients and, therefore, the real losers in the conflict. This "consumer as client" approach will help the consultant remain as objective as possible in analyzing the situation and will assist him or her to speak out honestly and frankly. The aim is to cause movement, alteration, and change in an intolerable organizational situation. To accomplish this, someone has to speak straightforwardly and this usually means the outside consultant, who is expendable to the ongoing situation.[23]

[23] This chapter is a revised version of Robert Sebring and David Duffee, "Who Are the Real Prisoners? A Case of Win-Lose Conflict in a State Correctional Institution," *Journal of Applied Behavioral Science* (February, 1977), pp. 23–40; reprinted by permission of the NTL Institute for Applied Behavioral Science.

12

Interorganizational Behavior and Correctional Programming

(David Duffee and Barbara D. Warner)

The case study presented in Chapter 11 can serve our interest in the management of interorganizational relations in several respects. First, it should point out the importance of coordination between organizations. This example of conflict between correctional agencies and other types of organizations is not unique. Correctional organizations of every type have a variety of interorganizational exchanges to deal with. Many involve other agencies in the "criminal justice system." Receiving offenders sentenced from court, consultation between a probation office and a sentencing judge or between the judge and the diagnostic center of a correctional department, the interaction between prison authorities and the parole board on parole granting and revocation, and the referral of prisoners to halfway houses serve as examples.

There are also many other exchanges that take the correctional manager away from the agencies of the criminal process itself. The involvement of outside educational organizations is a common one.

Many prisons run schools that have joint reporting and supervisory channels: one to the superintendent and one to a local or state education agency. In some systems the school teachers are employees of the department of correction and in some systems the teachers are employees of the educational agency. Lines of authority and advice obviously differ between these two cases, but, in either situation, cooperation is essential.

Because institutions house their charges almost entirely, a variety of other service organization exchanges are also crucial. Arrangements must be made with local hospitals for the care of seriously sick or injured offenders. Frequently, correctional institutions have arrangements with outside doctors, psychologists, and psychiatrists for services rendered on a contract basis. Most prison systems also have liaisons with various churches for the fulfillment of chaplaincies and with local civic groups, such as the Lions and the Junior Chamber of Commerce, for various inmate programs. Correctional departments also heavily rely on bureaus of vocational rehabilitation and state employment services for vocational programs in prison, employment counseling, and locating training and employment for released prisoners.

Correctional field organizations also have a great many interorganizational activities to conduct, although the nature of the collaboration and the nature of the exchange are likely to differ from those commonly found in prisons. Probation and parole organizations, particularly now that the reintegration policy has become popular, engage in many cross-agency contacts in order to obtain services for offenders. Halfway houses also frequently engage in the same referral for service activity. Correctional field staff frequently spend a great deal of time developing contacts for general organizational and program support. Probation and parole officials are constantly contacting employers to find opportunities for offenders, often simply to build support in the work community for the employment of offenders. More important still to probation and parole work, however, is that the officer must approach officials of other organizations in the daily routine of offender supervision.

Thus, interorganizational exchange between correctional agencies and other organizations is constant. Yet, there is little written about the management of interorganizational relations in corrections, and the amount of conflict between correctional and other types of agencies is generally considered high. There is also a great deal of complaint that outside organizations are often unwilling to deal with correctional clients, even when their own service mandates suggest that offenders are eligible for service.

It is extremely important that correctional managers begin to focus more directly on their interorganizational responsibilities. Doing so will require that these managers learn the differences between dealing with outside organizations and dealing with agencies and subunits that are directly under their command.

DISTINCTIONS BETWEEN INTERORGANIZATIONAL AND INTRAORGANIZATIONAL RELATIONS

The great majority of organizational theory and research focuses on the internal structure and dynamics of single organizations. Only recently has organizational theory shifted interest to examine the problems of interorganizational relations. One of the reasons for the slowness of this development is that interorganizational analysis requires, at least to some extent, a different frame of reference from that which seems productive for the analysis of intraorganizational behavior.

The greatest distinction, say Litwak and Hylton, is that intraorganizational theory has stressed the centralized location of power in American organizations and the types of structures that are generated by unitary, centralized forms of command over ordered, collective behavior.[1] They suggest that the opposite is necessary as a starting point in the analysis of interorganizational behaviors. Interorganizational analysis points up the possibility of maintaining acceptable amounts of social conflict as organizations interacting with each other attempt to achieve their own goals as they interact with the outside environment. Most interorganizational interactions are *not* governed by a central authority, and the extent to which the organizations will cooperate with each other is guided by voluntary association of two or more organizations for a joint purpose. The means of establishing and maintaining such voluntary, joint behaviors is very different from the means of getting two parts of the same organization to interact effectively.[2]

Litwak and Hylton's study of coordinating agencies in the health and social welfare fields suggests that the rise and survival of agencies to coordinate service agency activity is dependent on (1) the interdependence of the organizations to be coordinated, (2) the level of awareness among the organizations, (3) the extent to which the activities that join the organizations can be standardized, and (4) the number of organizations that are involved. They suggest, in relation

[1] Eugene Litwak and Lydia F. Hylton, "Interorganizational Analysis: A Hypothesis on Coordinating Agencies," *Administrative Science Quarterly* (March, 1962), pp. 395–420.
[2] Ibid.

to "interdependence," that organizational relations will vary curvi-linearly. If organizations have little interdependence, there will be little coordination of their activities. On the other extreme, if the two organizations are totally dependent on each other, it is very likely that they will merge rather than achieve some means of co-ordinating their activities on an interorganizational basis. The level of interorganizational awareness and the standardization of organiza-tional activities are positively related to coordination. The more that organizations are aware of each other, and the more that their activities can be summarized, transferred, and counted in discrete units and packages, the more coordination can exist.[3]

The number of organizations to be coordinated affects coordina-tion in varying ways. If there are few organizations to coordinate, it is unlikely that any formal means of coordination will arise. But if there are a great many organizations to coordinate, and if their interactions can all be catalogued in the same manner, it is more likely that coordination will entail legislated regulation rather than the establishment of an agency to coordinate activity.[4]

While Litwak and Hylton's study concentrated on the conditions under which formal types of coordinative arrangement would emerge, Levine and White have focused on the attempt to define the nature of organizational exchanges themselves, regardless of their frequency or the extent of coordination that emerges.[5] Levine and White define exchange between organizations as "any voluntary activity between two organizations which has consequences, actual or anticipated, for the realization of their respective goals or objectives."[6] They go on to enumerate four dimensions of the exchange relation that they feel are crucial in determining whether or not exchange will take place and what its outcomes will be. These dimensions are:

1. The parties to the exchange, or the nature of the organizations that will be interrelated;
2. The kinds of things, information, people, or other resources exchanged and the amount or quantities exchanged;
3. The type of agreement underlying the exchange—whether it is highly formal or an ad hoc arrangement—and the extent to which the organizations both want the exchange.

---

[3] Ibid.
[4] Ibid.
[5] Sol Levine and Paul E. White, "Exchange as a Conceptual Framework for the Study of Interorganizational Relationships," in Y. Hasenfeld and R. English, *Human Service Organizations* (Ann Arbor: University of Michigan Press, 1974), pp. 545–61.
[6] Ibid., p. 548.

4. The direction of exchange, in terms of whether one organization does the sending and the other the receiving (unilateral), both organizations trade elements (reciprocal), or both organizations send resources to another party (joint support for a separate program or agency).[7]

In a related article that focuses on exchange in health organizations, Levine, White, and Paul stress that organizational exchanges are inherently bound up with organizational goals and the attempts of an organization to achieve objectives.[8] They suggest that it is infrequent that an organization can carry out all of its goal-related activities to an optimum level and that achieving even partial goal attainment often requires a greater base of resources than the organization can muster internally. They feel that most organizational exchanges are attempts to get some or all three "organizational elements" that are crucial to goal achievement. These elements are: (1) recipients of services, (2) the equipment, knowledge, and funds to carry out the service, and (3) the service of personnel to render the service to clients.[9]

They suggest that

Kinds and degrees of interactions that go on among agencies are affected by (1) the functions that they carry out which, in turn, determine the elements they need, (2) their access to elements from outside the system of health and welfare agencies or, conversely, their relative dependence upon the local system of other health and welfare agencies.[10]

Transposed to correctional problems, one might suggest that correctional organizations will interact with other agencies to the extent that their goals require outside resources (and the types of resources required) and to the extent that the correctional organization can gather these resources from higher sources (such as access to taxes) or must rely on other agencies to meet some resource needs through an exchange relationship.

There are a variety of ways in which these concepts and hypothetical statements can be tested within the correctional field. Probably the most important interorganizational relationships for correctional managers are those involving other correctional agencies. Since the following chapter will examine in detail the exchanges between courts and correctional organizations, we have chosen in

[7] Ibid., pp. 558–59.
[8] Sol Levine, Paul E. White, and Benjamin D. Paul, "Community Interorganizational Problems in Providing Medical Care and Social Services," *American Journal of Public Health* (Aug., 1963), pp. 1183–95.
[9] Ibid., p. 1185.
[10] Ibid., p. 1190.

this chapter to examine relationships between prison and parole organizations as an example of interorganizational exchange within the criminal justice system. After looking at this system linkage, we will go on to examine the nature of interorganizational relations in community settings and the extent to which correctional agencies can become participating members of the interorganizational field or network at the community level. We will then examine how the formalization of relations with outside service agencies can influence the extent to which offender needs are fulfilled and some of the steps that correctional managers can take to improve relations with outside agencies.

EXCHANGE BETWEEN PRISON AND PAROLE ORGANIZATIONS[11]

In a number of states the prison and parole administrations have been combined under one superagency for the coordination of institutional and field services. In other states, and in the federal system, prison and parole administrations are formally separated. In some states the prison and parole systems may exist with equal status as departments. In other states the parole organization is included as an aspect of the governor's executive offices and may be attached directly to the parole board. The first parole in America was operated by prison administrators themselves as part of the program at the Elmira, New York, reformatory when it opened in 1876. However, frequent conflicts of interest between prison administration and the parole-granting decision later resulted in the establishment of an autonomous parole board. The separation of the board and the parole-granting decision from prison administration often resulted in the separation as well of the organization for the supervision of parolees and the organization for the supervision of inmates.

This separation solved, at least for a while, some problems such as claims that the paroling authority was too heavily swayed by the opinion held by prison staff about offender and/or prison maintenance needs. But the separation caused some other problems of the coordinative variety, for in the separated condition the prison and parole administrators had to coordinate their policies and their plans for offenders across the boundaries of their respective organizations. As the general organizational theory presented in Part One has demonstrated, organizations jealously guard their boundaries and the

---

[11] This section draws heavily on David Duffee, Frederick Hussey, and John Kramer, *Criminal Justice: Organization, Structure, and Analysis* (Englewood Cliffs, N.J.: Prentice-Hall, 1978), pp. 405–12.

extent to which outside organizations are given a part in the decisions about organizational goals and programs.[12] Hence, even though prison and parole organizations may have common overall goals (or value premises), they frequently differ in the ways in which these value premises are prioritized. Consequently, conflict between prison and parole organizations is frequent, and its consequences for effective offender supervision can be drastic.

To the extent that Levine and White are accurate in their analysis of the dimensions of organizational exchange, the goals of the prison and parole organizations in relation to each other should help to explain how various correctional agencies will interact with each other and explain the impact that this interaction will have on the offender. Because the correctional policy typology has demonstrated viability as a goal typology in both prison and parole settings, it may be useful to start with the examination of how the different policies can guide the way prison and parole organizations will interact with each other.

Figure 12.1 shows 16 possible combinations of prison and parole policy and the extent to which conflict among the policies might be observed. We would expect that organizations with identical policies would have little conflict. Obviously, differences of opinion may always arise over how an offender should be supervised, over who and how many people should be paroled and revoked, and so on. Nevertheless, we would expect that organizations in the main diagonal line of Figure 12.1 would at least have common philosophies, understand

Prison/Parole Policy and Possible Conflict

| | | Prison Policy | | | |
		Reintegration	Rehabilitation	Reform	Restraint
	Reintegration	Identical	Mild conflict	Open conflict	Open conflict
Parole Policy	Rehabilitation	Mild conflict	Identical	Mild conflict	Open conflict
	Reform	Open conflict	Mild conflict	Identical	Mild conflict
	Restraint	Open conflict	Open conflict	Mild conflict	Identical

Figure 12.1

[12] See especially James D. Thompson and William McEwen, "Organizational Goals and Environment: Goal Setting as an Interaction Process," *American Sociological Review* (February 1958), pp. 23-30.

each other's priorities and the reasons for differences, and might be able to work out conflicts that do arise in a mutually satisfactory manner.

Naturally, the type and frequency of exchange, even in the case of identical prison/parole policies, will be determined to a great extent by the policy in question. Exchange between restraint policy agencies is likely to be limited, since both agencies attempt to be self-sufficient and to minimize contacts with outside organizations. Restraint prison and parole organizations are thus likely to communicate with each other only as required by their own rules. The most obvious element of exchange will be the offenders themselves. Since both organizations do not consider it part of their function to provide services or to facilitate change for offenders, this exchange is likely to be highly routinized and unencumbered by a great deal of information about the offender. It is unlikely for these organizations to engage in a great deal of joint undertakings, and there will be little mutual planning or program sharing and very little in the way of sharing of staff.

Exchange between reform organizations is likely to be more complex, but still relatively slight. These organizations attempt to change offenders through the control of the external environment and the use of external sanctions. The information about offenders probably given the greatest importance will involve information about misbehavior and the sanctions applied and information about the types of rule infractions or criminal infractions expected from the offender as he or she is transferred from one organization to the other. Since reform organizations also rely heavily on the value of work, information about offender work skills and interests is likely to be highlighted. Again, there is likely to be little sharing of resources or personnel, except that parole officials may establish offices in the prison to expedite parole planning.

Exchange in rehabilitation organizations is likely to be more frequent and more complex because of the greater complexity perceived in the nature of the offenders' behavior. Hence, there is likely to be a great deal of sharing of information about diagnoses and prognoses. There may well be sharing of staff in the sense that both prison and parole officials may jointly consider cases and how they should be handled. It is unlikely, however, that there will be many joint programs between these organizations. The exchange is controlled in the sense that the prison will handle the offender during the most difficult stages of offender adjustment and the parole department will handle offenders as their "conditions" improve.

Exchange is likely to be greatest in reintegration organizations. Since reintegration organizations place high priority on testing an offender's behavior under real conditions, and on maximizing the match between the offender's goals and the means available to achieve them, there should be a good deal of joint planning and perhaps some joint programming between the two agencies. Reintegration organizations will attempt to minimize the extent to which prisons themselves have to be used and to minimize the distance between prison and community life. Hence, there is likely to be a great deal of exchange of offenders in the parole direction. Parole will be used frequently, and the differences between parole and institutional living will be reduced through the use of intermediate units, such as halfway houses, over which both organizations may exercise some control.

Under the conditions of mild conflict noted in Figure 12.1, the exchanges discussed above may not be too different, except that more conflict will enter the situation. In situations in which the parole office is more liberal than the prison is, the conflict may not be too difficult for either the organizations or the offenders to handle, although there will be some problems. It is possible, for example, that the more liberal parole office may consider offenders ready for parole before prison officials think they are ready. However, this may not create too much conflict since the more conservative prisons are likely to see the "dangers" of early release falling on the parole office instead of themselves. Other difficulties may include the inability of the parole office to obtain from the more conservative prison the information that is sought relevant to parole planning for the offender. For example, a restraint prison may not gather all of the psychological factors that a rehabilitation parole agency would think important.

Because of the sequential relation of prison and parole agencies in the criminal process, there may be greater administrative problems when the prison is slightly more liberal than the parole agency. In these situations, offenders will "stack up" in prison even though the prison officials believe they are ready for release. Morale for both prison staff and offenders may suffer under these circumstances. Similarly, if a reintegration or rehabilitation prison attempts to obtain joint planning or program supervision from reform or restraint parole offices, the prison officials are likely to become frustrated. Prison officials may feel that the types of training that they want to initiate in the institution will lack continuity with the offender's supervision on parole because the more conservative parole agents are either not interested in services or change activities for offenders or are more interested in surveillance than provision of service.

Finally, Figure 12.1 located six occasions of "open conflict," or instances when the policies of the prison and parole organizations are so far apart that little productive exchange may take place. About the only exchange that is likely to occur with any frequency in these instances is the passage of offenders themselves between organizations. But even in these instances, the policy and philosophical differences are so great that there is likely to be a great deal of misunderstanding concerning the offender and a great deal of other conflicts concerning matters of mutual interest. To take the most extreme cases, let us look very briefly at a reintegration prison attempting to cooperate with a restraint parole office, and vice versa, a reintegration parole office attempting to receive offenders from a restraint prison.

A reintegration-oriented prison is likely to be seen as a threat to a restraint-oriented parole department, because the prison officials will be eager to parole offenders at the earliest possible date and to intervene in the community on the behalf of offenders. The parole office is likely to see this as meddling by the prison staff. The parole agency, attempting to avoid adverse criticism from the community, is likely to see the prison official's behavior as troublesome to organizational stability. There will also be few ways in which the organizational officials can deal with each other effectively. To the reintegration staff, the restraint parole staff will appear conservative, unconcerned about the welfare of clients, and unconcerned as well about the protection of the community that could be brought about by successfully integrating the offender into community living. The restraint parole staff are likely to see the prison staff as overly idealistic, as conflict seeking, as underconcerned with constraints imposed by record-keeping tasks and the perceived nature of the community. Joint planning is unlikely to happen frequently in these instances, and joint programs are probably out of the question.

The opposite condition (a reintegration parole department facing a restraint prison) may be equally difficult, although the direction of exchange of offenders is likely to mean that the prison staff will not feel overly threatened by whatever the parole department wants to do in the way of community supervision. The prison staff simply will not help the parole department to obtain their reintegration goals. Hence, the parole department is likely to feel that offenders are not prepared for parole because the prison staff placed little emphasis on training programs and release preparation. Parole officials, even though they hold earliest possible release of offenders as an important priority, are likely to feel that there is insufficient information on inmates to allow early parole in some instances. More likely, however, the parole staff will simply feel that all the tasks of change are dumped on them and that any activities of job searching and other preparatory steps that could have taken place in prison have to begin on parole. Another possible conflict will be with offenders themselves. Experienced in the restraint atmosphere of the prison, offenders may feel that the reintegration parole staff expect and demand too much of them. If they are accustomed to "doing their own time" in prison and to being left alone if rules are obeyed, offenders may perceive the parole staff as idealistic meddlers who are out to "mess up their heads" or interfere with their style of life in the community.

The management tasks that are implied by these different prison parole relationships vary considerably, both in the nature of what managers can do to reduce conflict and in the decision of where that conflict resolution must start. The further apart the two organizations are in their basic policy, the greater will be the need for top-management intervention to solve conflicts. Front-line officials can do little to solve the problems that arise between themselves or with their clients if they are operating under the very different constraints imposed by reintegration and restraint policies. Hence, if conflict is to be reduced in these instances, it will require a great deal of basic philosophical discussion at the top levels of the organizations. In short, open conflicts will not be settled until there is a policy change in one organization or the other, or in both.

In some instances of such conflict, a third-party intervention may be necessary before policy conflict resolution can take place. Examples would be if a state planning agency, the governor's office, or some consulting group pressures for change in the way that the organizations get together. Often, this conflict resolution may entail wholesale personnel changes at the top level of both organizations.

When the conflicts are milder and basic policy differences are less extreme, it may be that the organizational top staff can delegate some conflict resolution to middle managers in both organizations. Basic philosophical differences may remain in these instances, but concerted effort among middle managers working across organizations may reduce the disruptiveness of these differences. Together they may be able to settle on a series of joint organizational agreements that formalize the procedures by which the organizations exchange elements, and by a series of compromises they may work to a situation in which each organization gives to the other something that the other wants in order to further its own ends. The type of conflict resolution may, in the end result, have the consequences of changing the policy of one of the organizations or both, as these operations change. But the extensiveness of change is likely to be less than in the previous case.

Finally, when organizations have joint or identical policies, the types of conflict present in exchange situations are not going to be disagreements about goals, but smaller disagreements about the means of achieving them. In these instances, middle management can probably handle almost all the questions that arise, and in the long run they may delegate much of the exchange issue to front-line personnel. Even in these instances, however, prison and parole organizations will experience more effective exchanges to the extent that formal channels for discussion are kept open, perhaps in the form of a standing joint committee or even in the form of as little investment as an annual joint meeting in which mutual problems can be investigated and the means of resolution initiated.

THE INTERORGANIZATIONAL FIELD

While the interaction between prison and parole organizations is very important in its own right, probably more important as time goes on is the total interorganizational field into which all correctional agencies must fit within the American community structure. Warren and his colleagues, in a study of six "community decision organizations" in nine American cities, remarked with some surprise that in virtually all cities above a certain size they could identify identical or almost identical community organizations at work.[13] "Such regularity of appearance documents the essential similarity of the formal organizational structure of the American community, sector by sector."[14]

Previous to the Warren study, many community power and decision experts concentrated on influential individuals in community settings and examined community decisions as functions of the influence exerted either by a single elite group or by a pluralistic set of power groups who came forward as different issues of importance to community living arose.[15] Warren's group countered this perspective with the decision to study what they titled the community decision organizations, the agencies on the community level that

[13] Roland L. Warren, Stephen M. Rose, and Ann F. Bergunder, *The Structure of Urban Reform* (Lexington, Mass.: Lexington Books, 1974).
[14] Ibid., p. 6.
[15] See Floyd Hunter, Ruth Conner Schaffer, and Cecil G. Sheps, *Community Organization: Action and Inaction* (Chapel Hill: University of North Carolina Press, 1956); Linton C. Freeman, Thomas J. Farara, Warner Bloomberg, Jr., and Morris H. Sunshine, "Locating Leaders in Local Communities: A Comparison of Some Alternative Approaches," *American Sociological Review* (Oct., 1963), pp. 791–98; and readings in Willis D. Hawley and Frederick M. Wirt, *The Search for Community Power* (Englewood Cliffs, N.J.: Prentice-Hall, 1974).

made decisions about urban policy and social services distribution. They argue that these organizations may be equally important as influential opinion leaders in the determination of how a community may respond to social problems and, moreover, that influential individuals and groups gain influence to the extent that they have access to these organizations.[16]

> [Community Decision Organizations] have, within their legitimated fields, inordinate power to control not only what is done about specific problems, but even more basically, how specific problems will be defined, and what choices of technology and professional expertise will be employed in addressing them . . . .[17]

Warren's team took a rather different approach to the analysis of social service organizations than we have described so far. While they highlight the work of Levine and White and Litwak and Hylton, they also suggest that the exchange approach, which we illustrated in the prison/parole example, is still too limited to do justice to the actual operations of community organizations. They suggest that instead of looking at the external relations of one organization, of the exchanges between two organizations, it is important to stress the influences of the "interorganizational field" itself on community structure and the allocation of social resources on the community level.

The seminal work in this area is the attempt to classify the organizational environments into several different types.[18] We have discussed this work previously in the attempt to understand why interorganizational relations and the management of the environment are increasingly becoming the most important aspects of the managerial role.[19] In brief, Emery and Trist argue that the nature of an organization's environment will itself determine to a great extent what the organization can do to achieve its goals and the kinds of management strategies that are appropriate to achieving them.[20] They suggest that all organizations desire to gain some measure of control over their environments in order to increase the effectiveness of operations, but that the means of obtaining control have changed. As organizational environments become more turbulent, they would suggest, organizations are forced to become more interdependent on outside forces (notably other organizations) to obtain their respective goals. In some instances, this interdependence may mean a greater

[16] Warren, Rose, and Bergunder, *The Structure of Urban Reform*, p. 6.
[17] Ibid., p. 170.
[18] F. E. Emery and E. L. Trist, "The Causal Texture of Organizational Environment," in F. E. Emery (ed.), *Systems Thinking* (Baltimore: Penguin, 1970), pp. 241-58.
[19] See Part Four and Chapters 3 and 10.
[20] Emery and Trist, "The Causal Texture of Organizational Environment."

amount of merger and coalition among organizations in order to "simplify" the environment. However, they also suggest that organizations can maintain their independence and also achieve some measure of placidness in the environment to the extent that related organizations can achieve a common normative framework concerning what each organization should be doing and how it should be done.

Warren et al. have expanded on this idea of a common normative framework. They suggest that in trying to understand why social service and urban planning organizations act as they do, it is important to examine the relations among all the organizations rather than single organizations themselves. Key elements in the interorganizational field, according to Warren et al., are domain, norms, and "institutionalized thought structure."[21] The importance of domain was discussed in Chapter 10 in which it was posited that the claimed domain of correctional organizations was shrinking and that other social agencies were expanding their domains to perform functions previously carried out by correctional agencies. Norms refer to the established means by which the several organizations settle their contests about domain. In the above discussion of prison and parole exchange, we could say that the commonality of norms increases as the similarity of policy increases, but that only in cases of open conflict (which would be rare) are the sharing of norms so low that rule-guided contest between organizations becomes very disruptive. In the more common cases of organizational disagreement, there are at least unspoken agreements between agencies concerning the proper sphere of each. For example, even if a rehabilitation prison staff disagree with a reform parole staff, the prison staff do not try to establish alternative paths by which to release offenders from custody.

Warren's team suggests that perhaps most important to the character of the interorganizational field in the social service field, however, is the institutionalized thought structure that undergirds the norms of exchange and predetermines the types and the scope of domain that is seen as legitimate by various agencies. The institutionalized thought structure has several elements. According to Warren, it consists of (1) a common belief value system about the value and functioning of American society, (2) basically similar strategies for addressing social problems, (3) basically similar ideologies or rationales for organizations working in the social sector, (4) basically similar authority

---

[21] Warren, Rose, and Bergunder, *The Structure of Urban Reform*, pp. 18-9.

structures for the organizations in question, and (5) similar sources of legitimation and power.[22]

A detailed examination of the organizations and programs established to deal with urban poverty and juvenile delinquency in the early 1960's tends to corroborate Warren's findings. Marris and Rein found that the available, or feasible, strategies for handling urban social problems were limited by the fact that

> The administrative and political structure of the United States explicitly intends that no power, at any level of government, shall claim authority broad enough to control all the social institutions of a community.[23]

Within this basic fact of political structure in the United States, they found that the principle means of social problem solving is delegated to a variety of autonomous organizations. A heavy interest exists in each organization with its own survival, particularly if the personnel believe strongly in what they are doing. Hence, almost as a matter of survival, and in an unplanned and informal way, the interactions of the various social agencies delimit the goals and strategies of each organization. The attempt to break this cycle by establishing new and innovative organizations frequently fails. Because the newcomer threatens the jurisdiction (domain) of the established authority, it has to struggle to survive. Survival becomes the most urgent purpose . . . " and round again.[24]

THE INTERORGANIZATIONAL FIELD AND SERVICE TO OFFENDERS

There is little question about the low level of need fulfillment among the American offender population or among the larger population from which they come. In most cases, offenders are recruited from the same class of persons who become the target of the social reforms headed by the agencies studied by Warren and by Marris and Rein. A high level of social problems is especially observable among offenders released from prison. This group not only has the typical problems associated with lower-class groups, but it has added to those the problems caused or exacerbated by the condition of its separation from community living for a significant period of time and the stigmatized conditions of the return itself.[25]

[22] Ibid., p. 20.

[23] Peter Marris and Martin Rein, *Dilemmas of Social Reform* (New York: Atherton, 1967), p. 137.

[24] Ibid., p. 42.

[25] See John Irwin, *The Felon* (Englewood Cliffs, N.J.: Prentice-Hall, 1970); Elliot Studt, *Surveillance and Service in Parole* (Los Angeles: UCLA Institute of Government and Public Affairs, 1972).

Almost every study of offenders returning from prison has emphasized the problems of poverty and lack of work. Lenihan, reviewing the financial condition of prisoners released in all 50 states, finds the financial resources of prisoners very inadequate (as low as $20 in gate money in some places, and no means of transportation away from the prison). The low level of gate money, low inmate wages, the small number of inmates admitted to work release, and the lack of loans to released prisoners all contribute to an impoverishment that can only excite a need to return to crime for financial reasons.[26]

Lack of money, of course, can often be symptomatic of other problems. It may indicate a low level of education, and therefore no means of obtaining a good job or establishing credit. And it has attendant with it all sorts of other lingering problems that money could alleviate, such as the need for expensive medical attention, transportation to and from work, educational training, legal services, and adequate housing.

There may be some things that the correctional system can do to correct this situation on its own, but it is surprising how little a correctional agency can accomplish to meet social problems, even within the prison setting, without the cooperation of outside organizations. Greater pay for inmate labor is, of course, connected to the willingness of the legislature to allocate funds, or at least the willingness of outside firms to accommodate prison competition in the market by which higher prices for prison produced goods could pay for higher wages. Meyer also documents the workings of the correctional–industrial complex in which the enforced poverty of offenders allows pharmaceutical companies to save millions each year by paying small wages to inmates to be guinea pigs in drug experiments.[27] Sacks' survey of the means of finding work release employers also underscores the importance (and the lack) of solid working relationships between correctional programs and outside organizations.[28]

The desperation of the correctional agency status in the social service field might be indicated by a recent article relating to subsidizing released offenders. Norman Colter argues that the offender's poor financial condition adds to his or her other problems and increases the chances of his or her return to crime. Stressing the amount of money that could be saved if additional crime were

[26] Kenneth J. Lenihan, "The Financial Condition of Released Prisoners," *Crime and Delinquency* (July, 1975), pp. 266-81.

[27] Peter B. Meyer, *Drug Experiments on Prisoners* (Lexington, Mass.: Lexington Books, 1975).

[28] Mason J. Sacks, "Making Work Release Work: Convincing the Employer," *Crime and Delinquency* (July, 1975), pp. 255-65.

avoided, Colter suggests that parole boards should subsidize the offender until the offender gets on his or her feet, perhaps for a period of 6 months. The suggestion itself makes sense; the surprising thing is the implication that the correctional system itself should (and would have to) bear the burden for the subsidy when other unemployed or needy citizens can apply to county boards for assistance.[29]

Meeting the direct needs of offenders is not the only service-related aspect of correctional work where greater integration of the correctional agency in the community would make programs either more possible or more effective. Several studies about the opening of group homes have found that the correctional agency may encounter a variety of difficulties in different communities. In middle-class communities, for example, the agency frequently has difficulty neutralizing the power of organized political resistance. In lower-class communities, establishing community programs may be easier, but the agency continually faces suspicion over the contents of the program as well as feelings that the agency is controlled by outsiders.[30]

A recent study of parole in Chicago illustrated the equal importance of interorganizational relations in parole work. McCleary found that parole officers were severely limited in their effectivenss in serving clients by their need to build reputations as competent and fair officers. "Competence" and "fairness" to outside agencies tended to mean that the officer would not advocate for his client in situations in which adverse publicity would result and that the agent's decisions to refer or sponsor a client for social programs would be balanced against the other agencies' desire for good risk, low-trouble clients.[31] McCleary is critical of the structural position that parole officers find themselves in, stating that the officers are so dependent on building their reputations, both inside their own agency and across agencies, that the reputations themselves rather than public protection or offender service become their primary concerns.[32] This situation seems very similar to the problems that Marris and Rein observed of new agencies moving into a social action

---

[29] Norman C. Colter, "Subsidizing the Released Inmate," *Crime and Delinquency* (July, 1975), pp. 282–85.
[30] Pedro Ruiz, John Langrid, and Joyce Lowinson, "Resistance to the Opening of Drug Treatment Centers: A Problem in Community Psychiatry," *The International Journal of the Addictions* (March, 1975, pp. 149–55; Robert B. Coates and Alden D. Miller, "Neutralization of Community Resistance to Group Homes," in Yitzhak Bakal (ed.), *Closing Correctional Institutions* (Lexington, Mass.: Lexington Books, 1974), pp. 67–84.
[31] Richard McCleary, "How Structural Variables Constrain the Parole Officer's Use of Discretionary Powers," *Social Problems* (Dec., 1975), pp. 209–25.
[32] Ibid., p. 224.

area: They threaten the domain of other organizations, and as a result must become defensively overconcerned with their own.

Wallace Mandell, in a frequently cited discussion piece, relates the difficulty in obtaining services for offenders to the difficulty that correctional agencies have had in entering the domain of social service work. Other, longer established community service agencies do not often recognize correctional agencies and staffs as legitimate members of the social service community.[33] This argument raises an interesting possibility that we will test later: that the difficulty of offenders in receiving services and resolving problems may be as much a function of their association with stigmatized agencies as it is a function of their own stigmatized position in the community.[34] In other words, it is possible that the offender's access to social services and resources will increase only as the correctional agencies improve relations with outside agencies or as the need fulfillment function for residents is totally dissociated from the correctional agencies that guard and exercise surveillance over the offender.[35]

> Organizations for specific clients have never done well because they cannot mobilize enough power to overcome the elites and their arguments for efficiency. Thus specialized organizations tend to become easily dominated by elite values and inevitably move toward rigid bureaucratic control and a concern for efficiency.[36]

If Hage's observation is essentially accurate, it would go a long way toward explaining the difficulty that correctional agencies have in obtaining sufficient resources to meet offender needs on their own, as well as help to explain the difficulties that correctional agencies have in joining a broader social service community. Aiken and Hage found that organizations with the greatest number of joint programs were agencies with the greatest amount of internal complexity, a greater amount of innovation, more active communication channels, and rather decentralized decision-making structures.[37] But, as we have already seen, correctional agencies often have stilted and limited communication networks (Chapter 7), have great difficulty innovating (Chapter 10), and tend toward autonomy, defensiveness, and

[33] Wallace Mandell, "Making Correction a Community Agency," *Crime and Delinquency* (July, 1971), pp. 281-88.

[34] Irwin has much to say about this possibility in *The Felon.*

[35] On the issue of separating service delivery entirely from corrections, see Chapter 15 of this book and Norval Morris, *The Future of Imprisonment* (Chicago: University of Chicago Press, 1974).

[36] Jerald Hage, "A Strategy for Creating Interdependent Delivery Systems to Meet Complex Needs," in A. Negandhi (ed.), *Interorganizational Relations* (Kent, Ohio: Kent University Press, 1974), p. 224.

[37] Michael Aiken and Jerald Hage, "Organizational Interdependence and Intra-Organizational Structure," *American Sociological Review* (Dec., 1968), p. 912.

centralization of authority (Chapter 11). In addition to these problems is the problem that the resource bases of the correctional agencies are limited to their legally constrained clientele; therefore, their ability to join in the established interorganizational field of human service agencies may be minimal indeed.

Hage states that

> There is little (interdependence) between organizations that are competitors, and it is precisely these organizations that one needs and wants in a delivery system for clients with multiple handicaps . . . [38]

Even if it might be beneficial for the offender (or anyone else with problems) to have available as a means of meeting those needs a cooperative network of social service agencies, even though it might be beneficial for the community containing these people to have their needs met, "coordination may not necessarily be advantageous to the agencies involved, as they define their goals and functions . . . ."[39]

Reid identifies three levels on which two agencies can cooperate with each other: (1) ad hoc case coordination, (2) systematic case coordination, or service integration, and (3) program coordination, or joint programming.[40] In reviewing cases of voluntary cooperation (Levine and White would call it exchange), Reid also emphasizes the importance of shared goals and complementary resources, but, unlike Levine and White, he adds that there must be efficient means to control the exchange.[41] In analyzing the means of control necessary for each level of coordination or exchange, he concludes that the heaviest cost of unmediated agency coordination is establishing routine exchange governing mechanisms. Creating such mechanisms, Reid cautions, may be more costly to the agencies and to the community than the benefit of the added or coordinated service can justify.[42]

This observation is extremely important because it underscores a general, common-sense point that is often overlooked by planners and critics, if not by agency executives themselves. Every benefit has its attendant costs, and unless resources are unlimited, correctional agencies and the outside agencies they wish to coordinate with will both have to pay for the coordination. The outside agencies

---

[38] Hage, "Interdependent Delivery Systems to Meet Complex Needs," p. 223.
[39] William Reid, "Interagency Coordination in Delinquency Prevention and Control," *Social Service Review* (March, 1964), p. 427.
[40] Ibid., pp. 420–21. See also Bertram T. Black and Harold M. Kase, "Interagency Cooperation in Rehabilitation and Mental Health," *Social Service Review* (March, 1963), pp. 26–32.
[41] Reid, "Interagency Coordination in Delinquency Prevention and Control," p. 421.
[42] Ibid., pp. 426–27.

frequently complain that the price of dealing with correctional agencies and clients is too high. Correctional managers may also find the cost too high. Interagency cooperation will demand that internal resources (principally manpower) be expended in outside coordinative efforts. Unless resources are unlimited (which would make co-ordination unnecessary anyway), managers may feel that the drain of manpower away from internal organizational roles is too costly under present organizational policy and structural arrangements.

Of course, the correctional organizations and/or the outside agencies can always change their internal policy and priorities to free up additional resources for interorganizational programs. But pursuing this possibility would take us back to Part Two of this book to reexamine the present policies in operation or ahead to Part Five in which we will examine the relationship between correctional policy change and general changes in American social structure. In the meantime, let us examine some other difficulties in the current interorganizational situation.

A common problem for correctional organizations as they confront the need to engage other organizations in meaningful exchanges is the difference in the structure between correctional organizations and other social service agencies operating at the community level. Correctional agencies, for example, state vocational rehabilitation departments and state departments of mental health, have a highly formalized vertical articulation between any local community action office and a central state office where policy is formulated, budgets are structured, and agency evaluations are performed. Many of the social service agencies that have the competence in social services needed by correctional clients are not so structured. They are either autonomous agencies making their own policy or they are agencies federated on the local level and gaining support from a community chest and/or local government.

Levine and White have observed that agencies with vertical ties to a state level department may often have conflicts with local service agencies who are more dependent on each other and on local support.[43] They point out that while the state level and local agencies may have common value premises (or goals), and, in Warren's terms, have the same institutionalized thought structure, the agencies operate in different and conflicting resource domains, the different constraints of which pull them apart.[44]

---

[43] Levine and White, "Exchange as a Conceptual Framework for the Study of Interorganizational Relationships," p. 550.
[44] Levine, White, and Paul, "Community Interorganizational Problems in Providing Medical Care and Social Services," p. 1184.

Levine, White, and Paul comment that this differential authority structure may influence interorganizational relations so strongly that "particular organizations may find it more difficult to legitimize themselves to other parts of the . . . agency system than to such outside systems as the community or the state."[45] Hence, if a state-run correctional system is to increase the ability of its local suboffices to integrate their services with outside agencies, the higher managers will have to devise means by which the local office executives can maintain sufficient discretion to accommodate the constraints operating in the other agencies without being cut off from the state level system that supports the local operation.[46]

Correctional agencies on the local level of government will not encounter this problem. Their managers will be more concerned with the conservative status quo thrust that their relations with other local agencies and with local government will give their programs and the range of experiences they can offer to offenders. Local correctional agencies will be tied to the institutionalized thought structure that exists in the interorganizational field at the local level, and they will encounter problems that correctional clients are "undeserving" of the expensive programs and services that are in short supply for even more "deserving" clients.[47]

INTERAGENCY COOPERATION AND OFFENDER PROBLEM RESOLUTION

We had the opportunity to test some of these general observations and assumptions about offender problems and means of problems resolution in 9 Pennsylvania cities in 1977. The study involved the survey of 148 residents in halfway houses administered by the Pennsylvania Bureau of Correction.[48]

A survey team polled all the residents in these centers who had at least 3 weeks experience in community living. They were asked whether they had encountered any difficulties in 3 separate problem areas, including 28 specific problems. The areas were classified as "hard" problems, such as having enough money to get started with and finding a job and transportation, "soft" problems, such as emotional adjustments and difficulties with family reunion after prison, and "center-related" problems, such as complying with center

[45] Ibid., p. 1192.

[46] See David Duffee, Peter B. Meyer, and Barbara D. Warner, *Offender Needs, Parole Outcome and Program Structures in the Pennsylvania Bureau of Correction Division of Community Services: A Terminal Evaluation Report* (Harrisburg, Pa.: Governor's Justice Commission, 1977), pp. 168–72.

[47] Ibid., pp. 152–54.

[48] For the complete study, which had many other facets, see footnote 46.

rules about curfew, weekend furloughs, and other conflicts that can occur only to people who are under control of a correctional bureaucracy.

In analyzing the resolution of residents' problems, we were concerned with the frequency of resolution, with differences in resolution rates for different problem types, and with the means used to resolve the problems. The third area, means of resolution, contained the bulk of the data. What we tried to determine here were the ways in which both the community and the correctional centers could help or hinder the residents in resolving their problems. Although the centers and their correctional staff are responsible for aiding the resident in fulfilling reintegration needs, this responsibility can often be met in indirect rather than direct ways. That is, community correctional agencies may function best as integration mechanisms rather than as service mechanisms. Since there are many agencies within the community that are capable of fulfilling the residents' needs, it is, of course, important that these services are available to residents. This availability is most important when these needs can *only* be met through the cooperation of an outside organization, as is true in cases of financial assistance, job training, and education. However, it is also important for other services for various reasons. First of all, it is not cost-effective for centers to be duplicating services that already exist within the community. Second, it is important to use as many community resources as possible in order that these services continue to be available to the resident for as long as necessary after the resident leaves the correctional agency jurisdiction. (If the center offered many services internally, the resident could easily become dependent on such support. The same would be true if parole departments offered direct services instead of making referrals; the offender at the termination of parole would need to avail himself or herself of a different source for the resolution of problems, many of which, such as job finding, are recurring for people in the lower and working classes.) Third, and particularly important, it seems that centers may use their interaction with other service agencies as a means of linking the offender and the center itself to the rest of the community. If the center is offering "separate but equal" services to offenders, the agency only widens the gap between the offender and the rest of the community, and, in this way, only serves as another roadblock to true integration.

However, the ability of a particular center to funnel residents toward other agencies may be contingent on many factors. The willingness or capacity of the other agencies within the community to work with correctional clients, certain characteristics of the offenders themselves, and some aspects of the correctional agency policy will all have some effect on each correctional center's ability to function as an integration mechanism for resident problem resolution.

In general, we found that approximately one-half of the problems reported by the center residents were, in their own estimation, resolved (311 problems, or 51 percent of the reported total). When the percentage of problems resolved was broken down by individual center, there was a surprising range from a low rate of 35 percent in one Philadelphia center to a high rate of 76 percent in another center in the same city. When the resolution rates were broken down by problem types, we found that "hard" problems were resolved more frequently than were either soft problems or center-related problems. (Of course, all center-related problems are temporary, since at parole the offender is free of that situation.) Roughly 57 percent of the hard problems were resolved, while only 45 percent of the soft problems and 36 percent of the center-related problems were reported as resolved. The ranking of resolutions by problem type varied somewhat, but only in 2 of 12 centers were the soft problems more frequently resolved than were the hard problems.

To analyze the means of problems resolution, responses were placed into three general categories. If the resident problem had been resolved by an outside agency, the response was coded an "agency" resolution. If either the center staff or another center resident was credited with the resolution by the resident, the response was coded a "center" resolution. The third resolution category was used if the resident claimed that he had solved the problem himself or had relied on family and friends.

In general, we found that outside agencies were responsible for the greatest number of resolutions (47 percent) and the centers were responsible for the fewest (18 percent). When the problems were broken down into our three categories of problems, a clearer picture of resolution strategies emerged. It then became evident that different problem resolution mechanisms were more effective with one type of problem than with another. Outside agencies were the chief means of resolving hard problems; and friends and relatives were the most effective means for the resolution of soft problems. These data show that the majority of resident problems that were resolved at all were resolved by sources outside the center (either by outside community agencies or by family and friends of residents) rather than directly by the center.

Therefore, we became interested in analyzing individual center interaction with various outside agencies, especially with those agencies that deal with hard problems, which is by far the largest category of resident problems. It was hypothesized that as center staff formalized their relations with outside agencies, those agencies would either be more willing or more capable of resolving offenders' problems.

In order to test this hypothesis, we interviewed relevant staff members in various community agencies that offered hard services within each center community. Thirteen questions concerned interaction frequency and types between outside agency staff and the staff of the correctional centers. Areas such as the agencies' awareness of the center's goals, their perspective on the value of the centers as a community service agency, ways in which the centers helped the agency to fulfill its own goals, and frequency and type of communication patterns between the agencies were covered. Responses from approximately four outside agencies per center were used to calculate the degree to which each center had formal means of exchange established with outside agencies.

We tried to get the same agencies in each center community to respond to the interview. Although there were some differences in the exact agencies measured, in all cases we obtained measures from agencies that were in use by center residents and offered the same types of services. Examples of the types of agencies measured were the local offices of the state employment service, the local office of the vocation rehabilitation service, the department of public assistance, and the Opportunities Industrialization Centers. Formalization scores ranged from a high of 11.8 in Erie, Pennsylvania, to a low of 7.2 in York, Pennsylvania.

The scores for each center were then correlated with the percentage of hard problems that were resolved by outside agencies. The correlation we found here was positive, but rather small (.36). However, it also occurred to us that the centers and their related service agencies might be confronting very different levels of problems with the various center residents. Obviously, easy problems can be resolved much more frequently than can difficult and complex ones, regardless of how well the correctional agency interacts with its outside agencies.

As a measure of offender problem difficulty, we used the length of time that each individual in our sample was incarcerated for the present crime. It seemed to us that this number not only had methodological benefits, but it also rather accurately symbolized a host of complicating factors for residents released from prisons. Offenders who had been incarcerated for long periods of time usually had committed very serious crimes, which would appear as stigmatizing to both outside agencies and to the community in general. Length of incarceration would also affect the complexity of an offender's problems, in the sense that long separation from the community would produce interlocking difficulties between low education, no family support, and no money, while offenders incarcerated for a short period of time might still have community contacts on which to rely.

We therefore correlated the average length of incarceration of residents in each center with the center's average percentage of hard problems resolved by agencies. As expected, we found a very strong negative correlation ($-.798$). This, in and of itself, is not surprising, but in examining this relationship, it became evident that the centers varied widely in the average length of incarceration and therefore on the difficulty of the problems that they or their outside agencies would have to handle. When the resolution/agency formalization scores were recorrelated, controlling for the length of incarceration, we found a very strong positive correlation ($.73$). At this point, we also correlated the length of incarceration and formalization scores to verify that these were independent factors; we found virtually no relationship ($-.07$).

These data suggest that if an offender is incarcerated for only a short period of time, correctional center formalization with service agencies may not be necessary. The community may well be capable of assimilating this type of offender without interagency coordination. But with those residents who have served extremely long periods of incarceration, the institutionalization of center-to-agency relations may not be of value either. These individuals may be so stigmatized or have such difficult problems to solve that the added effort of increasing the agency-to-center interaction, on the organizational level, will not increase the rate of problem resolution achieved without it. For the majority of offenders, however, with the average range of problems when released from prison, formalized center-to-agency interaction seems to have a great deal of influence on getting resolutions to resident problems.

IMPROVING THE CORRECTIONAL ORGANIZATION STATUS IN THE INTERORGANIZATIONAL FIELD

One might ask then what the correctional agency role should be in aiding offenders to resolve reintegration problems. Since the majority of problems encountered by offenders returning from prison are hard problems, and since the services needed to solve these problems exist in almost all communities with large offender populations, one important role for the correctional agencies should be building ties with the existing community agencies that offer such services. If offenders must face agencies that look unfavorably on servicing offenders, offenders may never have an adequate chance to avail themselves of those opportunities by which many citizens negotiate the difficulties of urban living. This research helps to clarify the notions espoused in the reintegration policy. Community attitudes toward offenders may have to be changed and a greater range of opportunities may have to be provided, but that work may well have to concentrate on the agencies of service rather than on more amorphous types of community resistance.

Correctional staff must begin by taking a realistic view of correction-to-agency interaction. Any form of interagency cooperation or coordination is based on reciprocity of service. It is not a one-way street. Each agency in the community has its own goals to fulfill, and some form of mutual aid in reaching those goals must be established if relationships between various agencies are to continue or to improve.

It is suggested here that correctional staff become more aware of the goals of the other agencies and that they also inform these agencies about the goals of the correctional agency. "A clearer knowledge of the problems and goals of the other organization would appear to be a first step in developing cooperation between two organizations which is based on mutual benefit."[49] The correctional and service agencies' mutual, human service goals, as well as the function of the correctional reintegration agencies in returning offenders to productive roles in society, should be emphasized.

The correctional agencies' function in building successful exchanges cannot be overlooked. "The sending agency is linking itself with the services of the receiving agency, and to the extent the referral is a successful one, may enjoy the good will of the satisfied client, of the receiving agency, and consequently of the community as a whole."[50] If an agency cannot handle a particular problem, or over a course of several referrals does not seem effective, it is obviously senseless for the correctional agency to continue to send clients with that kind of problem. But the correctional staff should expect wide variance between what an agency can do for a client referred from an unfamiliar source (and from a correctional one at that) and what the same agency may be willing and able to do if agency-to-agency staff exchanges have preceded the exchange of a client. As Vickers points

---

[49] Levine, White, and Paul, "Community Interorganizational Problems in Providing Medical Care and Social Services," p. 1193.

[50] Ibid., p. 1190.

out that in the area of human organization what an organization can do and what the organization wants to do are often synonymous.[51]

It is possible that when it is trying to build a relationship with another agency, the correctional organization should not send its hardest cases and reserve the easier ones for its own efforts. This tendency is a real problem that correctional managers should be aware of and watch for. Since correctional agency staff, especially those operating in the community, are themselves interested human service professionals, they may feel competition with outside agencies for the resolution of problems. If they, or their own managers, evaluate correctional work in terms of problem resolutions, they may well "dump" the more difficult case on outside agencies while dealing with other cases internally. This practice is common in many human service agencies, but it would seem particularly harmful in the long run to correctional agencies that are just entering a legitimate place in the interorganizational field. Hence, it may well be that correctional staff should be evaluated in the effectiveness of their linkage roles instead of in their ability to provide direct services. The most common need of other agencies that correctional agencies can continually fill is the need for clients. Hence, this resource should be offered at all times, not just in times of distress.

Correctional staff must be willing to give and take with other agencies in their communities and to offer aid to outside agencies in any ways that seem appropriate. If the resolution of resident problems is to improve, it seems crucial that staff allocate more of their time to building relationships to agencies in the communities that offer needed services and spend less time trying to resolve offender problems directly. In this way, correctional staff are not only helping the residents currently in their charge but also all future residents who will need those services.

---

[51] Geoffrey Vickers, *Making Institutions Work* (New York: Halsted, 1973).

13

Correctional Interaction with the Courts

The recent "explosion" in the area loosely defined as correctional law suggests that the interaction of the courts, notably the appellate courts, with the correctional system merits special attention as correctional administrators examine the nature of their organizational environment and the impact that it may have on the internal operations of their organizations. Yet the most helpful way to examine the new trend in the interaction between courts and correctional agencies is not totally clear. Some legal experts assume that it is helpful, to the courts if not to the correctional agencies, merely to present a series of recent court cases and elaborate the conditions that impelled the decisions and the possible consequences for correctional administration.[1] A variety of casebooks have recently been prepared with these apparent objectives in mind, although such works are more

[1] Robert J. Kutak, "Grim Fairy Tales for Prison Administrators," in George G. Killinger, Paul F. Cromwell, and Bonnie J. Cromwell, *Corrections and Administration* (St. Paul, Minn.: West, 1976), pp. 474–92.

likely to be used by criminal law students and lawyers than by correctional managers.[2]

Other observers of the court–corrections connection have been less optimistic about this "rational–informational" approach to the examination of correctional decisions by courts. They have stressed that it may well be the response of the administration rather than the content of the court opinions themselves that needs most serious study because it is that reaction, rather than the judicial one, that will most closely determine whether and what the impact of judicial opinion is on correctional administration.[3] These observers draw analogies between the present court interest in correctional operations with the high level of court concern for police operations in the 1960's. As some reports on that "due process revolution" demonstrated, the end result for organizational behavior is found not in the legally interpreted meaning of judicial action, but the consequences of the interaction between judicial opinion and command and the administrative ability, desire, and method of compliance or non-compliance.

Nevertheless, even these "realistic" or organizationally based analyses of judicial intervention in correctional operations have not often concentrated on the interorganizational nature of the correctional due process movement. It is this focus which this chapter seeks to provide. Hence, it will not concentrate on court opinions themselves, reviews of which are adequately available from other sources (and probably better provided through the justice department of any state than a textual review can render). Neither will it concentrate solely on the assumed, or even empirically demonstrated attitudes of correctional executives toward court opinions, due process, or the citizenship status of offenders. Instead, the concentration will be on the structure of interaction between the courts and correctional agencies and on the structure of correctional organization itself, since these constraints limit and shape the extent to which the courts can and will intervene in correctional organization and processes.

COURTS AND CORRECTIONS: A SPECIAL CASE OF ORGANIZATIONAL EXCHANGE

Examining the linkages between the several agencies of the criminal justice system became popular in the late 1960's with the activity of the President's Commission on Law Enforcement and the Administration

[2] Ted Palmer, *Constitutional Rights of Prisoners* (Cincinnati: Anderson, 1974); Hazel Kerper and Janeen Kerper, *The Legal Rights of the Convicted* (St. Paul, Minn.: West, 1974); Sol Rubin, *Law of Criminal Correction*, 2nd ed. (St. Paul, Minn.: West, 1973).
[3] Sol Rubin, "The Administrative Response to Court Decisions," *Crime and Delinquency* (1969), pp. 377–86.

of Justice.[4] It became apparent, as that tradition of systemic analysis developed, that even without an overarching authority structure to coordinate the activities of these loosely linked agencies, these agencies could and did affect each other greatly, particularly through manipulations of their own internal structures. For example, the police could influence prosecution effectiveness by the means in which they gathered evidence and handled investigations; prosecutors could influence police arrest policies by refusing to prosecute certain types of cases; prosecution could delimit the discretion of the judge and the probation staff at sentencing through the constraints placed on the range of sentence during plea negotiation; and courts could change the shape and focus of correctional operations by changing the proportions of offenders placed on probation or incarcerated and by the length of sentence imposed.

While many critics of criminal justice operation snubbed the criminal justice network by calling it a "nonsystem,"[5] such criticism is obviously naive about the interactions of the various agencies as well as it is ignorant of the range of input and output connections that can accurately and usefully be called systems.

Perhaps part of the confusion about what can be called systemic is clarified by the foregoing chapter on interorganizational relations. Litwak and Hylton stress that interorganizational systems often are structured to maintain certain levels of conflict. However dysfunctional or troublesome these conflicts may look to an observer who focuses on *internal* organizational states, they definitely serve identifiable functions within the larger social structure.[6] The writing of Marris and Rein[7] and William Reid[8] add support to this perspective: Critics of American public organization cannot lose sight of the fact that these often conflicting, competitive, and inefficient organizations are in many basic respects purposefully structured to manifest this low level of integration and concerted action. This high-noise, high-duplication, high-waste *system* does present many problems both to managers of specific agencies as well as to the citizenry that

[4] See, for example, President's Commission on Law Enforcement and the Administration of Justice, *Challenge of Crime in a Free Society* (Washington, D.C.: Government Printing Office, 1967).
[5] James S. Campbell, Joseph R. Sahid, and David P. Stang, *Law and Order Reconsidered* (New York: Bantam Books, 1970).
[6] Eugene Litwak and Lydia F. Hylton, "Interorganizational Analysis: A Hypothesis on Coordinating Agencies," *Administrative Science Quarterly* (March, 1962), pp. 395-420.
[7] Peter Marris and Martin Rein, *The Dilemmas of Social Reform*, (New York: Atherton, 1967).
[8] William Reid, "Interagency Coordination in Delinquency Prevention and Control," *Social Service Review* (March, 1964), pp. 418-28.

seeks of these organizations the performance of necessary community functions. And yet this system has also provided the structure for change and improvement within which criticism of the system is even possible.

There are obvious limits on the ways in which these loosely linked but systemically interacting agencies can modify each other's behavior or cooperate in order to accomplish a joint goal. It may surprise some that courts and corrections might be seen as having joint goals when one examines the recent amount of conflict between them and the high level of mutual criticism. Nevertheless, they obviously share many value premises or share the same institutionalized thought structure. Both agencies often agree that running a correctional organization requires a vast amount of discretion on the part of the administrators and decision makers,[9] both agree that there are legal and legitimate rationales for the constraints placed on offender behavior, both agree that administrators have acquired by experience or by education a sufficient level of expertise to justify the discretion used in constraining and controlling inmates, and both agree that correctional operations are necessary governmental functions. Both also seem to agree on the procedures by which complaints of one agency about the other agency will be lodged and negotiated: There are highly institutionalized forms within which the conflict is controlled and the compromises between the two organizations will be worked out.

Nevertheless, there are some obvious differences between the interaction of the court and a correctional agency compared to the interaction of the court with other courts or the interaction of the correctional agency with other community agencies. Two most pressing differences are related. The court and correctional agencies are components of different branches of government, as established by the Constitution of the United States. Most correctional agencies fall under the executive branch; the courts fall under the judicial branch. (Many probation departments, of course, are administered by the judiciary. This exception would not seem to alter the separation in function between judicial decision making and correctional program supervision.) These branches are theoretically separate, equal, and counterbalancing and they serve different functions. The courts cannot administer correctional agencies; they cannot tell correctional administrators or guards or inmates what to do. They

[9] See Marvin Frankel, *Criminal Sentences* (New York: Hill & Wang, 1972); Rubin, "Administrative Response to Court Decisions," p. 381.

can, however, tell the correctional agencies what not to do in limited situations.[10]

On the other hand, as a system that spans the judicial and executive branches, many have argued that the courts and correctional agencies together perform a similar social function. Many have titled this function "social control."[11] Others, notably Parsons,[12] suggest that the court correctional complex serves an "integrative" function for society by mediating the conflicts that result from the inherent strains in the economic and political systems. Presumably, this joint function is performed under the conditions that are now present in this system, and maintenance of the separation of powers and inter-organizational conflict may well be necessary to the effective performance of this integrative function.

Related to this separation of duties, however, is the fact that courts, unlike other executive agencies, *can* intervene in correctional operations without the assent (and most often because a particular correctional administration will not assent) to the types of changes that the court would like to see take place.

Most observers will agree that the capacity of the courts to act in this manner is not small and that the intervention activities of the courts have increased markedly in recent years. Kutak reviews what he considers four key cases in four different states and concludes that the appellate court decisions are unusual not only in the type of relief that they have offered the suing inmates, but also and more importantly in the fact that each court went far beyond the specific complaint and chose to review the entire prison system.[13] This trend may be widespread. In addition to the four cases cited by Kutak, a federal court in Pennsylvania has recently handed down a set of rules that must be followed when determining whether or not an offender should be placed in a halfway house program.[14] Another court has reacted similarly in relation to institutional furloughs.[15]

In addition, judicial review of prison conditions has also recently upheld prisoner actions that for years would have resulted not only in severe punishment but also in additional prosecution. Michigan and California courts have admitted that the threat of sexual assault

[10] Herbert Packer, *The Limits of the Criminal Sanction* (Stanford: Stanford University Press, 1968), pp. 172-173.

[11] Roland L. Warren, *Community in America* (Chicago: Rand McNally, 1963), pp. 9-12.

[12] Talcott Parsons, *Structure and Process in Modern Societies* (New York: Free Press, 1960), Chapter One.

[13] Kutak, "Grim Fairy Tales for Prison Administrators," p. 4.

[14] *Bryan* v. *Kane*, U.S. District Court for Middle District of Pennsylvania, Sept. 17, 1975.

[15] *U.S.* ex rel. *Meyers* v. *Sielaff*, 381 F. Supp. 840 (E.D. Pa., 1974).

may provide prisoners with a defense to escape charges.[16] In Massachusetts the state supreme court granted that inmates can utilize the defense of justification in a prosecution for striking a prison guard.[17] One commentator on that case toys with the inflagratory suggestion that such a decision may increase the willingness of prisoners to riot.[18]

It must also be recognized that the court's impact on corrections does not always have to be direct. It is evident that the increased judicial concern for the rights of offenders has influenced other organizations, which, in turn, may impact significantly on correctional operations. For example, a number of state legislatures, following the court attitude toward presentence investigations, have *legislated* the defendant's right to examine his presentence report.[19] The National Labor Relations Board in Tennessee held that work release inmates had a right to participate in a union representation election even though the institution was against it.[20]

Thus, there is little doubt that the court can influence the correctional process and organization and it can do so in situations in which other organizations would be effectively shut out if the correctional organization did not voluntarily allow the intervention. In reality, the more important questions are questions about when the court will intervene in such a manner and what will be the impact of such interventions.

THE LIMITS TO COURT CHANGE IN CORRECTIONS

Although to many it may seem too obvious to mention, it is important that the courts reject the opportunity to intervene in correctional operations far more often than they accept the opportunity. Or, stated in another way, the courts intervene only in the limited circumstances that they see correctional operations or conditions conflicting with the goals and functions of the courts. One of the most obvious functions of the courts is to protect the rights of citizens. When prison conditions are seriously criticized in the media, and the consciousness of the American public has been

[16] David Gilman, "Courts and Corrections," *Corrections Magazine* (Sept., 1976), pp. 51–53.
[17] David Gilman, "Courts and Corrections," *Corrections Magazine* (June, 1976), pp. 13–16.
[18] Ibid., p. 13.
[19] Sol Rubin and Jeffrey E. Glen, "Developments in Correctional Law," *Crime and Delinquency* (April, 1968), pp. 162–63.
[20] Ibid., p. 168.

raised concerning prisons and criminal justice in general, it is only natural that courts will pay more attention to the rights of prisoners than when interest in prisons is low. Higher visibility of correctional operations brings with it higher visibility of correctional conflicts with court goals, and thus a greater frequency of court response.

> (T)hough his rights may be diminished by the needs and exigencies of the institutional environment, a prisoner is not wholly stripped of constitutional protections when he is imprisoned for a crime. There is no iron curtain drawn between the constitution and the prisons of this country.[21]

There are two important organizational implications in this statement, as rhetorical and virtuous as it may sound. One is that the courts feel challenged by an organization that would flaunt its freedom from court overview. The other is that the courts are likely to step gingerly into this area, if at all, in the attempt to draw as clear a line as possible between the sphere of administrative interest and the sphere of court prerogative.

This second point can easily escape the correctional manager who has recently been surprised by a recent court decision affecting his operations. But the essential conservatism of the judiciary in the correctional area is incontrovertible. Rubin and Glen point out that even in an area in which the courts have been very firm on their stance toward rights, they have left ample room for administrators to maneuver. Decisions forbidding segregation in prison have always stopped far short of random cell assignments. While entire institutions cannot be segregated, the courts have continued to allow marked degrees of segregation within institutions.[22] Similarly, courts have not shut prisons down after declaring the conditions within them to be cruel and unusual.[23]

Rubin comments that, in many respects, the courts should be criticized for holding back rather than advancing either the rights of prisoners or the effectiveness of correctional administration. He notes that a federal appellate court refused to consider an inmate's complaint that the parole board did not have adequate information on which to base a parole release decision. The court used the outrageous rationale that the parole board did not need to demonstrate that it had such information or was competent to use it.[24]

---

[21] *Wolff* v. *McDonnell*, 15 CrL 3309, 418 U.S. 539 (1974).
[22] Rubin and Glen, "Developments in Correctional Law," pp. 167-68.
[23] Prisons systems in New Orleans, Philadelphia, and Arkansas have been declared in violation of the prohibition against cruel and unusual punishment and continue to operate.
[24] *Juelich* v. *U.S. Board of Parole*, 437 F.2d. 1147 (7th Cir., 1971).

The court said it does not matter that the parole board members are not qualified and it does not matter that the parole board records on which the decision is based is a pile of junk, or at least is hearsay . . .[25]

As late as 1967 the Supreme Court of Maine openly argued that parolees were not entitled to a hearing before the parole board.[26] Contrary to complaints that the courts have intervened too often, administrators reviewing these cases might complain that the courts have challenged their competence and authority, if not their power, by failing to review the matter before them.

Part of the courts' reluctance to intervene in correctional affairs is based on the adherence to the separation of powers principle. But, as many commentators have noted, the invocation of the separation powers doctrine really explains very little, since courts intervene in executive affairs to the extent that the executive branch has already stepped on the court domain, and more important, since the courts have a great deal of discretion to define where that separation takes affect anyway. Thus, it becomes necessary to wonder why that line between the judicial and the executive shifts as it does. Certainly not to be underestimated is the judicial accommodation of, or even its belief in, the rehabilitation and treatment functions of correctional agencies. Courts have frequently rejected offender complaints about unequal treatment on the grounds that correctional agencies have sought to individualize punishment.[27]

The fall of the rehabilitative ideal as a correctional guidepost probably has a great deal to do with the recent willingness of courts to look at cases that previously they would have ignored under the treatment rhetoric of the correctional agencies. But there are ample signs within the current leading case in institutional discipline that the United States Supreme Court continues to hold the treatment ideal up as a means of steering clear of some issues.

The insertion of counsel into the disciplinary process (in prisons) would inevitably give the proceedings a more adversary cast and tend to reduce their utility as a means to further correctional goals.[28]

Within the same opinion, the Court cites three leading works on behavior modification therapy as an excuse for allowing administrators to act quickly and without the orderly procedure that would

---

[25] Sol Rubin, "The Impact of Court Decisions on the Correctional Process," *Crime and Delinquency* (April, 1974), pp. 129–34.

[26] *Moltran v. State*, 232 A.2d. 809 (1967).

[27] Rubin, "The Impact of Court Decisions on the Correctional Process," p. 132.

[28] *Wolff v. McDonnell*, 15 CrL. 3314.

apply to even probation[29] and parole[30] discipline. "It may be essential that discipline be swift and sure," wrote the Court, rather than "simulate procedures of free society."[31]

This long-standing position of the courts in relation to rights of offenders has been summed up in the "hands off doctrine."[32] Indeed, at some points the court was so reluctant to intercede in correctional matters that it strained very real differences between various phases of the correctional process. For example, the court likened parole to incarceration within an extended prison, so that its feelings about prison discipline could also apply to parole.[33] Such visions of parole are contrary to what even the most conservative prison or parole administrator would describe and are contrary to the administrative purposes for which parole was established.[34] This strained view of correctional processes is still with us. In 1967 the Supreme Court contorted the nature of a probation revocation hearing, likening it to a deferred sentencing,[35] in order not to have its finding there apply to parole revocations.[36]

Kimberly and Newman sum up the hands off doctrine thus:

> The traditional self-definition of powers and functions in correction is that, once an offender has been convicted and sentenced . . . (he) may make *requests* not demands; he may be accorded *privileges* but he has no rights . . .[37]

It is not clear exactly where this doctrine started or exactly where it began to fall away. In fact, it is probably more accurate to say that it never really started and now has not really vanished. While many of the writers cited above place great importance on cases of the 1940's and 1950's to the formulation of the doctrine, others cite the following statement from *Coffin* v. *Reichard* (1945) as the first

---

[29] *Gagnon* v. *Scarpelli*, 411 U.S. 778 (1973).

[30] *Morrissey* v. *Brewer*, 408 U.S. 471 (1972).

[31] *Wolff* v. *McDonnell*, 15 CrL. 3312.

[32] Note "Beyond the Ken of the Courts: A Critique of Judicial Refusal to Review the Complaints of Convicts," *Yale Law Journal* (January, 1963), p. 506.

[33] See *Banning* v. *Looney*, 213 F.2d.771 (10th Cir.) cert. denied 348 U.S. 859 (1954); and *Strand* v. *Johnson*, 139 F.2d.771 (9th Cir., 1943); and the comments in Dennis Sullivan and Larry Tift, "Court Intervention in Correction: Roots of Resistance and Problems of Compliance," *Crime and Delinquency* (July, 1975), pp. 213–22.

[34] See, in general, David Dressler, *The Practice and Theory of Probation and Parole* (New York: Columbia University Press, 1959).

[35] *Mempa* v. *Rhay*, 389 U.S. 128 (1967).

[36] Fred Cohen, "Sentencing Probation, and the Rehabilitative Ideal: The View from *Mempa* v. *Rhay,*" *Texas Law Review* (Dec., 1968), pp. 1–59, and Rubin "The Administrative Response to Court Decisions," p. 380.

[37] E. L. Kimberly and D. J. Newman, "Judicial Intervention in Correctional Decisions: Threat and Response," *Crime and Delinquency* (January, 1968), p. 4.

chip in the wall:[38] "A prisoner retains all rights of an ordinary citizen except those expressly or by necessary implication taken away from him."[39]

It is probably more accurate to conceive of the interaction as a continual compromise and give and take process in which the courts activate their interest in corrections to the extent that at that point in time the correctional operation, as portrayed to them, threatens the courts' perception of their own goals and stature in the administration of justice. "There must be mutual accommodation between institutional needs and objectives and the provisions of the Constitution that are of general application."[40] Not surprising, in this view, is that one of the most guarded of all rights of prisoners is their access to the courts rather than their treatment within the prison.[41]

The observation that the courts really have no overarching doctrine about correctional cases, and instead respond to perceived threat to their own domain, can be bolstered by two recent court cases involving prison discipline[42] and interinstitutional transfer of prisoners.[43] Any believer of the "due process explosion" must have been startled by the very recent reiteration that "a wide spectrum of discretionary actions traditionally have been the business of prison administrators rather than the federal courts."[44] and the following reinvocation of the hands off policy: "The federal courts do not sit to supervise state prisons, the administration of which is of acute interest to the States."[45] Justice White, writing for the Court, has perhaps indicated that the Supreme Court feels threatened by the opportunity to intervene or that the Court is concerned far more with prison executive action that affects how and when offenders get to or are returned from the community rather than with equally questionable uses of administrative discretion within the confines of a set sentence or a prison system.[46]

Indeed, the Court's most recent correctional decisions seem to contradict the very understanding of the impact of due process on

[38] *Coffin* v. *Reichard*, 143 F.2d.443 (6th Cir. 1944), cert. denied 325 U.S. 887 (1945).
[39] Idem, at 445.
[40] *Wolff* v. *McDonnell*, 15 CrL. 3310.
[41] *Johnson* v. *Avery*, 393 U.S. 483 (1969).
[42] *Wolff* v. *McDonnell*, 418 U.S. 539.
[43] *Meachum* v. *Fano*, 19 CrL 3167, U.S. Supreme Court, June 25, 1976.
[44] Idem, at 3170.
[45] Idem, at 3171.
[46] See idem, at 3170; "The conviction has sufficiently extinguished the defendant's liberty interest to empower the state to confine him in *any* of its prisons," meaning that the conviction has extinguished the *Court's* interest in his liberty. *Wolff* v. *McDonnell*, 15 CrL. 3311, argues that parole revocation is an *immediate* loss of freedom while loss of good time is a future loss and only a probable loss, as opposed to a certain one.

the goals of rehabilitation that a few years earlier it had espoused very strongly. In *Kent* v. *United States* and in *In re Gault* the Supreme Court had nearly laughed at the suggestion that due process could interfere with the rehabilitative intents of the juvenile court.[47] Then Justice Fortas had remarked that the condition of being a boy was no excuse for making him suffer a kangaroo court, and further that he thought fair and orderly treatment by administrators would help rather than impede any rehabilitative process.[48]

The misused cites of behavior modification by the Supreme Court notwithstanding, any partially informed behavior modifier will attest to the importance of gaining the consent of the target of change to the methods applied, especially when those methods are aversive.[49] The present Supreme Court, ignoring its more reasoned position in 1967, states in *Wolff* v. *McDonnell* that the orderly procedure of due process, if applied to prison discipline in any significant way, would *raise* the level of antagonism in the prison and increase the frequency of retaliation by inmates against each other or against the administration.[50] In effect, the Court is now arguing that heavy-handed, secret procedures may be less conflict producing than are openness and formality. This new attitude of the Court seems to ignore any empirical evidence about prison organization, regardless of what it does to our basic notions of democracy.

A review of the impact of *Morrissey* by the American Bar Association seems to support the above argument that the Court is highly concerned with maintaining some distance from correctional matters and that its principal referents lately seem to be the cost to the state of changing administrative procedures and the protection of the correctional agency's capacity to continue its claim to rehabilitative effectiveness.[51] The A.B.A. notes that *Gagnon* v. *Scarpelli* rejects the across the board application of lawyers in the probation revocation process because of the "rehabilitative purposes" of revocation and because of the great expected cost that lawyers would entail. The association accurately points out that if the Supreme Court had really been interested in due process rather than the autonomy of the correctional organization, it could not have chosen this doctrine.[52]

Indeed, there might be some doubt about the role that the courts

[47] *Kent* v. *United States*, 383 U.S. 541 (1966); *In re Gault*, 387, U.S., 1, 1967.
[48] *In re Gault.*
[49] Norval Morris, *The Future of Imprisonment* (Chicago: University of Chicago Press, 1974).
[50] *Wolff* v. *McDonnell*, 15 CrL. 3311.
[51] American Bar Association, "Accelerating Change in Correctional Law" in W. Amos and C. Newman, *Parole* (New York: Federal Legal Publications, 1975), pp. 130–49.
[52] Ibid., p. 140.

play in shaping correctional processes altogether. A survey of prisons conducted just prior to *Wolff* found that of all the prison administrators responding to the questionnaire about prison discipline, 64 percent allowed confrontations, 57 percent allowed cross examinations, 37 percent allowed counsel, 80 percent allowed counsel substitutes, 59 percent allowed witnesses, and 88 percent provided written reasons for the decision in prison disciplinary procedures.[53] Many correctional administrators, it would seem, go beyond the courts in their attention to offender rights. It is possible that in some instances the courts' conservative stance may then encourage administrators to slow down the process of innovation instead of to take additional steps.

THE STRUCTURE OF THE COURT/ CORRECTIONS EXCHANGE

In order to understand the curious, two-forward-one-back give-and-take between courts and correctional agencies, it may help to examine the nature of the exchange that takes place over the long haul instead of examining any particular case.[54] The exchange structure, as Levine and White remind us, is made up of the parties to the exchange, the kinds and quantities exchanged, the agreement underlying the exchange, and the direction of the exchange.[55] Exchange itself is any interaction between two or more organizations that has consequences, real or intended, for the goals of the respective organizations. The goals, we must remember, are complex sets of constraints, not single objectives to be maximized.[56]

The parties to the exchange, as most readers are aware, are in actuality far more complex than the above accounts of previous court action might imply. The most frequently interacting units are the court and correctional units on the front line of the correctional process. Every day sentencing judges interact with probation staff over the possibilities of various sentence alternatives. Every day magistrates send bound-over defendants to jail when the defendant cannot post the required bond. Judges hear frequent cases by probation staff for revocations of probation or for changes in probation conditions. Sentencing judges send a continual flow of convicted

[53] American Bar Foundation, *Legal Status of Prisoners* (Chicago: American Bar Foundation, 1977), Section 3.2(c).
[54] Sol Levine and Paul White, "Exchange as a Conceptual Framework for the Study of Interorganizational Relationships," in Y. Hasenfeld and R. English (eds.), *Human Service Organizations* (Ann Arbor: University of Michigan Press, 1974), pp. 545–61.
[55] Ibid., pp. 558–59.
[56] Herbert A. Simon, "On the Concept of Organizational Goal," *Administration Science Quarterly* (June, 1964), pp. 1–22.

offenders to probation organizations for supervision in the community or to jail and prison authorities. With increasing frequency, judges today also send offenders to the diagnostic facilities of correctional departments for 60- or 90-day examinations prior to sentencing. Judges in many states receive from institutional executives daily requests for permission (or in some cases only notification) for the furlough of offenders or the placement of offenders in halfway houses. Judges are indirectly influenced by the new community-based programs in corrections. Many experts suspect that some judges now sentence to lengthier terms as a reaction to the expectation that the correctional authority will furlough an offender or place him or her on work release after a specified portion of the minimum sentence has been served.[57]

On this level, the parties to the exchange are on rather equal footing. Correctional agencies often complain that judges frequently pronounce sentences that are unwise or to conditions that the correctional authority cannot fulfill. It is also clear that judges often complain about the influence that the correctional conditions have on their power to sentence. Hence, there is undoubted conflict, but the conflict in many respects is worked out on this level of exchange just as it might be within *one* organization: The resolution of the conflict is passed onward and downward toward the offenders themselves, and the conflict is continually recurring.

But this is obviously not the only level on which exchange takes place. Most of the recent material on the court corrections interaction concerns appellate decisions. On this level, the exchange is informational and involves broader considerations of organizational conditions, policies, and practices. But all appellate decisions are based on and have the main purpose of reviewing the argument in a specific case. An offender may bring suit or ask for an injunction or for some other type of relief in his or her particular case. Most of these cases are resolved at the initial court level; they go no higher. But, of course, even on this initial court level, the court decision is an appellate review of previous "judicial" decisions taken by administrators within the correctional organization. And most offender grievances are handled at the administrative level and never reach court. We have no idea how many such cases are resolved to the offender's satisfaction. We would have to assume that most are not, but that the administrative procedures followed in these instances at least provide the semblance of fair and complete review and do not provide the offender with a valid complaint with which to enter court.

The main point here is that most appellate reviews of correctional

[57] Rubin and Glen, "Developments in Correctional Law," p. 168.

cases only occur when the internal, administrative performance of the judicial function breaks down. The exercise of judicial functions by executives is common. In fact, it is one of the manager's chief roles: the mediation of disputes between competing value premises and interests in the organizational units beneath the manager. And executives exercise this role as frequently in staff-to-staff conflict as in staff-to-offender conflict.

This judicial function of the executive is generated by the manager's rule-making power. In public organizations many procedures may be legislated, but in most internal organizational operations the legislature delegates to the executive the power to make additional rules by which to implement the legislated mandate. The executive, like a judge, must exercise judicial authority when the case or argument before him or her does not clearly fall within the rules that either he or she or the legislature has established. In most cases, an offender (or a complaining staff member) can appeal the executive judgment about rule application only when it can be demonstrated that the rules established were not followed,[58] or that the procedure used for determining which rule to follow was not accurate or fair,[59] or that the rules themselves violated basic notions of fairness,[60] or served no valid government purpose.[61]

Such instances of complaint are usually rare. One would suppose that when a valid complaint about any of these conditions arose, the manager, as much as the complainant, would welcome the judicial decision on what to do because such a valid complaint would indicate that the case at hand was so unclearly linked to the established rules or procedures for rule application that the organization itself needed some advice on how to proceed.[62] This is at least the position of Rubin who states: "Courts can and do make changes in correctional systems. The only reason they assume the importance they do today is that administration is not changing itself."[63] Similarly, McGregor, speaking of industrial management, not corrections, suggests that courts and legislatures change the internal executive procedures for rule making and rule application only when the managers have failed or refused to do so themselves.[64]

The management probably fails at this change less often than

[58] As is implied in *Wolff* v. *McDonnell.*

[59] As in *U.S.* ex rel. *Meyers* v. *Sielaff* or *Bryan* v. *Kane.*

[60] As in *Morrissey* v. *Brewer*, 408 U.S. 471 (1972).

[61] As in *Johnson* v. *Avery.*

[62] See William Chambliss and Robert Seidman, *Law Order and Power* (Reading, Mass.: Addison-Wesley, 1971).

[63] Rubin, "The Impact of Court Decisions on the Correctional Process," p. 134.

[64] Douglas McGregor, *The Professional Manager*, ed. by Caroline McGregor and Warren G. Bennis (New York: McGraw-Hill, 1967).

aggrieved parties would believe, since the stability of the organization depends rather heavily on management's ability to make such changes. On the other hand, appellate courts probably enter into this type of exchange with correctional agencies, on the policy level, with less frequency than they could because of their knowledge of the type of exchange that goes on below, that is, on the program level or on the front-line level.

Many observers of the current Supreme Court have attributed its vacillating position on civil rights, criminal procedure, and other matters that were firmly handled by the Warren Court to the Berger Court's own lack of a clear majority. To some extent this may be true, but it would seem that a structural analysis of the relationship of appellate courts to trial courts and front-line correctional work may offer a competing and equally important explanation. In brief, it would be this: Appellate courts today are far more aware of their limitations and constraints as policy-making agencies than was true of the previous, more liberal courts. Part of this awareness must come from the knowledge of how previous decisions, notably in the police area, were twisted by the police themselves and by the trial courts that cooperated with them. High court decisions about fairness within preconviction procedure more often than not either reiterated what agencies were already doing[65] or changed police explanations of their behavior rather than their behavior with suspects.[66] It also became obvious that the operational agencies could subvert the intent of the court rules altogether by relying on instant street adjustments, harrassment, and other such tactics rather than taking cases to court.[67]

The effect of correctional operations on the lower courts is not as immediate, or as visible, as the effect of the police on those same courts, because the police are in input agency to the court system while the correctional agencies are an output agency. Hence, the impact of correctional programs on the judiciary takes a longer and more tortuous route: The judge's behavior is changed as the judiciary receives feedback about correctional decisions.[68] For example, judges in several states have complained that institutional work release and furlough programs are usurping the judicial sentencing decision.[69]

[65] Rubin, "The Administrative Response to Court Decisions."
[66] Richard Kuh, The Mapp Case One Year After: An Appraisal of Its Impact in New York," *New York Law Journal* (Sept., 1962), p. 4.
[67] Jonathan Rubenstein, *City Police* (New York: Ballantine Books, 1973).
[68] Frank Remmington et al., *Criminal Justice Administration* (Indianapolis: Bobbs-Merrill, 1968), pp. 1–55.
[69] David Duffee, Thomas Maher, and Stephen Lagoy, "Administrative Due Process in Community Pre-parole Programs, *Criminal Law Bulletin* (Sept./Oct., 1977), pp. 383–400.

The end result is the same, however; the appellate review is always tempered by the knowledge that the correctional organization can react to the judicial direction in ways that are totally unintended or that trial level judges may react to the same decisions in ways that the appellate judiciary or the correctional administration both want to avoid. For example, the Supreme Court explicitly acknowledged in *Morrissey* that adding the due process elements to the parole revocation decision might reduce the number of paroles *given* since the board would find the taking away of parole status more difficult.[70] Other equally questionable practices are also possible and are a means of avoiding the courts' directives and yet achieving the objective of getting offenders off the street. In Pennsylvania the parole board added a vague catchall parole condition to the pre-*Morrisey* rules, so that now the evidence necessary to revoke might be less, at least in difficult cases. In the same state, the parole board routinely "detains" parolees for up to 23 months in county jails instead of holding a revocation hearing. The absence of revocation to state institutions does away with the complex *Morrisey* hearing and still allows the parole officer to get a parolee off the street for long periods of time.

Similarly, court impositions on decisions to revoke (or to grant) furlough status or halfway house status to offenders can mean that fewer offenders are placed in such programs in the first place.[71] Such alterations in the correctional process are probably unwanted by administrators, regardless of what judges want, and the end result may be that fewer offenders receive fair hearings, even if those who do receive hearings enjoy fairer hearings than would have been the case prior to judicial intervention. Hence, the appellate courts must approach the opportunity to intervene in correctional administrative procedure, at the policy level, with an open eye to the possibility that court advances in this part of its domain may well have an adverse effect on other parts of its domain.

On the other side of the coin, correctional administrators can probably approach the possibility of court encroachment on their power and discretion, and avoid the threat of it, with far more creativity than they have frequently displayed. Rubin catalogues three administrative responses to court decisions: (1) the provocative or openly defiant response, (2) the defensive, or minimally compliant response, and (3) the positive or policy leadership response.[72]

[70] *Morrissey* v. *Brewer.*

[71] Duffee, Maher, and Lagoy, "Administrative Due Process in Community Pre-parole Programs."

[72] Rubin, "The Administrative Response to Court Decisions," p. 377.

Rubin[73] and Sullivan and Tift would agree that by far the most common administrative response is defensive:

> Open rejection is rarely the reaction to external pressure. Rather, the organization stages a show of acceptance to mollify the external "threat" and, at the same time, rejects or modifies implementation so that it can continue to maintain its structure as well as previously negotiated coalitions, both external and internal.[74]

One of the important external coalitions is the connection between the trial courts and the front-line program level of the correctional organizations. Today the Supreme Court seems content to accommodate this defensive response from both correctional administrators and trial judiciary, allowing, at least as a matter of judicial policy, the high degree of discretion in decisions about offenders to continue.[75]

The defensive response from administrators and the trepidacious response from apppellate courts are interlocking. The greater change in the relationship between the courts and the correctional agencies will not come from the courts, which by their very nature are limited to the case-by-case judicial revamping of policy. The greatest amount of power to affect this relationship lies in the hands of the executives[76] and the legislature.[77] Rubin titles the executive capacity to change the domain boundaries between courts and correctional agencies the "positive response." This stance by administrators "would show awareness that court decisions are minimal, that they do not purport to solve administrative problems, and that they afford many hints to do more than the court has specifically demanded."[78] Some of these positive steps, such as the institution of ombudsmen in correctional agencies or the establishment of arbitration boards or grievance mechanisms, have already been implemented in a number of correctional settings.[79]

The basic logic in such administrative innovations is *not* constructed on the threat of additional court opinions; instead, it falls out *directly* from the recent advances in our knowledge of how to minimize organizational conflict in general and how to structure

---

[73] Ibid.

[74] Sullivan and Tift, "Correctional Resistance to Court Intervention," pp. 217–18.

[75] *Wolff* v. *McDonnell*, 15 CrL. 3313, "We are content for now to leave the continuing development . . . to the sound discretion of corrections officials . . . ."

[76] Rubin, "The Impact of Court Decisions on the Correctional Process."

[77] Paul Lerman, *Community Treatment and Social Control* (Chicago: University of Chicago Press, 1973), particularly Part II dealing with the California probation subsidy.

[78] Rubin, "The Administrative Response to Court Decisions," p. 381.

[79] Paul F. Cromwell, "Alternatives to Litigation of Prisoner Grievances," in George C. Killinger, Paul F. Cromwell, and Bonnie J. Cromwell (eds.), *Corrections and Administration* (St. Paul: West, 1976), pp. 510–20.

consensual rules for conflict resolution so that outside forces do not become involved.[80] Such positive steps by administration may in many respects be seen as a threat to court domain, since to the extent that administrators innovate prior to court intervention, the fewer are the valid cases that will go to court and the narrower will be the judicial scope of review when it does occur.

[80] Rubin, "The Administrative Response to Court Decisions," p. 386.

PART FIVE

THE ENVIRONMENT
OF CORRECTIONS
AND THE
MANAGEMENT
OF THE SYSTEM

INTRODUCTION

In 1911, in the first volume of the *Journal of Criminal Law and Criminology*, a Harvard law professor observed that public opinion had always affected the criminal law and the administration of punishment, but rarely had the examination of the consequences of punishment affected the criminal law or our designs for punishment.[1] Addressing the annual convention of the American Prison Congress, he concluded that in the twentieth century professional correctional officials and criminologists could change the unilateral impact of public belief on the administration of corrections. Sixty years later, when the author was a student in the first doctoral program in criminal justice, a Korean colleague issued with oriental wisdom,

[1] G. F. Kirchwey, "Crime and Punishment," *Journal of Criminal Law and Criminology* (Jan., 1911).

"Crime affects criminal justice; criminal justice does not affect crime." Little did I know at the time that his offhand observation was 60 years old and that its reissue was reinforcement of an age-old criminal justice characteristic. So much the difference, then, between professionalism in this field and professionalism in medicine or law in which the practitioners in the field lead public opinion.

Rare is the enterprise so unable to affect its basic constraints. Public belief and values still guide us, and limit us, in correctional work to a far greater extent than is true of many other public service endeavors. The relationship between correctional practice and the vicissitudes and basic ambivalence of public opinion should signal, perhaps, the extreme importance of the societal systems for punishment to the very nature of our culture and society. It suggests that punishment, unlike medicine and the law, let alone far less questioned undertakings such as sending human beings to the moon, is governed by ethics rather than technology of tasks, and it suggests that ethics in American culture has not changed a great deal.

Underscoring this observation requires little scholarly search. The "new" and controversial jurisprudential work of van den Haag, Packer, and Morris differ little in the concepts used or the conclusions derived from the far earlier works of McConnell.[2] The arguments for and against prison today seem only a reiteration of the equally vociferous controversy in the middle of the nineteenth century.[3]

Advances have been made in other branches of American enterprise in two ways. Technology can lead to opportunities, the taking of which are so far beyond the ethical ken of the culture that basic decisions about what to do are left to the technicians who raised the possibilities. In this way we achieved automotive travel—and the atom bomb. Somewhat different is the achievement by leaders in a field of a breakthrough in the conceptual paradigms with which we interpret social activity and thus change the very ethical standards by which public policy is judged. In this way, the American Constitution was a paradigmatic change in the way that people related to a central government, and Marxian economics was a paradigmatic change in the analysis of work.

Neither of these changes has guided the activity of punishment in the United States. Consequently, we cannot do much better or much worse (or to say it differently, we cannot do much differently) than

---

[2] Compare Ernest van den Haag, *Punishing Criminals* (New York: Basic Books, 1975); Herbert Packer, *The Limits of the Criminal Sanction* (Stanford: Stanford University Press, 1968); Norval Morris, *The Future of Imprisonment* (Chicago: University of Chicago Press, 1974); with Ray Madding McConnell, *Criminal Responsibility with Social Constraint* (New York: Scribners, 1912).

[3] Andrew T. Scull, *Decarceration* (Englewood Cliffs, N.J.: Prentice-Hall, 1977).

our predecessors did. There have been improvements, of course. Given our standards of decency, health, and fairness, corrections now is "better" than the corrections observed by the Harvard Law professor of 1911. But corrections is also sufficiently similar in its basic outlines, and especially in its basic cultural position, that we can turn in the 1970's to the discovery that coerced treatment fails[4] or that individualized treatment may conflict with general prevention and retribution[5] with an intellectual surprise that would have startled our predecessors. In short, we are caught in the same dilemmas that have constrained and shaped corrections for years.

There is, of course, always hope. The basic hope is that hindsight is perfect vision. The technological and ethical paradigmatic shifts that even a generation from now might seem extraordinary are far more difficult to realize when they are right under our noses. So perhaps we have made significant changes in corrections that have yet to be recognized.

The last part of this book, therefore, promises nothing new. Instead, the next two chapters are an attempt to examine some of the reasons for the lack of newness in corrections and some of the reasons why organizational management, the management of innovation, and the management of interorganizational relations progress as they do (to and fro and slowly). If major advances are to be made, they will probably be made in this last area of our inquiry: in examining the relationship between corrections and the general cultural and political climate of our country. As John Meyer has observed, the obstacles to change, once they are known and assailed, can become the facilitators to change.[6]

Chapter 14 examines the public values about correction and the ways in which these values can and do affect correctional policy. Some suggestions are made about correctional policy formulation that might aid correctional managers to address public concerns more satisfactorily and to implement correctional programs without infuriating and threatening major segments of the body politic. Then Chapter 15 draws together the material on organizational management in an attempt to assess the current conflicts in correctional policy between reintegration and restraint. This assessment leads to no hard and fast conclusions, but it does hold implications for the future of corrections and correctional management. Correctional managers will once again be called on to tackle the dilemmas of correctional policy or to follow its surface resolutions. In either case, the debate will take on new dimensions.

---

[4] Norval Morris, *The Future of Imprisonment*, Chapter Two.

[5] Ernest van den Haag, *Punishing Criminals*, Chapter Two.

[6] John C. Meyer, "Change and Obstacles to Change in Prison Management," *Federal Probation* (June, 1972), pp. 39–46.

14

Public
Opinion
and the
Formulation of
Correctional Policy

(David Duffee and R. Richard Ritti)

DEVELOPMENTS IN CORRECTIONAL POLICY[1]

A recent trend in penological research has been the emphasis on organizational and policy-making issues. The seminal collection by Cloward and others[2] on the social organization of the prison was followed by similar studies of parole organization and parole officer

---

[1] The first part of this chapter is a revised version of David Duffee and R. Richard Ritti, "Correctional Policy and Public Values," *Criminology* (Feb.,1977), pp. 449–60; reused here with the permission of Sage Publications.

[2] Richard Cloward et al., *Theoretical Studies in Social Organization of the Prison* (New York: Social Science Research Council, March, 1960).

styles,[3] institutions for juveniles,[4] probation,[5] and correctional system policy.[6] Within a matter of 20 years there was a major shift from research on the individual criminal to research on the social and organizational contexts within which criminals interact and are processed. Very recently this research reached a turning point at which the director of research for the California Department of Correction reported findings that the most effective correctional changes were not aimed at the offenders but at the system itself.[7]

A major component of this organizational research has been the study of variables that affect the ways in which agency officials behave and make decisions. The terms used to identify the constraints on policy making have varied depending on the particular officials involved and the specific decisions to be made at different points in the process. Nevertheless, a widely accepted model for explaining decision makers' correctional policy has been the ways in which the decision makers simultaneously accommodate (1) concerns about the individual offender and (2) concerns about the community.[8] This model has been successful both in training and in applied research situations.[9] However, as the reintegration correctional policy became predominant, there were some sharp reactions to its basic assumptions and practices.

There are two basic reasons for these recent reactions. The first reason is that the correctional policy model treats "concern for the community" as one variable. (The executive displays more or less concern through his or her elaboration of program structure.) As our knowledge of community increases, it is becoming evident that this model of executive concerns is too monolithic. The community is frequently a fragmented structure with several conflicting power and value bases to which the administrator must be attuned. For example,

---

[3] Daniel Glaser, *The Effectiveness of a Prison and Parole System* (Indianapolis: Bobbs-Merrill, 1969), pp. 289–315; Elliot Studt, *Surveillance and Service in Parole* (Los Angeles: U.C.L.A. Institute of Government and Public Affairs, 1972).

[4] David Street, Robert Vinter, and Charles Perrow, *Organizations for Treatment* (New York: Free Press, 1966).

[5] Leonard Scheurell, "Valuation and Decision Making in Correctional Social Work," *Issues in Criminology* (Fall, 1969), pp. 101–8.

[6] Vincent O'Leary and David Duffee, "Correctional Policy—A Classification of Goals Designed for Change," *Crime and Delinquency* (Oct., 1971), pp. 373–86.

[7] Lawrence Bennett, "Should We Change the Offender or the System?" *Crime and Delinquency* (July, 1973), pp. 332–42.

[8] Studt, *Surveillance and Service in Parole*; Don Gottfredson, *Measuring Attitudes Toward Juvenile Detention* (New York: National Council on Crime and Elinquency, 1968); Daniel Glaser, "The Prospect for Corrections," paper prepared for the Arden House Conference on Manpower Needs in Corrections, mimeographed, 1964; Clarence Schrag, "Contemporary Corrections: An Analytical Model," paper prepared for the President's Commission on Law Enforcement and Administration of Justice, mimeographed, 1966.

[9] See Chapters 4, 5, and 8 in this book.

the prison administrator may have to accommodate both politically influential lay people and university treatment consultants.[10]

A second reason for taking a different approach to policy constraints is that the correctional policy model treats "concern for the community" and "concern for the individual offender" as independent dimensions. While previous research supported the validity of this orthogonality assumption[11] one goal of the policy model was its utility as a guide in policy formulation. We would suggest at this juncture that policy-guidance instruments will be more helpful in the future if they do not reinforce administrative behavior that seeks to balance or to make trade-offs between the interests of the community and the interests of the offender. Irwin and Cressey suggested that criminologists overemphasized the situational explanations of the inmate subculture.[12] Similarly, we would suggest that the juxtaposition of "offender" and "community" may overemphasize some distinctions and downplay others. It is at least hypothetically arguable that there are two or more evaluative positions in the community that are relevant to correctional policy formulation. It is also true that many offenders are not social isolates. They have familial, peer group, and organizational ties with some community groups, and these connections can be as important to policy formulation as they are to individual classification and programming decisions.[13]

In summary, we thought it would be helpful to investigate the dimensions of public attitude toward corrections as these attitudes might influence current correctional policy. This investigation is based on the assumptions (1) that the correctional system has social control functions but (2) that the social control function can be implemented in a variety of ways. Concern for retribution or general deterrence[14] might imply a paramilitary organization, flat and lengthy prison sentences, and utilization of the *apprehended* offender as an example. Concern for rehabilitation or special deterrence, on the other hand, may also serve a social control function by reducing the probability that the offender would return to criminal activity when released.[15]

---

[10] Donald Cressey, "The Achievement of an Unstated Organizational Goal: An Observation on Prisons," *Pacific Sociological Review* (Fall, 1958), pp. 43–9.

[11] David Duffee, *Correctional Policy and Prison Organization* (Beverly Hills: Sage-Halsted, 1975).

[12] John Irwin and Donald Cressey, "Thieves, Convicts, and the Inmate Culture," *Social Problems* (Fall, 1962), pp. 142–55.

[13] Donald Clemmer, *The Prison Community* (Indianapolis: Bobbs-Merrill, 1958, reissue); John Irwin, *The Felon* (Englewood Cliffs, N.J.: Prentice-Hall, 1970); New York State Special Commission on Attica, *Attica* (New York: Bantam, 1972).

[14] Herbert Packer, *The Limits of the Criminal Sanction* (Stanford: Stanford University Press, 1968), pp. 37–45.

[15] Ibid., pp. 45–58.

We are not concerned in this study with other functions that the correctional system might perform within a social system. This study concentrates on conflicts between socially valued means to achieve one social end. Other studies may demonstrate equally important policy constraints related to other conceivable functions of the criminal process.

DIMENSIONS OF THE PUBLIC VIEW

To derive a preliminary structure of the public's views concerning some correctional policies, we constructed nine statements bearing on correctional policies and presented them to a representative sample of Pennsylvania households as part of a larger survey.[16] These statements were derived from recommendations of the National Advisory Commission on Criminal Justice Standards and Goals. Table 14.1 presents the results of this survey; percent agree represents those agreeing "completely" or "mostly" on a five-point scale, and percent disagree represents those agreeing "a little" or "not at all."

Correlational analysis of these statements shows that two dimensions very like those we have discussed can characterize the data adequately.[17] We found one clustering of responses related to incarceration and a second, equally clear clustering related to instances of rehabilitation that essentially ignore the question of punishment. Therefore, we have evidence to show that the public view is structured within at least two conceptually distinct categories that might be termed *retribution* and *rehabilitation*.

Two other statements, G and H, seemed to have elements of both concepts; that is, in the correlational analysis these statements related to both clusters. The wording of these items makes it apparent why they should evoke both punitive and rehabilitative responses. Statement H combines the generally unpopular suggestion of freedom for prisoners with the generally popular suggestion of a positive rehabilitation strategy. Statement G invokes the punitive dimension by suggesting criminals not be prosecuted, but it also combines elements of treatment or rehabilitation.

[16] The sample of households used is part of the basic statewide sample frame of the Pennsylvania Field Research Laboratory at The Pennsylvania State University. This is a four-stage clustered area probability sample of all Pennsylvania households (see L. Kish, *Survey Sampling*, New York: Wiley, 1965). Personal interviews lasting approximately one hour were conducted in respondents' homes during May and June of 1974.

[17] For example, items B and C representing the first cluster are strongly related showing a similarity coefficient of .88, and items D and E representing the second cluster are also strongly related with a similarity coefficient of .82. However, items representing one cluster are not highly related to items from the other. For example, C and D show a very low similarity of .24, C and E of .36. For the logic of the use of similarity coefficients, see R. Tryon and D. Bailey, *Cluster Analysis* (New York: McGraw-Hill, 1970), pp. 289–91.

Table 14.1 Public Attitudes Toward Correctional Strategies

	Percentage	
Retribution	Agree	Disagree
A. We should close down all our prisons and search for other ways to treat criminals	7	84
B. Most convicted criminals should be placed on probation or parole instead of being held in prison	10	70
C. Except for murder and for people who have already committed three or four crimes, no prison terms should be longer than 5 years	23	59
Rehabilitation		
D. Public drunkenness should not be handled as a crime if the person has a serious drinking problem	48	29
E. Job training programs for prison inmates should be the best possible even if it means increasing taxes	51	23
F. Juvenile delinquents should be sent to helping agencies instead of being sent to the reformatory	71	11
Both		
G. Criminals who are mentally retarded or who are mentally ill should not be prosecuted but should be handled by helping agencies	69	13
H. If he can find and hold a job in the community, a prisoner should be allowed out of prison during work hours	30	37
Other		
I. One of the major problems in preventing crime today is that we are making it too easy on convicted criminals	75	9

Note: Percentages based on valid responses from sample of 1426. Invalid responses, Don't Know's, and No Answer's range from 1.4% to 2.2% of sample base.

Finally, we have one statement (statement I) of broader normative content that is not clearly related to rehabilitative strategies but does seem to relate to an underlying punitive dimension.

To summarize, our conclusions about the *structure* of public attitudes suggest at least two conceptually distinct aspects.

1. A relatively broad, normative orientation toward retribution—society is being "too soft on criminals." The system strategies derived from this view place emphasis on the restraint of offenders.

2. A second aspect reflects a concern over treatment and re-habilitation. More generally, it might be interpreted as a concern over the genesis of criminal behavior, and consequently, its proper treatment.

WHAT THE PUBLIC SUPPORTS

Very obviously the norm of restraint or retribution is strongly supported. The notion of closing down prisons is flatly rejected. In fact, even the suggestion of limiting prison terms for those who are not major offenders finds support in less than one-quarter of the population. This emphasis on retribution as a normative stance is complemented by the overwhelming conviction that we are making it too easy for convicted criminals.

In view of this strong "lock 'em up and throw away the key" stance, the strong support accorded rehabilitation strategies by the public is perhaps surprising. Treatment for youthful offenders receives marked support. Job training programs, even at taxpayers' added expense, also receive better than two-to-one approval. In this context, note that statement G, dealing with the exemption from prosecution of mentally ill criminals, also receives strong support. Apparently norms concerning "responsibility" for behavior modify the normative prescription for retribution. This observation, incidentally, points up our woeful lack of understanding of public definitions of criminality in the normative sense. We will expand on this point momentarily.

Finally, we were surprised at the lack of public support for the statement dealing with work release (statement H). It seems to be one thing to provide special treatment for an offender whose *criminality* is in doubt, but quite another to suspend retribution for a prisoner who is assumed to be an ordinary offender. Therefore, in statement H the concern for rehabilitation clashed directly with the norm of retribution, resulting in split support for the correctional strategy of work release.

Our conclusions from this first inspection of the public's views of correctional strategies can be summarized under the topics of *structure* and *support*. Concerning structure, we have tentatively identified two conceptually distinct but not statistically unrelated categories—those of the normative concern for retribution and those concerning permissible strategies for rehabilitation and associated definitions of criminality. This conceptual distinctness is important because it suggests that high support for retribution as a normative stance does not necessarily preclude high support for rehabilitation.

That is, though the results of our correctional analysis indicate that citizens strongly supporting retribution will generally be less likely to support *liberal* rehabilitation strategies, the correlation is far from perfect.

Concerning *support*, we have observed that statements are worded at different levels of specificity. For example, statement H dealing with the particulars of a work release program is far more specific than statement I which directly evokes a normative concern for retribution. Put somewhat differently, the conceptual distinctness of the two clusters of statements, together with differences in the specificity of the statements, suggests the possibility of successfully integrating specific rehabilitative strategies within the overriding normative concern for retribution. It suggests the possibility of defining effective remedial strategies that satisfy (or at least leave inactive) strong normative concerns for retribution while appealing to existing support for rehabilitation.

SOME IMPLICATIONS FOR ACTION

At the outset of this chapter we suggested that the knowledge of community attitudes toward different correctional strategies might benefit professional and system executives. This was said not to suggest that the community is knowledgeable in justice alternatives, for other surveys suggest that most citizens are not. And it was not to suggest that the community is best qualified to be "right" in the sense of having some mystical understanding of what is and what is not efficacious in corrections. We are suggesting, however, that any strategy that totally ignores community opinion is likely to fail. It is likely to fail because the various representatives of the public whose support is needed for such programs, unlike the professional elites whose decisions are based on other considerations, are themselves members of their constituencies and are likely to represent and even amplify the misapprehensions of those constituencies. Thus, the problem is to define correctional changes that are normatively palatable and are also adjudged professionally to be efficacious.

From this limited study we can suggest some steps toward this goal. First, there is the need to construct a more complex view of public support than one that posits a single liberal–conservative dimension. This more complex view recognizes three facts:

1. Specific correctional strategies are subsumed under relatively broad normative dimensions. For example, the specific strategy of work release runs counter to the normative prescription for retribution.

2. The normative structure is multidimensional. Thus, at the very least, social values dealing with retribution and rehabilitation are conceptually distinct and represent *different* dimensions. We also have evidence that yet another dimension concerning values relating to individual vs. institutional rights may have to be considered in order to obtain an accurate view of the structure of public opinion.

3. Within a given dimension (e.g., retribution) the views of different social groupings are not consistently favorable or unfavorable, and they are not easily predictable. For example, upper middle-class respondents are considerably more liberal on statements invoking the normative posture of retribution, for example, the following statement: "One of the major problems in preventing crime today is that we are making it too easy on convicted criminals." Only 25 percent to 35 percent of the respondents classified as upper middle or middle class agree against 65 percent to 70 percent of the group of respondents in the lower or lower middle class.[18] However, when questioned about work release or about the disposition of juvenile offenders, we find the upper middle-class groups *less* liberal than the lower-class groups by almost two-to-one! Indications are that the more educated, more well-to-do respondents are typically more liberal when the dimension of retribution is invoked, but they also seem more conservative on questions of rehabilitation.

From this limited study we have succeeded better in raising questions than in providing answers. Still, it is clear that we have uncovered evidence of a structure considerably more complex than heretofore described. Also, while communities obviously are more than simple collectivities of individuals, making it difficult to infer how experiences in working-class as opposed to middle-class communities might differ, we have shown at least a basis for believing such differences may exist.

A second major issue that emerges from this work suggests the need to clarify the structure of public definitions of criminality and its genesis. We have seen evidence that the particular circumstances of the individual offender alter the evocation of a particular normative stance. So, for example, crimes by incompetents, by youth, by people with certain types of illness alter the normative stance taken

---

[18] Income and education were used in combined indices of social class, although in this particular example education is primarily responsible for the differences observed. Limitations on space prevent our going into further detail concerning this analysis which we hope to present in a subsequent paper.

by the public. One also suspects that the stance toward victimless crimes needs to be investigated.

A third possible area of exploration has to do with the public's understanding of the facts of the correctional system, of the extent to which "crime does not pay." We can be reasonably certain that the public is largely ignorant of the facts concerning the efficacy of the correctional system and the proportion of offenders "brought to justice." Knowledge of these areas of public belief would help our understanding of the normative stance toward criminal justice strategies.

What, then, is the use of this kind of information? The first benefit would be a better understanding of how to package public information and public relations programs to convey better to the public what is being attempted in the reform of our criminal justice system. The strategy here would be to reinterpret what has been deemed professionally to be efficacious to make it suitable within the existing normative framework. Put another way, alteration of values and norms is virtually impossible in a limited time span. But it is possible to emphasize aspects of programs and to redesign programs to make them suitable within the current normative context.

For example, our study of halfway houses administered by the Pennsylvania Bureau of Correction demonstrated that the Bureau encounterd especially strong resistance in four particular neighborhoods. In these instances, the administrators of the program either rode roughshod over community inquiries about the purpose of the program or they attempted to gain support by stressing the rehabilitative function of the planned facilities.[19] Our data would suggest that a more effective approach would involve emphasizing that community-center residents have reached this privileged status because of their good behavior while in prison and/or that these offenders have served their time and satisfied their debt to society. Both of these claims are as easily substantiated as the claims that community treatment will be efficacious, but neither claim arouses community resentment that retributive correctional functions have not been performed.

A second use of this kind of information can be the development of a methodology to monitor trends over time. Such data will be all the more necessary within the context of our knowledge that different social classes respond differentially to various correctional strategies.

[19] David Duffee et al., *The Evaluation of State Delivered Community Based Correctional Services* (Harrisburg, Pa.: Governor's Justice Commission, June, 1975).

Third, we suspect that the underlying community values that have strong impact on correctional policy are not correctional-specific. A number of scholars, including Goffman,[20] Wilkins,[21] and Szasz,[22] have argued that similar kinds of deviant behavior are frequently handled by different social control systems. If these observations are valid, the core values manifested here in terms of rehabilitation and retribution should also be displayed in community stances toward mental health and social welfare. A methodological consequence of such correlations would be that surveys of community attitudes toward criminal justice should be incorporated in instruments that also cover other social program areas.

Overcoming our current ignorance of community, as it relates to criminal justice, is likely to redefine some other major correctional problems or to rearrange completely our strategies for their solution. Korn once lamented that the public is a sacred cow often deferred to but never consulted.[23] Systematic investigation of community and of criminal justice agencies *as aspects of community* is one step in desanctifying the community beast to the extent that it might participate with state and national experts in the solution of its problems.

ADMINISTRATOR'S VALUES AND PUBLIC VALUES

It is true that examinations of public opinion, even as simple as the one reported above, could be of great use to correctional administration. Administrators armed with valid data on public belief and values would be in a far stronger position to deal with legislators and elected executives over issues of correctional programming. Without such data, elected officials are likely either to object to or to support correctional policy in accordance with their "hunches" about what the public will condone. The above data and other similar surveys[24] suggest that both administrators and elected officials are inaccurate in estimating the strength and shape of public attitude. It is obvious from the above data (e.g., closing prisons is not popular or work release encounters only mixed reactions) that many current programs favored by correctional officials will experience resistance from the public. Such data also make it clear that the sources of resistance are not spread randomly over the population and, that the public even

[20] Erving Goffman, *Asylums* (Garden City, N.Y.: Doubleday, 1961).
[21] Leslie Wilkins, *Social Deviance* (Englewood Cliffs, N.J.: Prentice-Hall, 1965).
[22] Thomas Szasz, *Ideology and Insanity* (Garden City, N.Y.: Doubleday, 1970).
[23] Richard Korn, "Of Crime, Criminal Justice, and Corrections," *University of San Francisco Law Review* (Oct., 1971), pp. 27-75.
[24] David Lewis Smith and C. McCurdy Lipsey, "Public Opinion and Penal Policy," *Criminology* (May, 1976), pp. 113-24.

supports some activities administrators have long supposed the public would resist.[25]

While the utility of public opinion sampling may be very important to any *particular* correctional program issue, the most startling finding of the Pennsylvania data is *not* the public support or opposition to any particular program but rather the sharp divergence between the structure of public value as indicated in direct survey of the public and the structure of public value as perceived by surveys of correctional administrator's policy.

The data from the public survey demonstrate that *two* underlying dimensions constrain public reaction to correctional policy. There is a concern for retribution, which may vary from strong to weak. There is also a concern for rehabilitation, which may also vary from strong to weak. While correctional practitioners and academicians alike have often conceptualized retribution (or punishment) and treatment (or rehabilitation) as opposites along *one* dimension, statistical analysis of the public data indicates that such is not the case. Upper middle-class communities were relatively weak on both the retribution dimension and on the rehabilitation dimension. Lower-class, urban communities were strong on retribution and were relatively strong on rehabilitation. Administrators have frequently felt it necessary either to "sell" the public on treatment or to sell the public on the disadvantages of punishment in order to advance their treatment goals because the administrators believed that strengthening the one set of values would automatically decrease the other set of values. The public has not responded as administrative strategy has theorized; the data indicate why.

As remarkable as it might seem, retribution and rehabilitation seem to be values that must be handled, accommodated, or satisfied independently of each other. By ignoring the fact that these are two separate value clusters, administrators have often militated against their own programs. They have often entered communities to initiate community programs with public statements that rehabilitation, rather than retribution, is the best means of punishing. The public's rebuffs to these messages are often interpreted by administrators as evidence that the public is too backward to accept modern correctional techniques or too uneducated to understand what is effective. Administrators might better have started with the strategy of satisfying demands for retribution and demands for rehabilitation separately.

Why have correctional administrators so often misconstrued the structure of public values? And why is their own structure for the formulation of correctional policy so markedly different? Recall that

[25] For example, Smith and Lipsey found strong support for conjugal visitation in two southern cities.

the large majority of correctional policy research demonstrates that correctional managers counterplay the concern for the individual offender and the concern for the community. For the administrator, these are the pressing constraints: how to handle the offender and how to handle the community simultaneously. Reintegration, rehabilitation, reform, and restraint are four model policy orientations by which correctional administrators attempt to handle these two concerns. A comparison of administrative and public structures of basic value premises indicates neither direct conflict nor contradiction; instead, it indicates the existence of two separate value paradigms within which correctional programming will either unfold or be judged (see Figures 14.1 and 14.2). The existence of these two separate paradigms should suggest that the primary characteristic of exchange between public and public administrators will be *not* heated *dialogue* but heated attempts to communicate that fail because the basic references are dissimilar.

If the ideological structures, or value structures, within which the public and correctional administrators think about corrections are indeed different, it is important to understand how it is that correctional managers' values have become this separate from public values.

Figure 14.1 The Structure of Public Value About Corrections

Concern for Retribution

		Low	High
Concern for Rehabilitation	High	Crime indicates Criminals cannot follow norms	Understanding of crime—criminal in doubt, state in flux
	Low	Crime of low public concern	Crime threatens community norms

Figure 14.2 The Structure of Administrative Value About Corrections

Concern for Community

		Low	High
Concern for Offender	High	Rehabilitation	Reintegration
	Low	Restraint	Reform

The questions implied in the need to gain such an understanding are far too many and far too complex for satisfactory coverage here. Are correctional administrators recruited from groups whose values are very different from those of the public in general? Do the constant study and practice of a particular social service program alter one's basic understanding of what should be done? Do correctional administrators become so overly concerned with the survival of their organizations that they lose the ability to judge the functionality of their enterprises for the public that created the organizations in the first place? Does the act of administering a public organization isolate it and its officials from the public itself?

The answers to such questions cannot be obtained *within* the study of correctional organization as it presently operates. These questions require a broader frame of reference that would allow asking questions about and measuring characteristics of an entire society at any one point and over time. However, there are probably few persons who could inform such study more intelligently than those who are currently engaged in correctional administration, once they were willing to, and able to, examine their environments with as much effort and commitment that they display in the internal affairs of their organizations. In order to answer such questions accurately, we will need to know in much more detail how managerial roles structure executive thought and how managerial roles structure the executive's interaction with outside groups, particularly with the citizens of a state whose being generates the public executive roles in the first place.

While such questions are too new and too complex for current managerial science, our previous exploration of organizational theory and behavior can offer some initial guidelines for the inquiry and hazard some rough guesses about what is taking place.

THE SEPARATION OF THE CORRECTIONAL MANAGER FROM PUBLIC VALUE

A number of organizational sociologists and systems theorists have identified several levels of system complexity in relation to task performance. For example, Roland Warren posits that there are five distinct auspices under which various social functions can be performed; they range from (1) the individual and families to (2) informal groups to (3) voluntary associations, to (4) business enterprises and, finally, to (5) government.[26] Katz and Kahn, concentrating

[26] Roland Warren, *The Community in America*, (Chicago: Rand McNally, 1963), p. 73.

on the elaboration of complex organizations, suggest that tasks or problems (1) are initially addressed as they occur through voluntary associations to achieve a common objective, (2) are then prepared for through the elaboration of maintenance structures to sustain production structures over time; and (3) are finally institutionalized in autonomous, permanent organizations whose boundaries and managerial structures attempt to organize the environment for the benefit of the organization.[27] Buckley distinguishes systems of any sort as the complexity of their feedback loops allows them to predict and learn rather than respond to external conditions. Of particular importance is his distinction between *goal-oriented systems* that alter internal system states in orientation to unchanging end goals and *goal-directed systems* that can alter end goals or functions as well as internal structures.[28]

While we could continue this list in the interest of building comparative morphological frameworks, these three versions of a common phenomenon, drawn as they are from community sociology, social psychology, and general systems theory, are perhaps diverse enough to make a general point. Organizations are initiated in response to commonly perceived, socially significant tasks. At that stage, they are only vaguely distinguished from other community or social groupings. Indeed, they are community property. As organizations elaborate, the first significant break with the community appears to be a goal-oriented stage in which the major managerial effort is the stabilization of the internal organizational climate.[29] During this process the organization takes on an identity of its own and is perceived as a socially distinct thing rather than as a community arrangement for the accomplishment of group-perceived goals. In other words, the organization achieves some independence from the community functions the performance of which provided its initial impetus.

As the organization continues through time, the policy relevant (or structure changing) questions more and more frequently arise from internal rather than from external sources. The organization rationalizes itself and top management becomes preoccupied with justifying its organizational structure to outside groups. This process has major consequences both for the efficiency of the organization and for the effectiveness of the organization as a contributor to the performance of community functions. As the organization becomes goal-directed, rather than goal-oriented, several things happen:

[27]Daniel Katz and Robert Kahn, *The Social Psychology of Organizations* (New York: Wiley, 1966), pp. 77–83.
[28]Walter Buckley, *Sociology and Modern Systems Theory* (Englewood Cliffs, N.J.: Prentice-Hall, 1967), pp. 187–91.
[29]See Chapter 5 for an elaboration.

1. Diffusely laid social values and traditions become very specific decision generators and tests.[30]
2. Contradictory goals are resolved in terms of organizational structures that stress one goal over another.
3. Routines and rituals that originated in the community phase of organizations are discarded as irrational or as not contributing to the manifest goals of the organization.
4. There becomes an overriding concern with the validity of the indicators of organizational achievement: organizations become concerned with modifying structure in relation to organizational outcomes instead of in relation to original purposes. In other words, the organization becomes concerned with meeting its own constraints, not those of community survival.

The consequences of these changes, stated in general terms, are extremely important to understanding the relation of the correctional organization to the performance of societal functions.

First, there would seem to be a narrowing of the scope of the organization's functional contributions to society, that is, a reduction in the ambiguity and complexity of outputs. For example, the tribal societies studied by Malinowski may have produced canoes in a highly ritualized manner in order that the ritual would contribute (latently) to communal integration. But the modern boat factory produces boats, not a ritually reinforced identity of a social group.[31]

Second, as the output narrows and is more rationally pursued, the latent community functions previously performed in the *community* accomplishment of the organizational task are either no longer attended to or become the basis of external political attacks on the purposes and values of the rationalized organization. In other words, as the organization becomes more effective in the scientific evaluation of a few specified objectives, it becomes less able to handle other outputs that were previously achieved symbolically in the course of achieving the primary tasks.

Third, as external pressures on the organization increase for change in its goals and processes, the trend toward increased internal organizational stability reverses. Organizational participants with different specialties and statuses will begin to attack the internal rationality of the organization in direct proportion to their sympathy for and membership in one external group or another.

---

[30] See Chapter 4 for an elaboration on this process.
[31] Bronislaw Malinowski, "Functionalism in Anthropology," in Lewis A. Coser and Bernard Rosenberg (eds.), *Sociological Theory: A Book of Readings*, 2nd ed. (New York: Macmillan, 1964), pp. 637–50.

The turbulence of both the internal and external organizational environments in the long run are directly related to the organization's incompetence to accommodate ambiguity, multiplicity, and conflict in goal structure. The more the organization rationally devises special competence as directed to specified objectives, the less it services other functions originally associated with the primary task. This problem is particularly relevant to corrections, since nearly all organized community activities associated with the communal task of punishment are legally monopolized by public organizations of the state.

To restate the foregoing in terms of its impact on correctional management, the social arrangements for punishment pass through several stages during which correctional management becomes progressively more involved in "solving" organizational problems, or putting several subobjectives into one system, and less involved with the extent to which public values are manifested in the interactive process of social disruption and stabilization. It becomes more important to the manager to resolve internal conflicts than to resolve societal conflicts. Moreover, because the manager has great personal and professional investment in the organization of correction, he or she is likely to equate the survival and growth of the organizational structure with the survival and growth of the social structure in general. Vickers and others have lain that assumption in its grave: Our social institutions now feed the very social conflicts that they were designed to reduce.[32]

The separation of our organizational executives and of social policy from the community problems and processes that generated them has been termed by Roland Warren the single most predominant characteristic of twentieth-century American community life.[33] A brief examination of Warren's community theory can help us untangle the nature of that separation and some of the reasons for the differences between organizational policy and public values. Warren points out that many community functions, corrections included, are now carried out by vertical arrangements in which local centers of action are guided by policy and are supported by resources located at extracommunity levels (in regional, state, or national government). The more attentive organizational managers are to these vertical arrangements of decision making and resource flow, the less they will be attentive to local community variations or to interconnections between the activities of their own organizations and those that perform other community functions. For example, Duffee, Meyer, and Warner have demonstrated the conflicts existing

---

[32] Geoffrey Vickers, *Making Institutions Work* (New York: Halsted Press, 1973).
[33] Warren, *The Community in America*, pp. 14–20.

between the vertical allegiances of halfway house executives to their central office command and their ability to interact effectively with local community groups.[34]

The impact of the increased verticalization of correctional organizations has made it progressively less likely that correctional executives can respond with immediacy to local conditions and values and more likely that they will implement programs that are relatively similar across the various community populations serviced by their organizations. This "verticalization" has decided advantages for some kinds of correctional activity. Deinstitutionalization has progressed most rapidly under the auspices of state and national executives who were well isolated from the conditions into which they placed the decarcerated offenders and who were isolated as well from the local objections to the programs that have been undertaken.[35] State level correctional executives in California successfully altered the shape of incarceration policy and state funding of institutional and probation programs, despite data suggesting that the new program was more expensive and less crime-effective than the policy and program that it replaced.[36] State administered halfway houses in Pennsylvania have been successfully implemented, but other forms of community correctional activity have been meager.[37] State bureaucrats in Massachusetts were able to close many institutions for juveniles despite opposition from local communities and labor unions.[38]

For other correctional programs or objectives, the vertically organized system has been less successful. Crime rates have gone up continuously despite the major federal activities and funds directed at crime and crime control. Recidivism has remained relatively stable, but at times it has gone up in the newer, supposedly more effective programs. Costs may have risen despite claims about the cheapness of new programs.[39]

Above all, vertically organized correctional systems have not dissuaded the communities of America about the value of retribution, and as a result, correctional administration is again feeling the effects

[34] See David Duffee, Peter B. Meyer, and Barbara D. Warner, *Offender Need, Parole Outcome and Program Structure in the Bureau of Correction Community Services Division* (Harrisburg, Pa.: Governor's Justice Commission, 1977), and Chapter 12 in this volume in which the interorganizational relations of these centers to human service agencies were examined.

[35] Andrew T. Scull, *Decarceration* (Englewood Cliffs, N.J.: Prentice-Hall, 1977).

[36] Paul Lerman, *Community Treatment and Social Control* (Chicago: University of Chicago Press, 1974).

[37] Duffee, Meyer, and Warner, *Offender Need, Parole Outcome and Program Structure in the Bureau of Correction Community Services Division.*

[38] Yitzhak Bakal (ed.), *Closing Institutions* (Lexington, Mass.: Lexington Books, 1974).

[39] See, in general, Scull, *Decarceration*; Lerman, *Community Treatment and Social Control*, and Chapter 10 of this book.

of political and economic backlash on programs and operating assumptions that seemed unassailable only a decade ago. Many factions of the American public have *not* preferred cheaper to more expensive punishment, they have not rejected expensive treatment in favor of cheaper or more expensive punishment, and they have not been willing, across the board, to settle for one or the other.

It is the hypothesis here that correctional executives have not been able to accommodate this complexity because correctional organizations have not heretofore been organized to accept several goals at the same time. Instead, correctional organization has been structured to "resolve" what executives have seen as a basic ambivalence between punishment and treatment. But the public has not been ambivalent: It has sought both rehabilitation *and* retribution.

That correctional managers perceive that retribution and rehabilitation are different means to the same goal, rather than different goals (or values) requiring separate means, is probably reinforced by many separate factors that are too disparate to enumerate. There is one important one, however, that requires special emphasis: the relationship of the correctional executive who is responsible to a vertically organized special system for handling individual offenders vis-à-vis specific local communities. Correctional executives, at least in our largest systems, are sufficiently distant from communities that not only can they afford to think of the "community" as a single entity, but also they cannot obtain the kind of information about communities that would enable them to do anything else. Communities, as entities, are relatively unimportant to the correctional executives' administrations in comparison to the correctional executives' relationships to state legislatures and federal program funds. (And this is probably true whether we are examining administrations in single large cities within which many diverse ethnic, cultural, and economic groups exist or we are examining administrations of regional and statewide systems.) Even large city correctional systems, such as those in Philadelphia and New York City, are sufficiently complex, large, and isolated from the various communities that executives are more concerned with their own organizations than they are with the communities that support them.

As a consequence, executive policy formulation can juxtapose the "concern for the offender" and the "concern for the community" as if these two concerns were independent and separate dimensions. The offender, after all, has been isolated from the community through his or her identification, conviction, and allocation to a correctional agency. For the correctional executive, the offender is as much or more a member of the *organization* than he or she is a member of the *community*, because it is in terms of organizational roles rather than community roles that the offender must play.

Correctional organizations have thus elaborated a variety of ways of handling offenders based on the structural differentiation of the organization into separate parts. By the time the organizational interaction with the offender is concluded the organization has invented a number of ways in which the offender is to be returned to the community; these ways depend on whatever offender changing technologies are in vogue in the organization at the time (i.e., parole, work release, furlough, sentence termination). But the American correctional organization has generally focused *on the offender* rather than on the meaning of crime and the criminal to communities. As such, the organization has concentrated on "rehabilitation" types of arrangements. It has rarely focused on activities suggested by communities that value retribution, and it has never really attempted to concentrate on both rehabilitation and retribution at the same time.

The current conflicts between reintegration and restraint policy and the newer attempts to isolate treatment from punishment should be understood in this context. To the extent that correctional management can devise ways to implement this separation and achieve goals related to both activities, correctional organization may indeed be on the threshold of significant change.

15

Bureaucracy, Equity, and Change in Correctional Organization

Any correctional executive, whether he or she would accept or reject the theoretical perspective presented here, should be aware that some of his or her greatest problems are not "manageable," in the sense that manipulation of the internal structure of the organization can solve the problems. These "unmanageable" problems derive from the *external* political economy of correctional organizations and from the larger systems in which corrections is embedded.

It is to these larger questions, of the political and social functions of corrections, that this chapter turns. A full discussion of such issues is far beyond the scope of this work, which has had the task of questioning the extent that administrators can be more effective managers within existing social conditions. Discussions of what our current organizations can and cannot do is extremely important now, because correctional agencies are under attack from a variety of parties holding separate ideological viewpoints. Such attacks can understandably anger correctional executives, as they do this author, when they are launched without regard for or sufficient knowledge of what correctional organizations are now doing and potentially can do.

Frustration with correctional organization is justified when policy makers promise too much and attempt too little *and* these deficiencies are integrally connected to addressing social needs that go unmet because our present social institutions frustrate the very social goals that they are assigned to achieve. Some of the claims that "corrections is a failure" are this type of criticism. They are made by persons who have long assumed that penal organizations can make a "better society" and have finally discovered that they cannot. As such, these evaluations of failure are really somewhat misdirected. A greyhound cannot fail by losing a horserace and an architect does not fail if the prison he designs is later found inappropriate for use as a hospital. Any such mismatch indicates the existence of failure, but they are failures in matching the right tools, processes, and structures to the objectives to be achieved rather than failures of the internal management of the system in question.

ASSESSING CORRECTIONAL FUNCTIONS

When correctional organizations are criticized for "not doing their job," several crucial questions should be raised prior to agreeing with this criticism. Failed at what? By whom and for what reasons was achievement in this area expected? How was the assessment of failure undertaken? Questions similar to these are reasonably asked by researchers when program administrators claim success. And they should be. But it is not apparent that such questions are rigorously pursued prior to the assertion of failure.

Some methodological reasons for this problem are clear. First of all, demonstration of program failure is generally not something one sets out to do. Failure of a program, or an organization, is generally the null hypothesis. Evidence to support it is not gathered. Instead, evidence is gathered to test the question whether the program has had the effects or outcomes it was intended to produce. The null hypothesis states that the program has made no difference or has had other (perhaps negative) effects. The way research is *usually* conducted, the evidence tested can lead to the failure to reject the null hypothesis, but such evidence is inappropriately used to demonstrate failure. A null hypothesis is *not* proven.

More important to the practice of correctional management, however, is that much correctional research does not ask the right questions, in the sense that researchers frequently do not ask questions whose answers can reasonably be expected to have an impact on the management of the organization. It has been researchers, much more frequently than administrators, who have been intrigued with recidivism. Not only is recidivism a very likely occurrence, but even high levels of it are unlikely to alter drastically the situation that the correctional executive has to manage. Research is just beginning on more practical matters. How to reduce prison violence or how to reduce custodial staff turnover are questions no less theoretically complex and interesting than those about recidivism.

It is noteworthy that while "corrections" (presumably *in toto*) is deemed a failure, corrections *in toto*, has rarely, if ever, been evaluated. Researchers seem preoccupied with the assessment of *programs* rather than with the assessment of organizations or systems. Some program evaluators may mention in their reports that the program might have been more successful if administrators had given more attention to it. These evaluators, however, infrequently follow up their own leads to ask what activities *did* take up the administrators' time and energy. Perhaps these unstudied activities have been more important to the explanation of correctional organization than the operation of a few "treatment" programs have been.

While it would be idiocy to go around claiming that corrections is, indeed, successful, it would seem high time to raise the question of what correctional organizations have actually been doing all this time if for all the outcomes investigated there has been no demonstrable impact. What *are* the social functions of correctional organizations? How are correctional organizations linked to other structures that together make up community or social systems? Or is it possible that correctional organizations are so isolated from society that they perform no useful purpose? That they exist for themselves? (This is, of course, a possibility, but it is unlikely).

Perhaps we can clarify the same point in another way by asking the same questions in reverse. Instead of asking what do correctional organizations achieve, apart from the treatment activities that are apparently unsuccessful, we might ask what correctional organizations manage to achieve (or what functions they perform for society) by *not* achieving those things which evaluators have expected.

To put it briefly, let us start with the assumption that correctional organizations have succeeded in *not* changing (persons, crime rates, public safety levels, etc.). Indeed, many critics of the system would suggest that the system has done very well in not producing change. Organizations that attempt not to produce change (in other words, produce stability, predictability, maintenance of existing relationships) are very common and apparently are necessary to the existence of complex systems. For example, personnel departments and budgeting departments in large organizations both tend to be conservative forces that concentrate on the ability of the organizations to survive under present conditions or within present definitions of objectives and present financial limitations. These parts of organizations tend to conflict with other units which do concentrate on change (such as research and development units and marketing and advertising units). Some *adaptive* or change-directed units are engaged in tasks of altering the internal structure and processes of the organization so that it may more effectively meet the demands of a changing environment. Other such units are engaged in active manipulation of different environmental units so that the environment of the organization will be more amenable to objectives and/or operational patterns that are already established.

To the extent that correctional systems are actually pattern-maintaining instead of change-inducing systems, "corrections" is obviously a very misleading term. Corrections *implies* change (granted, in a certain direction) and change implies a system that can and does create disorder, shakes up existing situations and interaction patterns, and builds to new situations and objectives. In terms of our correctional policies, rehabilitation and reform policies are probably examples of change induction that focus inwardly on the organization (i.e., like research and development units). They attempt to produce changes (e.g., in offenders) that will yield these "products" more acceptable to certain demand markets in the environment (most specifically to police, judges, parole officers, and probable employers). Reintegration policy, in contrast, may be similar to those change-inducing units that focus outward on the environment (i.e., marketing and advertising) and would allow the organization to manipulate the external factors to its advantage (e.g., create career lines attractive and feasible for offenders, create toleration in the community for stigmatized groups).

Although a variety of studies have sought to explain, or at least evaluate, correctional system operations *under the assumption that the system had change-inducing objectives*, fewer studies have sought to describe correctional organizations *under the assumption that the system had status-maintaining or stability objectives*. One of the few studies to do so was a remarkable investigation by Martin and Webster who were concerned with the *social consequences of conviction* in the English penal system.[1] Essentially, their unusual

[1] J. P. Martin and D. Webster, *The Social Consequences of Conviction* (London: Heinemann, 1971).

methodology dictated in-depth interviews with all offenders in one English court both directly after their conviction and subsequent to their completion of sentence. Their results are not surprising, in terms of their own hypotheses, but stand in marked contrast to many of the criticisms of the American penal system. In brief, they found that conviction (and/or the serving of sentence) had few consequences for the career pattern of the offender in question. Those offenders with relatively stable, supportive family relationships, a relatively satisfactory job and income, etc., returned after conviction to the same social circumstances. Those offenders whose preconviction social situation demonstrated marked decline, instability, etc., continued after conviction to manifest the same life career pattern. Contrary to American researches, which have rarely used the same methodology, Martin and Webster found that the penal system had few positive *or* negative effects. Instead, the system apparently operated like something of a vacuum in the offender's life, interrupting well-established and continuing life patterns for varying but temporary periods of time.

Paraphrasing the conclusion of this study in organizational terms, one might say that Martin and Webster found the *operational* goals of the system were to maintain present social situations. Regardless of the administrative objectives of the penal professionals, the system managed neither increases nor decreases in probability of criminal offenses, employability, family harmony, or other indicators of change.

It is incorrect, however, to suggest that such a system "does nothing" when we say it "maintains" present patterns or induces stasis is the social system. It is more accurate to understand the maintenance function of the system as a conservative force that slows down (or perhaps impedes altogether) the dissolution of existing institutionalized patterns of interaction and distributions of social rewards. In terms of its impact on the offenders processed, the system functions to *delay* the trends apparent in life career patterns. The unstable, emotionally troubled worker who will eventually quit his fifth job will not do so until the completion of his sentence for assault. The relatively happy junior executive who is about to marry his way into a better position will not do so until he has served his 30 days for drunken driving.

In terms of larger, system effects, pattern maintenance may mean that correctional processes retard social system change by focusing explanatory activity on individuals rather than on social reward (or control) systems. Or, as van den Haag suggests, a system of penal justice can only maintain the distributive justice system as it stands. Penal sanctions are incapable of inducing change in social organization.[2]

THE JUSTICE MODEL OF CORRECTION

We have alluded briefly throughout this book to the current shifts of emphasis in correctional policy. These shifts include the return to "straight time" or flat sentences, the return of sentencing authority from discretionary correctional boards to judges and legislatures, the abolition of coerced treatment program participation, etc. One leading proponent of this shift in emphasis is David Fogel, who has advanced what he calls "a justice model" of correction.[3] This model, he suggests, is less concerned with the administration of justice than with just administration.

The aim of the justice model is to inject more certainty into the administration of correction by establishing clearer rules of procedure and regulation and by extracting the present control practices in which rewards and penalties for offenders are contingent on administrative (a la "treatment") discretion. The forecasted outcomes of the implementation of the justice model include shorter amounts of time served, greater fairness (as perceived by offenders), and the availability of social services to offenders on a voluntary basis.

As a correctional administrator with academic credentials and long experience on the line, Fogel is a perceptive critic of the present system. He accepts the findings that treatment programs have failed to achieve their manifest goals of change, but he adds that they have probably succeeded in their latent, managerial functions of providing administration with more subtle ways of controlling inmates. It is Fogel's value position that this indirect form of control, while perhaps effective for the maintenance of stability, is manifestly unfair and has long-range dysfunctions for staff, offenders, and community that are gradually gaining recognition. That is, the maintenance structures that operate today in the correctional system necessitate the espousal of change goals that are not and cannot be implemented. As various groups in society, including those directly interacting in correctional organizations, increasingly favor change in the distribution pattern of social rewards, the use of change-committed language in the maintenance of stability appears (1) increasingly hypocritical or (2) increasingly incompetent. In either case, various segments of the community are thereby likely to lose faith in the

[2] Ernest van den Haag, *Punishing Criminals* (New York: Basic Books, 1975), p. 30.
[3] David Fogel, *We Are the Living Proof* (Cincinnati: Anderson, 1975).

correctional apparatus. Fogel's suggestion, then, is to admit to the maintenance functions of the correctional system and to strive for these objectives in a more straightforward (therefore just) manner.

RETRIBUTION, DETERRENCE, AND PUNISHMENT

Ernest Van den Haag starts at a different point, but his recent book on the purposes and means of punishment implies changes in the administration of correction that are somewhat similar to Fogel's. Van den Haag's work is divided into three parts and deals sequentially with the reasons for punishment, the relation between punishment and the control of crime, and types of punishment and their management.[4] Much like Morris (whose work we will discuss in a moment), Van den Haag concentrates on the conditions under which punishment should be prescribed, on the logic of punishment as a legal and social mechanism, and on the exclusion of nonpunitive programs (i.e., change-producing programs) from punitive organizations. Hence, in a sense, Van den Haag concentrates more on the external environment and preconditions to punishment than on how punishment would actually be administered. But such a work is directly relevant here, because so much of the criticism of today's correctional operations involves rethinking and redoing those preconditions rather than the organization of correction itself.

One of Van den Haag's key objectives, apparently, is the rehabilitation of the concepts of general deterrence and retribution or the demonstration of their legitimacy as social concerns. He begins by making a distinction between distributive justice, or the allocation of social rewards to members of a social group, and retributive justice, or the allocation of punishments to members of the social group who break the laws that regulate conduct within the group. He admits that unfair or highly differential distributions of rewards may play some role in increasing the probability that some persons in a social system will be more likely to break the criminal law than others. But he also believes that no administration of the penal law can correct defects in the distributive system and that all social systems will be characterized by differential distribution of rewards. Hence, he concludes that to the extent that persons value the present social system, rather than an alternative, the retributive system is both an important (and an inevitable) component of the social system.

Using these assumptions and values as a basis, Van den Haag sets about to attack the present system of criminal justice. He does so

---

[4] Van den Haag, *Punishing Criminals.*

by citing studies showing that rehabilitation and special deterrence do not seem effective, by citing other studies showing that general deterrence is or can be effective, and by arguing that no one has a right to change another's values, but that society does have a right to punish those whose behavior challenges the predominant values of the existing system.

He comments, as many other recent writers also have, that the general deterrent function of the criminal law is broader than many critics of the harshness of the system have supposed. General deterrence (others have called it general prevention)[5] must be recognized, he asserts, for its impact on the criminal and potential criminal. The fact that many persons do break the law, he argues, is no demonstration of ineffectiveness because we must realize that there are many others who have not broken the law partially because of the fear of punishment. Also, he argues that regardless of its immediate impact on restraining persons from criminal acts, the enforcement of the law is a reward to those persons who have not and perhaps would not have broken it any way.

To those who argue that the conditions of poverty, poor housing, poor education, unequal employment, etc., are causes of crime, and causes not addressed by the penal sanction, Van den Haag replies that the poor, like the rich, are rational and that it is rational, criminal behavior that the criminal law aims to control. He suggests that changes in poor social conditions may indeed be good things but that the need for these changes does not excuse crime and does not militate against the need for a strong, swiftly acting, and effective criminal justice administration.

Surprisingly enough, some of the penal recommendations that Van den Haag draws from these arguments might be seen as rather liberal. For example, he suggests that an effective criminal justice system might rely very heavily on a series of financial sanctions rather than punishment by incarceration. Furthermore, he suggests that prisons be limited in their enrollment to very serious offenders for whom lesser sanctions have repeatedly failed and for whom the prospect of further dangerous behavior seems likely.

He concludes that prisons should be hard and stern places, but not overtly cruel, and that there should be no connection between an offender's sentence and the participation in treatment of self-betterment programs while in prison. Finally, one of his most controversial recommendations is for the prolonged incarceration of the

[5] Jackson Toby, "Is Punishment Necessary?" *Journal of Criminal Law, Criminology and Police Science* (Sept., 1964), pp. 332–37; Johannes Andeneas, "General Prevention, Illusion or Reality?" *Journal of Criminal Law, Criminology and Police Science* (July/Aug., 1952), pp. 176–98.

dangerous person at the expiration of his or her sentence for a particular crime as a means of social protection. He bases this recommendation on firm faith that science has the competence to predict who will be dangerous in the future.

THE SEPARATION OF PUNISHMENT AND TREATMENT

Norval Morris' recommendations for reform are in many respects similar to Van den Haag's. The major difference is that Morris totally rejects that ability to predict dangerousness and would completely remove such predictions from the sentencing decision.[6] Morris perceives the principle problem with current prison administration to be the belief in coerced cure and the impact of that belief on both sentencing and parole decisions as well as on internal prison discipline and staff offender relations.

Morris clearly retains faith in the need for and the effectiveness of individual cures of behavior and/or emotional problems. He remarks that many individuals in the free world, including many who now strongly oppose treatment in prison, firmly believe that treatment programs of different types can help them with their own problems. Therefore, he sees no reason why offenders, simply because they are offenders, should be denied access to such treatment opportunities. The problem, he states, is not with treatment, but with coerced treatment, which is, as far as he is concerned, not only a contradiction in terms but unfair both to the taxpayer who is asked to waste money on it and to the staff and offenders who are forced to engage in it.

> The total institution has such massive impact on its charges, its authority is so annihilative of free choice, that it is essential for us to protect, so far as we can for his sake and ours, the prisoner's freedom not to be in any treatment programs.[7]

Much of Morris' book then is an attempt to spell out how the separation of treatment and punishment could take place without relegating the imprisoned offender to an institution where no change could be undertaken.

Much of this separation concentrates, as had van den Haag, on the way and the reasons for which one would arrive at the prison door rather than on prison organization itself. Morris believes that the key

[6] Norval Morris, *The Future of Imprisonment* (Chicago: University of Chicago Press, 1974).
[7] Ibid., p. 20.

to improved prisons lies in changes in sentencing policy. No one convicted of a crime should be incarcerated, he argues, unless (1) the prison was the least restrictive sanction available and (2) the sentence to imprisonment is not undeserved relative to the seriousness of the crime.[8] He feels that incarceration is the least restrictive option when a lesser punishment would debase the importance of the law broken, or incarceration for that crime was necessary for general deterrence of that type of behavior, or because lesser sanctions had been tried with that offender in the past and had failed to deter.[9]

Surprisingly, Morris does not recommend the abolition of parole, although it would seem that he could, given his objection to using prison behavior as a means of predicting behavior on release and his objection to the indeterminate sentence (under which parole is necessary). He recommends the retention of parole on several grounds, the largest of which is practical: He simply believes that the parole bureaucracy is so entrenched that any reforms that include its abolition are doomed to fail. However, he also sees some positive sides to parole, not the least of which is the ability to supervise the released offender in the community prior to the expiration of sentence, and in doing so to include conditions on that parole period behavior. Finally, he suggests that a paroling authority can take a fair hand in sentencing. By placing the ability to alter criminal sentences in a board removed from public pressure at a trial, we may achieve fairer sentences than would be imposed at such a trial. He stresses, however, that the parole date in such cases should be set within a month or two of entry to prison and should not depend on an offender's behavior in prison, with the exception that violent behavior by prisoners can be reason for changing a parole date and/or reducing good time credits.[10]

Finally, Morris sets out in his last chapter a model for a prison for repetitively violent offenders.[11] He suggests that such a prison should hold no more than 200 offenders and that there should be at least 150 staff for that number of offenders. He suggests that the presence of the offender in the specialized prison should be strictly voluntary: randomly selected violent offenders would have the option of serving their time in the special prison or remaining in the general prison population. Once in the special prison, these offenders would be required to work and to live in small units that served as discussion groups, but in no other way would therapy be required.

[8] Ibid., pp. 59–60.
[9] Ibid., p. 60.
[10] Ibid., pp. 30–40.
[11] Ibid., pp. 85–120.

He argues that all treatment, education, medical, and other programs should be made available to these offenders for their use on a voluntary basis.

POLICING OFFENDERS

Another set of recommendations for reform of the system stem from several years' work of a research team attached to the New York Governor's Special Committee on Criminal Offenders.[12] The now widely known conclusion of this research is that "With few and isolated exceptions, the rehabilitative efforts that have been reported so far have had no appreciable effect on recidivism."[13] One conclusion, writes Martinson, is the idea that "if we can't do more for (or to) offenders, at least we can safely do less."[14] He means that if treatments do not have beneficial effects, we should select the least costly of the equal treatments. This would mean decarceration for many offenders, he asserts, and incarceration for high-risk offenders in custodial institutions. He cautions, however, that decarceration may have negative impact on the deterrent effect of the criminal law, although he does not find, unlike van den Haag, any reasons to believe that general deterrence is effective.[15]

Following this research, and several reports of it, Wilks and Martinson offered some additional comments about a future correctional system in a recent issue of *Federal Probation*.[16] Emphasizing that certain California studies on intensive supervision of adult offenders demonstrated the effectiveness of deterring parolees through high revocation,[17] Martinson suggests that community supervision of offenders might concentrate on high surveillance. Instead of providing services, or treatments, parole officers and volunteer parole aides might decrease crime by offenders by concentrating on observing their behavior more closely and continuously and by letting the offender know that any infraction will lead to revocation. The highly surprising recommendation here is one of designating an individual to watch the offender whom the offender does not know. It is Martinson's belief that the secretiveness of the identity of the parolee's "big brother" might increase the threat

[12] Douglas Lipton, Robert Martinson, and Judith Wilks, *The Effectiveness of Correctional Treatment* (New York: Praeger, 1975).

[13] Robert Martinson, "What Works? Questions and Answers About Prison Reform," *Public Interest* (Spring, 1974), p. 25.

[14] Ibid., p. 48.

[15] Ibid., p. 50.

[16] Judith Wilks and Robert Martinson, "Is the Treatment of Criminal Offenders Really Necessary?" *Federal Probation* (March, 1976), pp. 3-9.

[17] Martinson, "What Works?" p. 47.

potential of the supervision system. He concludes this article with the non sequitur of doubtful historical veracity that reducing crime is a hallmark of democracy.[18]

RESTRAINT POLICY AND RECENT REFORM MODELS

There is a bothersome similarity between the restraint policy, as defined in Chapter 4, and the changes in correctional practice suggested by current reformers who are disillusioned and impatient with the deficiencies and excesses of correctional organizations as they presently operate. The fair and efficient administration of restraint and the absence of attempts to demand and/or facilitate change are the hallmarks of restraint policy. Such an approach to corrections does not seek changes in either correctional environment or in offenders. The interaction of staff and offenders is to be guided by regulations alone, because the adherence to regulations maintains order and predictability in the governing of human beings that other community groups and organizations have deemed to punish.

There is no doubt that a restraint system can be a "liveable" situation. Its demands on both staff and offenders are minimal, and the outputs promised for the social system, if necessary, are not exciting or disruptive.

Such a correctional system is perhaps the most bureaucratic and perhaps the most equitable in its ministration of punishment. Such a system may, indeed, be more desirable, under a variety of criteria, than rehabilitation or reform systems whose objectives and management processes seem to be mismatched. Furthermore, a restraint system is much less challenging, threatening, and disruptive than the reintegration system. In a time when so many other social institutions, values, and objectives are changing rapidly, a correctional system capable of slowing change down may be very desirable to dominant power groups in the United States.

However, the ascendancy of a restraint policy as the dominant correctional option should be recognized for what it is. Restraint, consistently implemented, will be a change of the system as it stands, a step toward emphasizing and embracing on a formal, political level tendencies that have always been present and relatively powerful in correctional organizations. Such a policy option is an admission, long overdue perhaps, that the administration of correctional organization is antithetic to social change and a means of reinforcing distributive

[18] Wilks and Martinson, "Is the Treatment of Criminal Offenders Really Necessary?" p. 9.

justice as it stands. Fogel anticipates that this sort of correctional system, while more obviously the tool of those in power, will also be more acceptable to those punished by it. This anticipation is unlikely to be fulfilled.[19] This author sees two other more probable options.

First, formalizing the goals of the system as ones of social maintenance will present the correctional system as a prime target to anyone considering fundamental social change. If the system does move toward consistently implemented restraint, the "reforms" of the restraint system will be coming from sources external to the organization, and the aims of these "reforms" will be to shut the system down entirely.

A second, and the more likely possibility, is that the correctional system will simply lose social and political importance. The major forums for social conflict resolution will move elsewhere, and the more subtle means of social control (such as rehabilitation, treatment, coerced personal change, etc.) will also move elsewhere, for example, into mental health, social welfare, and related policy areas. These other areas will continue to take on the processing of social problems and "problem people" at an increasing rate. This trend is already very strong (i.e., the decriminalization of alcoholism, civil commitments or treatment of drug addicts, the counseling of political dissidents, etc.).[20] Correctional (or more appropriately, *penal* organizations) are likely to find themselves with less to do and fewer problem people to manage. This occurrence is *not* decried by this author. He would only wish that both correctional administrators and social reformers would recognize the trend for what it probably is—that the social control functions never well dissembled in the correctional apparatus are finally moving into a growing number of other social institutions where they may be more effective, because they are less obvious in their occurrence.

Restraint policy is not in itself bad or good, just as the other policies current in correctional administrative thinking are in no absolute sense to be praised or damned. Their value is relative, and their relative value is now apparently changing. This may be well and good: When one does not get out of a system what is desired, and the demands that it produce have been enunciated over a sufficient period of time, it may be well to change one's expectations rather than the system in question. Hence, the resuscitation of restraint as a potentially predominant operating policy has much common sense to recommend it. But it would be unfair to both the current

[19] Fogel, *We Are the Living Proof.*
[20] Nicholas Kittrie, *The Right to Be Different* (Baltimore: Penguin, 1971); Andrew T. Scull, *Decarceration* (Englewood Cliffs, N.J.: Prentice-Hall, 1977).

reformers of the system and to the administrators who might have to manage the reformed system to let matters rest there. Just what changing the goals instead of changing the system and just what the restraint system consistently implemented might look like are both issues that deserve exploration.

The review of the above reform suggestions emphasizes that many if not all of them concentrate on the constraints under which the new system would operate instead of on the internal conditions and problems that the new organizational system itself would impose. This focus is all right if taken for what it is: suggestions for what the system should not do, and can be constrained from doing, rather than suggestions for how it would actually run. It may indeed be possible to separate from the correctional organization the individual change and treatment motives and demands that presently adhere to the organization and color its operations. It may be true that offenders and staff, disengaged from the task of conducting and/or undergoing change, can relate to each other and to themselves much more honestly. It may be true that a prison relieved of treatment-contingent release decisions can still conduct its internal affairs with a modicum of overt violence and misbehavior. And it may be that treatment programs, if engaged in voluntarily by offenders, will be much more effective for them and for the society that supports these programs.

But none of these possibilities makes terribly evident how it is that the correctional system (particularly the prison) will operate on a daily basis, how correctional administration will manage the organizations, or how the correctional system will relate to its external political economy, notably to other social service and control systems. This author assumes that correctional administrators will still be saddled with a variety of large and complex problems because they will still be guiding large and complex organizations whose basic structures and structural deficiencies relate to the nature of these organizations as organizations as much as to their nature as places of punishment. Hence, the author would assume that almost all, if not all, the organizational principles and management practices described and analyzed herein will still be immediately relevant to the operation of the system.

Moreover, some recurrent management problems that have already troubled correctional managers for years are likely to rise again in new and interesting forms. Will, for example, there be more or less conflict between custodial staffs (in either prisons or field settings) who are directly under the control of the correctional administrators and the social service staffs whose associations with offenders have become voluntary? If an offender in a prison or on parole decides to engage in some form of therapy or to obtain some form of training, will his or her relation to the police-like staffs of the correctional agency conflict any less with his or her relations with social service officials or with the therapeutic or learning milieus required for effective treatment or education?

With what behavioral and informational controls will correctional management limit the excesses of custodial staffs as they attempt to maintain offender conformity to rules and regulations? Rothman has catalogued with open horror the brutality and insensitivity to offenders that were possible in the 1860's in places like Sing Sing when all treatment goals of the prison were abandoned and the single objective of prison administration was maintenance of order.[21] On a more general level, Katz and Kahn have asserted that organizations that seek to control employee behavior by resort to rules and regulations rather than internal motivations in general tend to degenerate because the overt rules and regulations always become the maximal level of employee performance rather than the minimal acceptable level.[22]

Also, to the extent that a restraint system manifests for the social system the belief in retribution and deterrence as the primary functions, or sole functions, of criminal punishment, will arguments be made that persons punished under that rubric be segregated from beneficial, desired social service programs because offender access to these programs in themselves detracts from the strength of the deterrent threat or the weight of the retributive stigma? While many of the reformists at least hope not, and in some instances insist that offenders will have every right to voluntary self-betterment, there is not a great deal of historical evidence to support their optimism. At the very least, the legal and interorganizational means to achieve these relationships between offenders and social programs should be developed.

Lastly, attention must be paid to the possible negative consequences on correctional staff and correctional employment prospects that might result from the proposed changes in correction. Geis and Cavanaugh argue that "as a job comes to be defined as important in terms of these values regarded highly by the society, to that extent will it be treated well by society, and to that same extent will its personnel situation be enhanced."[23] Toby has cogently argued that the integration of the treatment ideology into corrections has played

---

[21] David Rothman, *The Discovery of the Asylum* (Boston: Little, Brown, 1971), pp. 101–105.
[22] David Katz and Robert Kahn, *The Social Psychology of Organizations* (New York: Wiley, 1966), p. 341.
[23] Gilbert Geis and Elvin Cavanaugh, "Recruitment and Retention of Correctional Personnel," *Crime and Delinquency*, (July, 1966), p. 239.

a role in corrections by changing the perception of both community groups and correctional officials about the nature of the enterprise.[24] In explaining its use, he suggests that the effectiveness of the offender's treatment is not so important as is its effect on the persons responsible for punishing. The treatment "myth" has been functional, one could add to this argument, because it has raised the cultural status of correctional work, as Geiss and Cavanaugh have suggested, and has tempered the level of coercion and brutality that are frequently attendant upon punitive organization. While maintenance of coerced treatment and continued belief in treatment as a purpose of correction are not justified by such latent functions, their dissolution as part of the operational rationale of the system should be presaged by other management devices that would play the same role vis-à-vis correctional jobs as valuable careers and the social psychology of correctional work.

REINTEGRATION AND RECENT REFORM MODELS

As the recent reform efforts gain strength, another important set of issues involves the relationship of the new policy changes to the reintegration policy that is also still widely popular and gives every evidence of also increasing strength, despite recent criticism about its ineffectiveness. As the review of recommendations by Morris, Martinson, and Fogel (if not van den Haag) have shown, many of the new ideas about correctional programs and policy leave much of the recent thrust into community settings untouched. Morris recommends prison as a sentencing option only when it is the *least* restrictive alternative available. Martinson states that the relative lack of differential effects for incarcerative and community programs should lead us to select the community alternatives because they are cheaper. Fogel begins his work with the flat assertions that the fortress prison has to go and that the revisions of the prison that he suggests are temporary measures designed to improve the current situation until new forms of correction can be invented. And while van den Haag would seem to place greater weight than the others would on the importance of maintaining the stigmatizing effect of prison as a part of punishment, he does recommend that the great majority of offenders could be punished in the community by a series of fines, the gravity of which should be set in accordance with the offender's ability to pay and the seriousness of the crime.

Thus, there is no direct conflict between the recommendations

[24] Toby, "Is Punishment Necessary?"

recently made for the reform of the correctional system and the continuing and increasing use of community forms of punishment. There may be, however, some indirect, less obvious conflicts. As we have seen in Chapter 12, it is likely that restraint-oriented and reintegration-oriented organizations will experience a variety of conflicts with each other. It is also likely that restraint-oriented correctional organizations will have a harder time formalizing relationships with outside service agencies. There may also be some conflict, on a more general level, between the assumptions of restraint that individual offenders may change their behavior only if they want to, and the assumptions under reintegration that change can be facilitated, although not demanded, through the activity of correctional staff.

Of the four men whose work is reviewed above, the one who addresses the relationship between reintegration and restraint most directly is Morris, who includes a system of graduated release within his new model for incarceration. While he is firm in his belief that release decisions should not be contingent on "treatment" conclusions or diagnoses about offenders, and that offenders who refuse treatment should be released as soon as those who accept it, he also argues that release from prison should be a gradual affair, beginning with several furloughs, followed by participation in work release programs, and then by placement in a community facility. He argues that these forms of reentry, which have become the hallmarks of the reintegration policy, should be included under the new forms of sentencing and punishment that he proposes. The major difference between these gradual reentry programs in his system and the systems that typically operate now is that Morris would have these reentry phases scheduled early upon the offender's admission to prison. They would become the rights of all offenders and would be subject to change only if the offender committed a crime or other major disciplinary infraction while in prison or while in one of these reentry programs. In other words, offenders would cease to be accepted to halfway houses and the like on the basis of a counselor's decisions about need, sincerity, maturity, dangerousness, or other treatment or quasi-treatment dimensions.

There is now some evidence to support the effectiveness of Morris' recommendations, ranging from the examination of the internal logic of the reintegration policy itself, to examinations of offender behavior when in community programs, to studies of community attitudes about community correction. Let us take these in order.

First, there is no inherent theoretical or policy related reason within reintegration policy that community correctional programs must be or should be attached to classification decisions based on offender personality or future predicted behavior. Reintegration policy argues that program decisions should be joint decisions between staff and offenders and that offender programs should be based on realistic attempts to meet offender goals within the means acceptable to society. If correctional staff in community settings can help offenders gain access to a variety of community opportunities, the offender is likely to fare better upon his return to the community than if he is left alone to negotiate reentry. But correctional staff should not coerce the offender to accept community programs as something that he or she needs in order to gain release or to ingratiate himself or herself with the staff. There is also a demand that rules for offender and staff behavior be clearly stated and rigidly adhered to and that the consequences for breaking the rules should be clearly stated.

Therefore, it is very possible that community reentry programs of the reintegration type would benefit from their attachment to the restraint-oriented sentencing guidelines and prison disciplinary code that Morris recommends. If chances of parole or early release were not affected by gaining entry to community programs, it is possible that there would be less gaming between staff and offenders over who should be selected. And if conditions of remaining in the program were limited to the offender's ability to abide by the law and obey minimal program behavioral rules, there might be less manipulation within such programs. Staff could not suggest, with coercive implications, that the halfway house resident should see such and such a counselor or engage in such and such a training or treatment program. Offenders in community programs could not utilize their participation in group therapy, training programs, or other internal or external treatment activities as a means of impressing the staff.

In terms of actual behavior of offenders in the community programs, much of the conflict between staff and offenders revolves around similar issues. Offenders frequently feel that staff should let them alone unless they seek assistance or advice, and they feel that their behavior should be self-determined unless they break laws or center rules about conduct.

Many community correctional staff still approach the offender, and their responsibility to the offender, in terms reminiscent of the rehabilitation model. Most offenders would prefer to understand community programs as something that they deserve for good behavior that can be taken away for prohibited behavior. Offenders see community placement as helpful, in the sense that it may give them time to get reestablished in a community, but they prefer to interpret their responsibilities to the program in retributive terms; they see such programs as part of their punishment, not as part of a necessary treatment.

Finally, administering gradual release programs under a system such as Morris proposes might easily be more acceptable to the public than it is under a "treatment" espousing system. As we have seen in Chapter 14, the public frequently makes a high demand that retribution be served through correctional organizations. When the correctional staff attempt to explain community programs in terms of treatment, they can easily heighten the demand that retribution be paid. If, however, the decision to release the offender were made early in the offender's correctional career, as part of his or her disposition, and given to all offenders who behave properly (rather than to those who "need" it), the public might be more accepting of community placements. It could be said then that offenders are placed in the community only after the appropriate length of prison time had been served and as a result of the conforming behavior while in prison. The treatment activities that took place in such programs would be, as Morris argues, not their purpose, but a separate set of activities that the correctional program might facilitate rather than direct or coerce.

DISTRIBUTIVE AND RETRIBUTIVE JUSTICE

If the above analysis is substantially correct, then there may be less evident conflict between community-based correctional programming and the objectives of restraint policy than would first be suspected. Moreover, there may be fewer problems in meshing the community programming and the continuing trend toward deinstitutionalization with the new version of restraint policy than there are problems in determining the specifics of the restraint organization and management patterns themselves and getting them to work right. Hence, the largest and most important questions in correctional management today, and in the years to follow, may not be whether and what the impacts of the new reform movement will be but the age-old question about whether or not the new reforms are really anything substantially new and different from what we have seen and experienced before.

One recent work by a macrosociologist answers this larger question with a resounding no. Andrew T. Scull insists that the new wave of deinstitutionalization, while it is advertised as more humane and more effective, is really engaged in because it is cheaper for the state and it is a more effective social control.[25] He argues that communities and government officials, and possibly the correctional staffs themselves, are being misled about the purposes and effects of decarceration because the managerial policy and the academic research to support it have focused on the effects of the labeling process and the minute detail of how individual deviants react to and are processed through the agencies of social control. This emphasis on the social processes of correction at the individual, face-to-face level have obfuscated the broader issues, such as the relation of the system of correction to other social institutions and the impact of the class system and the capitalist economy on the mechanisms of social control used within it. New correctional policy, Scull asserts, is shaping up in the way that it is, not because of concern with the offender or reduction in crime or safety to the public or the lack of it, but because the state can no longer afford the cost of isolating offenders in expensive institutions but it can afford the cost of dumping offenders and other deviants into certain communities that serve as the new walless "institutions" for the waste products of the political economic system that we value.

Scull does not address the new push toward restraint that we have just reviewed. But to the extent that the new restraint system is compatible with, or may even speed up the decarceration movement (by reducing the staff need to deliberate treatment decisions), then his criticism can be levied against the whole new shape of correctional policy rather than against the community programming that occurs within it. The fact that the restraint rules would take out of re-integration programming any direct responsibility for treatment would seem to support Scull's argument. Unless correctional organizations should suddenly start placing offenders in middle-class instead of in lower class neighborhoods, and unless they suddenly begin obtaining middle-class instead of marginal employment and welfare benefits for the offenders so released, new correctional programs may simply be intergrating offenders into the already large segment of the American populace that is segregated economically and politically from the mainstream of American life, rather than integrating offenders into "normal" American community living.

This argument may be backed up by the recent work of Rudolph Moos, a psychologist at Stanford.[26] Moos' empirically based classification of institutional and community correctional programs suggests that the two types of programs are not very different in purpose or

[25] Scull, *Decarceration.*
[26] Rudolph Moos, *Evaluating Correctional and Community Settings* (New York: Wiley, 1974).

structure.[27] He also suggests that community programs might guarantee the continuation of institutional programs, rather than threaten their existence, because while length of stay in institutions might be reduced, reincarceration rates may go up.[28] Commenting on the work of another community psychologist, Moos says:

> Sarason has cautioned against enthusiasm about what community-based correctional and/or psychiatric settings can become. He feels that these settings may not be as different from regular institutional programs as the current literature suggests. He concludes that "there is little reason to expect that the adverse consequences will be discernibly less."[29]

Moos goes on to modify that caution somewhat, but in terms that make the recent changes even more ambiguous. He relates that some community research suggests that community programs may have greater *differential* impact than institutional programs. "Thus we may expect both greater beneficial and greater harmful impact from community correctional programs."[30]

Such comments are not made to dull the enthusiasm for new trends in correctional policy and management, although dulling enthusiasm for "new" social programs in the United States has much to suggest it as both a critical and managerial guide. Such comments will not change correctional reform or stop it from happening, but they should be said to place such changes in proper perspective. Perhaps correctional managers have recognized one thing that is observable in these comments to a greater extent than the outside reformers who rail against current management practice and call for change. That one thing is that the changes that are often proposed should often be interpreted in terms of the proposing group rather than in terms of the group that will supposedly be served.

Both community corrections and the new restraint formulations are beneficial to the politicians, reformers, and organizational officials that propose them as much as and probably more than they are beneficial to some idealized version of "community" or "offender" that the proposers claim will benefit. And these proposals will probably be carried out *only* to the extent that the changes benefit the groups involved in initiating the change.

Perhaps it is because of this knowledge that in the past correctional managers remained out of the system reform business and concentrated on the management of their organizations. But this situation does not excuse correctional managers for maintaining a stance of

[27] Ibid., pp. 246–50.
[28] Ibid., pp. 250–51.
[29] Ibid., p. 250.
[30] Ibid., pp. 252–53.

plodding cynicism any more than it excuses reformers for calling for change without examining all the consequences. Since correctional managers have been and will be blamed for their self-interest in whatever they do, they stand to lose little by engaging more directly and more forcefully in the public forum on correctional policy and correctional change. An active and political correctional management may be able to make it clear to the public, as well as to various pressure groups, that correctional change is really insignificant except to the extent that correctional management can and will implement the change through the structural alteration of the system. Moreover, they might be able to clarify the connection between retributive and distributive justice in the United States in a way that outsiders have rarely been able to do. They might agree with van den Haag that tinkering with the retributive justice system in the United States will never substitute for changes in the distribution of social rewards and opportunities. But they can also help to contradict the notion that van den Haag and other restrainists seem to advance: that strengthening the retributive system and redoing the distributive system can proceed independently. If, indeed, our system of criminal punishment helps to maintain our social structure; then the only significant changes in that punitive system will be made through alterations in our basic notions of social justice rather than of criminal justice.

BIBLIOGRAPHY

ACKOFF, RUSSELL L. and FRED E. EMERY, *On Purposeful Systems.* Chicago: Aldine, 1972.

AIKEN, MICHAEL and JERALD HAGE, "Organizational Interdependence and Intra-Organizational Structure," *American Sociological Review*, 33 (December 1968), 912-30.

ALDRICH, H., "Cooperation and Conflict Between Organizations in the Manpower Training System: An Organization Environment Perspective," in *Conflict and Power in Complex Organizations: An Inter-institutional Perspective*, ed. Avant R. Negandhi. Kent, Ohio: Comparative Administration Research Institute Center for Business and Economic Research, Kent State University, 1972.

ALLEN, HARRY E. and CLIFFORD E. SIMONSEN, *Corrections in America: An Introduction.* Beverly Hills, Ca.: Glencoe Press, 1975.

American Bar Association, "Accelerating Change in Correctional Law," In *Parole*, eds. W. Amos and C. Newman. New York: Federal Legal Publications, 1975, 130-49.

American Bar Foundation, *Legal Status of Prisoners.* Chicago: Bar Foundation, 1977, sec. 3:2(C).

American Friends Service Committee, *Struggle for Justice.* New York: Hill & Wang, 1971.

ANDENEAS, JOHANNES, "General Prevention, Illusion or Reality," *Journal of Criminal Law, Criminology and Police Science*, 43, 2 (July/August, 1952), 176-98.

ARGYRIS, CHRIS, *Integrating the Individual and the Organization.* New York: John Wiley, 1964.

———, *Interpersonal Competence and Organization Effectiveness.* Homewood, Ill.: Dorsey, 1962.

———, *Intervention Theory and Method.* Reading, Mass.: Addison-Wesley, 1970.

———, *Personality & Organization.* New York: Harper & Row, 1957.

BAKAL, YITZHAK, ed., *Closing Correctional Institutions.* Lexington, Mass.: Lexington Books, 1973.

BANTON, MICHAEL, *The Policeman in the Community.* New York: Basic Books, 1964.

BARNARD, CHESTER I., *The Functions of the Executive.* Cambridge, Mass.: Harvard University Press, 1968.

BEER, STAFFORD, *Decision and Control*. New York: John Wiley, 1966.

BENNE, KENNETH D. and MAX BIRNBAUM, "Change Does not Have to Be Haphazard," *School Review,* 68, 3 (Autumn 1960), 5-41.

————, "Principles of Change," in *The Planning of Change* (2nd ed.), eds. K. D. Benne, W. G. Bennis, and R. Chin. New York: Holt, Rinehart & Winston, 1969.

BENNETT, LAWRENCE, "Should We Change Offenders or the System?" *Crime and Delinquency*, 19, 3 (July 1973), 332-42.

BENNIS, WARREN G., *Changing Organizations*. New York: McGraw-Hill, 1966.

————, "Theory and Method in Applying Behavioral Science to Planned Organizational Change," *The Journal of Applied Behavioral Science*, 4 (Oct/Nov/Dec 1965), 337-60.

BENSMAN, JOSEPH and ISRAEL GERVER, "Crime and Punishment in a Factory: A Functional Analysis," in *Mass Society in Crisis*, Bernard Rosenberg, et al. New York: Macmillan, 1964, 141-52.

BERKHARD, RICHARD, *Organizational Development: Strategies and Models*. Reading, Mass.: Addison-Wesley, 1969.

BLACK, BERTRAM T. and HAROLD M. KASE, "Interagency Cooperation in Rehabilitation and Mental Health," *Social Service Review*, 37 (1963), 26-32.

BLAKE, ROBERT and JANE MOUTON, *The Managerial Grid*. Houston: Gulf, 1964.

BLOOM, BERNARD C., *Community Mental Health: A Historical and Critical Analysis*. Montclair, N.J.: General Learning Press, 1973.

BLUMBERG, THOMAS, "Diversion: A Strategy of Family Control in the Juvenile Court Process, Florida State University, School of Criminology, 1975.

BRADLEY, HAROLD, "Designing for Change: Problems of Planned Innovations in Corrections," *The Annals of the American Academy of Political and Social Science*, 38 (January 1969), 81-91.

————, GLYNN SMITH and WILLIAM SALSTROM, *Design for Change: A Program for Correctional Management*, final report, Model Treatment Program, Institute for the Study of Crime and Delinquency. Sacramento, Ca.: The Institute for the Study of Crime and Delinquency, July 1965.

BRAYBOOKE, DAVID and CHARLES LINDBLOM, *A Strategy of Decision*. New York: Free Press, 1973.

BUCKLEY, WALTER, *Sociology and Modern Systems Theory*. Englewood Cliffs, N.J.: Prentice-Hall, 1967.

BURKE, W., ed., *Contemporary Organization Development: Conceptual Orientation and Interventions*. Washington, D.C.: National Training Laboratories, 1972.

BURNS, B. and G. M. STALKER, *The Management of Innovation*. London: Tavistock Publications, 1961.

CALVIN, JOHN J. and LOREN DORACKI, *Manpower and Training in Correctional Institutions*, Joint Commission on Correctional Manpower and Training, Staff Report. Washington, D.C.: Government Printing Office, 1969.

CAMPBELL, JAMES, JOSEPH R. SAHID, and DAVID P. STANG, *Law and Order Reconsidered*. New York: Bantam, 1970.

CHAMBLISS, WM. and ROBERT SEIDMAN, *Law, Order and Power*. Reading, Mass.: Addison-Wesley, 1971.

CHIN, R., "Models and Ideas About Changing," paper prepared for The Symposium on Acceptance of New Ideas, University of Nebraska, November, 1963.

CLEMMER, DONALD, *The Prison Community*. Indianapolis: Bobbs Merrill, 1958.

CLOWARD, RICHARD and LLOYD OHLIN, *Delinquency and Opportunity*. New York: Free Press, 1960.

———, et. al., *Theoretical Studies in the Social Organization of the Prison*. New York: Social Science Research Council, 1960.

COATES, ROBERT B. and ALDEN D. MILLER, "Neutralization of Community Resistance to Group Homes," in *Closing Correctional Institutions*, ed. Yitzhak Bakal. Lexington, Mass.: Lexington Books, 1974.

COFFEY, ALAN R., *Correctional Administration*. Englewood Cliffs, N.J.: Prentice-Hall, 1975.

COHEN, FRED, "Sentencing, Probation, and the Rehabilitative Ideal: The View from *Mempa* v. *Rhay*," *Texas Law Review* (December 1968), 1–59.

COHN, ALVIN, "The Failure of Correctional Management," *Crime and Delinquency*, 19, 3 (July 1973), 232–41.

COLTER, NORMAN C., "Subsidizing the Released Inmate," *Crime and Delinquency* (July 1975), 282–85.

"Comment: Beyond the Ken of the Courts: A Critique of Judicial Refusal to Review the Complaints of Convicts," *Yale Law Journal*, 72, 1963, 506–58.

CRESSEY, DONALD R., "Contradictory Directives and Complex Organizations: The Case of the Prison," *Administrative Science Quarterly*, 4 (June 1959), 1–19.

———— , "Limitations on Organization of Treatment in the Modern Prison," in *Theoretical Studies in Social Organization of the Prison*, Richard Cloward, et al. New York: Social Science Research Council, Pamphlet 15, March 1960.

———— , "The Achievement of an Unstated Organizational Goal: An Observation on Prisons," *Pacific Sociological Review*, 1 (Fall 1958), 43-49.

———— , "The Nature and Effectiveness of Correctional Techniques," *Law and Contemporary Problems*, 23 (Autumn 1958), 754-71.

———— , ed., *The Prison: Studies in Institutional Organization and Changes*. New York: Holt, Rinehart & Winston, 1961.

———— , "Professional Correctional Work and Professional Work in Corrections," *National Probation and Parole Association Journal*, 5 (January 1959), 1-15.

———— , "Social Psychological Foundations for Using Criminals in the Rehabilitation of Criminals," *Journal of Research in Crime and Delinquency*, 2 (1965), 44-55.

CRESSWELL, ERNEST, ed., *Proceedings of the Second International Symposium on Criminal Justice Information and Statistics Systems*. Sacramento, Ca.: SEARCH group Inc., 1974.

CROMWELL, PAUL F., "Alternatives to Litigation of Prisoner Grievances," in *Corrections and Administration*, eds. Killinger, Cromwell and Cromwell. St. Paul, Minn.: West, 1976, 510-20.

CROZIER, MICHAEL, *The Bureaucratic Phenomenon*. Chicago: University of Chicago Press, 1964.

CURRIE, ELLIOTT and JEROME SKOLRICK, "A Critical Note on Conceptions of Collective Behavior," *Annals of the American Academy of Political & Social Science* (September 1970), 34-45.

DAHRENDORF, RALF, *Class and Class Conflict in Post Industrial Society*. Stanford, Ca.: Stanford University Press, 1955.

DANIELS, ARLENE KAPLAN, "The Social Construction of Military Psychiatric Diagnoses," *Recent Sociology*, no. 2. New York: MacMillan, 1970.

DESSION, GEORGE, "Psychiatry and the Conditioning of Criminal Justice," *Yale Law Journal*, 47, 3 (January 1938), 319-40.

DEUTSCH, M., *The Resolution of Conflict*. New Haven, Conn.: Yale University Press, 1973.

DRESSLER, DAVID, *The Practice and Theory of Probation and Parole*. New York: Columbia University Press, 1959.

DUFFEE, DAVID, *Correctional Policy and Prison Organization*. Beverly Hills, Ca.: Sage-Halsted, 1975.

———, "The Correctional Officer Subculture and Organizational Change," *Journal of Research in Crime and Delinquency*, 11, 2 (July 1974), 155–72.

———, *The Use of Correctional Offices in Planned Change*, final research report, National Institute of Law Enforcement and Criminal Justice, NI-71-115 PG, September 1972.

———, and ROBERT FITCH, *An Introduction to Correction: A Policy and Systems Approach*. Santa Monica, Ca.: Goodyear, 1976.

———, FREDERICK HUSSEY and JOHN KRAMER, *Criminal Justice: Organization, Structure and Analysis*. Englewood Cliffs, N.J.: Prentice-Hall, 1978.

———, THOMAS MAHER and STEPHEN LAGOY, "Administrative Due Process in Community Preparole Programs," *Criminal Law Bulletin*, 13, 5 (September 1977), 383–400.

———, PETER B. MEYER, THOMAS MAHER and KEVIN WRIGHT, *Products, Issues and Problems in Community Placed Correctional Systems*, update report, Community Services Evaluation, DF-76-E-9D-740. Harrisburg, Pa.: Governor's Justice Commission, November 30, 1976.

———, PETER B. MEYER and BARBARA D. WARNER, *Offender Needs, Parole Outcome, and Program Structure in the Bureau of Correction Community Services Program*. Harrisburg, Pa.: Governor's Justice Commission, September 1977.

——— and R. RICHARD RITTI, "Correctional Policy and Public Values," *Criminology*, 14, 4 (February 1977), 449–60.

———, KEVIN WRIGHT and THOMAS MAHER, *Bureau of Correction Community Treatment Centers Evaluation, Refunding Evaluation Report*. Harrisburg, Pa.: Governor's Justice Commission, January, 1975.

———, et. al., *The Evaluation of State Delivered Community Based Correctional Services*. Harrisburg, Pa.: Governor's Justice Commission, June 1975.

Educational Systems and Designs, Inc., *Management Models: The Communication Process*. Westport, Conn.: Educational Systems and Designs, 1967.

EMERY, F. E. and E. L. TRIST, "Socio-Technical Systems," in *Systems Thinking*, ed. F. E. Emery. Baltimore, Md.: Penguin, 1969.

———, "The Causal Texture of Organizational Environments," in

Systems Thinking, ed. F. E. Emery. Baltimore, Md.: Penguin, 1970, 241–58.

EMPEY, LAMAR, *Alternatives to Incarceration,* Office of Juvenile Delinquency and Youth Development Studies in Delinquency. Washington, D.C.: Government Printing Office, 1967.

———, "Implications: A Game with No Winners," postscript to *The Time Game,* Mannochio and Dunn. New York: Dell, 1972.

———, "Offender Participation in the Correctional Process: General Theoretical Issues," in *Offenders as a Correctional Manpower Resource.* Washington, D.C.: Government Printing Office, 1967.

ETZIONI, AMITAI, *A Comparative Analysis of Complex Organizations.* New York: The Free Press, 1961.

Evaluation Unit of the Governor's Commission on Crime Prevention and Control, *Residential Community Correctional Programs in Minnesota.* St. Paul, Minn.: Governor's Commission, 1976.

FAIRWEATHER, GEORGE W., DAVID H. SANDERS and LOUIS G. TORNATSKY, *Creating Change in Mental Health Organizations.* New York: Pergamon Press, 1974.

FEELEY, MALCOLM M., "Two Models of the Criminal Justice System: An Organizational Perspective," *Law and Society Review,* 7, 3 (Spring 1973), 407–25.

FOGEL, DAVID, *We Are the Living Proof.* Cincinnati: Anderson, 1975.

FORRESTER, J. W., *World Dynamics.* Cambridge, Mass.: Wright Allen Press, 1971.

FOX, SANFORD, *The Law of Juvenile Courts in a Nutshell.* St. Paul, Minn.: West, 1971.

FOX, VERNON, *Community-Based Corrections.* Englewood Cliffs, N.J.: Prentice-Hall, 1977.

FRANKEL, MARVIN, *Criminal Sentences.* New York: Hill & Wang, 1972.

FREEMAN, LINTON C., THOMAS J. FARARO, WARREN BLOOMBERG, JR, and MORRIS H. SUNSHINE, "Locating Leaders in Local Communities: A Comparison of Some Alternative Approaches," *American Sociological Review,* 38 (October 1963), 791–98.

GARFINKEL, HAROLD and EGON BITTNER, " 'Good' Organizational Reasons for 'Bad' Clinic Records," in *Studies in Ethnomethodology,* ed. Garfinkel. New York: Basic Books, 1967.

GEISS, GILBERT, and ELVIN CAVANAUGH, "Recruitment and Retention of Correctional Personnel," *Crime and Delinquency,* 12, 3 (1966), 232–39.

GILMAN, DAVID, "Courts and Corrections," *Corrections Magazine* (June 1976), 13–16.

———, "Courts and Corrections," *Corrections Magazine* (September 1976), 51–53.

GLASER, DANIEL, *The Effectiveness of A Prison and Parole System*. Indianapolis: Bobbs-Merrill, 1969.

———, "The Prospect for Corrections," paper prepared for the Arden House Conference on Manpower Needs in Corrections, mimeograph, 1964.

GOFFMAN, ERVING, *Asylums*. Garden City, N.Y.: Doubleday, 1961.

GOTTFREDSON, DON, *Measuring Attitudes Toward Juvenile Detention*. New York: National Council on Crime and Delinquency, 1968.

GOTTFREDSON, D. M., LESLIE T. WILKINS, P. B. HOFFMAN, and S. M. SINGER, *The Utilization of Experience in Parole Decision Making: A Program Report Summary*. Davis, Ca.: National Council on Crime & Delinquency Research Center, Parole Decision Making Project, June 1973.

GOULDNER, ALVIN, "Reciprocity and Autonomy in Functional Theory," in *Symposium on Social Theory*, ed. Llewellyn Gross. New York: Harper & Row, 1959.

———, "The Sociologist vs. Partisan: Sociology and the Welfare State," *American Sociologist*, 3 (May 1968), 103–16.

GREENWOOD, PETER W., DALE MANN and MILBREY WALLIN MC-LAUGHLIN, *Federal Programs Supporting Educational Change, Vol. III: The Process of Change*. Santa Monica, Ca.: Rand Corporation, April 1975.

GREINER, LARRY E., "Antecedents of Planned Organizational Change," *Journal of Applied Behavioral Science*, 3 (Jan/Feb/ March 1967), 51–86.

GRIFFITHS, JOHN, "Ideology in Criminal Procedure or a Third Model of the Criminal Process," *Yale Law Review*, 79, 3 (January 1970), 359–417.

GROSS, NEAL, JOSEPH GIOCQUINTA, and M. GERNSTEIN, *Implementing Organizational Innovations: A Sociological Analysis of Planned Educational Change*. New York: Basic Books, 1971.

GRUSKY, OSCAR, "Role Conflict in Organizations: A Study of Prison Camp Officials," in *Prison Within Society*, ed. Lawrence Hazelrigg. Garden City, N.Y.: Doubleday, 1969.

GULICK, LUTHER and URWICK L., *Papers on the Science of Administration*. New York: Institute of Public Administration, 1927.

HAGE, JERALD, "A Strategy for Creating Interdependent Delivery

Systems to Meet Complex Needs," in *Interorganizational Relations*, ed. Avant Negandhi. Kent, Ohio: Kent University Press, 1974, 346-58.

HAGEN, CHARLES and CHARLES CAMPBELL, "Team Classification in Federal Institutions," *Federal Probation*, 32, 1, 1968, 30-35.

HALL, JAY, MARTHA WILLIAMS and LOUIS TOMAINO, "The Challenge of Correctional Change: The Interface of Conformity and Commitment," in *Prison Within Society*, ed. Lawrence Hazelrigg. Garden City, N.Y.: Doubleday, 1969, 308-28.

————, JERRY B. HARVEY, and MARTHA WILLIAMS, *Styles of Management Inventory*. Houston: Teleometrics, 1964.

HARRISON, ROGER, and RICHARD HOPKINS, "The Design of Cross-Cultural Training: An Alternative to the University Model," *Journal of Applied Behavioral Science*, III, 4 (1967), 431-60.

HARVEY, J. B. and D. R. ALBERTSON, "Neurotic Organizations: Symptoms, Causes, and Treatment," in *Contemporary Organization Development: Conceptual Orientations and Interventions*, ed. W. W. Burke. Washington, D.C.: NTL Institute for Applied Behavioral Science, 1972.

HASENFELD, YEZEKIEL, "People Processing Organizations: An Exchange Approach," *American Sociological Review*, 37 (June 1972), 256-63.

HAWLEY, WILLIS D. and FREDERICK M. WIRT, *The Search for Community Power*. Englewood Cliffs, N.J.: Prentice-Hall, 1974.

HOVLAND, C. E. and W. WEISS, "The Influence of Source Credibility on Communication Effectiveness," *Public Opinion Quarterly* (1951), 15.

HUNTER, FLOYD, RUTH CONNOR SCHAFFER and CECIL G. SHEPS, *Community Organization: Action and Inaction*. Chapel Hill, N. Carolina: University of North Carolina Press, 1956.

IRWIN, JOHN, *The Felon*. Englewood Cliffs, N.J.: Prentice-Hall, 1970.

————, and DONALD R. CRESSEY, "Thieves, Convicts, and the Inmate Culture," *Social Problems*, 10, 2 (Fall 1962), 142-55.

JACOBS, JAMES B. and HAROLD G. RETSKY, "Prison Guard," *Urban Life*, 4, 1 (April 1975), 5-29.

JOHNSON, LESTER DOUGLAS, *The Devil's Front Porch*. Lawrence, Kan.: The University of Kansas Press, 1970.

Joint Commission on Correctional Manpower and Training, *Ex-offenders on a Correctional Manpower Resource*. Washington, D.C.: Government Printing Office, 1966.

KALPMUTS, N., *Diversion from the Justice System*, National Council on Crime and Delinquency, 1974.

KATZ, DANIEL and ROBERT KAHN, *The Social Psychology of Organizations.* New York: John Wiley, 1966.

KELMAN, HERBERT, "Compliance, Identification, and Internalization: Three Processes of Attitude Change," *Journal of Conflict Resolution* (April 1958), 51-60.

KERPER, HAZEL and JANEEN KERPER, *The Legal Rights of the Convicted.* St. Paul, Minn.: West, 1974.

KIRCHWEY, G. F., "Crime and Punishment," *Journal of Criminal Law and Criminology,* 1 (January 1911), 718-834.

KITTRIE, NICHOLAS, *The Right to Be Different.* Baltimore: Penguin, 1973.

KORN, RICHARD, "Issues and Strategies of Implementation in the Use of Offenders in Resocializing Other Offenders," in *Offenders as a Correctional Manpower Resource.* Washington, D.C.: Government Printing Office, 1967.

——— , "Of Crime, Criminal Justice and Corrections," *University of San Francisco Law Review,* 6 (October 1971), 27-75.

KUH, RICHARD, "The Mapp Case One Year After: An Appraisal of Its Impact in New York," *New York Law Journal,* 148 (September 1962), 1-10.

KUTAK, ROBERT J., "Grim Fairy Tales for Prison Administrators," in *Corrections and Administration,* eds. G. Killinger, P. Cromwell and B. Cromwell. St. Paul, Minn.: West, 1976, 474-92.

LAWLER, EDWARD E. and JOHN GRANT RHODE, *Information and Control in Organizations,* Santa Monica, Ca.: Goodyear, 1976.

LAWRENCE, P. R. and J. W. LORSCH, *Organization and Environment.* Cambridge, Mass.: Harvard University Press, 1967.

LEAVITT, HAROLD J., "Applied Organizational Change in Industry: Structural, Technological, and Humanistic Approaches," in *Handbook of Organizations,* ed. J. G. March. Chicago: Rand McNally, 1965.

LENIHAN, KENNETH J., "The Financial Condition of Released Prisoners," *Crime and Delinquency,* (July 1975), 266-81.

LERMAN, PAUL, *Community Treatment and Social Control.* Chicago: University of Chicago Press, 1975.

LEVINE, SOL and PAUL E. WHITE, "Exchange as a Conceptual Framework for the Study of Interorganizational Relationships," in *Human Service Organizations,* eds. Y. Hasenfeld and R. English. Ann Arbor, Mich.: University of Michigan Press, 1974, 545-61.

——— , and BENJAMIN D. PAUL, "Community Interorganizational Problems in Providing Medical Care and Social Services,"

American Journal of Public Health, 53, 8 (August 1963), 1183-95.

LEWIN, KURT, "Frontiers in Group Dynamics," *Human Relations*, 1 (June 1947), 5-41.

——, "Group Decision and Social Change," in *Readings in Social Psychology*, eds. Macoby, et. al. New York: Holt, Rinehart & Winston, 1958.

——, *Resolving Social Conflicts*. New York: Harper & Row, 1948.

——, "Studies in Group Decision," in *Group Dynamics*, eds. Cartwright and Zander. Evanston, Ill.: Row Peterson, 1953.

LIKERT, RENSIS, *New Patterns of Management*. New York: McGraw-Hill, 1961.

——, *The Human Organization*. New York: McGraw-Hill, 1967.

LIPPIT, R., J. WATSON, and B. WESTLEY, *The Dynamics of Planned Change*. New York: Harcourt, Brace & World, 1958.

LIPTON, DOUGLAS, ROBERT MARTINSON, and JUDITH WILKS, *The Effectiveness of Correctional Treatment*. New York: Praeger, 1975.

LITWAK, EUGENE and LYDIA F. HYLTON, "Interorganizational Analysis: A Hypothesis on Coordinating Agencies," *Adminstrative Science Quarterly*, 6 (March 1962), 395-420.

MC CLEARY, RICHARD, "How Structural Variables Constrain the Parole Officer's Use of Discretionary Powers," *Social Problems*, 23, 2 (December 1975), 209-25.

MC CLEERY, RICHARD, "Correctional Administration and Organizational Change," paper presented at the annual meeting of the American Political Science Association, Washington, D.C.: September 1972.

MC CONNELL, RAY MADDING, *Criminal Responsibility and Social Constraint*, New York: Scribner's, 1912.

MC CORKLE, LLOYD, ALBERT ELIAS and F. LOVELL BIXBY, *The Highfields Story*. New York: Holt, Rinehart & Winston, 1958.

MC GREGOR, DOUGLAS, *The Human Side of Enterprise*. New York: McGraw-Hill, 1960.

——, *The Professional Manager*, eds. Caroline McGregor and Warren Bennis. New York: McGraw-Hill, 1967.

MALINOWSKI, BRONISLAW, "Functionalism in Anthropology," in *Sociological Theory: A Book of Readings*, (2nd ed.), eds. Lewis A. Coser and Bernard Rosenberg. New York: Macmillan, 1964, 637-50.

MANDEL, NATHAN GARY and WM. H. PARSONAGE, "An Experiment in Adult Group Supervision," *Crime and Delinquency*, 11, 4 (October 1965), 313-25.

MANDELL, WALLACE, "Making Correction A Community Agency," *Crime and Delinquency*, 17 (1971), 281-88.

MANN, FLOYD, "Studying and Creating Change," in *The Planning of Change*, W. Bennis, K. Benne and R. Chin. New York: Holt, Rinehart & Winston, 1961.

MARRIS, PETER and MARTIN REIN, *Dilemmas of Social Reform*. New York: Atherton, 1967.

MARTIN, J. P. and A. WEBSTER, *The Social Consequences of Conviction*. London: Heinemann, 1971.

MARTINSON, ROBERT, "What Works? Questions and Answers about Prison Reform," *The Public Interest*, 35 (Spring 1974), 22-54.

MASLOW, ABRAHAM, *Eupsychian Management*. Homewood, Ill.: Richard D. Irwin, 1965.

MAYO, ELTON, *The Human Problems of an Industrial Civilization*. Boston: Division of Research, Harvard Business School, 1946.

MENNINGER, KARL, *The Crime of Punishment*. New York: Viking, 1969.

MERTON, ROBERT, "Social Structure and Anomie," in *Social Theory and Social Structure* (enlarged ed.) ed. Merton. New York: Free Press, 1968, 185-214.

MEYER, JOHN C., "Change and Obstacles to Change in Prison Management," in *Issues in Corrections and Administration*, eds. George G. Killinger, Paul F. Cromwell, Jr., and Bonnie J. Cromwell. St. Paul, Minn.: West, 1976.

MEYER, MARSHALL W., "Organizational Domains," *American Sociological Review*, 40 (October 1975), 599-615.

MEYER, PETER B., "Communities as Victims of Corporate Crimes," paper presented for the Second International Symposium on Victimology, Boston, September 8, 1976.

———, *Drug Experiments on Prisoners*. Lexington, Mass.: Lexington Books, 1975.

——— and DAVID DUFFEE, "Alternatives to Incarceration: Humane Corrections or Low Cost Social Control?" paper presented at The National Conference on Criminal Justice Evaluation, Washington, D.C., March 10, 1977.

MOOS, RUDOLPH, *Evaluating Correctional And Community Settings*. New York: John Wiley, 1975.

———, "The Assessment of the Social Climates of Correctional Institutions," *Journal of Research in Crime and Delinquency*, 4, 2 (July 1965), 174-88.

———, "Changing the Social Milieus of Psychiatric Treatment Setting," *Journal of Applied Behavioral Science*, 9, 5 (1973), 575-93.

MORE, HARRY W., Jr., *Criminal Justice Management*. St. Paul, Minn.: West, 1977.

MORRIS, NORVAL, *The Future of Imprisonment*. Chicago: University of Chicago Press, 1974.

National Advisory Commission on Criminal Justice Standards and Goals, *Corrections*. Washington, D.C.: Government Printing Office, 1973.

NELSON, E. K. and CATHERINE LOVELL, *Developing Correctional Administrators*. Washington, D.C.: Joint Commission on Correctional Manpower and Training, November 1969.

New York Governor's Special Committee on Criminal Offenders, *Preliminary Report*. New York: State of New York, November 1969.

New York State Special Commission on Attica, *Attica*. New York: Bantam, 1972.

NORD, WALTER R., "The Failure of Current Applied Behavioral Science—A Marxian Perspective," *Journal of Applied Behavioral Science*, 10, 4 (1974), 557-78.

OHLIN, LLOYD, HERMAN PIVEN and DONNELL PAPPENFORT, "Major Dilemmas of the Social Worker in Probation and Parole," *National Probation and Parole Association Journal* (July 1956), 211-25.

O'LEARY, VINCENT, "Correctional Assumptions & Their Program Implications," *Proceedings of the National Conference on Pre-release*. Huntsville, Tex.: Institute of Contemporary Corrections and the Behavioral Sciences, November 1967.

———, *The Correctional Policy Inventory*. Hackensack, N.J.: National Council on Crime & Delinquency, 1970.

———, and DAVID DUFFEE, "Correctional Policy: A Classification of Goals Designed for Change," *Crime and Delinquency*, 17, 4 (October 1971), 373-86.

——— and DONALD J. NEWMAN, "Conflict Resolution in Criminal Justice," *Journal of Research in Crime and Delinquency*, 7 (July 1970), 99-119.

———, DAVID DUFFEE, and ERNEST WENK, "Developing Relevant Data for a Prison Organizational Development Program," *Journal of Criminal Justice*, 5, 2 (Summer 1977), 85-104.

ORENSBERG, CONRAD M., "Behavior and Organization: Industrial Studies," in *Social Psychology at the Crossroads*, eds. John H. Rohrer and Musafer Sherif. New York: Harper, 1951.

PACKER HERBERT, *The Limits of the Criminal Sanction*. Stanford: Stanford University Press, 1968.

PALMER, JOHN, *Constitutional Rights of Prisoners*. Cincinnati: Anderson, 1974.

PARSONS, TALCOTT, *Structure and Process in Modern Societies*. New York: Free Press, 1960.

PERLSTEIN, GARY and THOMAS PHELPS, eds., *Community Alternatives to Prison*. Santa Monica, Ca.: Goodyear, 1975.

PERROW, CHARLES, "A Framework for the Comparative Analysis of Organizations," *American Sociological Review* (1967), 194-204.

PIVEN, HERMAN, "Professionalism and Organizational Structure, Training and Agency Variables in Relation to Practitioner Orientation and Practice," unpublished doctoral dissertation, Columbia University, 1961.

PONDY, L. R., "Organizational Conflict: Concepts and Models," *Administrative Science Quarterly*, 12 (2), (1967) 296-320.

POPE, CARL E., "Sentence Dispositions Accorded Assault and Burglary Offenders: An Exploratory Study in Twelve California Counties," paper prepared for the annual meetings of the Society for the Study of Social Problems, New York, 1976.

President's Commission on Law Enforcement and the Administration of Justice, *Challenge of Crime in a Free Society*. Washington, D.C.: Government Printing Office, 1967.

———, *Task Force Report: Corrections*. Washington, D.C.: Government Printing Office, 1967.

PRESSMAN, JEFFREY and AARON WILDAVSKY, *Implementation*. Berkeley, Ca.: University of California Press, 1973.

REID, WILLIAM, "Interagency Coordination in Delinquency Prevention and Control," *Social Service Review*, 38 (March 1964), 418-28.

REITH, CHARLES, *The Blind Eye of History: A Study of the Origins of the Present Police Era*. Montclair, N. J.: Patterson Smith, 1974.

REMINGTON, FRANK, et. al., *Criminal Justice Administration*. Indianapolis, Ind.: Bobbs-Merrill, 1968.

ROBINSON, CYRIL, D., "The Mayor and the Police—The Political Role of the Police in Society," in *Police Forces in History*, ed. George L. Mosse. London: Sage, 1975.

ROETHLISBERGER, F. J. and W. J. DICKSON, *Management and the Worker*. Cambridge, Mass.: Harvard University Press, 1949.

ROTHMAN, DAVID, *The Discovery of the Asylum*. Boston: Little, Brown, 1971.

RUBENSTEIN, JONATHAN, *City Police*. New York: Ballantine, 1973.

RUBIN, SOL., *Law of Criminal Correction* (2nd ed.). St. Paul, Minn.: West, 1973.

———, "The Administrative Response to Court Decisions," *Crime and Delinquency* (1969), 377–86.

———, "The Impact of Court Decisions on the Correctional Process," *Crime and Delinquency* (April 1974), 129–34.

——— and JEFFREY E. GLEN, "Developments in Correctional Law," *Crime and Delinquency* (April 1968), 155–70.

RUIZ, PEDRO, JOHN LANGROD and JOYCE LOWINSON, "Resistance to the Opening of Drug Treatment Centers: A Problem in Community Psychiatry," *The International Journal of the Addictions*, 10, 1 (1975), 149–55.

RUTHERFORD, ANDREW, "The Dissolution of Training Schools in Massachusetts," Academy for the Study of Contemporary Problems, Battell Institute, 1973.

SACKS, MASON J., "Making Work Release Work: Convincing the Employer," *Crime and Delinquency* (July 1975), 255–65.

SARASON, SEYMOUR, *The Creation of Settings*. San Francisco: Jossey-Bass, 1972.

SCHEIN, E., *Process Consultation: Its Role in Organization Development*. Reading, Mass.: Addison-Wesley, 1969.

———, "The Mechanisms of Change," in *Interpersonal Dynamics*, eds. W. Bennis, E. Schein, F. Steele and D. Berlew. Homewood, Ill.: Dorsey, 1964, 342–78.

SCHEURELL, ROBERT P., "Valuation and Decision Making in Correctional Social Work," *Issues in Criminology*, 4, 2 (Fall 1969), 101–108.

SCHRAG, CLARENCE, "Contemporary Corrections: An Analytical Model, " paper prepared for the President's Commission on Law Enforcement & Administration of Justice, mimeograph, 1966.

SCULL, ANDREW T., *Decarceration, Community Treatment and the Deviant*. Englewood Cliffs, N.J.: Prentice-Hall, 1977.

SEBRING, ROBERT and DAVID DUFFEE, "Who Are the Real Prisoners? A Case of Win-Lose Conflict in a State Correctional Institution," *Journal of Applied Behavioral Science*, 13 (1977), 23–40.

SELZNICK, PHILIP, *T.V.A. and the Grassroots*. New York: Harper, 1948.

SHOVER, NEAL, "Experts and Diagnosis in Correctional Agencies," *Crime and Delinquency*, 20, 4 (October 1974), 347–58.

SIGURDSON, HERBERT R., A. W. MCEACHERN, and ROBERT M. CARTER, "Administrative Innovations in Probation Services," *Crime and Delinquency*, 19, 3 (1973), 353–66.

SILVER, ALLAN, "The Demand for Order in Civil Society: A Review of Some Themes in the History of Urban Crime, Police, and Riot," in *The Police*, ed. David Bordua. New York: John Wiley, 1967.

SIMON, HERBERT, "On the Concept of Organizational Goal," *Administrative Science Quarterly*, 9 (June 1964), 1–22.

SKOLNICK, JEROME, *Justice Without Trial*. New York: John Wiley, 1966.

SMITH, DAVID LEWIS and C. MCCURDY LIPSEY, "Public Opinion and Penal Policy," *Criminology*, 14, 1 (May 1976), 113–24.

SMITH, GILBERT, *Social Work and the Sociology of Organizations*. London: Routledge and Kegan Paul, 1970.

STREET, DAVID, ROBERT VINTER and CHARLES PERROW, *Organization for Treatment*. New York: Free Press, 1966.

STUDT, ELLIOT, "Reintegration from the Parolee's Perspective," in *Reintegrating the Offender in to the Community*, Criminal Justice monograph. Washington, D.C.: Government Printing Office, 1973.

——, *Surveillance and Service in Parole*. Los Angeles: University of California at Los Angeles Institute of Government and Public Affairs, 1972.

——, SHELDON MESSINGER, and THOMAS WILSON, *C-Unit: The Search for Community in Prison*. New York: Russell Sage, 1968.

SUDNOW, DAVID, "Normal Crimes: Sociological Features of the Penal Code in a Public Defender's Office," *Social Problems* (Winter 1965).

SULLIVAN, DENNIS C., *Team Management Probation*. Hackensack, N.J.: National Council on Crime and Delinquency, 1971.

—— and LARRY TIFT, "Court Intervention in Correction: Roots of Resistance and Problems of Compliance," *Crime and Delinquency* (July 1975), 213–22.

SYKES, GRESHAM, *The Society of Captives*. Princeton, N.J.: Princeton University Press, 1971.

SZASZ, THOMAS, *Ideology and Insanity*. Garden City, N.Y.: Doubleday, 1970.

TAYLOR, FREDERICK WINSLOW, *The Principles of Scientific Management*. New York: Norton, 1967.

TEETERS, NEGLEY, "State of Prisons in the U.S.: 1870–1970," in *Penology*, George C. Killinger and Paul F. Cromwell, Jr. St. Paul, Minn.: West, 1973.

TERRYBERRY, SHIRLEY, "The Evaluation of Organizational Environments," *Administrative Science Quarterly*, 12, 4 (March 1968), 590-613.

THERSTROM, STEPHAN, "Yankee City Revisited: The Perils of Historical Naivete," in *The Structure of Community Power*, eds. M. Aiken and P. Mott. New York: Random House, 1970.

THOMPSON, JAMES, *Organizations in Action*. New York: John Wiley, 1967.

———— and WILLIAM MCEWEN, "Organizational Goals and Environment: Goal Setting as an Interaction Process," *American Sociological Review*, 23, 1 (1958), 23-30.

TOBY, JACKSON, "Is Punishment Necessary?" *Journal of Criminal Law, Criminology and Police Service*, 55, 3 (September 1964), 332-37.

TOCH, HANS, *Violent Men*. Chicago: Aldine, 1970.

————, DOUGLAS GRANT and RAYMOND GALVIN, *Agents of Change: A Study in Police Reform*. New York: Schenkman-Halsted, 1975.

TRYON, R. and D. BAILEY, *Cluster Analysis*. New York: McGraw-Hill, 1970.

United States Department of Health, Education, and Welfare, *Experiment in Culture Expansion*, Report on the Proceedings of a Conference on "The Use of Products of a Social Problem in Coping with the Problem," California Rehabilitation Center, Morco, Ca., July 10, 11, and 12, 1963.

URWICK, L. F., *Scientific Principles and Organization*. New York: American Management Association, Institute of Management Services, November 19, 1938.

Van DEN HAAG, ERNEST, *Punishing Criminals*. New York: Basic Books, 1975.

VICKERS, GEOFFREY, *Making Institutions Work*. New York: Halsted, 1973.

VON HIRSCH, ANDREW, "Prediction of Criminal Conduct and Preventive Confinement of Convicted Persons," *Buffalo Law Review*, 21 (1972), 717-58.

WALLACE, ROBERT, "Ecological Implications of a Custody Institution," *Issues in Criminology*, 2, 1 (Spring 1966), 47-60.

WALTON, R., *Interpersonal Peacemaking: Confrontations and Third-Party Consultation*, Reading, Mass.: Addison-Wesley, 1969.

WAMSLEY, GARY L. and MAYER N. ZALD, "The Political Economy of Public Organizations," *Public Administration Review*, 33, 1 (January 1973), 62-73.

WARREN, ROLAND L., *Community In America*. Chicago: Rand McNally, 1963.

———, "The Interorganizational Field as a Focus for Investigations," *Administrative Science Quarterly*, 12, 3 (December 1967), 396–419.

WARREN, ROLAND, STEPHEN M. ROSE and ANN F. BERGUNDER, *The Structure of Urban Reform*. Lexington, Mass.: Lexington Books, 1974.

WEBER, G. H., "Conflicts Between Professional and Non-professional Personnel in Institutional Delinquency Treatment," *Journal of Criminal Law, Criminology, and Police Science*, 48 (1957), 26–43.

WENK, ERNST, *The Assessment of Social Climates in Correctional Institutions*. Davis, Ca.: National Council on Crime and Delinquency, June 1973.

——— and RUDOLPH MOOS, "Social Climates in Prisons: An Attempt to Conceptualize and Measure Environmental Factors in Total Institutions," *Journal of Research in Crime and Delinquency*, 9, 2 (July 1972), 134–48.

WENKS, H. ASHLEY, "The Highfields Project and Its Success," in *The Sociology of Punishment and Correction*, eds. N. Johnston, L. Savitz and M. Wolfgang. New York: John Wiley, 1970.

WHYTE, WILLIAM FOOTE, ed., *Money and Motivation*. New York: Harper & Row, 1955.

WILDAVSKY, AARON, "If Planning is Everything, Maybe It's Nothing," *Policy Sciences*, 4 (1973), 127–55.

WILINSKY, HAROLD, *Organizational Intelligence*. New York: Basic Books, 1965.

WILKINS, LESLIE, *Evaluation of Penal Measures*. New York: Random House, 1969.

———, *Social Deviance*, Englewood Cliffs, N.J.: Prentice-Hall, 1965.

WILKS, JUDITH and ROBERT MARTINSON, "Is The Treatment of Criminal Offenders Really Necessary?", *Federal Probation*, (March 1976), 3–9.

WILSON, THOMAS, "Patterns of Management and Adaptation to Organizational Goals: A Study of Prison Inmates," *American Sociological Review*, 74, 2 (September 1968), 146–57.

WRIGHT, KEVIN, "Correctional Effectiveness—The Case for an Organizational Approach," unpublished doctoral dissertation, Pennsylvania State University, 1977.

ZALD, MAYER, "Power Balance and Staff Conflict in Correctional

Institutions," *Administrative Science Quarterly*, 7 (1962), 22–49.

———— , "The Correctional Institution for Juvenile Offenders: An Analysis of Organizational 'Character'," in *Prison Within Society*, ed. Lawrence Hazelrigg. Garden City, N.Y.: Doubleday, 1969, 229–46.

ZAX, M. and E. L. COWEN, "Early Identification and Prevention of Emotional Disturbance in a Public School," in *Emergent Approaches to Mental Health Problems*, eds. E. L. Cowen, E. A. Gardener and M. Zax. New York: Appleton-Century-Crofts, 1967.

NAME INDEX

SUBJECT INDEX